The Theatre o

CW00632117

Jacqueline Mulhallen has studied and worked as an actor and writer in both England and Australia and won a scholarship to study drama in Finland. She worked as performer and writer with Lynx Theatre and Poetry and her plays *Sylvia* and *Rebels and Friends* toured England and Ireland (1987-1997). Publications include 'Focus on Finland', *Theatre Australia*, 1979; (with David Wright) 'Samuel Johnson: Amateur Physician', *Journal of the Royal Society of Medicine*, 1982; 'Sylvia Pankhurst's Northern Tour', www.sylviapankhurst. com, 2008; 'Sylvia Pankhurst's Paintings: A Missing Link', *Women's History Magazine*, 2009 and she is a contributor to the *Oxford Handbook of the Georgian Playhouse 1737-1832* (forthcoming).

Jacqueline Mulhallen

The Theatre of Shelley

Cambridge
OpenBook
Publishers

2010

OpenBook
Publishers

Open Book Publishers CIC Ltd.,
40 Devonshire Road, Cambridge, CB1 2BL, United Kingdom
http://www.openbookpublishers.com

© 2010 Jacqueline Mulhallen.

Some rights are reserved. This book is made available under the Creative Commons Attribution-Non-Commercial-No Derivative Works 2.0 UK: England & Wales License. This license allows for copying any part of the work for personal and non-commercial use, providing author attribution is clearly stated. Details of allowances and restrictions are available at:

http://www.openbookpublishers.com

As with all Open Book Publishers titles, digital material and resources associated with this volume are available from our website:

http://www.openbookpublishers.com

ISBN Hardback: 978-1-906924-31-7
ISBN Paperback: 978-1-906924-30-0
ISBN Digital (pdf): 978-1-906924-32-4

Acknowledgment is made to the The Jessica E. Smith and Kevin R. Brine Charitable Trust for their generous contribution towards the preparation of this volume.

All paper used by Open Book Publishers is SFI (Sustainable Forestry Initiative), and PEFC (Programme for the Endorsement of Forest Certification Schemes) Certified.

Printed in the United Kingdom and United States by
Lightning Source for Open Book Publishers

To William Alderson

Contents

List of Illustrations

Acknowledgements

This study started life as a Ph.D. thesis for the English Department of Anglia Ruskin University. I would like to thank the staff of the English Department for their warm academic support and also for awarding me a major research bursary and further bursaries to attend conferences and to study in Italy. I owe a great debt to Professor Nora Crook, not only for her meticulous supervision of my thesis but also to both her and Dr. Keith Crook for all their encouragement, generosity and hospitality.

I am most grateful to the staff of Anglia Ruskin University Library, the British Library, Cambridge University Library, Eton College Library, Horsham Museum. I am especially grateful to the London Library, which granted me membership under the Carlyle Scheme. I had a great deal of help from the staff of Archivio Storico del Teatro La Fenice, Biblioteca Nazionale Marciana, Biblioteca Casa Goldoni, Biblioteca Nazionale di Firenze, Gabinetto Vieusseux, Teatro della Pergola and Museo della Scala who encouraged and advised me and tolerated my inadequate Italian. The Committee of the British Association for Romantic Studies (BARS) granted me the Stephen Copley Award (2006) for travel to Italy. I would like to thank the following organisations and individuals for kindly allowing me to reproduce their material as illustrations: the Garrick Club, Senate House Library Special Collections, the Huntington Library, the Pennsylvania Academy of the Fine Arts, Ivor Guest and Dance Books and Anthony Speaight. David McGowan, BBC Written Archives Centre, helped me locate Shelley's *Hellas* (1976), which the British Library Sound Archive allowed me to hear.

Dr. Hilary Porriss, University of Cincinnati, Dr. Kai Merten, University of Giessen, Professor Jacky Bratton and Dr. Gilli Bush-Bailey, University of London and Professor Angela Esterhammer, University of Western Ontario, all gave me generous advice. I am particularly grateful to Professor Marcello de Angelis, Università di Firenze for his help in tracing a performance which Shelley might have seen. Many thanks to Colin Blumenau, Director of the Theatre Royal, Bury St Edmunds, for inviting me to become voluntary researcher for the 'Restoring the Repertoire' project (2004-2006).

All my friends and family have been very supportive, but I would not have completed the work without the optimism and enthusiasm of my husband, William Alderson. I benefited in a practical way from his knowledge of Greek and Greek drama, his passion for secondhand bookshops, his computer literacy and our discussions, but of course I owe him far more than this. Hope Stallybrass found me many out-of-print books on the theatre which proved invaluable, David Bookallil sent me, from Australia, a score of the overture to Thomas Dibdin's *The Cabinet* and Stephanie Shaw read chapters with the eagle eye of a professional sub-editor. I especially thank Jane and Felix Blunt for their wonderful hospitality while I was in Italy, Jane in particular. She not only took me to see places which Shelley knew, but without her help in contacting Italian libraries by phone before my visit, I could not have accomplished anything there in the two weeks available.

Last but not least, my thanks to Rupert Gatti, William St. Clair, Alessandra Tosi and Corin Throsby of Open Book Publishers, who have all been sympathetic and very generous with their time. I am grateful for their encouragement, enthusiasm and advice.

Note on the Text

Since there is no complete modern edition of Shelley's drama, I have used a variety of texts.

For *Prometheus Unbound, Tasso* and *The Cenci* I have used *The Poems of Shelley* edited by Kelvin Everest and Geoffrey Matthews, but I have also noted the stage directions in *BSMIX* which comprises the intermediate fair copy of *Prometheus Unbound* which Shelley transcribed into three notebooks for safe-keeping.[1] For *Hellas* I have used *Shelley's Poetry and Prose* edited by Donald H. Reiman and Neil Fraistat (2002), supplemented by *The Hellas Notebook; Bodleian MS adds e.7* edited by Donald H. Reiman and Michael Neth. I have used *The Poetical Works of Shelley* edited by Thomas Hutchinson and revised by Geoffrey Matthews, for *Swellfoot the Tyrant*, since it is based on the *editio princeps*.

However, as the version of *Charles the First* in *The Poetical Works of Shelley* is inaccurate and the new editions of *Charles the First* in the Longman and the Johns Hopkins editions have not yet appeared, I have derived a text based upon *The Charles the First Draft Notebook: a facsimile of Bodleian MS adds. e.17*, edited by Nora Crook, *Shelley's 1821-1822 Huntington Notebook : a facsimile of Huntington MS. HM 2111*, edited by Mary A. Quinn and the notes in the *Hellas Notebook*. I have received helpful information from Nora Crook on certain doubtful points and about her latest thoughts and revisions through which I have modified some of the readings, but the responsibility for the quotations remains mine. I have adopted the reading that appears to be Shelley's latest intention. I have not shown cancels where a cancelled word is needed to complete the sense and I have expanded ampersands and silently corrected Shelley's misspellings and miswritings, supplying minimal punctuation. This also applies to the text of the *Fragments of an Unfinished Drama* where I have used a text based on *The Faust Draft Notebook: a facsimile of Bodleian MS adds. e. 18*, edited by Nora Crook and Timothy Webb.

---

1   *BSMIX*, p. lxii.

I have used *Shelley and His Circle, Vol. VI*, edited by Donald H. Reiman for *A Philosophical View of Reform*, and *Shelley's Poetry and Prose* edited by Donald H. Reiman and Neil Fraistat for *A Defence of Poetry*. For other prose extracts, I referred to *Shelley's Prose, or, The Trumpet of a Prophecy*, ed. by David Lee Clark.

I have also used a number of contemporary collections of plays such as those published by Dolby, Cumberland or Longman, where an example will illuminate Georgian stage practice. In these collections, pages are either not numbered, or the numbering is confusing, so I have not given any numbers. The dates I give for Shelley's own plays are when they are generally agreed to have been written rather than publication dates. Unless otherwise stated, the translations in the text are mine.

Page number for the facsimile edition are reversed where the manuscript commences at the end of the Notebook.

List of Abbreviations

BLJ   *Byron's Letters and Journals*, ed. by Leslie Marchand, 12 vols (London: John Murray, 1973-1994)

BSM   *The Bodleian Shelley Manuscripts*, gen. ed. Donald H. Reiman, 22 vols (New York and London: Garland, 1986-1997)

BSMIX   *Volume IX: The Prometheus Unbound Notebooks: a facsimile of Bodleian MSS. Shelley e. 1, e. 2, and e. 3*, ed. by Neil Fraistat (New York: Garland, 1991)

BSMXII   *Volume XII, 'Charles the First' Draft Notebook, A Facsimile of Bodleian MS Shelley adds. e. 17*, ed. by Nora Crook (New York: Garland, 1991)

BSMXIX   *Volume XIX: The Faust draft notebook: a facsimile of Bodleian MS. Shelley adds. e. 18*, ed. by Nora Crook and Timothy Webb (New York: Garland, 1997)

BSMXVI   *Volume XVI: The Hellas Notebook, A Facsimile of Bodleian MS. Shelley adds. e. 7*, ed. by Donald H. Reiman and Michael Neth (New York: Garland, 1994)

CCJ   *The Journals of Claire Clairmont*, ed. by Marion Kingston Stocking (Cambridge, MA: Harvard University Press, 1968)

MWSJ   *The Journals of Mary Shelley, 1814-44*, ed. by Paula R. Feldman and Diana Scott-Kilvert (Baltimore: The Johns Hopkins University Press, 1995)

MWSL   *The Letters of Mary Wollstonecraft Shelley*, ed. by Betty T. Bennett, 3 vols (Baltimore and London: The Johns Hopkins University Press, 1980-1988)

MYR   *Manuscripts of the Younger Romantics: Percy Bysshe Shelley*, gen. ed. Donald H. Reiman, 9 vols (New York and London: Garland, 1985-1997)

[handwritten annotations:]
KSMB Keats-Shelley Memorial Bulletin
KSJ Keats-Shelley Journal → KSR Keats-Shelley Review
ELN English Language Notes
ELH English Literary History

MYRVII   *Volume VII: Shelley's 1821-1822 Huntington notebook: a facsimile of Huntington MS. HM 2111*, ed. by Mary A. Quinn (New York: Garland, 1996)

OSA   *The Poetical Works of Shelley*, ed. by Thomas Hutchinson, corr. by G.M. Matthews (Oxford: Oxford University Press, 1970)

SC   *Shelley and His Circle, 1773-1822*, ed. by Kenneth Neill Cameron, Donald H. Reiman and Doucet Devin Fischer, 10 vols (Cambridge, MA: Harvard University Press, 1961-2002), vols 1-4 ed. by Kenneth Neill Cameron, vols 5-8 ed. by Donald H. Reiman, vols 9-10 ed. by Donald H. Reiman and Doucet Devin Fischer

SP   *The Poems of Shelley*, ed. by Geoffrey Matthews and Kelvin Everest, 2 vols (London: Longman, 1989, 2000)

SPP   *Shelley's Poetry and Prose*, ed. by Donald H. Reiman and Neil Fraistat (New York: Norton, 2002)

Wolfe   *The Life of Percy Bysshe Shelley*, 2 vols (London: J.M. Dent & Sons, 1933)

PBSL ⟶ copy entry Jones, ed., letter

PMLA   Publications [Journal] of the Modern Languages Association

SIR   Studies in Romanticism

Introduction

There has never been a full-length, in-depth study of Shelley's dramatic work as a whole, nor one which places it fully in the context of the theatre of the late Georgian, or Romantic, period, 1780-1830. It has long been considered that Shelley rarely attended the theatre, disliked it when he did and was therefore unable to write successfully for the stage. This, however, is not a description of Shelley's views and abilities and is based on assumptions about both Shelley and the Georgian theatre which are gradually being shown to be misunderstandings. Shelley not only had a knowledge of practical theatrical techniques and dramatic criticism current in his lifetime but evolved a theory of drama consistent with this knowledge and used them as a framework for writing his own dramatic works.

The first difficulty encountered in writing about Shelley's drama is the argument that the Romantic poets disdained the stage as being too popular for their intellectual and artistic abilities and instead wrote 'closet drama'. Among those holding this view are Allardyce Nicoll and Michael Booth who praise playwrights such as James Planché and Edward Fitzball whose work accorded with popular culture; Marilyn Gaull, who thinks that 'closet drama helped playwrights to overcome the restrictions of the theater'; and Joseph W. Donohue who believes the poets refused 'to accommodate the relationship between private reality and [...] human action'.[2] While there is some truth in these views, they underestimate the extent to which theatre interested the Romantic poets, and indeed the majority of their contemporaries.

'Closet drama' is often taken to be drama written for reading but not for performance, but as Jeffrey N. Cox remarks, it 'does not define a specific

---

2   Allardyce Nicoll, *A History of English Drama: 1600-1900, IV: Early Nineteenth-Century Drama 1800-1850*, 2nd edn, 6 vols (Cambridge: Cambridge University Press, 1955), pp. 60-63; Michael R. Booth, *English Melodrama* (London: Herbert Jenkins, 1965), p. 47; Marilyn Gaull, *English Romanticism: The Human Context* (New York: Norton, 1988), pp. 103-104; Joseph W. Donohue, Jr., *Theatre in the Age of Kean* (Oxford: Blackwell, 1975), p. 172.

form'.[3] Yet he himself describes *The Cenci* as 'published as closet drama', thereby suggesting that publication defines the genre. On the other hand, Philip Cox suggests that author's intention is what differentiates it, since he states that *Prometheus Unbound* 'can clearly be seen to reject the possibility of stage performance' unlike *The Cenci* which was 'written with intention of theatrical production'.[4] The present definitions of closet drama seem to have been chosen with hindsight. That given by Donohue is:

> stage drama manqué, drama aspiring to a state of performance either actual or imagined, but not produced, or producible, on the contemporary stage because of some special circumstance (for example: its language is insufficiently intelligible or unsuited to the spoken voice, the effects it calls for cannot be realized, the kind of stage it requires no longer exists, its subject matter is indecorous, the author fears it will be damned, or praised, and so on).[5]

This definition happens to cover the drama of the Romantic poets: George Gordon Noel, Lord Byron, Samuel Taylor Coleridge, John Keats, Sir Walter Scott, Percy Bysshe Shelley, Robert Southey and William Wordsworth, all of whom wrote plays. Byron and Scott are examples of those who feared being 'damned', while 'indecorous' applied to Shelley whose play, *The Cenci*, was turned down for its subject-matter. Donohue adds that 'certain plays were written frankly for the stage but not produced (at least, not in their authors' lifetimes)'.[6] But, as Timothy Webb discusses in his pioneering 1985 essay, 'The Romantic Poet and the Stage', the Romantic poets did not universally turn their backs on the stage of their day and each had different experiences in writing for it. Byron's *Marino Faliero* (1821) was performed against his wishes but Keats's *Otho the Great* was accepted, but shelved by Drury Lane, then rejected by Covent Garden. Coleridge's *Osorio* was also initially rejected but, after much reworking, it was staged as *Remorse* (1813). Wordsworth was 'angered and upset' when *The Borderers* was rejected by Covent Garden in 1797, but later claimed to have 'no thought of the Stage when he initially wrote the play'.[7] Clearly, even in an author's lifetime, the

3   Qtd in Philip Cox, *Reading Adaptations, Novels and Verse Narratives on the Stage, 1790-1840* (Manchester: Manchester University Press, 2000), p. 12.
4   Philip Cox, *Reading Adaptations*, pp. 12-13.
5   Joseph W. Donohue, Jr., *Dramatic Character in the English Romantic Age* (Princeton, NJ; Princeton University Press, 1970), p. 160.
6   Donohue, *Dramatic Character*, p. 160.
7   Timothy Webb, 'The Romantic Poet and the Stage' in *The Romantic Theatre: An International Symposium*, ed. by Richard Allen Cave (London: Colin Smyth, 1986), pp. 12, 14-15, 18; *Seven Gothic Dramas 1789-1825*, ed. by Jeffrey N. Cox (Athens: Ohio University Press, 1992), p. 38; Philip Cox, *Reading Adaptations*, p. 13.

attitude of author or theatre to the play may change.

The attitude of Byron and Scott appears ambivalent. Byron repeatedly stated that he did not want his plays performed. *Manfred* was 'the very Antipodes of the stage', *Marino Faliero*, 'unfit for the stage', 'written solely for the reader', 'not for acting'.[8] David Erdman, however, believed he desired success on stage but that the possibility of failure made him deeply apprehensive.[9] On the other hand, what he imagined to be the simplicity of the Greek theatre appealed to Byron, who disliked both the scenic effects which Shelley admired and the tendency of contemporary theatre to make love the main interest.[10] His criticisms imply a genuine desire to reform the British theatre, meanwhile allowing his vision to take the form of a 'mental theatre' in the way Jeffrey N. Cox suggests as a blueprint for the theatre of the future.[11] Scott, who apparently inspired Byron's fear,[12] may have been put off writing for the stage by his first attempt, a play, *The House of Aspen*, which went into production but was terminated mid-rehearsal.[13] He did not, however, object to his novels being 'terryfied', i.e., adapted for the stage by the actor, Daniel Terry, and he encouraged the playwrights, Joanna Baillie and Charles Maturin, author of *Bertram*. His *Essay on Drama* praised the theatre.Catherine Burroughs suggests that closet drama was a choice made by women when writing or performing drama by women was discouraged; for her, just as closets might vary in size and use, 'closet drama' can be used to include any kind of sketch or dialogue read or performed privately by and for women.[14] She does not distinguish between writing for and reading aloud in a private space, although as the second may be part of a process of eventual public performance the definition is unclear. The writers she gives as examples of closet playwrights, Baillie and Elizabeth Craven, wrote drama for performance in a public or semi-public situation. Craven's private theatre therefore could be classed in the

---

8   *BLJV*, p. 194; *BLJVIII*, pp. 59, 60, 68.
9   David V. Erdman, 'Byron's Stage Fright: The History of his Ambition and Fear of Writing for the Stage' *ELH* 6 (1939), 219-243 (pp. 232-233).
10   *BLJVIII*, pp. 56, 78.
11   Philip Cox, *Reading Adaptations*, p. 12.
12   Robertson Davies, 'Playwrights and Plays' in *The Revels History of Drama in English, 1750-1880* ed. by Michael R. Booth, Richard Southern, R. Davies, and F. and L.L. Marker, pp. 194-195.
13   Information from Dr. Kai Merten, University of Giessen, private communication, 23 August 2006.
14   Catherine Burroughs, *Joanna Baillie and the Theater Theory of British Romantic Women Writers* (Philadelphia: University of Pennsylvania Press, 1997), pp. 11-12, 21-22, 177 (for descriptions of closets).

tradition of aristocratic private theatres and she herself with such gifted amateur aristocratic performers as Richard, Earl of Barrymore. Baillie may have feared that 'it may perhaps be supposed, from my publishing these plays, that I have written for the closet rather than the stage',[15] but she made it clear she would have preferred them performed. Indeed, she wrote *De Monfort* for Sarah Siddons and her brother, John Philip Kemble, which they performed at Covent Garden; thus she belongs with writers such as Henry Hart Milman, who hoped his *Fazio* would be staged, though he 'printed it in case it was not a success'.[16]

The weakness of these definitions may be seen when one considers that a play intended for performance on the public stage may also be read or performed privately and that, until they are performed, all plays are 'closet plays'. There is a collaborative process in producing a play; many playwrights have found, like Coleridge, that the cuts and adaptations suggested by the theatres can help the success of the play. Since the reaction of an audience can be assessed by performing or reading plays in a small private circle, such as referred to by Burroughs, this should be borne in mind, given the Shelleys' habit of reading plays aloud and their projected amateur drama in Pisa in 1822. On the other hand, if a play is published, and most are not, the writer may alter it to a more literary style, as Ben Jonson and, probably, Shakespeare, did, or re-insert the text excised by the censor, as Thomas Holcroft did with *Love's Frailties*.[17] The intention of the author, therefore, cannot be the sole criterion of a closet play. If authors claim that a play was never intended for the stage, they need not take responsibility for its failure in performance, but if it is a success they can take the credit.

A play may survive until, or be revived in, another era. An 'unperformable' drama, such as Lorca's *El Pubblicò* or Strindberg's *A Dream Play*, may well become performable in another period because the complexity of the text becomes better understood, because of changes in public opinion towards a taboo subject or technical changes in the theatre, but there must be inherent qualities which make it stageable. Jeffrey N. Cox's description of the closet play as 'the theatre of the future' may not always be appropriate

---

15   *Joanna Baillie's Plays on the Passions (1798 edition)* ed. by Peter Duthie (Peterborough, Ont.: Broadview Press, 2001), pp. 108-109.

16   Thomas Campbell, *Life of Mrs. Siddons*, 2 vols (London: Effingham Wilson, 1834), p. 254; Henry Hart Milman, Preface to *Fazio*, 4th edn (London, 1816).

17   Lukas Erne, *Shakespeare as Literary Dramatist* (Cambridge: Cambridge University Press, 2003; Thomas Holcroft, *Love's Frailties* (London: Shepperson & Reynolds, 1794), p. A2.

since many plays were, and are, written which are merely unstageworthy, and of course some were written to be deliberately so. However, it may be applicable in cases such as Byron's and, indeed, Shelley's.

Fashions in style may also change; some which were successful in their time are later thought best forgotten and others considered undeservedly neglected, but falling out of favour cannot define a closet play. Furthermore, later assumptions about poor taste or overwriting may be found to be mistaken. When, in 2004, the Theatre Royal, Bury St Edmunds began rehearsed readings of late Georgian plays which had not been performed for many years, they were found to be more effective than they appeared to be on the page, even though only semi-staged. Stage directions and effects which appeared clichéd to the reader proved very moving when performed.

The relationship between 'closet' drama and the stage among theatre critics of the late Georgian period was fluid and complex. Readers of plays were also theatre-goers and amateur performers, while dramas were sometimes first published in the hope of attracting a theatre manager. A.W. Schlegel believed that 'the very form of dramatic poetry' implied 'the theatre as its necessary complement' but conceded that 'there are dramatic works which were not originally designed for the stage [...] which nevertheless afford great pleasure in the perusal'.[18] This might apply to Baillie's *De Monfort*, which two biographers of Siddons imply was more suitable for the closet since it was 'a beautiful poem' but 'on the stage [...] no spectator wished it a longer life' and required 'more stirring incidents to justify the passion of her characters'.[19] The performability of a new play was considered important by reviewers, at least when discussing plays by women.[20] To the actor, John Bernard, a closet play was merely a bad one whose author lacked 'the power of invention, and the capability of embodying what he invents'.[21] Suggesting that plays would work in the closet, if not on stage gave theatre managements a useful formula for softening the blow when returning scripts. John Fawcett, manager at Covent

---

18   A.W. Schlegel, *Lectures in Dramatic Art and Literature*, trans. by John Black, 2nd edn, rev. by Rev. A.J.W. Morrison (London: Geo. Bell & Sons, 1904), p. 32.
19   James Boaden, *Memoirs of Mrs. Siddons*, 2 vols (London : Henry Colburn, 1827), II, p. 330; Thomas Campbell, *Life of Mrs. Siddons*, 2 vols (London: Effingham Wilson, 1834), p. 254.
20   Greg Kucich, 'Revising Women in British Romantic Theatre' in *Women in British Romantic Theatre: Drama, Performance and Society, 1790-1640*, ed. by Catherine Burroughs (Cambridge: Cambridge University Press, 2000), pp. 59-60.
21   John Bernard, *Retrospections of the Stage*, 2 vols (London: Henry Colburn, 1827), I, p. 137.

Garden in 1822, rejected *The Promise*, a play by Shelley's friend, Edward Williams, saying that it had 'poetical beauties but not dramatic'.[22] But it should be borne in mind that many plays, regardless of their dramatic skill, could not be performed because the Examiner of Plays would not grant them a licence, or the theatre feared that one would not be granted, as was the case with *The Cenci*.

As a professional actress and playwright, Elizabeth Inchbald, when editing *The British Theatre*, carefully considered the question of which plays succeeded better on stage and which in the closet. In her preface to *The Dramatist*, she said that 'plays of former times were written to be read' but that nowadays they are both read and performed. Despite *Antony & Cleopatra* and *As You Like It* having been written for the stage, she classes them among those she finds more successful in the closet. Although Hannah Cowley and John O'Keeffe were both professional playwrights writing for the stage, Inchbald considers Cowley's *A Bold Stroke for a Husband* equally successful in both areas, but believes 'a reader must be acquainted with O'Keeffe on the stage to admire him in the closet'. She suggests that Colley Cibber's *A Careless Husband*, although written for the stage and frequently performed, does not satisfy 'the present demand for perpetual incident' on stage, and that *As You Like It* will only succeed if 'some actress of very superior skill performs the part of Rosalind', like 'Mrs. Jordan'. Her position is clear when she describes 'that fine play', *De Monfort*, as 'both dull and highly improbable in the representation... its very charm in the reading militates against its power in the acting' despite the 'most appropriate performances' of Siddons and Kemble.[23] A 'closet' play is one which cannot convince in performance.

James Henry Leigh Hunt originally intended his masque, *The Descent of Liberty*, for the stage, but 'as he proceeded however he found himself making so many demands on the machinist [...] that he gave up his wish and set himself with no diminution of self-indulgence, to make a stage of his own in the reader's fancy'.[24] Hunt, as a theatre critic, knew the theatre

---

22   Gisborne & Williams, p. 124.
23   Remarks by Elizabeth Inchbald, *The British Theatre*, 25 vols (London: Longman, Hurst, Rees and Orme, 1808): *Antony and Cleopatra*, IV, *As You Like It*, III, *A Bold Stroke for a Husband*, XIX, *A Careless Husband*, IX, *The Castle of Andalusia*, XXII, *The Dramatist*, XX, *De Montfort*, XXIV, and qtd in Ellen Donkin, *Getting into the Act* (London: Routledge, 1995), p. 163. Inchbald's comments on these and other plays leads Burroughs to a different conclusion. Burroughs, *Closet Stages*, p. 84.
24   James Henry Leigh Hunt, *The Descent of Liberty* (Philadelphia: for H. Hall, 1816), p. 44.

sufficiently to be aware that his stage directions required the machinists to follow one set of scenic effects with another so soon that they would have had difficulty in finishing one in time to perform the next, while the repetition of so many groups might have wearied rather than delighted the audience. The idea of a masque being written especially to be read when in its seventeenth-century heyday it was appreciated for scenic effects rather than literary content, no doubt appealed to his sense of humour. The definitions of Inchbald and Hunt show their relationship to their theatre; they consider the demands upon actors and machinists and the preferences of audiences, the performability rather than the author's intention. However, their definitions applied to their own day; audience tastes are not static and technical advances might render Hunt's masque performable.

The meaning of 'closet drama' for Shelley's contemporaries, therefore, was a play unsuitable for performance on stage which might have literary merit. Although not mentioned by modern critics, this meaning has coloured the term ever since. The literary merit of Shelley's drama is not in question, but its performability has been, although Shelley is said to have thought it 'affectation' not to write a play for the stage and nowhere stated it his intention to write 'closet drama'.[25] If this is defined as his contemporaries suggest, a play unsuccessful on stage, then an exploration of Shelley's drama should show how far it would achieve success in the theatre, whether Georgian or later. My analysis is therefore based on how successful Shelley's plays have been or would have been in performance, taking into account criteria which are more appropriate to performance than to reading: dramatic qualities such as dialogue which lends itself to delivery, dramatic incident, characterisation, suspense, mystery and opportunities for dance or song.

Shelley long enjoyed the reputation of being the only major Romantic poet to write a performable play, *The Cenci* (1819), 'the best play of its period', but this judgement was usually counterbalanced with the reservation that its success was due to what Donohue describes as 'intuition' rather than to dramatic skill.[26] The opinions of, among others, Booth, Robertson Davies and Gaull, have perpetuated the view that Shelley's poetic genius and intellectuality prevented him from writing successfully for the stage in an era of melodrama, hippodrama and pantomime.[27] Yet it was Shelley's very

25   Wolfe, II, p. 198.
26   Cox, *Seven Gothic Dramas*, p. 58; Donohue, *Theatre in the Age of Kean*, p. 172.
27   Booth, *English Melodrama*, p. 47; Michael R. Booth, *Prefaces to English Nineteenth-Century Theatre* (Manchester: Manchester University Press, 1980), pp. 18-19; Davies,

intellectual capability and open mind which allowed him to acquire the skills of theatre writing without serving the long apprenticeship of an Elizabeth Inchbald or a Thomas Holcroft. He appreciated the skills of performers, whether acrobats, dancers, musicians or actors, and understood that their talents need not be limited to these genres, but could be combined to serve a poetic drama.

Shelley's dramatic ability was noted as long ago as 1936 by a leading theatre critic, St John Ervine.[28] *The Cenci*'s first professional performance in England in 1922, with no less an actress than Sybil Thorndike playing Beatrice, was enormously successful. Following this, it has been performed frequently but not by a major British theatre company since 1959.[29] Despite Curran's 1970 full-length study of *The Cenci*, subsequent studies of Shelley's drama have been directed away from the theatre and it has been classed as 'closet drama' or 'mental theatre'.[30] It has been discussed from the point of view not of dramatic technique but psychology, morality or imagery.[31] While these studies all, of course, illuminate the play, they do not address the questions of the effectiveness of Shelley's dramatic technique or how he envisaged its staging. Still less has this been done in the case of his other dramas. Although Curran and Nora Crook have discussed aspects of staging,[32] other studies of *Charles the First* (1822) have tended to ignore its theatrical qualities.[33] *Hellas* (1821), *Prometheus Unbound* (1819) and *Swellfoot*

'Playwrights and Plays' in *The Revels*, p. 193; Gaull, *English Romanticism*), pp. 103, 104.

28   St John Ervine, 'Shelley as Dramatist' in *Essays by Divers Hands*, xv, ed. by Hugh Walpole (London: Humphrey Milford, Oxford University Press, 1936).

29   Stuart Curran, *Shelley's Cenci: Scorpions Ringed with Fire* (Princeton, NJ: Princeton University Press, 1970), pp. 225, 248; there have been no productions by the Royal Shakespeare Company or the National Theatre <http:/www/dswebhosting.info/ Shakespeare/dserve> [accessed 17 September 2004]; <http://www.nationaltheatre. org.uk> [accessed 17 September 2004].

30   William Jewett, *Fatal Autonomy: Romantic Drama and the Rhetoric of Agency* (Ithaca: Cornell University Press, 1997); Michael Simpson, *Closet Performances: Political Exhibition and Prohibition in the Dramas of Byron and Shelley* (Stanford, CA: Stanford University Press, 1998); Alan Richardson, *A Mental Theatre* (University Park and London: The Pennsylvania State University Press, 1988), p. 100.

31   Anne McWhir, 'The Light and the Knife: Ab/Using Language in The Cenci' *KSJ*, 38 (1989), 145-161; Julie A. Carlson, *In the Theatre of Romanticism; Coleridge, Nationalism, Women* (Cambridge: Cambridge University Press, 1994); Ronald L. Lemoncelli, 'Cenci as Corrupt Dramatic Poet' *ELN*, 16 (1978), 103-117; Donna Richardson, 'The Harmatia of Imagination in Shelley's Cenci' *KSJ*, 54 (1995), 216-239; Stephen Cheeke, 'Shelley's The Cenci: Economies of a "Familiar" Language' *KSJ*, 47 (1998), 142-160.

32   *BSMXII*, p. xlvi; Curran, 'Shelleyan Drama' in *The Romantic Theatre*, pp. 68-69.

33   Jewett, *Fatal Autonomy*; Kenneth R. Johnston and Joseph Nicholes, 'Transitory

the Tyrant (1820) have not been discussed, even hypothetically, as stageable dramas until Jeffrey N. Cox's recent essay.[34] This is most welcome as it claims Shelley as dramatist, but, necessarily, because of its brevity, does not allow him to amplify the pertinent points that it makes. My study provides the details of Shelley's dramatic techniques and their relationship to the writers, performers, managers, scene painters, mechanists and audience of late Georgian England and, to a lesser extent, Italy. It can be seen that the drama Shelley saw influenced his own and that he wrote in such a manner as to make his work stageable in the theatre of his own time. This includes *Prometheus Unbound* and *Hellas*, which are modelled on plays successfully staged, even if in fifth-century Greece, and are influenced by contemporary theatrical practice. Shelley may not have expected them to succeed in a commercial London theatre and made no attempt to submit them. While I do not suggest that he did not wish them to be read, I consider them performable and shaped by experience of theatrical performance.

As there is no performance history of Shelley's drama from his own period, and little from other periods for any but *The Cenci*, there are difficulties in suggesting how Shelley himself envisaged his drama being performed. However, by imaginatively relating them to the stage technique of late Georgian theatre and taking note of his stage directions or descriptions within the text, some of his intentions hitherto ignored or misunderstood become clear. I have discovered that the stage effects which he specifies were not only achievable with late Georgian theatre technology, but also frequently used, which suggests that he was aware of the required results. His having written *The Cenci* with particular actors in mind led me to consider what other actors he might have contemplated for other dramas. Shelley's excellent powers of memory and observation would have enabled him to bear in mind performances he had seen when creating his own drama. I have been able to trace some of these influences.

Shelley was neither employed in the theatre like the actor-playwrights, Inchbald and Holcroft, nor involved in other ways, like his friends, Hunt, as theatre critic, or Byron, as member of the Drury Lane Committee, but that does not preclude a dramatic sense or an ability to understand stagecraft. This study reveals that Shelley attended the theatre more frequently than was hitherto supposed and shows that the theatrical techniques he learnt,

Actions: Men Betrayed' in *British Romantic Drama*, ed. by Terence Allan Hoagwood and Daniel P. Watkins (London: Associated University Presses, 1998).
34   Jeffrey N. Cox, 'The Dramatist' in *The Cambridge Companion to Shelley*, ed. by Timothy Morton (Cambridge: Cambridge University Press, 2006), pp. 65-84.

and used, would be redundant in drama only intended to be read. Shelley was able not only to structure a play to reveal its meaning through dialogue and action rather than description, but also to understand the practical exigencies of scenery, lighting, actors' abilities and audience response. It is necessary to put his work in the context of late Georgian theatre — very different in style and stage mechanics from that of the Victorian, twentieth century and present-day — to show that, far from despising the theatre audience, Shelley saw the possibilities for communicating his ideas by using it to reach a wider public. The frequent dismissal of him as a 'closet dramatist', with its suggestion of ignorance of theatre, therefore becomes questionable.

The second difficulty in discussing the work of the Romantic poets for the theatre is, as Jeffrey N. Cox points out, the entrenched prejudice against the plays of this period which has resulted in little study having been done.[35] Though he himself has done much to correct this view in his introduction to *The Broadview Anthology of Romantic Drama* and in 'Re-viewing Romantic Drama',[36] it is still influential in current studies of Romanticism.[37] In the last fifteen years, however, valuable selections of drama and studies of playwrights and the theatre of Shelley's period have been published. Through the editions of Paul Baines, Barry Sutcliffe and Cox himself, there has been a realisation that late Georgian theatre has been judged by unsuitable criteria.[38] Melinda Finberg's edition and the studies by Ellen Donkin and Tracey C. Davis, for example, have made students aware of women dramatists who were successful in the theatre of their day but subsequently largely ignored.[39] Julia Swindells has drawn attention to the links between political movements and plays such as *Inkle and Yarico* and

---

35   Cox, *Seven Gothic Dramas*, pp. 2-4.
36   *The Broadview Anthology of Romantic Drama*, ed by Jeffrey N. Cox and Michael Gamer (Toronto: Broadview Press, 2003), pp. vii-xxiv; Jeffrey N. Cox, 'Re-viewing Romantic Drama' *Literature Compass* 1.1, doi:10.1111/j.1741-4113.2004.00096.x (2004).
37   Gaull, *English Romanticism*, p. 88; Jane Stabler, *Burke to Byron, Barbauld to Baillie 1790-1830* (Basingstoke: Palgrave 2002), p. 47; Richardson, *A Mental Theatre*, p. 100; Simpson, *Closet Performances*, p. 377.
38   Cox, *Seven Gothic Dramas*; *Five Romantic Plays 1768-1821*, ed. by Paul Baines and Edward Burns (Oxford: Oxford University Press, 2000); *Plays by George Colman the Younger and Thomas Morton*, ed. by Barry Sutcliffe (Cambridge: Cambridge University Press, 1983).
39   *Eighteenth Century Women Dramatists*, ed. by Melinda C. Finberg (Oxford: Oxford University Press, 2001); Tracy C. Davis and Ellen Donkin, *Women and Playwriting in 19th Century Britain* (Cambridge: Cambridge University Press, 1999); Ellen Donkin, *Getting into the Act*.

The Rent Day.[40] Marc Baer has confirmed the link between political activism
and theatre in Georgian England and developed our understanding of the
backgrounds of the audience by his study of the 1809 Old Price protests
against raised seat prices at Covent Garden.[41] The connections between
Shelley, the radical press and Spencean meetings have been explored by
Steven E. Jones and Iain McCalman and those of the radicals with the
theatre by David Worrall.[42]

These studies have given some of the background required for discussion
of the drama. For an understanding of the context in which Shelley wrote,
however, I found no substitute for studying the plays themselves and the
biographies and memoirs of those involved in the theatre, such as James
Boaden, John Bernard, Michael Kelly and Thomas Dibdin.[43] Although
Inchbald's plays have been collected by Paula Backscheider and the *British
Women Playwrights* website has made others available, much of the foremost
drama of the period remains out of print and inaccessible to a modern
audience or reader.[44] Some can only be read in the collection preserved by
John Larpent, Examiner of Plays (1741-1824), in the Huntington Library, also
available on microfilm in the British Library. Moreover, literary historians
writing about late Georgian theatre have rarely written with an awareness
of the exciting developments in theatre history of the previous 50 years,
such as the work on theatre architecture by Richard Southern and Richard
Leacroft,[45] on scene painting and amateur theatre by Sybil Rosenfeld and

40   Julia Swindells, *Glorious Causes, the Grand Theatre of Political Change, 1789 to
1833* (Oxford: Oxford University Press, 2001).
41   Marc Baer, *Theatre and Disorder in Late Georgian London* (Oxford: Clarendon
Press, 1992).
42   Steven E. Jones, *Shelley's Satire, Violence Exhortation and Authority* (Illinois: De
Kalb Northern Illinois University Press, 1994), pp. 4, 47; Iain McCalman, *Radical
Underworld* (Cambridge: Cambridge University Press, 1988), pp. 80-82; David
Worrall, *Theatric Revolution: Drama, Censorship and Romantic Period Subcultures, 1773-
1832* (Oxford: Oxford University Press, 2006), pp. 249-252.
43   James Boaden, *The Life of Mrs. Jordan* (London: Edward Bull, 1831); Boaden,
Memoirs of Mrs. Siddons; Bernard, *Retrospections of the Stage*; Thomas Dibdin, *The
Reminiscences of Thomas Dibdin*, 2 vols (London: H. Colburn, 1827; repr. New York:
AMS Press, 1970); Michael Kelly, *Reminiscences*, ed. by Roger Fiske (London: Oxford
University Press, 1975).
44   *The Plays of Elizabeth Inchbald*, ed. by Paula Backscheider (New York: Garland,
1980); *British Women Playwrights around 1800*, gen. eds: Thomas C. Crochunis and
Michael Eberle-Sinatra <http://www.etang.umontreal.ca/bwp1800/essays/crochu-
nis_nassr99.html> [accessed 13 January 2007].
45   Richard Southern, *The Georgian Playhouse* (London: Pleiades, 1948); Richard
Southern, *Changeable Scenery* (London: Faber & Faber, 1952); Richard Leacroft, *The
Development of the English Playhouse* (London: Eyre-Methuen, 1973).

on costume by Diana de Marly, which give a more complete picture of the technology and knowledge which informed the Georgian theatre.[46] Helpful work on the management and production of these theatres has been done by Donohue and others.[47] Since I commenced this study in 2000, Jane Moody has given due credit to the work of the minor theatres and extended the work of Booth and George Taylor to enlarge current understanding of their architecture, audience and of 'illegitimate' drama such as burletta.[48] Jeffrey N. Cox, Michael Gamer and Jacky Bratton have given valuable general overviews.[49] Bratton, with Gilli Bush-Bailey,[50] and Paul Ranger have conducted illuminating experiments with their students.[51] With the exception of Cox and Gamer, however, writers eager to emphasise the vigour and popularity of the burletta and melodrama tend not to see the drama as a whole or the connection between the genres and the 'major' and 'minor' theatres.

Just as a playwright with no interest in the theatre is not considered an effective dramatist, so a writer on drama should not conduct research solely in the library. In order to understand the practical aspects of the type of theatre Shelley knew, including the machinery and techniques available, I took backstage tours of the recently restored Georgian Theatre, Richmond, North Yorkshire (1788), the Theatre Royal, Bury St Edmunds, Suffolk (1819) and the Teatro della Pergola, Florence (1656). At La Pergola I was able to

46   Sybil Rosenfeld, *Georgian Scene Painters and Scene Painting* (Cambridge: Cambridge University Press, 1981); Sybil Rosenfeld, *Temples of Thespis: Some Private Theatres and Theatricals in England and Wales, 1700-1820* (London: The Society for Theatre Research, 1978); Diana de Marly, *Costume on the Stage 1600-1940* (London; B.T. Batsford, 1982).
47   Donohue, *Theatre in the Age of Kean*; *The London Theatre World, 1660-1800* ed. by Robert D. Hume (Carbondale & Edwardsville: Southern Illinois University Press, 1980); *The Stage and the Page: London's "Whole Show' in the Eighteenth Century Theatre* ed. by Geo. Winchester Stone Jr (Berkeley: University of California Press, 1981); W.G. Knight, *A Major London 'Minor': The Surrey Theatre (1805-1865)* (London: The Society for Theatre Research, 1997).
48   George Taylor, *The French Revolution and the London Stage, 1789-1805* (Cambridge: Cambridge University Press, 2000); Jane Moody, *Illegitimate Theatre in London* (Cambridge: Cambridge University Press, 2000); Booth, *English Melodrama*; Booth, *Prefaces to English Nineteenth-Century Theatre*.
49   Cox and Gamer, *Broadview Anthology*; Cox, 'Romantic Drama'; Jacky Bratton, *New Readings in Theatre History* (Cambridge: Cambridge University Press, 2003).
50   Jacky Bratton, Gilli Bush-Bailey and DT 2323A semester 97/8B, 'The Management of Laughter; Jane Scott's Camilla The Amazon in 1998' in *Women in British Romantic Theatre*.
51   Paul Ranger, *'Terror and Pity Reign in Every Breast': Gothic Drama in the Patent Theatres, 1750-1820* (London: Society for Theatre Research, 1991).

see *le guide*, the grooves in the stage for moving the scenery and observe the amount of backstage space available. I was involved from its beginning in April 2004 until December 2006 with the project of 'Restoring the Repertoire' at the Theatre Royal, Bury St. Edmunds, in which rehearsed readings with professional actors of plays by Shelley's contemporaries were given. As I was providing specific background research on the original actors, I was able to enlarge my knowledge of those whom Shelley might have seen, and, by attending rehearsals, I gained a better understanding of how the techniques differ from accepted styles of the twentieth and twenty-first centuries.

The theatre of Shelley's lifetime was an art form of high quality encompassing a great variety of work, for which writers he admired, such as William Godwin, Matthew Gregory ('Monk') Lewis, Holcroft and Coleridge had written. It was also a period of change and developing technical skills, which, given Shelley's interest in progress, could hardly have failed to attract him. I have linked these changes to his recorded theatre-going at different periods to show that he was able to observe them and to provide a context in which his drama can be assessed. Because theatre is a three-dimensional art involving more than a literary text and because Shelley himself, who referred to drama as a 'prismatic and many-sided mirror', was aware of the importance of these other components, I describe the acting styles, music, dancing, scenery, lighting, the stage and the auditorium. Since the stage illusion of 1819 cannot be replicated with the same effect in 2010, it is important to understand what Shelley himself expected to see in order to identify what stage effects he envisaged in his own drama. Nevertheless, there are certain techniques of playwriting which do not change with the times, and my own background as a professional actress, writer and co-manager of a touring theatre company allows me to bring an understanding to a play-text not readily available without such experience. Raymond Williams's *Drama and Performance* makes the primary point that 'play and performance' are all too often treated 'in separate compartments' rather than 'as the unity which they are intended to become'.[52]

The third barrier to assessing the quality of Shelley's drama is the generally accepted assertion by his friend, Thomas Love Peacock and his cousin, Thomas Medwin, that he was not a frequent theatre-goer and, indeed, disliked it. This has led to the persistent belief that he was unable

---

52   Raymond Williams, *Drama in Performance* (Harmondsworth: Penguin, 1972), p. 4.

to learn stagecraft from first-hand experience.[53] The critics who have been least subject to this belief and who have most emphasised Shelley's talent as a dramatist, Kenneth N. Cameron, Curran and Jeffrey N. Cox, have not established what performances at the theatre Shelley actually saw and they differ among themselves on this point. Despite Cox's belief that Curran's reference to entries in Mary Shelley's journals suffices, Curran himself was not sure that Shelley saw the performances in question, stating that he 'educated himself in the study'.[54] Cameron assumes that Shelley saw all the performances while Donohue believes that the entries cannot be relied upon.[55]

I have clarified the usefulness of Mary Shelley's journals by cross-checking them with those of her stepsister, Claire Clairmont, and the memoirs of Shelley's friends, Peacock, Edward John Trelawny and Edward Williams. For performances from an earlier period, I have included the evidence supplied by his cousins, Harriet Grove and Medwin. Despite the efforts of Shelley's friend, Thomas Jefferson Hogg, to insist on the contrary, his *Life of Shelley* provides illuminating anecdotes which show that Shelley himself had dramatic and humorous talents, while the drama Shelley read aloud to his own circle is an important indicator of his knowledge and taste. A study of newspapers and playbills in English and Italian libraries has enabled me to show that his experience of contemporary performance was more extensive than previously supposed. Appendix I gives a list of plays seen by Shelley while in England and Italy — the first time, to the best of my knowledge, such a list has been made. Shelley's theory of drama can be inferred from *A Defence of Poetry* and the prefaces to the dramas themselves, where they exist, supplemented by his letters, and anecdotes from the memoirs of friends, although these have to be sifted and compared for reliability. Schlegel has been referred to by Webb, Cox and others, but I believe that this study makes the fullest acknowledgement of the extent of the debt to Schlegel's work in Shelley's theory of drama as set out in *A Defence of Poetry*.[56]

It might have appeared, after Curran's full-length study of *The Cenci*,

---

53   Wolfe, II, p. 330; Thomas Medwin, *The Life of Percy Bysshe Shelley*, 2 vols (London: Thomas Cautley Newby, 1847), I, p. 52.

54   Cox, 'The Dramatist', p. 83n; Curran, *Cenci*, p. 158.

55   Kenneth N. Cameron, *Shelley: The Golden Years* (Cambridge, MA: Harvard University Press, 1974), pp. 394-395; Donohue, *Dramatic Character*, p. 181.

56   Cox 'The Dramatist', p. 71; Webb, 'The Romantic Poet and the Stage' in *The Romantic Theatre*, p. 25.

that there was nothing to add about the relation of this play to the theatre. However, because of its twentieth-century performance success, both Curran and Richard Cave suggest that *The Cenci* is more suitable for the modern stage. This opinion allows the persistence of the idea that Shelley was out of step with plays successful on the stage of their time.[57] The work on the late Georgian theatre which I have carried out enabled me to consider the question of how in tune Shelley was with the technical and artistic requirements of the Covent Garden Theatre to which he sent the play. My study of Milman's *Fazio*, generally agreed to have had an influence on *The Cenci*,[58] and my discovery of the manuscript of *The Italian Wife*, the version of *Fazio* adapted by Thomas Dibdin and performed at the Surrey Theatre, not only enabled me to extend Cox's suggestion that the offerings of both major and minor theatres were often alike in character but also shows Shelley's craftsmanship to be superior to Milman's.[59] Shelley was sufficiently competent both to avoid Milman's defects and to suggest effects obtainable with late Georgian theatre techniques. It is thus possible to make an informed conjecture on the impact which *The Cenci* would have made on the 1819 audience for which it was intended. I have traced the discussion of the performability of *The Cenci* from Hunt's original review[60] through the unfavourable comments of Nicoll and Davies to Cave's more sympathetic assessment taking into account its varied performance history,[61] in order to assess exactly why views on the play's performability differ so widely and to provide a possible explanation.

As it is unfinished, the manuscript of Shelley's historical tragedy, *Charles the First*, does not contain detailed notes or directions as to staging, but it is possible to work out something of what he intended by referring to the resources of Covent Garden and by analogy with other plays of the period, supported by Shelley's theoretical stance in the *Defence of Poetry*. By studying his notes with an awareness of the focus he had given to the scenes he had

---

57   Curran, *Cenci*, p. 253; Richard Allen Cave, 'Romantic Drama in Performance' in *The Romantic Theatre*, p. 104.
58   Donohue, *Dramatic Character* pp. 171-177.
59   Cox and Gamer, *Broadview Anthology*, p. xxiv.
60   R. Brimley Johnson, *Shelley-Leigh Hunt: The Story of a Friendship* (London: Ingpen and Grant, 1928), pp. 48-57.
61   Nicoll, pp. 196-197; Booth, *English Melodrama*, p. 47, for Booth's comments on Shelley and the Romantic poets in general; Robertson Davies, 'Playwrights and Plays' in *The Revels*, p. 193; K.N. Cameron and Horst Frenz, 'The Stage History of Shelley's The Cenci' *PMLA*, 60 (1945), 1080-1105; Curran, *Cenci*; Marcel Kessel and Bert O. States, 'The Cenci as a Stage Play' *PMLA*, 72 (1960), 147-149; Bert O. States, Jr, 'Addendum: The Stage History of Shelley's The Cenci' *PMLA*, 65 (1957), 633-644.

already concluded, I have been able to suggest events which would have been included in the play because of their dramatic possibilities, and to make a reasonable projection of its planned structure. Inevitably, this part of my work is speculative but it is underpinned by textual and contextual evidence. My assessment of the importance which *Charles the First* holds in Shelley's work has been achieved by considering its relationship to his reading of histories and memoirs of the Civil War and seventeenth-century plays. The timeliness of the subject and the likelihood of the acceptance of Shelley's play by Covent Garden in 1823 is demonstrated by their commissioning Mary Russell Mitford's *Charles the First* that year.[62] I believe that it would have been an effective stage play, both for the Georgian stage and for the stage of today. My work corroborates and extends the view of Cameron and Crook that, whatever the cause of Shelley's abandonment of *Charles the First* in early 1822, it was not because it was proceeding in the direction of unstageability and that, had it been completed, it would have been an important and lasting work of art.

Prometheus Unbound and *Hellas* are great poems which are usually neither performed nor considered as drama and were published with no intention or expectation of their immediate performance, but their writing is rooted in actual theatrical practices. Shelley was aware that the theatre was a dynamic art form and his 'lyrical dramas' accord with his theory of drama sufficiently to suggest that he thought them performable.[63] I therefore consider the ways in which they show his qualities as an effective dramatist rather than a poet. Rather than analysing *Prometheus Unbound* for literary or mythmaking features, I look at Shelley's introduction of song, scenic effect or suggestions of dance. It has been argued that *Prometheus Unbound* has a metaphorical and structural relationship with ballet and opera.[64] I have been able to show that this was a practical performance relationship too, resulting from the influence of contemporary work in these forms. In a performance, there is no reason why Shelley's stage directions should not be followed and dancing and singing take place. Curran and Lilla Crisafulli have suggested the influence upon Shelley of the great composer of ballets, Salvatore Viganò.[65] The pre-eminence of his work and the popularity and

62   M.R. Mitford, 'Original Preface' to *Charles the First : An Historical Tragedy* in *The Dramatic Works of Mary Russell Mitford*, 2 vols (London: Hurst and Blackett, 1854), I. p. 243.
63   *A Defence of Poetry* in *SPP*, pp. 520-521.
64   Ronald Tetreault, 'Shelley and the Opera' *ELH*, 48 (1981), 144-171.
65   Stuart Curran, 'The Political Prometheus' *SIR*, 25.3 (Fall 1986), 429-455; Lilla

vigour of ballet and opera in both England and Italy have been described more fully by dance and music historians.[66] I have studied the libretti of the Viganò ballets which Shelley saw to show the ways in which he conceived drama as being developed through dance. I have been able to establish not only that the scenery, lighting and spectacular stage effects which would have been required to stage *Prometheus Unbound* were achievable by theatres at the time, but that Shelley had seen in Italy the possibilities of a state-subsidised theatre as opposed to the commercial English theatre.[67] He may have published the 'lyrical dramas' as poems while considering that they could be staged when political conditions became more favourable in a less censored, less commercial future theatre, that hinted at by Schlegel.[68] These dramas would combine the best of ancient and modern; moral and political philosophy and poetry accompanied by acting, music, dancing and spectacular scenic effects. Since Shelley had studied Greek drama, visited the theatre at Pompeii and read contemporary authorities on Greek theatre, *Prometheus Unbound* drew upon ideas of classical Greek stagecraft as it was understood by the best lights of his day. His dramatic art was flexible enough to accommodate Aeschylus, Shakespeare and Viganò, and allowed him to combine effects from several eras.

The influence of Aeschylus' *The Persians* has been often mentioned in connection with *Hellas*, but it has not been considered before that Shelley used the structure of *The Persians* to write a modern, performable play.[69]

Maria Crisafulli, 'Il viaggio *olistico* di Shelley in Italia: Milano, la Scala e l'incontro con l'arte di Salvatore Viganò' in *Traduzione, Echi, Consonanze: Dal Rinascimento al Romanticismo*, a cura di Roberta Mullini e Romana Zacchi (2002), pp. 163-183.

66   Mercedes Viale Ferrero, 'Staging Rossini' in *The Cambridge Companion to Rossini*, ed. by Emanuele Senici (Cambridge; Cambridge University Press, 2004); Carlo Gatti, *Il Teatro alla Scala: nella storia e nell'arte, 1778-1963*, 2 vols (Milano: Ricordi, 1964); Ivor Guest, *The Romantic Ballet in England* (London: Pitman, 1954); Ivor Guest, *The Romantic Ballet in Paris* (London, Pitman, 1966); Ivor Guest, *The Ballet of the Enlightenment* (London: Dance Books, 1996); Luigi Rossi, *Il Ballo alla Scala 1778-1970* (Milan: Edizione della Scala, 1972); William C. Smith, *Italian Opera and Contemporary Ballet in London 1789-1820* (London: The Society for Theatre Research, 1955); Marian Hannah Winter, *The Pre-Romantic Ballet* (London: Pitman, 1974).

67   John Rosselli, *The Opera Industry in Italy from Cimarosa to Verdi* (Cambridge: Cambridge University Press, 1984), pp. 49-50.

68   Schlegel, pp. 41-42, 488.

69   Timothy Webb, *Shelley: A Voice not Understood* (Manchester: Manchester University Press, 1977), pp. 198-200; Earl R Wasserman, *Shelley; A Critical Reading* (Baltimore: Johns Hopkins University Press, 1971), pp. 377-378; Constance Walker, 'The Urn of Bitter Prophecy: Antithetical Patterns in Hellas ' *KSMB*, 33 (1982), 36-48 (pp. 37-38).

Shelley suggests in his preface that *Hellas* should be considered as a drama, while calling it a 'mere improvise.'[70] This is not as contradictory as it first appears since, having seen the improvisations of Tommaso Sgricci which were structured in the Greek style, he knew that this style was effective on stage. *Hellas* was also influenced by *The Bride of Abydos* by William Dimond (1818). Shelley completed *Hellas* shortly before Greek drama came into vogue on the London stage; the support for the very cause for which it was written brought stagings of Greek drama throughout the following decades.[71] Had *Hellas* been performed, Shelley would have emerged at the forefront of theatrical innovation.

Swellfoot the Tyrant has been described as a humourless failure, although such critics as Cameron, Seymour Reiter and Jennifer Wallace have acknowledged its comic and political qualities.[72] Its similarity to prints and pamphlets relating to the Queen Caroline case has long been established, but recent studies of the political background have shown a connection between private theatre and political 'spouting clubs'.[73] While there is no evidence that Shelley had performance in mind, the stage techniques used are in line with theatre practice of the time. Since its style lends itself to mimicry, I was prompted by Bratton's discussion of Charles Mathews to consider a probable actor who may have inspired Shelley.[74] *Swellfoot* has its roots in Aristophanes but Shelley appears to have also used elements of *commedia dell'arte* and its descendants, Punch, pantomime and burlesque, which his contemporaries believed to be direct descendants of ancient comedy.[75] The most valuable work on the pantomime is still David Mayer's and, on Punch, George Speaight's.[76] I was fortunate enough to see an

70   *SPP*, pp. 430-431.
71   Edith Hall and Fiona Macintosh, *Greek Tragedy and the British Theatre 1660-1914* (Oxford: Oxford University Press, 2005), p. 270.
72   Cameron, *The Golden Years*, p. 362 ; Seymour Reiter, *A Study of Shelley's Poetry* (Albuquerque: University of New Mexico Press, 1967), p. 253; Jennifer Wallace, *Shelley and Greece: Rethinking Romantic Hellenism* (London: Macmillan, 1997), p. 75; Webb, *The Violet in the Crucible* (Oxford: Oxford University Press, 1976), p. 137; Ronald Tetreault, *The Poetry of Life: Shelley and Literary Form* (Toronto: University of Toronto Press, 1987), p. 158.
73   N.I. White, 'Shelley's Swellfoot the Tyrant in Relation to Contemporary Political Satires' *PMLA*, 36 (September 1921), 332-346; Worrall, *Theatric Revolution*; Jones, *Shelley's Satire*; McCalman, *Radical Underworld*; John Earl, 'The Rotunda; Variety Stage and Socialist Platform', *Theatre Notebook*, 58.2 (2004), 71-90.
74   Bratton, *New Readings*, pp. 100-110.
75   Schlegel, p. 202; Lady Morgan, *Italy*, 3rd edn, 3 vols (London: H. Colburn, 1821) II, pp. 291n, 292n.
76   David Mayer, *Harlequin in His Element: The English Pantomime 1806-1836*

Opera Restor'd production (2001) of *The Dragon of Wantley*, an eighteenth-century burlesque included in Simon Trussler's helpful collection, which showed that in performance this genre is much funnier, and more fun, than in reading.[77] In considering the performance possibilities of *Swellfoot the Tyrant*, rather than its form as literary text, the nature of its humour is more fully revealed. It is worth considering how timely Shelley's dramatic works were; in three cases, they were written at the point when the London theatre required a drama on just such a theme.

As the purpose of the study is to place Shelley in the context of the theatre, I have not attempted to make any detailed comparison with the drama of other poets, such as Goethe, Byron or Schiller, despite the importance of their own work and their influence on Shelley, nor have I discussed Shelley's translations of drama. I conclude, however, that each of Shelley's dramas exhibits a different aspect of his knowledge of stagecraft and that, if performed, they could be successful with audiences. Because of the close connection between *A Philosophical View of Reform* and *A Defence of Poetry*, I have also considered how Shelley re-interpreted his political philosophy in his dramas, all of which deal with the overthrow of a tyrant.[78] They could therefore be seen as Shelley's attempt to reach the mass audience he believed had eluded him when writing in other forms, such as the essay or narrative poem.

(Cambridge, MA: Harvard University Press, 1969); George Speaight, *Punch and Judy: A History* (London: Studio Vista, 1970).

77   *Burlesque Plays of the Eighteenth Century*, ed. by Simon Trussler (Oxford: Oxford University Press, 1969).

78   Cox arrives at a similar conclusion; see Jeffrey N. Cox, 'The Dramatist', p. 67.

Chapter One
The Theatrical Context –
the Georgian Theatre
in England

When Shelley's play, *The Cenci,* received its first professional performance in 1922, the theatre for which he wrote it no longer existed. Critical assessment of Shelley's writing as theatre writing rather than poetry, therefore, has been based on staging and acting styles which were not what he could have had in mind. Stage effects designed for theatres of one period do not necessarily transfer to another since a theatre director presenting a play of an earlier era must adapt and set the text to suit a contemporary understanding if it is not to be the 'dry exhibition' Shelley dreaded.[79] So, before discussing Shelley's effectiveness in writing for the theatre, it is important to establish what kind of a theatre existed in the late Georgian period (1780-1832) and understand the possibilities and restrictions it offered to a dramatist.

This period, which encompassed Shelley's short lifetime, was one of exciting changes in the theatre. There were technical innovations in architecture, lighting and scenery; many new theatres were built in London and elsewhere, including Shelley's home town of Horsham; and there were artistic changes towards a greater realism in scenery design and costume. The theatre was popular and widespread. The theatres of major towns toured to theatres in smaller towns. For example, the theatre at Richmond in Swaledale toured to Beverley, Harrogate, Kendal and Ulverston. The Norwich circuit 'included Yarmouth, Lynn, Bury St Edmund's [sic], as the principal towns, and other smaller ones as subsidiary to the greater planets […] Swaffham, East Dereham, North Walsham, Eye, &c., were visited'. [80]

79   *SPII,* p. 729.
80   Sybil Rosenfeld, *The Georgian Theatre of Richmond and its Circuit: Beverley,*

There were theatres set up in booths at fairs and groups of strolling players who performed in barns, inns or private houses. The quality of performance provided by these companies should not be dismissed. Mary Russell Mitford describes her enjoyment of them. John Bernard, who worked with them as an actor, tells comic anecdotes about his experiences, but not without sympathy and respect, for example, for their 'clever stage managing'.[81] The company of Roger Kemble produced the greatest acting family of the period as well as one of its most influential playwrights, Thomas Holcroft.[82]

Apart from professional companies there were many amateur societies. 'There were apprentices' theatricals, military and naval theatricals, children's and school theatricals, and small theatres in which amateurs could try out their histrionic abilities for a modest fee.'[83] Families of the nobility and gentry performed in private theatres and at the public schools. There is evidence that the popularity of the theatre at this period was akin to that of sport today. Most people, regardless of class or occupation or income, would have known enough about the subject for it to be a topic of conversation one could enter into with a complete stranger.[84]

Shelley's interest in technological progress suggests that he would have noticed the radical transformation in the theatre in England, begun in the late 1780s. This can be illustrated by describing some of his theatrical experiences before he left England in 1818.

Richmond, Surrey, 1802

According to Shelley's cousin Medwin, Shelley paid his first visit to the theatre when he and Medwin crossed the river by boat from Syon House School to the Richmond Theatre on the Green and saw Dorothy Jordan, the

---

Harrogate, Kendal, Northallerton, Ulverston and Whitby (York: The Society for Theatre Research in association with William Sessions, 1984), p. 49; Bosworth Harcourt, *Theatre Royal, Norwich: The Chronicles of an Old Playhouse* (Norwich: Norfolk News Co., 1903), p. 8.

81   Mitford, *Works*, I, p. viii-ix; Bernard, *Retrospections*, I, p. 12.

82   *The Life of Thomas Holcroft Written by Himself Continued by William Hazlitt* (Oxford: Oxford University Press, 1926), p. 87.

83   Sybil Rosenfeld, 'Jane Austen and Private Theatricals', *Essays and Studies* n.s. XV (London: John Murray, 1962), 40-51 (p. 42).

84   Baer, *Theatre and Disorder*, p. 193; 'On Actors and Acting', *The Selected Writings of William Hazlitt*, ed. by Duncan Wu, 9 vols (London: Pickering & Chatto, 1998), II, p. 152.

foremost comedy actress of her generation, in *The Country Girl*. Shelley left Syon House before 1804, Medwin earlier. Jordan performed at Richmond regularly in the summer from 1789, but Boaden, her biographer, mentions 1802 in particular, a year in which it is possible that all three would have been present. [85]

The great eighteenth-century actor manager, David Garrick, adapted Wycherley's Restoration comedy, *The Country Wife*, re-naming it *The Country Girl*, intending to 'clear one of our most celebrated comedies from immorality and obscenity'. The opinion of the theatre historian, John Genest, was that Garrick had 'removed all the exceptionable parts, but he has in great measure destroyed the vigour of the Original.'[86] Restoration comedy and Jacobean plays, including Shakespeare, were seldom performed in their original versions. This censorship of sexual matters was to affect the stageability of *The Cenci*.

By 1802, *The Country Girl* was out of date, and the actress, though a star, past her heyday. The theatre, too, was old-fashioned; built in 1765, it was tiny but with the typical features of a larger Georgian theatre. The outside was plain, the inside, simply panelled and painted green. The entry door led to a landing with the pay box and steps to a foyer with access doors to the boxes and pit and separate stairs to the gallery. The pit was the floor of the auditorium, furnished with backless, green baize-covered benches and the boxes ran right around the interior of the auditorium encircling the pit. The number of tiers of boxes depended on the size of the theatre. The theatre at Richmond, Surrey, had a 'creditable tier of Georgian boxes round the little pit, together with upper side boxes and a gallery facing the stage'.[87] There were also boxes directly above the proscenium doors through which the actors made their entrances and exits. The stage was raked and the actors largely performed on the forestage, which projected into the auditorium.[88]

Part of the excitement of going to the theatre was the spectacular effect of seeing one scene replace another as scenery was changed in full view of the audience. Often the scene changed behind the actors, so they were instantly transported to their new location without the delay of entrance

85   Medwin, *Life*, I, p. 52; Boaden, Mrs. Jordan, II, p. 105.
86   David Garrick, *The Plays of David Garrick*, ed. by H.W. Pedicord and F.W. Bergmann, 8 vols (Carbondale and Edwardsville: Southern Illinois University Press, 1982), VII, pp. 199, 415.
87   Southern, *Georgian Playhouse*, pp. 30-42, figs 10-14.
88   Richard Southern, 'Theatres and Actors' in *The Revels*, p. 65.

and exit. Paired shutters which moved across the stage in grooves met in the middle to form the back scene and when the scene changed they slid back and another pair slid across. It was necessary for 'long' and 'short' or 'very short' scenes, in terms of stage depth, to alternate.[89] A large theatre had seven or more grooves but, even at Richmond, Shelley would have seen several scene changes in *The Country Girl*, for example: Harcourt's Lodgings (I. i), different parts of the park (III. i and III. ii), Moody's house (IV. i and IV. ii) and Bellville's lodging (IV. iii).

The backstage was reserved for the scenery, often painted by wellknown artists.[90] For the actors to appear within it would have spoiled the perspective created by a series of graduated wings towards a back scene, although an actor might run, dance, leap through, or otherwise use the scenery for a special effect, as Harlequin did in pantomime, and John Kemble in Sheridan's *Pizzarro* (1799).[91] It was also used for processions, such as in Colman the Younger's 1798 melodrama, *Bluebeard*. Michael Kelly describes the pasteboard horses in the second Act which 'answered every purpose for which they were wanted', and says, 'The Blue Beard, who rode the elephant in perspective over the mountains, was little Edmund Kean'.[92] The most distant part of the procession was created by models moving across the back scene, then small children, representing adults, crossed over between the next grooves, and the principals appeared on the forestage. This technique is preserved in the Český Krumlov theatre, Czech Republic.[93] Pieces were added, representing hedges, walls, rocks or bridges, to mask a ramp, a row of lights or a trap, or the scenery was cut out to create layers of trees for 'a cut wood' or a cavern, which would break up the perspective. Painted cloth drop scenes, on rollers, were also used. Theatres had a repertory of perhaps 100 plays, so scenery was kept in stock and re-used, not designed for every production.[94]

The stage was candlelit by a central chandelier, a row of footlights

---

89   Colin Visser, 'Scenery and Theatrical Design', p. 83; Southern, *Georgian Playhouse*, pp. 20-24; Ferrero, 'Staging Rossini', pp. 206-207.
90   Sybil Rosenfeld, *A Short History of Scene Design in Great Britain* (Oxford: Blackwell, 1973), p. 60.
91   Colin Visser, 'Scenery and Theatrical Design' in *London Theatre World*, p. 85.
92   Kelly, *Reminiscences*, pp. 246-247.
93   Information from Professor Petr Pirina, Chairman, Český Krumlov Foundation, private conversation at the Congress of Perspectiv, the Association of Historic Theatres in Europe, Bury St Edmunds, 4 October 2007.
94   Colin Visser, 'Scenery and Theatrical Design', p. 84; Southern, *Changeable Scenery*, p. 256; Rosenfeld, *Georgian Scene Painters*, p. 23; Rosenfeld, *Scene Design*, pp. 98, 103.

and some lights concealed on battens in the wings. The auditorium was fully lit.[95] Scenery changes were rapid and easy in comparison with later innovation. The box set replaced the earlier system of wings and flats, but it requires a much longer and more complicated mechanical operation and was not completely introduced until 1881.[96] The actor together with the scenery then formed a brightly lit picture placed behind a proscenium arch at a distance from an audience sitting in darkness, the forestage no longer used. The stage picture when Shelley was going to the theatre differed since the size of the eighteenth-century theatre, the position of the stage and the lighting laid the emphasis on the actor and created an intimacy between actor and audience. Actors wore their own clothes or were given them by rich patrons, with the exception of some leading Shakespearean characters in period costume, and concessions to the Orient made by turbans or to classical times by Roman-style armour.[97] George Romney painted Jordan as Peggy in *The Country Girl*, hair flowing, in a white dress with sash and large straw hat. Costume in general was that of the day, especially for a comedy.

In a century which had produced Garrick and other great and still-remembered talents, Jordan, who 'burst upon the Metropolis' with 'elastic spring' in 1785, was one of the greatest. 'Nature had formed her in her most prodigal humour', said Hazlitt. She had 'unbounded humour and unaffected sensibility' and her voice was 'a cordial to the heart'.[98] Versatile enough to play both Rosalind and Angela in *The Castle Spectre* but, having a figure 'made to assume the male attire', she was most popular in the roles where this was required, such as Peggy in *The Country Girl*. Her success was not merely because of her beauty, but also because she 'infused herself more completely' into a character' than any other actress. 'The great mistress of comic utterance',[99] she had a natural and hearty laugh which did not finish on cue but, as Hunt said, 'when you expect it no longer according to the usual habit of the stage, it sparkles forth at little intervals […] this is the laughter of the feelings.'[100] In the letter scene (*The Country Girl*, IV. ii), 'the very pen and ink were made to express the rustic petulance of the writer of

---

95   Edward A. Langhans, 'The Theatres' in *London Theatre World*, p. 50.
96   Bamber Gascoigne, *World Theatre* (London: Ebury Press, 1968), p. 248.
97   de Marly, *Costume on the Stage*, pp. 11-12, 41.
98   Hazlitt, III, p. 83; Boaden, *Mrs. Jordan*, I, pp. 71, 28, 19.
99   Boaden, *Mrs. Jordan*, I, pp. 139, 347, 72, 55, 70-71.
100   James Henry Leigh Hunt, *Critical Essays on the Performers of the London Theatres* (London: [n. pub.], 1807), p. 165.

the first epistle and the eager delight that composed the second'. It is clear from this that Jordan was able to physicalise her character's emotions, that is to express them through her physical actions.[101]

Changes to the London theatres

In the 1790s, Drury Lane and Covent Garden were respectively rebuilt and renovated to accommodate an audience of approximately 3,000 each. However, they retained many features in common with the Richmond theatre. Even when they both burnt down, Covent Garden in 1808 and Drury Lane in 1809, they were rebuilt to a similar plan; in the 1808 Covent Garden the forestage still projected 12.3 ft from the curtain line. In 1812 'commercial aspects' required the neo-classical architect, Benjamin Wyatt, to design the new Drury Lane with increased auditorium capacity. To reduce the size of the forestage he designed a picture-frame stage, the artistic grounds being that the actor could 'appear (as he certainly should do) among the scenery'. But Wyatt omitted the proscenium doors and put bronze lamps in their place, which was not a success: the actors refused to remain behind the 'frame', the lamps were always being blown out and the doors were restored after the first season (1812/1813).[102]

While such writers as Torrington and Richard Cumberland regretted the inevitable loss of intimacy between actor and audience, feeling that the skills of Garrick would be neither seen nor heard in the larger theatres,[103] they were comparing the size with the smaller theatres they had superseded. It is unwise to judge by the numbers they held, as Jane Stabler does, that they were 'more than three times the size of the largest venue at the Royal National Theatre today.'[104] Theatres were not subject to modern health and safety regulations; the Theatre Royal, Bury St Edmunds was licensed for 780 in 1819, but the same space may now hold only 350.[105] Contemporary

101 *Plays of David Garrick*, VII, p. 236; Boaden, *Mrs. Jordan*, I, p. 72.
102 Rosenfeld, *Georgian Scene Painters*, p. 92; Leacroft, *English Playhouse*, pp. 139, 155, 166-167, 170; George Saunders, 'The Treatise on Theatres', qtd in Leacroft, *English Playhouse*, p. 166; Simon Tidworth, *Theatres: an Architectural and Cultural History* (New York: Praeger, 1973), p. 128.
103 Qtd in A. Langhans, 'The Theatres' in *London Theatre World*, pp. 53-54.
104 Stabler, *From Burke to Byron*, p. 53.
105 Colin Blumenau, Director, Theatre Royal, Bury St Edmunds, speaking at the congress of Perspectiv, Association of Historic Theatres in Europe, Bury St Edmunds, 4 October 2007.

prints show the gallery and pit crammed with people. Crowds of people tend to muffle the sound of actors' voices, but, during this period, sound was not lost in a flying tower above the stage, since there was none, or behind the proscenium arch, since the actors played on the forestage, although contemporary comment suggests that they had to make an effort for their voices to reach the gallery.[106] The encircling auditorium was a more intimate space and provided a warmer atmosphere before it was broken up by division into stalls, circle and upper circle and entrances at the rear in the mid-nineteenth century. The actors were not separated from the audience but performed in the same physical space. As Donohue points out, an audience in which members can see each other is 'one very much aware of itself and more easily inclined towards generally vocal behaviour'.[107] The actor required a strong presence and rapport with the audience in order to keep their attention.

During the late eighteenth century, scenery and lighting techniques developed. The popular pantomime required frequent and smooth trick scenery changes for spectacular and magical effects such as trees growing out of rocks, burning palaces which collapsed, earthquakes, thunder and lightning. There was a particular taste for erupting volcanoes. Free-standing pieces of scenery had become more common, allowing actors to peep through windows and open doors, climb mountains and shelter in arbours. Hinged flaps enabled Harlequin to leap through windows and ceilings. The scenery room produced mountains and torrents, oriental temples and palaces, Gothic abbeys, gardens, ballrooms, illuminated cities, frozen Arctic regions and burning forests. Waves were turned on spindles and mechanical soldiers marched across the stage, which 'was adapted for scenic processions leaving an extraordinary depth in the rear, as likewise large spaces on the sides'.[108]

Sunsets could be created by gradually changing lights behind coloured glass or silk. Gauze could be used for mists or the appearance of a ghost, as can be seen by an illustration for *Richard III.*[109]

---

106 Alan S. Downer, 'Players and the Painted Stage', *PMLA*, 61 (1946), 522-570, (529-530, 529n); Leacroft, *English Playhouse*, p. 155.
107 Michael Booth, 'The Theatre and its Audience' in *The Revels*, pp. 21-22; Donohue, *Theatre in the Age of Kean*, p. 156.
108 Rosenfeld, *Georgian Scene Painters*, pp. 51-55, 63, 93; *Scene Design*, pp. 77, 91, 88, 103; qtd in Rosenfeld, *Georgian Scene Painters*, p. 92.
109 Illustration to *Richard III, A Tragedy, in Five Acts by W. Shakspeare* (London: T. Dolby, 1824).

. *R. Cruikshank, Del.*   *White, Sc.*

King Richard the Third.

1. 'Richard III', engraving by John White from a drawing taken in the theatre
by Mr. R. Cruikshank, c. 1824, from Cumberland's British Theatre,
private collection.

Transparencies, a linen or calico drop painted with transparent dyes which 'could be lit from the front to produce an opaque effect or from behind to give a transparency or vary the image' were used, as, for example, in the pantomime of *Harlequin and Humpo* (Drury Lane, 1812).[110] 'Burning towns' and 'hell scenes with flames', were commonly used effects, normally achieved by dropping a painted transparency, the main scenery kept throughout the act. The noise of thunder was technically created by running balls down 'the thunder run', a wooden trough, while the sound of wind was made by 'a piece of silk held taut by a weight stretched over a revolving drum with wooden teeth which scraped against the silk'. Bird song was created with off-stage pipes.[111]

When the Argand lamp, a powerful oil lamp equivalent to the light of 10 candles, was adopted at Drury Lane in 1784, the centre of the stage was well illuminated, allowing actors more freedom of movement.[112] John Kemble encouraged accuracy in scene painting, closely collaborating with the scene painter, William Capon, who 'reproduced remains of actual buildings with

110 *Harlequin and Humpo* in Cox and Gamer, *Broadview Anthology*, p. 209.
111 Rosenfeld, *Georgian Scene Painters*, pp. 61-62, 120; Colin Visser, 'Scenery and Theatrical Design', pp. 108-109, 116-117.
112 Colin Visser, 'Scenery and Theatrical Design', p. 116; Gösta Bergman, *Lighting in the Theatre* (Totowa NJ: Rowman and Littlefield, 1977), pp. 200, 203.

meticulous care'. For the oratorio which opened the new Drury Lane in 1794, Capon built a huge chapel with illuminated stained-glass windows and borders carved like a fretted roof.[113] For Baillie's *De Monfort:*

> Capon painted a very unusual pile of scenery, representing a church of the fourteenth century, with its nave, choir, and side aisles, magnificently decorated, and consisting of 7 planes in succession. In width this extraordinary elevation was about 56 ft. 52 in depth, and 37 in height. It was positively a building.[114]

It had 'practicable side ailes [aisles], and an entrance into a choir'.[115] Kemble also began to introduce authenticity in costume.[116]

As 'hardly a theatrical production of any type was put on in London without including some music',[117] Drury Lane and Covent Garden employed a full orchestra and ballet company. Roger Fiske remarks that *Macbeth* was never performed without Leveridge's music, and that 'when Shelley as a boy at Eton was 'singing with buoyant cheerfulness in which he often indulged, as he might be running nimbly up and down stairs, the Witches' Songs in Macbeth' these were composed by Matthew Locke.[118] There was a numerous backstage staff: from orchestra, chorus and ballet masters to wardrobe, scene painters and property men as well as carpenters and machinists.[119] The results of their work were so good that when Sheridan joked that, for *Bluebeard*, he ought to send for a real elephant from 'the 'Change', the machinist replied that he 'would be ashamed not to make a better'.[120] Real horses were indeed used when *Bluebeard* was revived in 1811 in imitation of the popular 'hippodrama' of Astley's, and for other extravaganzas such as *Timour the Tartar*.[121]

---

113 Rosenfeld, *Scene Design*, pp. 97-99.
114 Thomas Campbell, *Mrs. Siddons*, p. 252.
115 Rosenfeld, *Georgian Scene Painters*, p. 38.
116 Rosenfeld, *Scene Design*, p. 98.
117 Bruce Carr, 'Theatre Music 1800-1834' in *Music in Britain: The Romantic Age, 1800-1914*, ed. by Nicholas Temperley, 6 vols (Oxford: Blackwell, 1988), V, p. 288.
118 Roger Fiske, *English Theatre Music in the Eighteenth Century* (Oxford: Oxford University Press, 1986), pp. 26-29.
119 '...four principal painters constantly employed, exclusive of accessory principals, colour grinders, and attendants [...] property maker, machinist, master carpenter, 6 or 8 carpenters, 24 to 30 scene men [...] master tailor and keeper of the gentlemen's wardrobe, etc., mistress of the ladies' wardrobe, both with assistants, and dressers of both sexes [treasurer, under treasurer, housekeeper and attendants, lamplighters, firemen, porters, and watchmen.' Henry Saxe Wyndham, *The Annals of Covent Garden Theatre*, 2 vols (London: Chatto & Windus, 1906), I, pp. 336-337.
120 Kelly, *Reminiscences*, p. 247n.
121 Cox and Gamer, *Broadview Anthology*, p. 76.

R. *Cruikshauk, Del.*   *White, Sc.*

2. 'Macbeth', engraving by John White from a drawing taken in the theatre
by Mr. R. Cruikshank, c. 1824, from Cumberland's British Theatre,
private collection.

The new resources were seized upon by the younger dramatists such
as Thomas Morton, George Colman the Younger and M.G. Lewis.[122] These
playwrights used the scenery and lighting effects to move on the action
of their plays. In *Columbus* (III. v), Morton used the scenic device of an
earthquake and falling masonry to bring about a meeting of the lovers.[123]
Lewis, in *The Castle Spectre*, created a Gothic atmosphere with such settings
as a Cedar Room and an Armoury with folding doors opening to reveal
the ghost, enhanced by music selected by Michael Kelly, resident composer
at Drury Lane.[124] When these popular plays were performed in provincial
theatres with fewer resources, the scenery was adapted. An inventory of
early nineteenth-century scenery includes a drop of a 'Cedar Room' with
an 'Armoury' on the reverse, presumably intended for *The Castle Spectre*.[125]

122 Shelley was to meet Lewis in 1816, and the 'mysteries of his trade' Shelley
refers to may have been stagecraft. *MWSJ*, p. 126.
123 Thomas Morton, *Columbus* (London: W. Miller, 1792), p. 35.
124 M.G. Lewis, *The Castle Spectre* (London: J. Bell, 1798), II.i., IV.ii, pp. 24, 79; also
see Fiske's 'Introduction' to Kelly, *Reminiscences*, p. x.
125 Southern, *Changeable Scenery*, p. 307. I believe that this scenery has not

Playwrights and censorship

The new plays, with their scenes of excitement, terror and pathos, were not easily categorised into comedy and tragedy, and with Holcroft's adaptation from the French, *A Tale of Mystery* (1802), a new category arose which, because of the music which accompanied it, became known as melodrama. The form subsequently changed greatly. Traditionally, a playwright had been obliged to depend on a benefit on the third night but the fee which the playwright received at Covent Garden and the Haymarket greatly exceeded what might have been expected from that. It was therefore not surprising that poets such as Coleridge and Keats wished to write for the theatre since it was rewarding financially. This may also have been a motivation for Shelley but another was the possibility of reaching a wide audience. With the increased size of the theatres, a greater cross-section of the London population was able to visit the theatre. Plays such as Colman's *Inkle and Yarico* (1787) or Morton's *Speed the Plough* (1800) expressed anti-tyranny or anti-slavery views which allowed the urban working class to respond to the 'new rhetoric of radical egalitarianism'. Playwrights were obliged, however, to avoid the strict censorship by balancing these sentiments with patriotic lines and having their villains repent and be forgiven. Holcroft and Inchbald, both radicals, were no longer writing after 1800.[126]

All plays had to be submitted to the Examiner of Plays as they were to be performed with alterations made by the theatre. Dewey Ganzel has discussed the powers of the Examiner of Plays to censor statements regarded as anti-religious or politically dangerous in plays and the absurd lengths to which this censorship was taken.[127] Cox, building on the work of Nicoll, has shown how John Larpent, the Examiner during Shelley's lifetime, allowed his wife to gradually take over his work; both censored plays in accordance with their own religious prejudices.[128] According to Ganzel, Larpent's successor in 1824, the playwright, Colman the Younger, would not allow God to be mentioned at all or even, as Sutcliffe explains,

---

previously been identified as intended for this play.

126 Sutcliffe, *Plays by Colman and Morton*, pp. 15, 11, 5; E.P. Thompson, qtd in Baer, p. 66.

127 Dewey Ganzel, 'Patent Wrongs and Patent Theatres: Drama and the Law in the Early 19th Century', *PMLA*, 76 (September 1961), 387-398.

128 Nicoll, p. 17; Jeffrey N. Cox, 'Baillie Siddons Larpent: Gender, Power and Politics' in Burroughs, *Women in British Romantic Theatre*, pp. 40-41.

3. 'Bernard Blackmantle reading his play in the Green Room of Covent Garden Theatre', drawn and engraved by R. Cruikshank, 10 June 1824, from *The English Spy* (1825). Private collection.

the word 'thighs'.[129] Although Colman was not Examiner while Shelley was alive, he ensured that Mitford's *Charles the First* did not receive a licence, so his attitude to that play is important in considering Shelley's work.[130]

The jealousy with which the 'major' theatres, or Theatres Royal, Covent Garden and Drury Lane, regarded their monopoly, the patents which had been originally granted them by Charles II, has been well documented by Sutcliffe, Donohue and, more recently, Worrall. Under the 1737 Licensing Act, the only theatres in London to perform spoken drama were the 'patent' or 'legitimate' theatres, and the Little Theatre in the Haymarket in the summer only.[131] The 'minor' or 'illegitimate' theatres which opened in the late eighteenth century were permitted to present programmes of song, dance, acrobatics, clowning or pantomime, equestrian entertainments and burletta, originally a light musical play with mime and dialogue displayed

---

129   Ganzel, 'Patent Wrongs', p. 393; Sutcliffe, *Plays by Colman and Morton*, p. 13.

130   Dominic Shellard & Steve Nicholson with Miriam Handley, *The Lord Chamberlain Regrets: A History of British Censorship* (London: The British Library, 2004), pp. 29-33.

131   Donohue, *Theatre in the Age of Kean*, pp. 10-11.

on banners.[132] Theatres on the South Bank, such as the Coburg, later Victoria, now 'Old Vic', and the Surrey, were outside London in 1737; they did not have to submit their scripts to the Examiner but they had to be licensed by a magistrate. Although they were not licensed to perform plays, they began to interpret the term 'burletta' more broadly until it was hardly distinguishable from 'play'. 'Melodrama', a recent theatrical innovation with musical accompaniment, had not yet become the Victorian theatre style associated with it today.

The 'minor' theatres

The talent at the minor theatres was not inferior to that of the patent theatres: all employed the same musicians, writers and managers. Despite suggesting that scene painting at the minors was second-rate, Rosenfeld tells us that painters such as Clarkson Stanfield, David Roberts and Charles Tomkins worked at several minor theatres.[133] Thomas Dibdin, sometimes concurrently, managed both the Surrey and Drury Lane and wrote for Covent Garden.[134] Joseph Grimaldi, the most famous clown in English history, was employed by Sadler's Wells — and later became proprietor — before working at Drury Lane.[135]

The 'minors', like the patent theatres, had a cross-section of the population for their audience. In 1832, G.B. Davidge, manager of the Coburg, was to claim that his audience included the working class on Monday, 'the better classes' later in the week, 'even the nobility, most of the royal family' while D.E. Morris, proprietor of the Haymarket, said, 'There are persons of good condition visiting those minor theatres'.[136] The minor theatres often anticipated the patent theatres in stage effects and ideas. As Sadler's Wells did not have to submit a script to the Examiner of Plays, it produced a version of the fall of the Bastille based on eyewitness reports, while Drury Lane's play on the same theme was turned down. The 1794 Drury Lane used waterfalls and lakes on the stage to publicise the two tanks in its roof for firefighting, and was the first to introduce water drama

132   Ibid., p. 50.
133   Rosenfeld, *Georgian Scene Painters*, pp. 115, 127-129.
134   Dibdin, *Reminiscences*, I, p. 420, II, pp. 52, 108.
135   Dennis Arundell, *The Story of Sadler's Wells* (London: Hamish Hamilton, 1965), p. 92.
136   Donohue, *Theatre in the Age of Kean*, p. 157.

in *The Caravan* with a 'REAL DOG' which dived into a tank to save a 'child' from drowning.[137] At Sadler's Wells, however, under the management of Thomas Dibdin's brother Charles, the Younger, a pipe was connected to the New River and spectacular naval battle scenes and horse fights in the water were staged.[138] The Dibdins began to evade the ban on spoken word plays by producing 'burletta' versions of favourites such as *Macbeth* or *Douglas*, set to music, which were so successful that at the run of Thomas Dibdin's version of *The Heart of Midlothian* at the Surrey 'carriages of the first nobility graced the road in nightly lines, sometimes double'.[139] Although these productions showed the weakness of the law, it was not repealed until 1843, and meanwhile the patent theatres had the advantage. Donohue considers that by 1800 they provided the same variety as was available at the minor theatres, as well as all the great plays of the past and present.[140]

Private theatres

In addition to the major and minor theatres, the period boasted 'private' theatres such as the Catherine Street, Berwick Street and Rawstone Place theatres, where both 'political speechmaking' and acting took place. Worrall suggests the links these 'spouting clubs' had with the world of radical politics, but his description of them as 'rough', 'dubious', and 'strongly associated with crime' may not be universally applicable. Of necessity, as Worrall points out, their 'twilight world of legality' makes their activities difficult to recover.[141] Edward Stirling described the last-named, the 'Thespian Temple in Rawstorne street, Goswell Road [where] we paid to act 17/- for the privilege of enacting an innocent ostler, wrongfully accused of murder'.[142] Many other actors, such as Charles Lee Lewes, began successful careers in similar venues.[143] The Tottenham Street Theatre, later the West

---

137 Booth, 'Public Taste, the Playwright and the Law' in *The Revels*, p. 31; Arundell, *Sadler's Wells*, p. 44, Derek Forbes 'Water Drama' in *Performance and Politics in Popular Drama*, ed. by David Bradby, Louis James and Bernard Sharratt (Cambridge: Cambridge University Press, 1980), p. 92.

138 Arundell, *Sadler's Wells*, pp. 72, 98.

139 Ibid., pp. 96, 89; Moody, *Illegitimate Theatre*, p. 36; Donohue, *Theatre in the Age of Kean*, pp. 46-50; Dibdin, *Reminiscences*, I, p. 157.

140 Donohue, *Theatre in the Age of Kean*, p. 34.

141 Worrall, *Theatric Revolution*, pp. 263, 250-251, 258.

142 E. Stirling, *Old Drury Lane*, 2 vols (London: Chatto & Windus, 1881), I, p. 6.

143 *A Biographical Dictionary of Actors, Actresses, Musicians, Dancers, Managers and*

London, was well-respected and was to put on *Oedipus Tyrannus* in 1821.[144] By the late 1820s private theatres, 'free and easies' and singing clubs were putting on plays which attracted similar groups to those attending Deist chapels; it is not certain that this happened in Shelley's lifetime.[145] The usual choice for performance appears to have been a popular piece such as *The Wheel of Fortune, Who Wants a Guinea* or *Othello*, but Stirling's account suggests that new material was also performed. It is possible that Shelley had some knowledge of these theatres, as he knew some of the Spencean radicals. Extracts from *Queen Mab* were published in Thomas Cannon's *Theological Inquirer* and read aloud at Deist chapels, although McCalman believes it unlikely that Shelley attended these meetings.[146] He is recorded as having visited the British Forum, a 'spouting club', at the Crown and Anchor in 1811 but this appears to have been a debating society only. He recommended the tavern as a meeting place for reformers in 1817. Its respectability is suggested as, in the same year, Hazlitt held his lectures on the living poets there, while in 1798 the famous Whig orator, Charles Fox, chose it to hold his birthday party.[147]

Aristocratic amateur theatres

Amateur theatricals being popular among all classes, some of the richer aristocracy built large theatres in their grounds, while others converted part of their house or took over a barn, orangery or drawing room for their theatricals. Although not a commercial venture, they issued tickets and had sometimes quite large audiences of relatives, friends, local dignitaries, tenants and servants. Well-known theatres were at Wargrave, Woburn Abbey and Little Dalby Hall, and Richard, Earl of Barrymore and Lord Derby were accounted very good actors. Professionals, including George Colman the Elder at Wynnstay in 1779, Priscilla Kemble at Bentley Priory and Elizabeth Farren at Richmond House, were called in to coach

---

Other Stage Personnel in London, 1660-1800, ed. by Philip H. Highfill, Jr, Kalman A. Burnim and Edward J. Langhans, 22 vols (Carbondale: Southern Illinois University Press, 1963), IX, p. 270.

144   Hall & Macintosh, *Greek Tragedy*, pp. 239-240.

145   Earl, 'The Rotunda', p. 87n.; Bratton, *New Readings*, pp. 48-49.

146   McCalman, *Radical Underworld*, pp. 90, 276n., 17, 189.

147   Wolfe, I, p. 197; Stephen C. Behrendt, *Shelley and His Audiences* (Lincoln: University of Nebraska Press, 1989), p. 32.

them, and sometimes professional scene painters such as 'the celebrated Loutherbourg' painted the scenery. Michael Kelly described the annual theatricals at Lord Guilford's in 1811 in which he and the Kembles took part with the Earl, his family and guests.[148] The amateurs could be counted on to provide sumptuous costumes, although sometimes the expense of mounting the plays ended in financial disaster. Popular plays were *The Beaux' Stratagem* and *The Rivals*. It was thought that taking part in private theatricals encouraged young gentlemen to be good orators; Fox had taken part in amateur theatricals as a child.[149] Although there is no record of Shelley taking part in them, his cousins, the Groves, did.[150]

The audience

After Covent Garden was destroyed by fire in 1808, it was very quickly rebuilt, and re-opened in October 1809. John Kemble, now the manager, sought to pass some of the costs of the rebuilding on to the audience, doubling the price of the gallery seats and taking more space for expensive private boxes. The Old Price riots were a well-organised response to this price rise by the radical working and artisan class. There was little personal violence or destruction of property, but the rioters, the OPs, were determined not to allow the play to proceed and prevented it by singing, dancing and using the so-called OP rattle. Their cause attracted a great deal of sympathy and eventually Kemble was obliged to concede. Unlike the riots initiated by the aristocratic Mohawks in the eighteenth century, these differed, as Baer remarks, in being social protest rather than criminality. Shelley could not have failed to know about them, as they were in the news constantly at the time, but he may not have heard the radical point of view until he met Leigh Hunt, who supported the OPs, and Francis Place, the radical reformer, who was one of their leaders.[151]

Davies asks, 'What had a Byron, a Shelley, even a Scott, to say to an audience of which an important part might be made up of coal heavers, sweated milliners and semptresses, costermongers, rat-catchers, dolls'

---

148 Rosenfeld, *Temples of Thespis*, pp. 16, 111,163, 145, 36, 79, 74; Kelly, *Reminiscences*, pp. 315-316.
149 Rosenfeld, 'Jane Austen', p. 45; Rosenfeld, *Temples of Thespis*, pp. 39, 32-33, 20, 28, 163, 122-125.
150 *SCII*, pp. 568, 595, 597.
151 Wyndham, *Covent Garden*, I, p. 330; Baer, *Theatre and Disorder*, pp. 84-85, 61, 115.

eye-makers, dog stealers'. However, he draws this audience from Henry Mayhew's *London Labour and the London Poor* (1864), written after Shelley's death and after the monopoly of the patent theatres had been broken in 1843.[152] The audience of Shelley's day were a cross-section of society with average nightly attendance of 1500 which, despite tastes changing in the direction of the minor theatres and the Italian opera, remained constant.[153] Although the poorest of Londoners would not have been able to go to the Theatres Royal, cutlers, joiners, saddlers, shoemakers, knife grinders, hairdressers, apprentices, clerks and labourers could afford the shilling for the gallery. There was a considerable working-class audience for theatre, especially for Shakespeare,[154] and Charles Lamb's essay, *Old China*, suggests that people of taste could be found in the gallery.[155] It appears that the OPs considered themselves to be better lovers of drama than the wealthy patrons of the private boxes, since one of their main objections was that the occupants of these used them for assignations rather than for watching the play.[156] Donohue believes that Shelley could not write an 'effective tragedy aimed at an audience for whom he feels nothing other than dislike and mistrust', but there is no evidence that this was Shelley's attitude.[157] Moreover, Stephen Behrendt has described Shelley's ability to write for different audiences, citing *The Cenci* as one example.[158]

The early nineteenth-century audiences were not decorous and silent, but lively and vociferous, and reacted by weeping, cheering and hissing. At times they fought each other and threw things on the stage, and gallery-goers were 'never too inhibited to call out for what pleased them most'.[159] Reactions were usually spontaneous, although plays were sometimes hissed off stage as part of a plan by rival players or managers, but reports of the audience show that their criticism of acting was quite sophisticated.[160] A lack of inhibition in response is not indicative of an inability to appreciate good drama. Cave suggests that the 'prevailing theatrical taste [was]

152   Davies, 'Playwrights and Plays' in *The Revels*, p. 193.
153   Baer, *Theatre and Disorder*, pp. 167-168, 172; Donohue, *Theatre in the Age of Kean*, p. 17; Sutcliffe, *Plays by Colman and Morton*, p. 7.
154   Baer, *Theatre and Disorder*, pp. 141, 183; and see Stirling, *Old Drury Lane*, I, p. 77-78, for playing Shakespeare to mill hands.
155   Charles Lamb, *Old China*, in *The Works of Charles and Mary Lamb*, ed. by E.V. Lucas, 3 vols (London: Methuen, 1903), II, p. 250.
156   Baer, *Theatre and Disorder*, p. 33.
157   Donohue, *Theatre in the Age of Kean*, p. 172.
158   Behrendt, *Shelley and His Audiences*, p. 2.
159   Donohue, *Theatre in the Age of Kean*, pp. 154-155.
160   Charles Inigo Jones, *Memoirs of Miss O'Neill* (London: D. Cox, 1816), p. 91.

popularist and subsequently indifferent towards attempts to create new forms of tragedy,' but his comparisons of the relative success of Byron's *Marino Faliero* or *Werner* with Moncrieff's *Tom and Jerry* and Jerrold's *Black Ey'd Susan* more properly shows that there was as much room then for both these types of drama as there was in the twentieth century for that of Beckett and Pinter and the musicals of Rodgers and Hammerstein. As Somerset Maugham remarked, 'Hazlitt would not have troubled to write now and then a careful analysis of a popular actor's performance in a well-known play if he had not been assured that this subject was of concern to his readers'.[161] Inchbald's analysis of Baillie's *De Monfort*, shows that she expected attention and an intelligent reaction from members of the audience since she speaks of 'the most attentive auditor, [who] whilst he plainly beholds effects, asks after causes'.[162]

The received idea that, for the foremost critics of the Romantic period, reading plays was more satisfying than theatrical experience is evident in Gaull's statement that 'Coleridge, Hazlitt, Hunt, Lamb and other critics further enriched the reading experience with lectures and essays that dealt with text rather than performance' and her implication that this preference for text was compounded by 'the discomfort of the theaters, the vulgarity of the audiences, or the criminal element that surrounded the theaters'.[163] Hazlitt and Hunt were professional theatre critics who both wrote with great understanding of the art of acting and Coleridge, who attended the theatre regularly from Highgate, wrote a successful tragedy, *Remorse*. Their lectures were for a theatre-loving audience. Lamb shows nostalgia for the theatre of his youth in his essays *On Some of the Old Actors*, *On the Artificial Comedy of the Last Century* and *Stage Illusion*, but it is clear that he had a deep love of theatre and actors.[164] Furthermore, the theatres were comfortable, as Moody points out.[165] Gaull herself also remarks that, 'to the vast contemporary audiences of all ages, classes, and intellectual achievement, the theater was [...] interesting enough to justify 160 newspapers, magazines, and journals devoted exclusively to the theater between 1800 and 1830, and in 1825, 29

161 Somerset Maugham, Introduction to Raymond Mander and Joe Mitchenson, *The Artist and the Theatre* (London: Heinemann, 1955), p. xx.
162 Elizabeth Inchbald, 'Remarks' on De Montfort in *The British Theatre*, XXIV. Despite Baillie's original spelling, the title is spelt De Montfort on the playbill and by all contemporary theatre writers.
163 Gaull, *English Romanticism*, p. 104.
164 Lucas, *Works of Charles and Mary Lamb*, pp. 132-141, 141-147, 163-165.
165 Moody, *Illegitimate Theatre*, p. 151.

daily theatrical periodicals'.[166] It is unlikely that this interest could have been aroused if it was as impossible to hear or see as she states.

Gaull suggests that the existence of popular editions of plays shows that audiences preferred to read rather than see plays, but those she refers to were published after the plays had been performed from the text used by the theatre with contemporary cast lists.[167] Two other editions, Dolby's *British Theatre* and those of John Cumberland, were advertised as being 'printed under the authority of the managers from the prompt book with an authentic description of the costume and the general stage business' and with engravings 'from original drawings made in the theatre' often by I.R. Cruikshank. The details given for the costumes is typified by the following description of the Duke's costume for *The Honeymoon:*

> 1st. Crimson velvet circular cloak white satin doublet and breeches, faced with crimson velvet, and embroidered with gold; white silk tights; black shoes; black beaver hat, white and red feathers. 2nd Dark velvet jacket and breeches, ornamented with small white buttons; brown leather gaiters; shoes; sombrero. 3rd. Same as 1st, with coronet of gold and jewels, and state robe.

Furthermore, the time was given: 'Time in performance, Two Hours and Fifteen Minutes; When played in Three Acts, one hour and Forty Minutes.'[168]

Such details were not for those preferring to read rather than to see a play, but for amateur performers or readers with a knowledge of performance who would read a play before going to see it, as Julian Charles Young suggests they do.[169] Shelley also read plays which he later saw, such as *Fazio* and *Rosmunda.*[170] This interest in both reading and seeing plays accounts for the fact that a play successful with the reading public could transfer to the stage and that plays successful on stage were published.

166   Gaull, *English Romanticism*, pp. 81-83.
167   Ibid., p. 104.
168   Tobin, *The Honeymoon* (London: Samuel French, undated but with 'Remarks' by D-G (George Daniel) dated 1827), title page.
169   Julian Charles Young, 'Others and Mrs. Siddons', in *Specimens of English Dramatic Criticism, XVII-XX Centuries*, ed. by A.C. Ward (London: Humphrey Milford 1945), pp. 90-91.
170   *MWSJ*, pp. 662, 632, 193; Gisborne & Williams, p. 145.

The actors

This was 'a century of great and individual acting'.[171] Donohue describes the
audience going to see a play in order to compare different actors in famous
roles, although 'it was expected, of course, that the entire play would be
well cast and that a good deal of ensemble playing would happily coexist
with a somewhat greater emphasis on leading roles.' There was no director
though the prompter would rehearse the actors in the few rehearsals there
were. 'It was left to the performer to introduce new shade of meaning or
even an entirely new concept of the role by means of changes of vocal
inflection, pauses, gesture, movement — "business" in general'.[172] The
techniques used to achieve a performance differed from those used since
the nineteenth century. The study of sculpture was recommended to actors
to create an attractive picture on stage.[173] Siddons, for example, 'arose and
placed herself in the attitude of one of the old Egyptian statues';[174] her
brother, John Philip Kemble's 'attitudes were stately and picturesque, but
evidently prepared; even the care he took in the disposition of his mantle was
distinctly observable';[175] and Eliza O'Neill's 'attitudes might have afforded
a gallery of statues for the court of Virtue'.[176] This skill was, however, seen
only as a part of the training which an actor should undertake and not
more important than the power of the actor to represent the character he
was playing and the audience's response to this.

Boaden particularly stresses this aspect while acknowledging Siddons's
mastery of gesture. It is clear from what he says of the sleepwalking scene
(*Macbeth*, V. i) that her movements were made not for their own sake but for
a truthful portrait. 'She laded the water from the imaginary ewer over her
hands — bent her body to listen to the sounds presented by her fancy, and
hurried to resume the taper where she had left it'. Boaden also remarks on
her energy and its effect on the audience: 'the amazing burst of energy upon
the words "shalt be"' (I. v. 16) which 'perfectly electrified the house'; the
'triumphant hurry and enjoyment in her scorn, which the audience caught

171 Michael Booth, 'The Theatre and its Audience' in *The Revels*, p. 8.
172 Donohue, *Theatre in the Age of Kean*, pp. 62-64.
173 Alan S. Downer, 'Nature to Advantage Dressed: Eighteenth Century Acting',
PMLA 58 (1943), 1002-1037 (p. 1028).
174 Boaden, *Mrs. Siddons*, II, p. 388.
175 Macready, *Reminiscences*, I, p. 136.
176 'Desultory Reminiscences of Miss O'Neil' *Blackwood's Edinburgh Magazine*, XX-
VII (1832), qtd in Downer, 'The Painted Stage', p. 529.

as electrical, and applauded in rapture for at least a minute' in *The Grecian Daughter*. He contrasts her performance with that of Mrs. Yates, whose beauty he compares to a Greek statue, but who 'had but little expression to animate a form and countenance almost as perfect'. Siddons's acting had so much power that 'the sobs, the shrieks, among the tenderer part of her audiences; or those tears, which manhood at first struggled to suppress, but at length grew proud of indulging' were something impossible 'I should ever forget!'[177] Her gestures did not appear artificial to Hunt, who said, 'one can hardly imagine there has been any such thing as a rehearsal for powers so natural and so spirited'.[178]

The acting of the company as a whole was also of a high standard. In March 1812, *Julius Caesar* filled Covent Garden twice a week. The whole male cast were costumed in white togas, in which it might be difficult to distinguish individual actors. In Julian Charles Young's description, he suggests not only that their acting would have allowed Shakespeare's characters to be recognised, but that theatre-goers also read the plays they were to see:

> any intelligent observer, though he had never entered the walls of a theatre before, if he had but studied the play in his closet, would have had no difficulty in recognizing in the calm, cold, self-contained, stoical dignity of John Kemble's *walk*, the very ideal of Marcus Brutus; or in the pale, wan, austere, 'lean and hungry look' of Young, and in his quick and nervous *pace*, the irritability and nervous impetuosity of Caius Cassius; or in the handsome, joyous face and graceful tread of Charles Kemble — his pliant body bending forward in courtly adulation of 'Great Caesar' — Mark Antony himself; while Fawcett's sour, sarcastic countenance would not more aptly pourtray 'quick-mettled Casca', than his abrupt and hasty *stamp* upon the ground when Brutus asked him 'What had chanced that Caesar was so sad?'[179]

Young's description shows that these actors fully embodied the characters they played and were valued for it. Cast lists of Drury Lane or Covent Garden productions show a tendency to cast to type in the similarity of role offered to, say, Mary Ann Davenport or Henry Johnston, but the ability to play against type was also highly valued.[180] Tate Wilkinson, the manager of the York circuit who brought Jordan and others to the fore, remarks:

---

177 Boaden, *Mrs. Siddons*, II, pp. 144, 133; I, 317, 327.
178 Hunt, *Critical Essays*, p. 20.
179 *Leigh Hunt's Dramatic Criticism 1808-1832*, ed. by L.J. and C.W. Houtchens (New York: Columbia University Press, 1949), p. 65; Young, 'Others and Mrs. Siddons', pp. 90-91.
180 See, e.g., the cast lists for *Lovers' Vows* by Elizabeth Inchbald (Dublin: Thomas Burnside, 1798) and for *Speed the Plough* in *Plays by Colman and Morton*, p. 211.

you perceive the skill of the artist perhaps more when he is out of his walk, than when in; for there are not only many tragic and comic actors who possess, with justice, great-approved merit, yet it is Mr. Such-a-one still, because too much of the same man serves to represent a variety of characters, without paying that necessary difficult attention, to discrimination, which should, of course, demand an alteration of voice, action, motion, &c.[181]

In *The Life of Holcroft*, which Shelley read in 1816,[182] there is a description of the actor, Thomas Weston:

While the audience was convulsed with laughter, he was perfectly unmoved: no look, no motion of the body, ever gave the least intimation that he knew himself to be Thomas Weston [...] it was always either Jerry Sneak, Doctor Last, Abel Drugger, Scrub, Sharp [...][183]

Shelley may also have heard from Hunt his theory of 'natural acting':

A natural actor [...] may be correct in the representation of nature, or he may be called correct in the representation of deviations from nature, and either of these correctnesses is natural, in its relation to any appearance in life, natural or artificial, involuntary or assumed.[184]

It appears to me that the countenance cannot express a single passion perfectly unless the passion is first felt [...] a keen observer of human nature and it's effects will easily detect the cheat.[185]

Critics of the day referred to 'rant' with disapproval.[186] Although the criticism by Hunt and others shows that actors did not always meet their standards, what they considered to be good acting was 'natural' acting. John Bernard acknowledged that the concept of what was 'natural' could change and therefore acting styles change in accordance with the changes in the manners of the day, also saying, 'The actor must give the mind with the manner; he is a creature of sympathy; the imitator is merely one of discernment'.[187] The actor interacted with the audience but Hunt advocated the 'fourth wall' theory of drama in which actors perform as if an invisible wall exists between them and the audience.[188]

---

181 Wilkinson, *The Wandering Patentee or a History of the Yorkshire Theatres from 1770 to the present time*, 4 vols (York: Wilson, Spence and Mawman 1795), IV, p. 15.
182 *MWSJ*, p. 96.
183 *Life of Holcroft*, p. 100.
184 Hunt, *Critical Essays*, pp. 97-98.
185 Ibid., p. 17.
186 Ibid., pp. 23-25.
187 Bernard, *Retrospections*, I, pp. 226, 170.
188 Hunt, *Critical Essays*, Appendix, p. 2.

The theatres in 1809 and 1810

By the time of Shelley's next recorded visits to the theatre in April 1809, Drury Lane had also burnt down. Both companies were performing in other theatres, Covent Garden at the King's Theatre, Haymarket (usually the Opera House), and Drury Lane at the Lyceum.[189] At the King's Theatre on 17 April Shelley and his cousins, the Groves, saw *Richard III*, given at this period in the Colley Cibber version.[190] The actor playing Richard that season was G.F. Cooke as Kemble never appeared as Richard 'for fear of comparison' with Cooke.[191] Cooke, who influenced Kean, carefully wrote out blank verse in the form of prose to break up a tendency to rhythmic delivery. Alan S. Downer has noted that 'Kean followed Cooke in destroying the rhythm of blank verse, and made great use of "transitions", sudden shifts in tone.'[192]

Richard III was followed by Thomas Dibdin's pantomime, *Mother Goose*, which had established Grimaldi as 'the standard by which all later clowns are judged' and 'through which Clown was to become the principal figure in pantomime in place of Harlequin'.[193] A description has survived of Grimaldi as he would have appeared to Shelley:

> a red shirt frilled and decorated with blue and white facings which is cut away at the chest and waist to reveal an ornamental shirt beneath; his blue-and-white-striped breeches end above the knee with a red-white-and-blue ribbon which is repeated at his wrists; and beneath his blue-crested wig, his whitened face is daubed with red triangles on either cheek.[194]

200,000 people came to see him, for 'We can in no way describe what he does […] he must be seen.' Shelley's future enemy, Lord Eldon, the Lord Chancellor, saw *Mother Goose* twelve times, saying, 'Never never did I see a leg of mutton stolen with such superhumanly sublime impudence as by that man'.[195]

Grimaldi was also a brilliant mime, his Italian background allowing him a knowledge of *commedia dell'arte*, and, his father being ballet master at Drury Lane and his mother a dancer, he was also a talented dancer. The

---

189   Wyndham, *Covent Garden*, I, pp. 330, 224.
190   *SCII*, p. 517.
191   Mander and Mitchenson, p. 235.
192   Downer, 'The Painted Stage', p. 533.
193   Knight, *Surrey Theatre*, p. 31.
194   Highfill, VI, p. 411.
195   Ibid., p. 411.

famous *pas de deux* from *Mother Goose* between Clown (Grimaldi) and Harlequin, in women's clothes, when 'Clown tries to steal fruit from the basket of a St. Giles street-girl', was a parody of that of Achilles and Ulysses 'bordering on the acrobatic' in the ballet *Achille et Deidamir*.[196] Shelley was also later to see *Harlequin Gulliver* (16 February 1818), in which Grimaldi parodied a song from *The Padlock*, Charles Dibdin, the Elder's wellknown opera.[197]

Shelley also learnt the power of scenic effects. At the Lyceum on 19 April, the party saw *The Cabinet*, also by Thomas Dibdin, a comic opera with an absurd, disconnected story, patriotic jokes and splendid scenery, which has never been noticed in connection with Shelley. The other items in the programme were a farce by Henry Fielding, *The Virgin Unmask'd* (with *The Favourite Song of Timothy* an extra song originally written for Dorothy Jordan) and a ballet *Love in a Tub*. [198] If the ballet was based on George Etherege's Restoration play of the same name, the whole programme had a theme of young lovers outwitting the mercenary designs of the older generation which would have appealed to teenagers in love, like Shelley and his cousin, Harriet. But it is *The Cabinet* which has the most interesting stage feature. In Act II, the heroine is rescued from an island:

> Peter appears in a boat and lands. Boats with lights appear in the distance.
>
> Bianca: As I live, it's some pretty water-show! and coming this way too.
>
> *Music from the water heard louder. Large gallies drest in rich flags, with lanterns at the stern — gallies pass across — Orlando, Lorenzo, and the rest of the characters and attendants, with lights, land and arrange themselves round the flags.*[199]

When *The Cabinet* was first performed on 22 February 1802, a review in the *Theatrical Repertory* remarked:

> Some illuminated boats are introduced at the close of the opera, which came down the stage. We could not but smile at the invention — they display astonishing mechanical powers — The painted canvases intended to represent the waves, have the appearance of the bottom part of double doors left on their hinges, which very conveniently open for the boats to pass.[200]

---

196   Marian Hannah Winter, *The Pre-romantic Ballet* (London: Pitman, 1974), p. 200.

197   *MWSJ*, p. 193n.; Mayer, *Harlequin in his Element*, p. 80.

198   *The Favourite Song of Timothy*, as sung by Mrs. Jordan… in the Farce of the Virgin Unmask'd as revived at Drury Lane Theatre (London: Printed for S.A. & P. Thompson, [1790?]); *SCII*, p. 517.

199   Thomas Dibdin, *The Cabinet: A Comic Opera, in Three Acts, etc.* (London: Longman, Hurst, Rees and Orme, 1805), pp. 81-83.

200   Nicoll, pp. 32-33.

Ten years later, Shelley associated love, music and enchanted boats when he was writing *Prometheus Unbound*.

The following year when the Grove and Shelley families met once again in London, Covent Garden had been rebuilt by Robert Smirke based on the Parthenon with 'four fluted columns of the Doric portico', on each side of which were bas-reliefs by John Flaxman. There was a circle of private boxes with three tiers of dove-coloured boxes above, and 'the large arch of the proscenium, with its magnificent red velvet curtain, had a span of over fortytwo feet'. In the foyer was a statue of Shakespeare.[201]

The theatres in 1817 and 1818

Apart from Kean's performance of *Hamlet* in 1814, Shelley's next recorded theatre visits are in 1817. By then, Siddons had retired and the new stars were Kean and Eliza O'Neill. Covent Garden was 'pre-eminent for scenery', and scene painters created exotic locations with great verisimilitude: Italian carnivals, Arabian deserts, skating in Holland and a Hindu temple. John Philip Kemble attempted to be accurate by consulting an antiquarian; his brother Charles was eager to go one better not only as to the scenery, but also 'with an attention to Costume Never Before Equalled on the London stage', as described on his playbill in 1823.[202] The stage was also gaslit. Hunt described it as 'the most beautiful lustre of gas light we have ever seen […] everyone as visible as daylight'.[203] Experiments with gas lighting at the Lyceum in 1803, the first theatre to adopt it in both stage and auditorium when it re-opened as the English Opera House in 1817, showed that 'the soft and rapid changes between light and darkness over the stage […] had the greatest effect on the audience' and that these gradual changes were 'really magical, and one does not have to make something offendingly improbable when action passes from day to night'.[204] When they were concealed behind the wings at Drury Lane 'their effect, as they appear suddenly from the gloom, is like the striking of daylight'.[205] Many innovations had also been made in below-stage mechanisms and trapdoors to effect sudden

---

201 Mary Cathcart Borer, *The Story of Covent Garden* (London: Robert Hale 1984), p. 120; *Hunt's Dramatic Criticism*, pp. 26-27.
202 Rosenfeld, *Scene Design*, p. 102.
203 *Hunt's Dramatic Criticism*, pp. 314-315.
204 Bergman, *Lighting in the Theatre*, p. 256.
205 *Hunt's Dramatic Criticism*, p. 153.

appearances and disappearances and ghosts were accompanied by blue, white or red fire.[206] All these advances had a great effect on Shelley's own drama. If staged, sudden appearances and disappearances of ghosts and spirits are required for *Swellfoot the Tyrant*, *Prometheus Unbound*, and *Hellas*; the last two also require a gradual change of light.

In 1817 Shelley saw Kean as Shylock in *The Merchant of Venice*.[207] Donohue describes Kean's talent as 'wonderful for making his auditors think that what he did came on the spur of the inspired moment', although 'Kean's "secret", if he had one, was the same as Garrick's and Kemble's and Siddons's: minute, tireless preparation of the role'.[208] Kean's 'keynote was violence'. He startled both the audience and the other actors, one of whom he greeted at rehearsal with the words, 'We'll run through the scene, Mr. Wilton, because I'm told that if you don't know what I'm going to do I might frighten you.' Kean also had his detractors: one view was that 'his studied play of physiognomy becomes grimace and his animation of manner becomes incoherent bustle; what is spirited savors of turbulence and what is passionate of phrensy', while another was that 'his limbs have no repose or steadiness in scenes of agitated feeling; his hands are kept in unremitting and most rapid convulsive movement; seeking as it were, a resting place in some part of his upper chest and occasionally pressed together on the crown of his head.'[209] Yet Kean was undoubtedly as much the greatest actor of his generation as Siddons was of hers. The actor, George Vandenhoff, described his style as 'fitful, flashing, abounding in quick transitions; scarcely giving you time to think, but ravishing your wonder, and carrying you along with its impetuous rush and change of expression.'[210]

Despite his innovatory technique, there are indications that Kean owed much to the tradition of the previous generation. Kean pronounced G.F. Cooke, whom Shelley had seen as Richard III, 'a perfect actor'. Like Kean, Cooke had made the roles of Richard III and Shylock his own, and as Shylock, Cooke was thus described:

> The different ways in which he repeated the 'let him look to his bond', now
> with a tone of threatful decision, now with a malicious chuckle; and the
> torrent of passion with which he poured forth the magnificent speech which
> follows, giving its fullest effect to every change in the colouring, were felt and

206 Booth, *English Melodrama*, p. 64.
207 *MWSJ*, p. 164.
208 Donohue, *Theatre in the Age of Kean*, pp. 64, 60.
209 Downer, 'The Painted Stage', pp. 533-534.
210 Qtd in Donohue, *Theatre in the Age of Kean*, p. 60.

acknowledged by most enthusiastic applause. The best part of the passage, because an improvement on himself, was his manner of saying 'Shall we not revenge.' There was nothing of rant or fury in it. It was dignified, but mighty. … Then his running from one passion to the other in the next dialogue with Tubal… Then the intenseness of his ejaculation 'I thank God! I thank God!' on hearing of Antonio's misfortune; and the little fiend-like laugh which preceded the eager question which follows on it 'Is it true? Is it true' — There is no such acting to be met with nowadays except in Kean.[211]

Hazlitt felt Kean was unequalled as Shylock. The very first scene 'shewed the master in his art, and at once decided the opinion of the audience'. Kean had a 'lightness and vigour in his tread, a buoyancy and elasticity of spirit, a fire, an animation' and showed the character in:

varied vehemence of declamation, in keenness of sarcasm, in the rapidity of his transitions from one tone or feeling to another […] presenting a succession of striking pictures, and giving perpetually fresh shocks of delight and surprise […] The character never stands still; there is no vacant pause in the action: the eye is never silent.[212]

These descriptions show where Kean followed Cooke in playing Shylock and Richard. Kean adopted the range of emotion and passion, the variety, the sarcasm, the restlessness which characterised Cooke's performance. Shelley, having seen both actors, would have been able to compare them.

Opera and ballet in England

The Italian Opera (the King's Theatre, Haymarket) chiefly produced operas by Italian composers. *Il Matrimonio Segreto*, which Shelley was to see in Pisa, had already been performed in London.[213] The singers were also Italian. Shelley heard Violante Camporesi as Donna Anna in *Don Giovanni* and would hear her again at La Scala. Angelica Catalani, whom he had heard in *La Vestale*, was to settle in Pisa in 1821.[214] It had also benefited from the exodus of French ballet composers and dancers both before and certainly after the Revolution. Although ballet as an art form was developed in France, the first *ballet d'action* was created in England by John Weaver, *Loves of Mars*

---

211 Downer, 'The Painted Stage', pp. 535, 536.
212 Hazlitt, III, pp. 9-10.
213 *Il Matrimonio Segreto* premiered on 11 January 1794 and was regularly revived. Smith, *Italian Opera*, pp. 28, 48, 53, 68,129, 154.
214 Gino dell'Ira, *I teatri di Pisa (1773-1986)* (Pisa: Giardini Editori 1987), p. 14.

and Venus ('a Dramatic Entertainment of Dancing, Attempted in Imitation of the Pantomimes of the Ancient Greeks and Romans') at a time when, in France, ballet was confined to a dance within or following an opera, and dancers restricted by heavy costumes, wigs, corselettes and masks. Garrick knew of the work of Jean-Georges Noverre, the 'father of modern ballet', through his wife, a former dancer, and invited him to London in 1760 with his ballet *Fêtes Chinoises*. Although anti-French sentiment at the time prevented it from being a success, there was mutual admiration between Garrick and Noverre.[215]

Noverre had advanced the theory in his *Lettres sur la Danse et les Ballets* (1760) that ballet had 'the power to speak to the heart', believing that in a *ballet d'action* steps and gestures were 'to convey passions [...] in a gripping narrative' aiming for a pictorial but natural beauty, telling a story in dance and mime.[216] Acting talent was important. Prevented by the bureaucracy of the *ancien régime* from progressing in France, he worked in Germany and Austria, returning to London in 1788, where he was once more joined by French dancers. By this time there were some outstanding French 'composers of ballet'. They were not choreographers in the modern sense since they did not write down the steps, but they wrote what they wanted conveyed in the mime and dance. Among these were Pierre Gardel, whose *ballet d'action*, *Psiché*, Shelley saw in 1810, and Jean Dauberval, ballet master at the Pantheon in London in 1790-1791, when Viganò worked with him.[217] Viganò, whose ballets were to be a great influence on Shelley, 'was to profit enormously from Dauberval's teaching'. By the 1790s dance technique had changed. The dancers had begun to wear soft slippers and the very flimsy costumes now allowed to the *ballerina* enabled her to take up more acrobatic dancing, thus becoming the equal of the *ballerino*.[218] However, the male dancer remained the star. What is generally understood as the Romantic ballet is not considered to have properly begun until the 1827 Paris debut of Marie Taglioni. She was initially considered too sickly to become a dancer, but her ethereal style and use of dancing *en pointe* created the fashion for the *ballet blanc*; such ballets as *La Sylphide* and *Giselle* followed in which

---

215 Leo Hughes, 'Afterpieces or That's Entertainment' in Stone, *The Stage and the Page*, p. 68; Guest, *Romantic Ballet in England*, pp. 13-14.
216 Guest, *Ballet of the Enlightenment*, p. 6.
217 For *Psiché*, see *The Times*, 3 May 1810 and *SCII*, p. 577; Inspired by a contemporary painting, Dauberval created *La Fille Mal Gardée*, a version of which is still in the repertoire. Guest, *Ballet of the Enlightenment*, pp. 386-389, 388n.
218 Winter, *Pre-Romantic Ballet*, pp. 3-4.

4.1 'La Sylphide'. Scene from Act I, showing Madge reading Girn's fortune, James with arms crossed, and Effie leaning towards him. Engraving by T. Williams, c. 1832.

4.2. 'La Sylphide'. Scene from Act II: James placing the magic scarf on the Sylphide's shoulders. lithograph from a drawing by A. Laederich, c. 1832.

the primacy of the ballerina was established, but Marian Smith's *Ballet and Opera in the Age of Giselle* shows, from a close examination of the manuscript of the original ballet, that even at this time a ballet was not fully danced but included many scenes of mime.[219]An early print of *La Sylphide* throws light on the ballet as it was performed in the pre-Romantic period since it shows the characters posed as in a scene from a play.

One ballet, *Le Retour du Printemps*, Shelley saw at least three times, as it followed the operas *Don Giovanni* and Paër's *Griselda*. Claire Clairmont remarked on the 'Beautiful Dancing' of the principal dancer, Mélanie,

219 Guest, *Romantic Ballet in Paris*, pp. 1, 18; Winter, *Pre-Romantic Ballet*, p. 259; Marian Smith, *Ballet and Opera in the Age of Giselle* (Princeton: Princeton University Press, 2000).

with whom Peacock said Shelley was 'enchanted', saying 'he had never imagined such grace of motion'.[220] Dancers had long careers, as she did: 'all performed until they could not'. They worked internationally and 'almost all had worked together at some point'.[221] Among the French dancers who were in London in 1809 was Auguste Vestris, who was said to have invented the pirouette with Gardel.[222] Shelley saw his son, Armand, the velocity and duration of whose 'spinning round on one foot' was said to be 'like the motion of a top'.[223]

The scope of theatrical art available was very varied and rich, and there were new developments in playwriting, scenery and architecture. The skills of performers, whether actors, dancers or singers, were high, while the architects, scene painters, machinists and costumers were able to give them excellent support. There was a theatre-going population drawn from all classes, some of whom were radical in their politics. Theatre managers operated under the frustrating restrictions of the system of 'legitimate' and 'illegitimate theatres', not abolished until 1843, and strict, often unreasonable censorship which prevented writers for the theatre, including major Romantic poets, from treating controversial subjects. To anticipate this, writers operated self-censorship or set plays in Roman or medieval times.

In the Victorian period, as a commentator wrote, 'Boxes have been altered, the old partitions taken down, pit seats re-arranged, entrance in the centre, instead of that long passage, and the emerging from under the stage, and a middle gangway where none existed. The Orchestra has robbed the stage of several feet. The gallery raised'.[224] This difference in theatre structure led to late Georgian drama being regarded as out-of-date and impossible to perform because there were too many scene changes for the ultra-realistic sets. Music was also discarded. Although this had been criticised earlier and 'broke down under Phelps', Mayer believes that the influence of the 'pioneering playwrights' with the 'so-called New Drama' led to a twentieth-century view that serious drama could not include music. Reconsideration of late Georgian drama is beginning, and, with a better understanding of

---

220 *CCJ*, p. 85; Wolfe, p. 330; For Mélanie's talent and career, see Tetreault, 'Shelley and Opera', pp. 162-165.
221 Winter, *Pre-Romantic Ballet*, p. 162.
222 Guest, *Romantic Ballet in Paris*, p. 17.
223 Smith, *Italian Opera*, p. 99; Ethel L. Urlin, *Dancing Ancient and Modern* (London: Simpkin, Marshall, Hamilton Kent & Co., n.d.), p. 144.
224 Harcourt, *Theatre Royal, Norwich*, p. 90.

the theatre of this period, may be valued very differently.[225]

Despite the perennial distrust of some for theatre as an art form as opposed to literature, contemporary critics felt the Georgian theatre was capable of a drama as excellent as Jacobean or Athenian, if only the writers who might make it so would emerge. In 1820, two reviewers of *The Cenci* suggested that one such writer was Shelley.[226]

Shelley's experience of the Georgian theatre, its technical and architectural development, its innovations in the arts of performance, writing and scene and costume design, its exuberance and popularity with a large cross-section of society, was to deeply influence him. For his two great tragedies, *The Cenci* and the unfinished *Charles the First*, he drew directly upon this experience, writing for actors he had seen and stages and audiences he knew. Perhaps more surprisingly, this influence extended to the dramas he wrote in the style of classical Greece, *Prometheus Unbound*, *Hellas* and *Swellfoot the Tyrant*, for although these are based on Athenian drama some of their features are unmistakeably derived from plays which Shelley had seen on the London stage.

---

225 Carr, 'Theatre Music 1800-1834' in *Music in Britain*, p. 288; David Mayer, 'The Music of Melodrama' in Bradby, et al., p. 49.
226 *The Theatrical Inquisitor and Monthly Mirror*, 1 May 1820 and *The Edinburgh Monthly Review*, May 1820, qtd in *Shelley: The Critical Heritage*, ed. by James E. Barcus (London: Routledge, 1995), pp. 180, 189.

Chapter Two
Shelley's Theatregoing,
Playreading and Criticism

The classification of Shelley's plays as closet drama, which has been so often repeated, depends in part on the idea that he only rarely attended the theatre and did not like it or the audience when he did. His alleged lack of understanding of the theatre thus led to an inability to write performable drama. Shelley's friend, Peacock, said he 'had a prejudice against theatres' and his cousin Medwin said he 'rarely went to the play'.[227] However, Medwin was not with Shelley in London and not for long in Italy, while Peacock wrote his memoir over forty years after Shelley's death. The comment must also be put into the context of the theatre-loving period in which Shelley lived. His contemporaries would not have described Shelley as an 'avid theatre-goer', as Judith Pascoe does, on the basis of the theatre-going entered in Mary Shelley's journal.[228] Francis Place, the radical reformer, regarded himself as having 'little interest in theatre', yet he had 'seen most of our best acting [including] Tragedies and Comedies some of them twice or thrice'.[229] Mary Shelley, however, explains that Shelley was 'not a playgoer' because he 'was easily disgusted by the bad filling-up of the inferior parts', a judgment which an infrequent theatregoer, ignorant of the art of acting, would be unable to make.[230]

Neither Cameron nor Curran, who both emphasised Shelley's talent as a dramatist, established whether he had actually seen the performances mentioned in Mary Shelley's journal, although Cameron assumed that he had. Cox refers to Curran's citation of Mary's journal, but Curran himself

---

227 Wolfe, II, p. 330; Medwin, *Life*, I, p. 52.
228 Judith Pascoe, 'Proserpine and Midas' in The *Cambridge Companion to Mary Shelley*, ed. by Esther Schor (Cambridge: Cambridge University Press, 2003), p. 181.
229 Baer, *Theatre and Disorder*, p. 120.
230 Mary Shelley, 'Note on The Cenci', *OSA*, p. 336.

was not sure that Shelley had seen the performances, saying that he 'educated himself in the study.' Donohue felt that he could be certain of only four dramas that Shelley saw.[231] Performances mentioned by Edward Williams and Claire Clairmont were not included in these assessments.

Shelley's youth: Horsham and Windsor

Shelley grew up as a member of the land-owning aristocracy whose way of life consisted of field sports, balls, assemblies, visits to Bath and London, theatre and opera. Although later friends like Peacock may have known little about it, a glimpse of this life can be seen from the diary of Harriet Grove, Shelley's cousin and sweetheart for over two years, and from his 1808 letter to James Tisdall, a friend to whom he mentions the local balls and duck-shooting. A family such as the Shelleys was expected to patronise the Horsham Theatre as the Groves did the Salisbury Theatre. Timothy Shelley was a political associate of the Duke of Norfolk, who was a friend of Sheridan, and certainly went to the theatre. William Maddocks, M.P., who was to play an important part in Shelley's life in 1812-1813, wrote a farce for an amateur company and often invited professional actors and musicians to his house at Tremadoc.[232] Visiting the theatre was part of the upbringing of a young person of this class.

There was no theatre building at Horsham in 1785 when Charles Osborne had to open the Town Hall 'as a theatre',[233] but it clearly formed part of the touring circuit since there were a number of applications for licences to perform there. By the year of Shelley's birth, 1792, 'The Theatre, Horsham' had been built, from which E. Everard wrote inviting T.C. Medwin, Shelley's uncle, to his benefit.[234] By 1798, it had become an institution in the town, managed by a Mr. Ellin,[235] and was successful enough for another to be built in the 1820s.[236] The usual procedure was for companies to tour to certain towns at the same time each year when the

231 Cameron, *The Golden Years*, pp. 394-395; Curran, *Cenci*, p. 158; Cox, 'The Dramatist', p. 83n; Donohue, *Dramatic Character*, p. 169.
232 *SCII*, p. 509-520, for theatre, p. 514; *PBSLI*, p. 2; Kelly, *Reminiscences*, pp. 310-311, 265, 275.
233 Horsham Museum MS 333 X.2001.333.1.
234 Ibid. MS 333 X.2001.333.5.
235 Ibid. MS 333 X.2001.333.6.
236 Playbill in exhibition at Horsham Museum.

season at the main theatre finished, so it is likely that the same companies were regular visitors. Applications were made in two consecutive years by the Theatre Royal, Brighton,[237] the theatres at 'Lewes, Eastbourne etc.' (one of whose managers was Sampson Penley)[238] and the Theatre Royal, Windsor,[239] which was open only when the King was in residence.[240] Its manager, Thornton, who applied for the licence to tour to Horsham, also managed the theatre at Reading and had assisted the Earl of Barrymore's 1789 Wargrave theatricals.[241] The Penley family also managed a number of theatres in the south of England, including one at Peckham, near Camberwell, where Timothy Shelley's solicitor, William Whitton, lived. A close relationship between the theatres in Horsham and Windsor, the Penleys and Thornton, is therefore suggested, particularly as a Penley took over the Windsor theatre. It opened on 21 August 1815, when Shelley was living nearby at Bishopsgate, with *A School for Scandal*. It is possible that Shelley attended this performance with Peacock, since Peacock records seeing the play with Shelley without giving a date or place; if so, it may explain the report by Whitton, whose informant was a Mr. Penley, that Shelley had performed in the Windsor theatre since there was a strong likelihood of the actors recognising Shelley.[242] The close relationship of the actor to the audience with the possibility of dialogue between performers and those in the stage boxes may have caused confusion, or Whitton may have been the butt of a joke by Penley, perhaps with Shelley's knowledge that the information would be passed on to his father.

Such a version of events is consistent with several anecdotes about Shelley's boyhood and youth. Shelley's younger sister Hellen says he was 'full of cheerful fun, and had all the comic vein so agreeable in a household'. She relates an anecdote of his disguising himself and being hired as a gamekeeper, which, if true, would show considerable acting ability and liking for a hoax. 'He would act', she says, when he was obliged by their

---

237 Horsham Museum MS 333 X.2001.333.8; Horsham Museum MS 333 X.2001.333.11.
238 Ibid., MS 333 X.2001.333.7.
239 Ibid., MS 333 X.2001.333.2.
240 Nicoll, p. 238.
241 Rosenfeld, *Temples of Thespis*, p. 19.
242 Wolfe, II, p. 330; Roger Ingpen, *Shelley in England* (London: Kegan, Paul, Trench, Trubner, 1917), p. 458 [Jonas and Penley — Windsor, Henley, Folkstone, Peckham, Rye], *Authentic Memoirs of the Green Room* (London: J. Roach, [1815?]), p. 256; William C. Bebbington, 'Shelley and the Windsor Stage', *Notes and Queries*, n.s. 2 (May 1956), 213-216, p. 215.

father to 'repeat long Latin quotations, probably from some drama', and her memory of 'the expression of his face and movement of his arm' indicates that he did it well.[243] Her opinion that he was a good storyteller was confirmed by his friend at Eton, Walter S. Halliday, a 'delighted and willing listener to his marvellous stories of fairyland, and apparitions, and spirits, and haunted ground'.[244] Another schoolfellow, Andrew Amos, remembered Shelley entering 'with great vivacity' into composing and performing plays with him for the entertainment of the younger boy in the house they shared at Eton.[245] The King's Scholars at Eton performed their versions of plays such as *The Rivals* regularly in the Long Chamber, and Shelley would have had the opportunity to see them, although as he was not a King's Scholar himself he would not have taken part.[246] Hogg recalled Shelley's ability to 'relate or even act [joyous funny pranks] over again, in a vivacious manner, and with a keen relish and agreeable recollections of his own mischievous raillery', such as Shelley's re-enactment of an incident when he had frightened an old woman in a stage coach by reciting from *Richard II*: 'with a fiendish yell, he started up, threw open the window, and began to call, "Guard! Guard!"'[247]

Writing for the theatre was part of Shelley's literary activity in 1810. In August, he wrote to his father's protégé, Edward Graham, who was studying music in London with the musician, Joseph Woelff, asking him for information about sending a tragedy 'which is not yet finished' to Covent Garden and a farce to Drury Lane. He sent the farce to Graham on 14 September, saying it had been written by a friend, and wanted Woelff to write an overture for it. Hellen Shelley says that her brother, 'with my elder sister, wrote a play secretly, and sent it to Mathews, the comedian; who, after a time, returned it, with the opinion, that it would not do for acting'.[248] This suggests that Shelley had already seen Mathews perform, since reputation alone would have justified sending it to a number of other actors.

This may have been in April/May 1810, when the Shelleys and Groves met in London. Harriet Grove recorded visits to plays on 26 and 27 April and

243 Wolfe, I, pp. 25, 28, 23.
244 Ibid., p. 41.
245 Edward Dowden, *The Life of Percy Bysshe Shelley* (London: Kegan Paul, 1908), pp. 12-13.
246 Michael Meredith, *Five Hundred Years of Eton Theatre* (Eton College, 2001), p. 10.
247 Wolfe, II, pp. 23-24.
248 *PBSLI*, pp. 14, 16; Wolfe, I, p. 26.

5. Covent Garden, 1828, unknown artist, from *Fanny Kemble* by Dorothie de Bear Bobbé, private collection.

2 May, but not the titles or the theatre. It is unlikely, however, that visitors from the country would miss the newly opened Covent Garden Theatre, an attraction in itself, since London theatregoers like Crabb Robinson went to the newly opened theatres for the 'house not the performance'.[249]

Siddons was playing some of her most popular roles there: Lady Randolph in *Douglas*, Euphrasia in *The Grecian Daughter* and Lady Macbeth.[250] Although she was on the point of retirement, Boaden considered her to have lost little of her power. Indeed, in 1806/1807 her 'Volumnia, her Katharine, her Lady Macbeth, were at their *nil ultra*'.[251] The Drury Lane company, on the other hand, was still playing in the small, borrowed, Lyceum. Their programme on 26 April was *Riches*, a not particularly well received version of Philip Massinger's *The City Madam*, 'judiciously pruned' by Sir James Bland Burgess; and on 27 April, Tobin's *The Honeymoon*.[252] Although Elliston's performance in this was described by Hunt as 'one of the few [...] that might absolutely be termed complete',[253] the Groves had already seen

---

249 Eluned Brown, ed; *The London Theatre 1811-1866 Selections from the Diary of Henry Crabb Robinson* (London: The Society for Theatre Research, 1966), p. 48.
250 *The Times*, 3 May 1810.
251 Boaden, *Mrs, Siddons*, II, p. 354.
252 John Genest, *Some account of the English stage*, 10 vols (Bath: H.E. Carrington, 1832), VIII, p. 163.
253 Hunt, *Critical Essays*, p. 99.

R. *Cruikshank, Del.*   *White, Sc.*

6. 'Henry IV Pt I', engraving by John White from a drawing taken in the
theatre by Mr. R. Cruikshank, c. 1824, from Cumberland's British Theatre,
private collection.

both it and *No Song No Supper* by Stephen Storace and Prince Hoare, the
afterpiece which followed these plays, so it seems more likely they would
have preferred Covent Garden's programme.

On 26 April, this was *Henry IV Pt 1* with Charles and John Kemble
and G.F. Cooke as Falstaff, which Shelley quoted from when writing to
his father on 15 October 1811; and on 27 April, *The Grecian Daughter*, with
Siddons.[254] According to Boaden, she 'settled *once* and *for ever* all the great
points of the character' and did not change her performance.[255] If Shelley
saw it, he would have seen the gesture mentioned by Hunt to explain
how she compensated for the dramatist's inadequacy in what he called an
'insipid tragedy':

> This heroine has obtained for her aged and imprisoned father some
> unexpected assistance from the guard *Philotas*: transported with gratitude,
> but having nothing from the poet to give expression to her feelings, she
> starts with extended arms and casts herself in mute prostration at his feet.[256]

254 *SCII*, pp. 514, 577; *The Times*, 26 April 1810, 27 April 1810; *PBSLI*, p. 149.
255 Boaden, *Mrs. Siddons*, II, p. 159.
256 Hunt, *Critical Essays*, p. 20.

On 2 May, the Covent Garden benefit, in aid of the Fund for the Relief of Aged and Infirm Actors, was more likely to attract the well-heeled and fashionable audience of which the Groves and Shelleys formed a part than the Drury Lane benefit for the popular actor, William Dowton. Siddons played Lady Randolph in *Douglas* and the operatic stars, Angelica Catalani and John Braham, were singing between the acts. It is disappointing not to be able to record that Shelley saw Kemble and Siddons perform *Macbeth* on 30 April, but Harriet, who had injured her foot the previous year, 'Staid at home all day on account of my foot the rest of the Party went to the Play all but Mama and Percy.'[257] *Macbeth*, a favourite play of Shelley's from childhood, was very often performed, Lady Macbeth being Siddons's most famous role. It was the first play to be performed in the new Drury Lane (21 March 1794) and to open the new Covent Garden in 1809, and Shelley may have seen it already.[258] On 3 May the party went to Catalani's benefit opera, Pucitta's *La Vestale*, followed by Gardel's ballet *Psiché*.[259]

Theatregoing 1811-1818

When Shelley broke with his family, he rejected many aspects of the aristocratic way of life. Between 1811 and 1815 he lived in an unsettled fashion, sometimes in isolated places in Wales and Devon, which would not have allowed for theatregoing, but at others he was in London or Bath and he may have visited the Windsor theatre. Although Mary Shelley's stepsister, Claire Clairmont, remarked to Byron in 1816 that Shelley never went to the theatre, she was then talking of a stage career for herself and might have felt 'never' was the equivalent of 'rarely'.[260] Mary Shelley's letter to Hunt (5 March 1817), however, does imply that the Shelleys had not been to the theatre for some time:

> When a child I used to like going to the play exceedingly […] afterwards […] I went seldom principally from feeling the delight I once felt wearing out — but this last winter it has been renewed — and I again look forward to going to the theatre as a great treat quite exquisite enough, as of old, to take away

257 *The Times*, 27 April 1810; *SCII*, p. 577.
258 Drury Lane opened with an oratorio since it was Lent (12 March 1794), Kelly, *Reminiscences*, pp. 207, 311.
259 *The Times*, 3 May 1810; *SCII*, p. 577.
260 *The Clairmont Correspondence*, ed. by Marion Kingston Stocking (Baltimore: Johns Hopkins University Press, 1995), p. 29.

my appetite for dinner.[261]

On the other hand, Shelley's reference, when describing the theatre at Herculaneum, to 'two equestrian statues [...] occup[y]ing the same place as the great bronze lamps did at Drury Lane'[262] suggests that he must have visited the theatre in 1812/13, since after that season the lamps were removed.

Shelley's critique of Kean's Hamlet is often quoted to reveal his dislike of the theatre and acting:

> Go to the Play. The extreme depravity & disgusting nature of the scenes. The inefficacy of acting to encourage or maintain the delusion. The loathsome sight of men of personating characters which do not & cannot belong to them. Shelley displeased with what he saw of Kean.[263]

While it is an emphatic rejection of Kean's performance and the theatre, it would be unwise to conclude, as Donohue does, that this was 'inveterate distaste' and that 'Shelley's animosity toward the theater ran high throughout his life'. Shelley, particularly when younger, tended to react vehemently yet change his mind readily when shown to be wrong. On 17 December 1812, he ordered Herodotus, Thucydides and Xenophon on Godwin's recommendation, yet he had told Godwin in July that he had '*no* doubts on the deleteriousness of classical education'.[264] Moreover, Shelley was not the only one to disapprove of this performance. Among Kean's admirers, Hazlitt said, 'We think his general delineation of the character wrong. It was too strong and pointed. There was often a severity, approaching to virulence, in the common observations and answers' and George Daniel said, 'Mr. Kean's performance has many beauties, but they are the beauties of the *actor*, not *Hamlet*'. Crabb Robinson, in 1819, found Kean as *Hamlet* 'never pleased me so little'.[265] According to the *Theatrical Courier*, it was an 'uneven' performance and his 'stopwatch' rendering of "To be or not to be" 'merited no applause'.[266]

Mary Shelley, as Donohue says, 'seldom reveals whether Shelley

261 *MWSLI*, p. 33.
262 *PBSLII*, p. 71.
263 *MWSJ*, p. 35.
264 Donohue, *Dramatic Character*, pp. 169,168; *PBSLI*, pp. 316, 342.
265 Hazlitt, III, p. 17; 'D — G —' [George Daniel] 'Remarks' *Hamlet: A Tragedy In Five Acts* by William Shakespeare (London: John Cumberland, [n.d.]), p. 12; Crabb Robinson, p. 90.
266 'Theatrical Courier', qtd in *CCJ*, p. 50.

accompanied her to the theater on every visit she records.'[267] Nevertheless, while her entries seldom include a complete list of the theatre party or a full programme, they are usually supported by entries in Clairmont's journal, Peacock's memoir and, in 1821 and 1822, the journal of their friend, Edward Williams. As prostitutes often used the theatre for picking up clients, a young woman at this time did not go to the theatre unescorted, and, unless there is information to the contrary, her companion was likely to have been Shelley.[268] Perhaps she did not note his presence because she took it for granted, while she noted others because she wanted to remember theirs, as when she notes 'Go to the play in the Evening with Peacock — Fazio & the pantomime.' There is no doubt Shelley was there since Peacock recorded his 'absorbed attention to Miss O'Neill's performance'.[269]

It is usually clear when the Shelleys did *not* go to the theatre together:

C. & S. go to the opera — (Don G[iovanni])
H. Mrs. H. & I go to the opera — Figaro — I am very much pleased.[270]

They saw *Figaro* together on 24 February 1818.[271]

In March 1817, Mary's jotting 'See Manuel' must include both of them as she had made a flying visit to London expressly in order to spend a couple of days with Shelley, and would have been unlikely to see the second play by Maturin, author of *Bertram*, without him. When she went to see *Barbarossa* (27 May 1817), however, he had returned to Marlow.[272] When she was in Marlow and he in London, she did not record his theatre-going, one such occasion being 29 January 1818, when Shelley went to *La Molinara* with Claire, the Hunts, Peacock and Hogg. Another appears to have been to *Don Giovanni* with Peacock in 'the season of 1817' when Peacock quotes him as asking, 'if the opera was comic or tragic' and, 'after the killing of the Commendatore, he said: "Do you call this comedy?"'[273] Mary Shelley notes seeing *Don Giovanni* with Shelley on 23 May 1817, the day she arrived from Marlow to join him in London and again on 10 February 1818, when she joined him for the month in London before they left for Italy, suggesting it was chosen as a celebration, but, during February and March 1818, Shelley saw *Don Giovanni* three more times before Mary Shelley mentions Peacock

---

267 Donohue, *Dramatic Character*, p. 169.
268 Donohue, *Theatre in the Age of Kean*, p. 150.
269 Wolfe, II, p. 330; *MWSJ*, p. 193.
270 *MWSJ*, pp. 193, 161.
271 Ibid., pp. 195.
272 Ibid., pp. 166, 171.
273 *CCJ*, p. 82; Wolfe, II, p. 330.

accompanying them (7 March 1818). Shelley would not have asked the questions Peacock attributes to him on his sixth visit, which suggests confirmation of the 1817 date. This raises the possibility that Shelley made other unrecorded visits to the theatre when staying in London with the Hunts. Hunt had published *Critical Essays on the Performers of the London Theatre* in 1807 and was theatre reviewer for *The Examiner*, which Shelley read. He had described Hunt as 'a man of cultivated mind, & certainly exalted notions', and from 1817 they were to become close friends; Shelley called Hunt his 'best' friend.[274] Hunt may have been influential in arousing or renewing Shelley's interest in theatre.

Shelley had the opportunity of learning Hunt's attitude towards the performance of Shakespeare, his preference for 'natural' acting and admiration of Siddons. The first play Hunt ever saw, *The Egyptian Festival*, included 'a trap which opens on to a subterranean passage leading to the sea', and, he said, 'the scenery enchanted me'. He continued to appreciate this art,[275] a taste that he shared with Shelley, who told Hogg that the scenery at the opera house, San Carlo, Naples, 'exceeds any thing of the same kind in theatrical exhibition I ever saw before.' After Shelley's death, Mary Shelley wrote to both friends about the scenery for *Der Freischütz*, to Hogg adding that it 'would have made Shelley scream with delight'.[276]

At the Hunts, the Shelleys met the great theatre critic, William Hazlitt. Although no discussion of theatre with Hazlitt is noted, it is interesting to observe that shortly afterwards, they went to see *The Beggar's Opera* and Kean in *The Merchant of Venice*. Hazlitt was an admirer of both Kean's Shylock and Gay's comedy.[277]

Peacock emphasises his own role in introducing Shelley to the theatre and opera: 'I induced him one evening to accompany me to [...] the *School for Scandal*'; 'I persuaded him to accompany me to the opera'; 'With the exception of *Fazio*, I do not remember his having been pleased with any performance at an English theatre. Indeed I do not remember his having been present at any but the two above mentioned.'[278] These are confident, authoritative remarks and the final sentence appears to clinch his argument by implying that Shelley went to only two performances, but he confesses

---

274 *MWSJ*, pp. 170, 192; *PBSLI*, p. 77; *PBSLII*, p. 382.
275 Hunt, *Critical Essays*, p. v.; Colin Visser, 'Scenery and Theatrical Design', p. 99; Reviews of 1816, 1820 and 1831, *Hunt 's Dramatic Criticism*, pp. 138, 231, 288.
276 *PBSLII*, p. 69; *MWSLI*, pp. 445, 450.
277 *MWSJ*, p. 163; Hazlitt, III, pp. 9, 155; *MWSJ*, pp. 164-165.
278 Wolfe, II, p. 330.

7. 'Cut wood with bay and mountains', watercolour (artist unknown). Set design for 'Winter's Tale', undated.

his uncertainty in the phrase 'I do not remember'. Since Shelley had seen at least two operas, *La Vestale* and *Teresa e Claudio*, before they met, Peacock's role might not have been as important as he implies.[279] This, coupled with the possibility that he may have forgotten visits made so long ago, calls into question the reliability of his opinions.

Peacock may also have been a victim of Shelley's practical jokes, as he was to be in 1821, when Shelley told him that Byron's menagerie consisted of 'ten horses, eight enormous dogs, three monkeys, five cats, an eagle, a crow, and a falcon', and 'on the grand staircase, five peacocks, two guinea hens, and an Egyptian crane'.[280] There were actually only nine horses, two monkeys, two or three dogs, and a few birds.[281] It is quite possible that he was also teasing Peacock with this reaction to *A School for Scandal*:

When, after the scenes which exhibited Charles Surface in his jollity, the

279 *SCII*, pp. 517, 577; *The Times*, 18 April 1809, 3 May 1810.
280 *PBSLII*, pp. 330-331; for the popularity of telling tall stories or 'bamming' among Shelley and his contemporaries, please see Nora Crook and Derek Guiton, *Shelley's Venomed Melody* (Cambridge: Cambridge University Press, 1986), pp. 11-12.
281 Doris Langley Moore, *Lord Byron – Accounts Rendered* (London: John Murray, 1974), p. 260.

R. *Cruikshank, Del.*   G. *W. Bonner, Sc.*

The School for Scandal.

Charles. S. What! my old guardian!—What! turn inquisitor, and take evidence incog? O, fie! O, fie!

Act. IV. Sc. III.

8. 'The School for Scandal', wood engraving by Mr. Bonner from a drawing taken in the theatre by Mr. R. Cruikshank, c. 1824.

scene returned, in the fourth act, to Joseph's library, Shelley said to me: 'I see the purpose of this comedy. It is to associate virtue with bottles and glasses, and villany with books.'[282]

It is very unlikely that Shelley had no knowledge of one of the most popular plays of his day, both on the professional and amateur stages, before seeing it with Peacock. Shelley's criticism appears innocent and naive, but it is witty and accurate. Sheridan did wish to associate the virtue of warm-hearted affection with hard-drinking, spendthrift Charles and Joseph's villainy is associated with books by its revelation in a library even if the intention was to show his hypocrisy. In performance, this association had a strong visual emphasis. Scenery was an added audience attraction, often included in playbills, and the scenery for the library was wellknown and reproduced in prints.[283] If this was the occasion at the Windsor Theatre mentioned earlier, Shelley might have been in a mischievous mood and willing to tease both his father and Peacock.

Opera

Peacock goes on to say that Shelley 'from this time till he finally left England [...] was an assiduous frequenter of the Italian Opera' and Shelley would hear Camporesi and Catalani again in Italy. Of Shelley's recorded visits to the opera, six were to *Don Giovanni*. According to Peacock, Shelley said that Ambrogetti, as the Don, 'seem[ed] to be the very wretch he personates'.[284] Although Hazlitt disagreed, saying that 'we neither saw the dignified manners of the Spanish nobleman, nor the insinuating address of the voluptuary', Shelley's opinion of Ambrogetti's ability to embody the character accorded with the critics of *The Theatrical Indicator*, August 1817, who described him as 'the representative of a dissolute yet finished cavalier', and the *Morning Chronicle* (14 April 1817), for whom the part 'was performed in the most perfect manner by Ambrogetti, both as an actor and as a singer.' Shelley saw Ambrogetti again in *La Molinara* when 'he drew repeated plaudits by his exquisite humour, and was not less successful in his singing.' Fodor took the title role 'with a charming *naiveté*'. Shelley had heard her as Zerlina in *Don Giovanni* and in Paër's *Griselda*. When he saw

282 Wolfe, II, p. 330.
283 Rosenfeld, *Georgian Scene Painters*, p. 25.
284 Wolfe, II, p. 330.

Fazio, he would also have seen *The Libertine* which followed it, a version of Shadwell's *Don Juan* by Isaac Pocock with Mozart's music. Charles Kemble played the Don, 'as tame as any saint', according to Hazlitt; his arias were sung by another artist who the Shelleys were to hear again in Italy, John Sinclair. Hazlitt also describes the impressive use of machinery and spectacle from this production which Shelley appears to have recalled it in *Prometheus Unbound*.[285] After the departure of Armand Vestris as ballet-master at the King's Theatre in 1817, however, the London ballet declined because of mediocre choreography, despite excellent artistes. Shelley's unfavourable comparison with La Scala, 'We have no Miss Millani here — in every other respect, Milan is unquestionably superior' was entirely accurate.[286]

Shelley therefore can hardly have been as ignorant of opera, ballet or drama as Peacock implies, although he was neither a professional nor a *connoisseur*. Unlike an evening at the theatre today, an evening at the theatre in the Georgian era was an introduction to a variety of styles, since it was 'a regular programme of a tragedy or a comedy or a ballad opera followed by a farce or pantomime, songs, dances, other speciality numbers or orchestral music before during and between the individual pieces'.[287] As Mary Shelley sometimes noted these afterpieces in her journal as well as or instead of the mainpiece, it is clear that the Shelleys stayed for the whole programme. Shelley benefited from seeing this variety, from tragedy to burlesque and performers like the Kembles, Siddons, G.F. Cooke, Kean, Grimaldi, O'Neill and Jordan.

In all, Shelley's recorded theatre attendances before he left England in 1818 total 25. He saw most of the plays listed in Mary Shelley's journal, but there are evident gaps in the records before they met, when they were apart or when a journal is missing. It is evident that Shelley's theatre-going was not limited to what they record since the journals and memoirs of his friends provide extra information. The choice of theatre was perhaps decided by others or influenced by the availability of free entry through Hunt's theatrical connections, but, if the pattern reflects Shelley's own taste, it does not accord with Peacock's picture of one who disliked theatre and comedy. Shelley saw the tragedies *Richard III*, *Hamlet*, *Fazio* and *Manuel*, and, assuming the plays referred to by Harriet Grove in 1810 were at Covent

---

285 For visits, see *MWSJ*, p. 196; *CCJ*, p. 85; for reviews, see Hazlitt, III, p. 205; Smith, *Italian Opera*, pp. 103, 142-145; for information on performances in Italy, see dell'Ira, *I teatri di Pisa*, p. 14; .

286 Guest, *Romantic Ballet in England*, pp. 30-31; *PBSLII*, p. 4.

287 Michael R. Booth, 'Public Taste, the Playwright and the Law' in *The Revels*, p. 30.

Garden, *Douglas*, *The Grecian Daughter* and *Henry IV Pt 1*. The rest were comedies or light opera.

Despite his lack of admiration for Vittorio Alfieri's style, *Fazio's* morality and Maturin's poetry, Shelley attended performances of Milman's *Fazio* and Alfieri's *Rosmunda*, both of which he had already read, and a second play by Maturin, *Manuel*, whose *Bertram* he had read but missed when it was performed in 1816.[288] This indicates a desire to see how the actual performance compared with the experience of reading the play. Critics such as Michael Rossington and Julie Carlson have seen the influence of Lewis's *The Castle Spectre* and Coleridge's *Remorse* on *The Cenci*, so it is surprising that, given their frequent performance and Shelley's admiration for their authors, no attendance at either is recorded.[289] To *Don Giovanni*, Viganò's ballets and *Fazio*, he went more than once, which supports the view that the performances greatly interested him.

Shelley's theatre-going in Italy

The Shelleys, on their very first night in Italy, attended the Teatro Regio, Turin, 'the admiration of Europe', but they did not understand the opera they saw or even 'get at its tit[t]le'.[290] Thereafter, they were to visit theatres in all the major cities. Most often they saw opera, but they also saw ballet, plays and the *improvvisatore* Sgricci. It should be remembered that at this period before the unification of Italy, each Italian city had its own laws, including censorship restrictions. When Rossini's operas were performed, they were changed in accordance with the different cities' regulations. The recent background of each city was also different, affecting the way the theatre had developed.[291] Not all these theatres were equal in quality, either in architecture or musicianship. The large foyers were given over to gambling and hosted the masked balls which ended the carnivals. Nevertheless Italy had been at the forefront of theatrical architecture from the sixteenth

---

288   *MWSJ*: for *Fazio* see pp. 193, 196, 662, for *Bertram* and *Manuel* see pp. 131, 166, for *Rosmunda* see p. 632, *PBSLII*, pp. 8, 349.

289   *SPII*, p. 720; Carlson, *In the Theatre of Romanticism*, p. 193.

290   Tidworth, *Theatres*, p. 86; *MWSJ*, p. 202, 202n.; *CCJ*, p. 89.

291   Maria Grazia Amidei, *Il Teatro Goldoni di Venezia* (Università degli Studi di Urbino Anna Accademico, 1969-1970), p. 150; Lucia Zambelli and Francesco Tei, *A teatro con i Lorena: feste, personaggi e luoghi scenici della Firenze granducale* (Firenze: Edizioni medicea, 1987), pp. 84-88.

century and was still 'the leading nation as far as theatre architecture was concerned' where they 'experimented with different shapes [...] to attain best acoustic effects'. English theatre buildings, with the horseshoe-shaped or rectangular auditorium, derived from the Italian model.[292] Italian scene painters had led the way in this art and had invented the system of movable flats changed in full view of the audience, which was in use in London theatres, and stage tricks such as collapsing walls, termed *diroccata*. There was a system applied of using stock scenes for *opera buffa* but new designs for *opera seria* and historical and geographical accuracy was sought in set design and costume.[293] Italy had given the world two outstanding theatrical art forms, opera and the *commedia dell'arte*. As in England, there were touring circuits, for example: Florence, Lucca, Pisa, Leghorn, Siena, Perugia, Foligno.[294]

Milan had been Napoleon's capital of Italy, when it had developed a theatre-going middle class (1796-1814) and La Scala had become the centre of Italian musical life. There were boxes of up to six tiers, miniature drawing rooms, and, unlike other Italian theatres, a gallery, as in London. The auditorium was darkened with only the stage lit. Italian audiences appeared to pay little attention to the opera, only pausing in their gossip and eating for favourite arias, but their frequent attendance meant they knew the operas well. At La Scala, the favourite performing art in the early nineteenth century was ballet, but this was perhaps because of the genius of Viganò, whose ballets made a profound impression on Shelley, one which will be more fully described in Chapter 5.[295]

Under Austrian occupation, the censorship laws in Venice banned anything considered to be political or licentious, to undermine the dignity of royalty or nobility, or to allude to suicide or prostitution. Carlo Goldoni's work was accepted *in blocco* except for a few references considered 'too libertine'. Equestrian and acrobatic acts were popular, and there were separate theatres for prose and opera.[296] At this period, La Fenice was only open for the carnival season, so the Shelleys saw Rossini's *Otello* at San

292 John Rosselli, *Music and Musicians in Nineteenth-Century Italy* (London: Batsford, 1991), p. 57; Tidworth, *Theatres*, pp. 65-67; Bergman, *Lighting in the Theatre*, p. 208.
293 Ferrero, 'Staging Rossini', pp. 204-206; Colin Visser, 'Scenery and Technical Design', p. 83.
294 Rosselli, *The Opera Industry*, p. 34.
295 Rosselli, *Music and Musicians*, pp. 21, 54-57,60-61; Rosselli, *The Opera Industry*, p. 43; *MSWJ*, pp. 203, 205; Morgan, *Italy*, I, p. 159
296 Maria Grazia Amidei, *Il Teatro Goldoni di Venezia*, pp. 149-150.

Benedetto.[297] The librettist, Francesco Beria di Salsa, had to take into account the censorship laws[298] and the result, according to Mary Shelley, was 'a wretched piece of business'.[299] Byron, who saw it the previous February, complained that 'the first singer would not black his face'.[300] Their criticism may have referred to the story being unlike Shakespeare, however, and not to the music. A review in *La Gazzetta Privilegiata di Venezia* also describes 'Otello' as 'questo Moro del corpo bianco' (this Moor with the white body), but particularly praises the singing and concedes that Rossini's music was exciting. David Kimbell considers that 'Act III of *Otello* surpasses all earlier Italian operas' whose music 'impede[s] as little as possible the thrust of the drama'[301] and as Shelley seems to have been particularly responsive to music, elements of this production may have influenced *The Cenci*. Otello was sung by Nicola Tacchinardi, one of the leading singers of the time whom the Shelleys were to hear again in Pisa.[302]

A celebrated company, formed in Trieste in 1830, was that of Natale Fabbrici and Luigia Petrelli. It appears they had collaborated as early as October 1818, when 'comica compagna Petrelli e Fabrizi' were playing at the Teatro Vendramin S. Luca (now Teatro Goldoni). On 23 October, they performed *Arlecchino flagellò dei cavallieri serventi*. The title suggests it was satirical and topical and, as it was neither a Gozzi nor a Goldoni play, it must have been a *commedia dell'arte* scenario, perhaps created by the company, but now lost. Mary Shelley noted 'Arlequino' that night but added that Shelley 'spent the evening with' Byron. This need not, however, preclude his (or Byron's) prior visit to the theatre. Byron kept very late hours, and the phrase 'spent the evening' after a theatre performance also occurs in Edward Williams's journal in January 1822: 'T— and I go to the opera and afterwards passed the evening with him'. Shelley may have seen other *commedia* performances when absent from Mary Shelley in Venice during August and October 1818.[303]

---

297 Nicola Mangini, *I teatri di Venezia* (Milano: Mursia, 1974), pp. 86-89.

298 *Lo spettacolo maraviglioso: il Teatro della Pergola, l'opera a Firenze,* catalogo a cura di Marcello De Angelis (Firenze: Pagliai Polistampa, 2000), p. 197.

299 *MWSJ*, p. 230.

300 *BLJVI*, p. 18.

301 David Kimbell, *Italian Opera* (Cambridge: Cambridge University Press, 1991), p. 458.

302 *La Gazzetta Privilegiata di Venezia,* N. 224, 8 October 1818.

303 Luigi Rasi, *I comici Italiani,* 2 vols (Firenze: Fratelli Bocca, 1905), I, pp. 853-854; II, p. 265; *La Gazzetta Privilegiata di Venezia,* N. 229-237, 13-22 October 1818; *MWSJ*, p. 233; Gisborne & Williams, p. 127.

In contrast to the large and elegant opera houses which were subsidised by the government in Naples, Turin and Milan, there were no professional orchestras in Rome: 'Rome was for churches, not for theatre; […] the Pope acknowledged no such establishments.' [304] In 1816, Rossini found that the barber who shaved him was playing in the orchestra, and the players were as likely to be a goldsmith or upholsterer by day. The buildings were wooden and the hygiene appalling. Mary Shelley experienced 'the worst [opera] I ever saw' in Rome on 22 November 1819, one impossible to trace since she gives no theatre, title, composer or artist. [305]

At San Carlo, Naples there were six tiers of boxes and all the audience was seated, unlike at other court theatres where many had to stand. It had a proscenium 50 ft. broad and high, a stage 114 ft. deep with eight sets of wings ending in a backstage where the scenery could be built up independent of wing trolleys. Shelley's admiration for the scenery extended to the Opera House which he found 'very beautiful'. Like Stendhal, he thought the ballet at Naples 'inferior to that of Milan, where that species of exhibition called a serious ballet is conducted with incomparable effect' and thought that he would not be able to attend often since 'the boxes are so dear and the pit so intolerable'. [306] The ballet master at Naples whose ballets were inferior to Viganò's at Milan was Salvatore Taglioni, Marie Taglioni's uncle. [307]

The Shelleys lived in Florence from October 1819 to February 1820. Ferdinand III was a popular and relatively liberal ruler who had permitted a number of theatres before the French occupation, during which period they were very restricted and suspected of subversive activity. Upon Ferdinand's restoration he immediately gave them more liberty and they were beginning to increase in number. The chief were the beautiful La Pergola for opera and ballet and Il Cocomero, which Alfieri had attended, for plays. [308]

On 9 October 1819, Mary Shelley noted 'Go to the opera and see a beautiful ballet', [309] without giving the title. Unfortunately, it cannot be identified as the October number of *La Gazzetta di Firenze* is missing, but as Viganò's company toured, and had performed *Mirra* and *La Spada di*

304 Morgan, *Italy*, II, pp. 443-444.
305 Rosselli, *Music and Musicians*, p. 50; Rosselli, *The Opera Industry*, p. 62; *MWSJ*, p. 238.
306 Rosselli, *Music and Musicians*, p. 57; Bergman, *Lighting in the Theatre*, p. 209; Stendhal, *Correspondance (1816-1820)* (Paris: le Divan, 1934), pp. 300, 331; *PBSLII*, p. 69.
307 Guest, *Romantic Ballet in Paris*, p. 162.
308 Zambelli and Tei, *A teatro con i Lorena*, pp. 84, 87.
309 *MWSJ*, p. 298.

Kenneth at La Fenice during the 1819 carnival season, it may have been one of theirs.[310] The ballet *Otello*, most probably Viganò's, was shown following Giovanni Simone Mayr's *La rosa bianca, e la rosa rossa* (*The White Rose and The Red Rose*) at La Pergola on 2 January 1820, when Shelley went to the theatre with 'with Mr. Tomkins'.[311] Il Cocomero was showing a comedy by Nota, *La Lusinghiera* (*The Flattering Woman*),[312] but it is more probable that *Otello* was the choice. Shelley was unlikely to have been attracted by the subject of the comedy and tended to see favourite works again, while Tomkins, an English artist perhaps not fluent in Italian, may have preferred a visual representation and perhaps to see the famed scenery of Sanquirico.

The Shelleys lived in Pisa longer than anywhere else in Italy, and went to the theatre more frequently there than in other Italian cities. Although Mary Shelley's record seldom provides titles, the journals of Edward Williams and Claire Clairmont sometimes do. After Angelica Catalani made Pisa her home in 1821, Clairmont heard her sing in Rossini's *Aureliano in Palmira*.[313] Mary Shelley noted hearing Tacchinardi sing on 2 April 1821, probably his most highly praised role in *I Misteri Eleusini*, which was in the repertoire of the Teatro Rossi, Pisa and was given on 27 April 1821.[314] They heard Mercadante's *Maria Stuarda* on 13 January 1822. They also heard the *improvvisatore* Sgricci perform. Apart from *Rosmunda*, Shelley saw another play with Williams on 18 March 1822; Williams comments upon the acting not the singing.[315]

Schlegel's influence upon Shelley

Hazlitt, Hunt and Godwin were all familiar with Schlegel's *A Course of Lectures on Dramatic Art and Literature*, which Shelley read aloud on the coach to Italy.[316] Shelley's *A Defence of Poetry* reflects a view of the drama

310 Archivio Storico La Fenice <http://www.archiviostoricolafenice.org:49542/ArcFenice/> [accessed 9 December 2010]; Stendhal, *Correspondance*, pp. 300, 331.
311 *MWSJ*, p. 304, 304n.
312 Information from Professor Marcello de Angelis, Dipartimento di Storia delle Arti e dello Spettacolo, Università degli Studi di Firenze, email 26 June 2006. See Appendix I.
313 *CCJ*, pp. 132-133.
314 *MWSJ*, p. 359, 359n.; dell'Ira, *I teatri di Pisa*, pp. 38, 39.
315 Ibid., pp. 343, 349-350; Gisborne & Williams, p. 135.
316 Ibid., p. 199; for Hunt's familiarity, see *Hunt's Dramatic Criticism*, p. 296; for Godwin's, see Michael Scrivener, *Radical Shelley* (Princeton, NJ: Princeton University

that is very similar to Schlegel's, suggesting that his opinion of theatre was influenced by these lectures.

After speaking of the potential influence of the dramatist, Schlegel remarks:

> The theatre, where many arts are combined to produce a magical effect; where the most lofty and profound poetry has for its interpreter the most finished action, which is at once eloquence and animated picture, while architecture contributes her splendid decorations, and painting her perspective illusions, and the aid of music is called in to attune the mind, or to heighten by its strains the emotions which already agitate it [...] has an extraordinary charm for every age, sex and rank, and has ever been the favourite amusement of every cultivated people.[317]

Shelley says in *A Defence of Poetry*:

> The drama being that form under which a greater number of modes of expression of poetry are susceptible of being combined than any other, the connexion of poetry and social good is more observable in the drama than in whatever other form [...] The connexion of scenic exhibitions with the improvement or corruption of the manners of men, has been universally recognised: in other words, the presence or absence of poetry in its most perfect and universal form, has been found to be connected with good and evil in conduct and habit.[318]

Schlegel's discussion of Greek drama is fuller than Shelley's, but there are many parallels. Schlegel admired Aeschylus and Sophocles more than Euripides and Shelley classed Euripides below the earlier dramatists.[319] Schlegel believed that the large scale of Greek drama and the inclusive nature of the audience derived from 'the republican notion of the Greeks' and that 'the theatre was invented in Athens and in Athens alone was it brought to perfection'. Shelley said 'it is indisputable that the art itself never was understood or practised according to the true philosophy of it, as at Athens' and connected the value of the art with the social and political background, saying a drama 'of the highest order' teaches 'self-knowledge and self-respect'; the greatness of the drama at Athens corresponded to the greatness of the society it reflected. [320]

Shelley believed that human endeavour had reached its highest point so far in fifth-century Athens when the arts, sciences and political thought had

---

Press, 1982), p. 248; for Hazlitt's, see Hazlitt, I, pp. 271-306.
317 Schlegel, p. 41.
318 *SPP*, p. 521.
319 Schlegel, p. 120; *MWSJ*, p. 246; *SPP*, p. 517.
320 Schlegel, p. 34; *SPP*, pp. 520, 518.

flourished as never before or since and that, through its poetry, the 'energy, beauty and virtue' of that era could be transmitted and understood by other ages. The greatness of Athenian culture would be reborn in a democratic future and would be even better because of moral advances such as the abolition of slavery and the improvement in the position of women. Like Godwin and Schlegel, he attributed these to the influence of the Christian religion.[321]

His admiration for Greek drama was partly due to its political significance, first associated with his own political ideas when he wrote to Hogg (May 1811) of *Antigone*, 'Did she wrong when she acted in direct in noble violation of the laws of a prejudiced society.' The works recommended by Godwin, which he ordered in December 1812, included Aeschylus and Euripides, and in October 1814 he quoted *Prometheus Bound* in Greek, linking it to his own personal situation. He read the Greek dramatists continually.[322] He seems to have thought Aeschylus the greatest of the Greek dramatists, classing him with Homer. Mary Shelley's journal, although it cannot be a complete record of Shelley's re-reading of favourite authors, shows that he read Aeschylus more frequently than Sophocles or Euripides.[323] While he never lost his admiration for Sophocles' *Antigone*, both the depiction of the character and the choruses, it is 'the choruses of Aeschylus' he cites in *A Defence of Poetry* as examples of the 'highest poetry'.[324]

In the 21st century, audiences, while they may not read Greek, are familiar with Greek drama in performance. Greek drama appears on the curriculum of drama schools and university drama departments; tourists see performances at Epidaurus; and productions of *Antigone* or the *Oresteia* are given at the National Theatre or form part of the touring circuit in Britain. But those of Shelley's contemporaries who could read Greek did not see it performed. Edith Hall and Fiona Macintosh have shown that, although there was a tradition of performance of Greek drama in schools in the eighteenth century, it was considered impossible to perform in the theatre partly because of the chorus, which seemed unrealistic to theatre practitioners even after the Greek War of Independence had aroused

---

321 *SPP*, pp. 518, 525; 'On the Manners of the Ancient Greeks' in *Shelley's Prose, or, The Trumpet of a Prophecy*, ed. by David Lee Clark (London: Fourth Estate, 1988), p. 220; Scrivener, *Radical Shelley*, p. 248; Schlegel, p. 156.
322 *PBSLI*, pp. 342, 271; *PBSLII*, p. 360.
323 *PBSLII*, p. 53; *MWSJ*: for Aeschylus see pp. 631-632, for Euripides see p. 646, for Sophocles see pp. 676-677.
324 *PBSLII*, p. 364; *SPP*, p. 513.

popular interest. Their belief that William Mason's drama *Caractacus* included a 'singing, dancing, involved and interactive chorus' is based on the 1796 edition, but when Mason himself adapted and shortened the version for performance at Covent Garden (6 December 1776), he reduced the chorus to occasional four-line musical interludes (by Thomas Arne).[325] It is notable that Byron, while insisting that he wanted his plays to be 'like the Greeks', emphasised 'of course, *no* chorus.' Since the chorus was an integral part of most Greek drama, the remark shows Byron's bias towards the neo-classical tradition followed by Racine and Alfieri rather than that of ancient Greece itself.[326]

During the Renaissance, a belief arose that the classical Greek drama had to conform to the rules of the 'three unities', the Unity of Time, Place and Action. This was supposed to have derived from Aristotle, but it is a misunderstanding of what he wrote. Greek drama does not so conform and, as Schlegel points out, Aristotle discussed only Unity of Action 'with any degree of fulness', 'with respect to the Unity of Time, he merely throws out a vague hint; while of the Unity of Place he says not a syllable.'[327] Although Shelley does not discuss this in *A Defence of Poetry*, he appears to have observed the truth of what Schlegel said.

Schlegel discusses the parallels between the reign of Charles II and what he perceives to be the decline of drama: 'The influence which the government of this monarch had on the manners and spirit of the time' led to 'undisguised immorality'. The drama of Dryden and Davenant was technically innovative, but their desire to provide 'light and brilliant entertainment' for the monarch led to the 'offensiveness' of Restoration comedy and the lack of real tragedy. *Cato*, 'a tragedy after the French model', was 'a feeble and frigid piece.'[328] Shelley wrote, 'When society decays the drama sympathizes with that decay [...] The period in our own history of the grossest degradation of the drama is the reign of Charles II'. It is then that 'comedy loses its ideal universality' and, referring to *Cato* as an example of neo-classical drama, he continues, 'tragedy becomes a cold imitation of the great masterpieces of antiquity divested of all

325 Hall & Macintosh, *Greek Tragedy*, pp. 222-226, 245-256 (schools), 197-199 (chorus), 184, 187n.; William Mason, *Caractacus, a Dramatic Poem... Altered for Theatrical Representation* (London: [n. pub.], 1777); Wyndham, *Covent Garden*, I, p. 211-212.
326 *BLJVIII*, p. 57.
327 Schlegel, p. 237; *SPP*, p. 518, 520.
328 Ibid., pp. 476-479, 483-484.

harmonious accompaniments of the kindred arts, and often the very form misunderstood'.[329] The misunderstanding referred to is presumably the idea of 'the Unities'. Shelley's opposition to the neo-classical drama is clear from his letter to Horace Smith (14 September, 1821):

> He [Byron] is occupied in forming a new drama, and, with the views which I doubt not will expand as he proceeds, is determined to write a series of plays, in which he will follow the French tragedians and Alfieri, rather than those of England and Spain, and produce something new, at least, to England. This seems to me the wrong road; but genius like his is destined to lead and not to follow. He will shake off his shackles as he finds they cramp him. I believe he will produce something very great, and that familiarity with the dramatic power of human nature, will soon enable him to soften down the severe and unharmonising traits of his 'Marino Faliero'.[330]

To Mary Shelley he said that *Marino Faliero* had been written 'from a system of criticism fit only for the production of mediocrity'.[331] It is to be expected that he had discussed these ideas with Byron himself. Byron said that he wrote with the idea of 'producing *regular* tragedies like the *Greeks* — but not in *imitation* — merely the outline of their conduct adapted to our own times and circumstances'. He had met Schlegel at Mme. de Staël's home at Coppet and described him as her 'Dousterswivel' (swindler), so he may have had some impatience with his ideas.[332]

Schlegel gave a detailed description of Greek theatre, including the structure of the stage and auditorium, which had relied on the description of Vitruvius but was later confirmed by his examination of the theatres of Herculaneum and Pompeii. These he describes as 'quite open above, and their drama were always acted in day, and beneath the canopy of heaven [...] The Greeks [...] lived much more in the open air than we do, and transacted many things in public places which with us usually take place within doors.' He added that 'they carefully made choice of a beautiful situation' for the theatre.[333] Shelley also saw, with keen interest, the ancient Greek theatres at Pompeii and Herculaneum:

> We entered the town from the side towards the sea, & first saw two theatres, one more magnificent than the other, strewn with the ruins of the white marble which formed their seats & cornices wrought with deep bold sculpture. In the front between the stage & the seats is the circular space

---

329 *SPP*, p. 520.
330 *PBSLII*, p. 349.
331 Ibid., p. 317.
332 *BLJVIII*, p. 57; *BLJV*, p. 86; *BLJIX*, p. 26.
333 Schlegel, pp. 53-54, 53n.

occasionally occupied by the chorus. The stage is very narrow, but long; and divided from this space by a narrow enclosure parallel to it, I suppose for the orchestra. On each side are the consuls boxes, & below in the theatre at Herculaneum were found two equestrian statues of admirable workmanship occup[y]ing the same place as the great bronze lamps did at Drury Lane. The smallest of these theatres is said to have been covered, though I should doubt it. From both you see, as you sit on the seats, a prospect of the most wonderful beauty.[334]

He added, 'Their theatres were all open to the mountains and the sky.' The detailed examination and the conclusions he arrives at are very close to Schlegel's. His 'doubt' that the smaller had actually been covered, was due to not realising it was a music theatre or *odeum*. [335]

From his reading of Schlegel and his examination of the theatres of Pompeii and Herculaneum, Shelley had a good understanding of how Greek drama was performed: to an audience composed of the entire population, familiar with poetry and the legends it drew on, in masks, with dancing and music, in the open air with a view of wonderful beauty. He wrote:

> the Athenians employed language, action, music, painting, the dance, and religious institution to produce a common effect in the representation of the highest idealisms of passion and of power; each division in the art was made perfect in its kind by artists of the most consummate skill, and was disciplined into a beautiful proportion and unity one towards the other. On the modern stage a few only of the elements capable of expressing the image of the poet's conception are employed at once. We have tragedy without music and dancing; and music and dancing without the highest impersonations of which they are the fit accompaniment, and both without religion and solemnity. Religious institution has indeed been usually banished from the stage.[336]

Contemporary drama in England, although it still attracted a wide cross section of the community in the 1810s and 1820s, was a commercial venture performed indoors. Music and dancing had become separate and more frivolous art forms. The universal religious feeling which informed the Athenian drama had been replaced by the hypocritical morality of plays such as Milman's *Fazio*. Nevertheless, Shelley did not believe that the Athenian drama should be slavishly and unimaginatively replicated.

---

334 *PBSLII*, p. 71.
335 Ibid., p. 74; Baldassare Conticello, *Pompeii Archaeological Guide* ([n.p.]: Officine Grafiche De Agostini, 1989), p. 80.
336 *SPP*, p. 518.

Writing to Medwin, he said, '"Prometheus Unbound" is in the merest spirit of ideal Poetry, and not, as the name would indicate, a mere imitation of the Greek drama, or indeed if I have been successful, is it an imitation of anything'.[337] Schlegel, too, believed that poetry, 'the fervid expression of our whole being, must assume new and peculiar forms in different ages' but believed that Greek tragedy was 'beyond the comprehension of the multitude'. Shelley, however, found ways of making it understood by adapting it to the new age. He did not attempt to revive Greek drama in its original form in the nineteenth century but to emulate its spirit: 'the plant must spring again from its seed'.[338] *Prometheus Unbound, Hellas* and *Swellfoot the Tyrant*, have their seed in Aeschylus and Aristophanes but differ in that they take account of the way in which theatre had developed. Shelley weaves into the Greek fabric elements of the stage and performance techniques of his own time: the arts of opera and ballet are incorporated to compose the 'many-sided mirror' and even the street theatre of Punch or the folkdance of the tarantella. He was therefore attempting something entirely new, but which connected to the Greek dramatists of the great age of Athens who did not 'adhere to the common interpretation' of a story. His own versions were given with the same intention, to accord with modern needs.[339]

Shelley considered Greek drama only equalled by Shakespeare and Pedro Calderón de la Barca. Schlegel had described Calderón as 'a poet if ever any man deserved that name'; he and Shakespeare were 'the only two poets who are entitled to be called great'; his wish was for English writers to emulate Shakespeare.[340] In May 1818, Shelley lent his copy of Schlegel to the cultivated and multilingual Gisbornes, perhaps to allow them to see the discussion of Calderón. In April 1818, Italian was still 'half-intelligible' to him, but by July 1819, with the help of Maria Gisborne, Shelley had also learnt Spanish. He called Calderón 'a kind of Shakespeare' and was to read at least 12 of Calderón's plays and translate part of *El Magico Prodigioso*.[341]

The emphasis of Schlegel's lectures is on performance. He discusses the importance of 'action' and believes that 'visible representation is essential to the very form of the drama'. He suggests that an actor must 'assume [the] entire personality' of 'his fictitious original' and considers how far a

---

337   Ibid., p. 518; *PBSLII*, p. 219.
338   Schlegel, pp. 50, 528; *SPP*, p. 514.
339   Preface to *Prometheus Unbound* in *SPII*, p. 472.
340   Schlegel, pp. 494, 342, 488.
341   *PBSLII*, pp. 17, 4, 115, 105.

drama is 'poetical, and how far it is theatrical', a distinction of category not degree. To become theatrical, the dramatist should 'transport his hearers out of themselves', 'rivet their attention, and [...] excite their interest and sympathy,' avoiding 'whatever exceeds the ordinary measure of patience and comprehension.' This is done by using a 'strongly-marked rhythm [...] perceptible in the onward progress of the action', 'the effect of contrasts' from 'calm repose' to 'tumultuous emotions'.[342] Since performance is the test of whether a drama is successful or not, Schlegel's definition allows a considerable freedom in the interpretation of the term 'drama', which does not exclude a 'lyrical drama' such as *Prometheus Unbound*. Shelley found ways of introducing scenes which were 'riveting' or 'transporting' in all his dramas and appears to have borne this definition in mind while writing *The Cenci*.[343] Like Schlegel, who saw the dramatic elements in Plato's dialogues, Shelley thought the *Symposium* almost entitled to be called a drama 'from the lively distinction of the characters & the various & well wrought circumstances of the story'; from this it is clear that Shelley wished to write distinctive characters and a wellwrought plot.[344] It seems probable that Shelley was sufficiently influenced by Schlegel's lectures to consider the importance and effectiveness of drama as a moral and political tool. In 1818, he researched and sketched scenes for *Tasso* and began *Prometheus Unbound.*

Shelley's writing on politics and drama

On 9 November 1818, Shelley wrote to Peacock that if material works of art perish:

> They survive in the mind of man, & the remembrances connected with them are transmitted from generation to generation. The poet embodies them in his creation, [...] men become better & wiser, and the unseen seeds are perhaps thus sown which shall produce a plant more excellent even [than] that from which they fell.[345]

The similarity of these words to phrases appearing in *A Defence of Poetry*, written in 1821, suggests a continuity of thought. In January 1819,

---

342 Schlegel, pp. 30, 31, 36-38.
343 *SPII*, pp. 733-734.
344 Schlegel, p. 30; Michael O'Neill, 'Emulating Plato: Shelley as Translator and Prose Poet' in *The Unfamiliar Shelley*, ed. by Alan M. Weinberg and Timothy Webb (Farnham: Ashgate, 2009), p. 247.
345 *PBSLII*, p. 53.

he told Peacock he considered 'poetry very subordinate to moral & political science' and desired to write a political work.[346] In November 1819, he commenced *A Philosophical View of Reform* which discussed ways of resisting the government in England which feared and repressed the demands for reform as revolutionary, but meanwhile he had completed both *Prometheus Unbound* and *The Cenci*. This suggests the importance of the political ideas in the two dramas, both of which discuss resistance to tyranny but with the protagonists taking different approaches. This close connection between the political writing and the dramatic suggests that Shelley believed that ideas of resistance to tyranny can be discussed metaphorically in a play, thus avoiding censorship, and be communicated to a mass audience able to react together and discuss the ideas after the performance. In the Preface to *The Cenci* he describes himself as 'one newly [...] awakened' to the drama,[347] which was, in part, through his reading of Schlegel. It is clear from *A Defence of Poetry* that Shelley, like the Greeks, considered drama to be a highly important poetic form:

> The drama, so long as it continues to express poetry, is as a prismatic and many-sided mirror, which collects the brightest rays of human nature and divides and reproduces them from the simplicity of these elementary forms, and touches them with majesty and beauty, and multiplies all that it reflects, and endows it with the power of propagating its like wherever it may fall.[348]

The 'prismatic and many-sided mirror' is also a good description of drama which incorporates 'language, action, music, painting, the dance, and religious institutions' and shows Shelley's awareness of the impact of combining these into a three-dimensional art form.[349]

Shelley's Reading of Drama

Shelley's continued interest in drama is also indicated by his reading. In Greek he frequently read Aeschylus, Sophocles and Euripides, and in 1818 he also read Aristophanes.[350] He read and translated Calderón and

---

346 Ibid., p. 71.
347 *SPII*, p. 734.
348 *SPP*, p. 520.
349 Ibid., p. 518.
350 *MWSJ*: for Aeschylus see pp. 631-632, for Euripides see p. 646, for Greek tragedians see p. 651, for Sophocles see pp. 676-677, for Aristophanes see p. 633.

Goethe.[351] It would be surprising if Shelley had not read the complete works of Shakespeare and Jonson and the whole of the Beaumont and Fletcher canon, since these names appear in Mary Shelley's journal each year from 1817-1821, many titles more than once.[352] In 1821, 'Old Plays' is often noted, almost certainly *Ancient English Drama*, Scott's edition of Dodsley's *Select Collection of Old Plays* (1744). Shelley may have read Dodsley before leaving England, but by 1821 he was familiar with the work of the great playwrights of the Elizabethan and Jacobean periods and owned a 1605 copy of John Marston's *The Dutch Courtesan*.[353]

Peacock remembered Shelley's skill when reading Shakespeare aloud in 1817 at Marlow. He not only read *Othello* and *Antony and Cleopatra*, but also Beaumont and Fletcher's *The Faithful Shepherdess* and Jonson's *The Alchemist* and *Volpone*,[354] continuing the practice with these authors in Italy. It is clear from his reference to 'that one lovely scene to which you added so much grace in reading to me' in *The Two Noble Kinsmen*, that Mary Shelley also read aloud.[355] Playreading was more than a pastime, as the Shelleys learnt from it practical theatrical techniques. Rehearsal periods in the professional theatre begin with the cast reading the play aloud in order to discover weaknesses and strengths and to estimate its length. In the Georgian theatre, a new play was given a reading by the actors. It may be assumed that Shelley read his own plays to his circle, as he did his *Ode to Liberty* and as Edward Williams read his play, *The Promise*.[356] Performance was also considered, first *Othello*, then Shelley's *Fragments of an Unfinished Drama* (1822).[357]

Despite Byron's opinion of himself as 'a good actor' and his position on the Board of Drury Lane,[358] he claimed that:

> My dramatic Simplicity is *studiously* Greek — & must continue so — *no* reform ever succeeded at first. — I admire the old English dramatists — but this is quite another field — & has nothing to do with theirs. — I want to make a *regular* English drama, no matter whether for the Stage or not — which is not my object — but a *mental theatre*.[359]

351 *MWSJ*, pp. 296-297; *PBSLII*, p. 475; *OSA*, pp. 731-748, 748-762.
352 *MWSJ*: for Beaumont and Fletcher see pp. 635-636, for Jonson see p. 656, for Shakespeare see pp. 673-674.
353 *MWSJ*, p. 370; *SCX*, p. 728.
354 Wolfe, II, p. 315; *MWSJ*, pp. 175-179.
355 *PBSLII*, p. 34.
356 *OSA*, p. 410; *MWSJ*, p. 377; Wolfe, II, p. 188.
357 Gisborne & Williams, p. 131; *OSA*, p. 482.
358 *BLJIX*, pp. 37, 35.
359 *BLJVIII*, pp. 186-187.

The correspondence of Shelley and Byron on their plays *The Cenci* and *Marino Faliero* shows their disagreement about the drama. Byron said:

> I read *Cenci* — but, besides that I think the *subject* essentially *un*dramatic, I am not an admirer of our old dramatists as *models*. I deny that the English have hitherto had a drama at all. Your *Cenci*, however, was a work of power, and poetry. As to *my* drama, pray revenge yourself upon it, by being as free as I have been with yours.[360]

Shelley did, saying to Hunt, 'Certainly, if "Marino Faliero" is a drama, the "Cenci" is not'. In the preface to *The Cenci*, he states that 'The ancient English poets [...] might incite us to do that for our own age which they have done for theirs'. When these remarks are combined with his critique of Byron's drama in the letter to Horace Smith, they suggest that, despite Shelley's admiration for Byron, he not only differed from him on the question of the drama but was proud of doing so.[361]

The subject was further discussed with their friends, Williams and Trelawny, in Pisa when both poets resided there (1821-1822). Trelawny remembered Shelley saying 'I am now writing a play for the stage. It is affectation to say we write a play for any other purpose.'[362] This quotation appears reliable in the light of the disagreement on the drama between the poets. Williams recorded:

> Mary read to us the two first acts of Lord B's "Werner" — (the name he has given to the drama that he told me he had commenced on Dec' 21st. The tale is a most interesting one, but I do not think he has treated it so well as might have been expected for the subject. The scenes are all too long and the action seems rather to be repressed than brought forward. For representation, however, a greater part of the second act may safely and judiciously be cut out, and, contrary to all expectation, it will probably have gre[ater] success on the stage than in the closet.[363]

Williams's remarks show him to have had a practical sense of the stage since *Werner* was greatly cut and altered when Macready performed it in the 1830s. He gives more praise to the play Shelley was working on, *Charles the First*, which he compares to Shakespeare.[364] The comparison suggests Williams believed that Shelley was writing for the stage; he makes no reference to the closet in connection with *Charles the First*.

---

360 *PBSLII*, p. 284n.
361 Ibid., pp. 345, 349; *SPII*, p. 734.
362 Wolfe, II, p. 198.
363 Gisborne & Williams, p. 123.
364 Davies, 'Playwrights and Plays' in *The Revels*, p. 195; Gisborne & Williams, p. 123.

Despite the remarks of Peacock and Medwin and those who followed them in believing that Shelley did not appreciate theatre, the facts show that Shelley had seen the foremost artists of his age in drama, ballet and opera, not only in England but also in Italy. Shelley had sufficient familiarity with the theatre to enable him to make critical judgments of performances and had the knowledge to construct a play bearing in mind what an actor requires in developing character and in terms of vocal and physical demands, the interaction of characters, dialogue, suspense, unexpected events and dramatic irony. He was able to construct a stage picture, suggest scenic and lighting effects and see where music would add to the atmosphere, if a dance or song would be appropriate or humour effective. He was not connected to the theatre professionally, but playwrights do not come solely from within the profession, and Shelley had developed a taste in the theatre and a theory of drama distinct from that of Byron or Peacock, one which he could use in the creation of his own plays. Shortly after his arrival in Italy in 1818, he set about this. He planned, researched and started to write a drama based on the life of Tasso.

Tasso

Shelley had intended in April 1818 to 'devote[d] this summer & indeed the next year to the composition of a tragedy on the subject of Tasso's madness, which [...] is, if properly treated, admirably dramatic & poetical'. His comparison of his proposed tragedy to the popular verse dramas, *Bertram* (Drury Lane, 1816) and *Fazio* (Covent Garden, 1818) shows his ambition for performance on the London stage, and the style of the completed scene supports this. In preparation, he read Tasso's work in July 1818 and two biographies, and dedicated a notebook to the purpose.[365] He never completed the play despite later visiting Tasso's dungeon in Ferrara, where he saw his manuscripts, and writing a song which would have been suitable for inclusion as a dramatisation of Tasso's poetic ability and love for Leonora.[366] He may have still been intending to finish the play at this stage. He had made notes for scenes and characters, such as 'the malvaggio [the wicked one] and 'Laura the poetess'. This thoroughness of research as

---

365 *PBSLII*, p. 8; *MWSJ*, pp. 203, 209; G.M. Matthews, 'A New Text of Shelley's Scene for Tasso', *KSMB* XI, 39-47.
366 *PBSLII*, pp. 47-48; *SPII*, pp. 366, 445-447.

a basis for a play was to be replicated when he turned to *Charles the First*.

The first scene for *Tasso* is very short, but may not have been intended to be much longer since it is an efficient exposition as it stands. Two other scenes were planned but not written although they contain dramatic potential and would arouse the curiosity of a theatre audience. Both play on disguise and revelation. In the first, the 'scene where he reads the sonnet which he wrote to Leonora to herself as composed at the request of another', it is Tasso's love which is disguised and may be revealed. The possibilities are that she may acknowledge or guess it, remain in ignorance (as in Rostand's *Cyrano de Bergerac*), pretend ignorance, or confess her own love. In the second sketch, 'His disguising himself in the habit of a shepherd & questioning his sister in that disguise concerning himself & then unveiling himself',[367] Tasso is literally disguised, in potential danger of betrayal, and there is an actual and presumably emotional revelation.

From the first 15 lines of 'Scen 1.', we know that the Duke should see Pigna on state business but has cancelled the appointment and that Malpiglio, whose poetry is bad and mocked by Leonora, has bribed Albano, who shows his contempt for the petitioners by repeating, perhaps inventing, the Duke's remarks. Albano's subsequent unfinished speech cannot be judged from Geoffrey Matthews's two versions but his description introduces the appearance and character of Tasso, whose 'eyes/inwardly burn'd like fire' (34-35) and of the Duke, bored by Pigna and embarrassed by Maddalo (45-48). A relationship between Tasso and Leonora is implied in the description of her hidden face, and hands 'clasped, veinèd, and pale as snow/And quivering', followed by the mention of 'young Tasso' (25-27). In performance, such descriptions build anticipation for a sight of the characters, and would probably have been followed by the scene in which Tasso reads his sonnet. In the theatre, the first scene would have been easy to set up with stock scenery for an anteroom, and the wings would have been drawn back to reveal a grand Ducal apartment for the second scene. Shelley handles the dialogue between four characters well and does not labour his exposition. As early as 1818, therefore, it seems that he had grasped these essentials of the craft of playwriting, and also that he had given consideration to the staging.

It is puzzling that Shelley, having commenced *Tasso* so promisingly, discarded it. One answer may lie in Shelley's remark to Peacock that Tasso's 'sonnets to his persecutor [...] contained a great deal of what is

---

367 *SPII*, p. 366.

called flattery'. He was sympathetic to Tasso's situation, which was 'widely different from that of any persecuted being of the present day, for from the depth of dungeons public opinion might now at length be awakened to an echo that would startle the oppressor' but a play with a hero who flattered his oppressor could never be a vehicle for Shelley's views on politics and morality. Another related reason might be that, as Neil Fraistat believes, he was already interested in writing about a hero who did defy his oppressor — Prometheus — from March 1818.[368] Curran suggests that he had begun research on the themes as early as 1817. His creative impulse to write this may well have been stimulated by seeing the ballets of Viganò in April 1818.[369] If this were the case, ideas for *Prometheus Unbound* may have so interrupted work on *Tasso* that in September 1818 he gave into them and allowed himself to begin *Prometheus Unbound*. However, the style of this 'ideal' drama owed much to the plays of classical Greece, which were not at that time performed in London theatres. A more popular form would have to be selected for a first London success and so Shelley carried out his intention of writing for the London theatre instead with *The Cenci*. Like *Tasso*, it is set in Renaissance Italy and, like *Tasso*, its central characters belong to the all-powerful nobility. Beatrice Cenci was not an ideal but a 'sad reality' whose situation had parallels with Tasso's, but she defied rather than flattered her oppressors.[370]

368 *PBSLII*, p. 47; *BSMIX*, p. lxii.
369 Stuart Curran, *Shelley's Annus Mirabilis: The Maturing of an Epic Vision* (San Marino, CA: Huntington Library, 1975), p. xvii.
370 *PBSLII*, p. 96.

Chapter Three
Practical Technique – *The Cenci*

Since 1922, when it was produced by the leading British theatrical couple of the first half of the twentieth century, Sybil Thorndike and Lewis Casson, it has been difficult to deny that *The Cenci* is a performable play, yet the idea that it is a 'closet drama' has been extraordinarily persistent. Moody's excellent *Illegitimate Theatre in London* describes it so, and it is included in two recent studies of closet drama, although Alan Richardson's claim that *The Cenci* 'resembles *Prometheus* in its thematic development' seems a dubious reason, since thematic development does not define a genre, and Michael Simpson's that it 'was published, complete with a preface disclaiming any such ambition [as the stage]' appears based on a misunderstanding. Shelley does not 'disclaim' the stage, only a 'dry exhibition', and the author of a play would hardly mention in its preface that it had been rejected by a theatre.[371]

Earlier critics, like Davies and Nicoll, disparaged Shelley's dramatic skill, citing Shakespearean imitation as a reason for Shelley's supposed failure. Curran and Bryan Shelley, however, have shown that Shelley's echoes of Shakespeare or the Bible are intentional and work in the play's favour. Nicoll describes *The Cenci* as 'defective', while Davies says that it is 'slow to get under way, and the powerful scenes [...] cannot redeem it'. His claim that the play loses interest after Count Cenci's death shows that he believes Cenci to be the central character, which he is not; he has therefore missed the point of the play. On the other hand, Gaull believed Shelley 'brought too much talent to the stage' while Donohue, like Ervine, thought he worked with 'intuition'.[372] Curran and Cave suggested that

---

371 Moody, *Illegitimate Theatre*, p. 3; Richardson, *A Mental Theatre*, p. 100; Simpson, *Closet Performances*, p. 377.
372 Gaull, *English Romanticism*, p. 103; Davies, 'Playwrights and Plays' in *The Revels*, p. 196; Nicoll, pp. 196-197; Curran, *Cenci*, pp. 39-40, 177; Bryan Shelley, *Shelley and Scripture: the Interpreting Angel* (Oxford: Clarendon Press, 1994), pp. 83-86; Ervine,

9. 'Eliza O'Neill as Juliet in *Romeo and Juliet* by William Shakespeare, Act II, Scene ii', lithograph after George Dawe (1781-1829) by F.C. Lewis.

smaller stages and Stanislavskian acting style are more compatible with Shelley's psychological insights.[373] These do allow greater concentration on characterisation, but the play loses something by not being performed with late Georgian spectacular scenery and grand costumes, with the size

'Shelley as Dramatist', p. 96; Donohue, *Theatre in the Age of Kean*, p. 172.
373 Curran, *Cenci*, pp. 276, 277; Cave, 'Romantic Drama in Performance' in *The Romantic Theatre*, p. 104.

of stage and cast which Covent Garden was able to provide. In the banquet and trial scenes a show of grandeur and crowds of people would reveal Beatrice's weakness, isolation and courage in the face of such power more clearly. To achieve dramatic effect, Shelley used the techniques of the theatre of his time, following Schlegel's suggestions. He was more successful in this than was Milman in *Fazio*, a play popular in the nineteenth century but unperformed since.

The Cenci is Shelley's second mature attempt to write for the theatre. From an artistic point of view, he had 'newly been awakened' to the importance of the drama through reading Schlegel's lectures. In a practical sense, he may have realised that a successful play would bring financial reward and the reputation which he believed had eluded him. Shelley was later to write of his 'despair of rivalling Lord Byron', and a successful theatre production was something Byron had not achieved. Shelley would have gained a much larger and more popular audience for that than for a publication, particularly if Eliza O'Neill played Beatrice since if she was performing the theatre could sell out. Byron certainly knew of the difference her acceptance of a role could make. A play in which she starred could potentially reach 3,000 people per night in London, enter the repertoire and reach many more in the provincial theatres.

A role especially written for an actor was an advantage in getting a play by an unknown writer accepted. This had happened when Baillie's *De Monfort* included parts ideal for Kemble and Siddons. Kemble adapted it for the stage, providing it with superb, innovatory scenery, and Siddons asked Baillie to write her 'some more Jane De Montforts'.[374]

Shelley had learnt from his Roman acquaintances the interest which the story of Beatrice aroused. He thought its potential popularity in England so great that he was afraid that someone else might use it before his own play came out.[375] Indeed, his contemporaries, Stendhal and Merimée, were soon to do so. George Yost suggests Shelley may have known Pieracci's *Beatrice Cenci*, published in Florence in 1816 but never performed. Although it caused little stir and Yost admits that 'there is a great deal of Pieracci that Shelley does not use', he sees similarities in Beatrice denying that she knew the assassins and fearing her father after his death and the use of the

---

374 *SPII*, p. 734; *PBSLII*, p. 323; Macready's *Reminiscences*, I, ed. by Frederick Pollock, 2 vols (London: Macmillan, 1875), p. 86; *BLJV*, p. 261; Donkin, *Getting into the Act*, p. 166.
375 *PBSLII*, p. 103.

name 'Cammillo' (in Pieracci an elderly man who tries to rescue Beatrice).[376] Yost also finds a similarity in Beatrice's lines 'The beautiful blue heaven is flecked with blood!/The sunshine on the floor is black!' (III. i. 13-14) to Pieracci's:

il sole
stamane alzossi nero si, ma notte
Tremenda più scende coll'ira il sangue

(*The sun this morning rose so black, but a more fearful night will descend with anger and blood*).[377]

Whether or not Shelley knew this play, he preferred to follow what he believed to be the historical account. There were various versions of the story. Shelley said that he heard the story told in Rome and another contemporary visitor, Charlotte Eaton, gives a slightly different one from the one Shelley uses as the basis for *The Cenci*. This was a manuscript belonging to John Gisborne, the details of which are available in many studies.[378] To adapt it for the stage, he compressed the timescale, strengthened elements of characterisation and included elements of Gothic drama — found in, say, *De Monfort*, *Fazio* and *Bertram* — such as the storm, the castle and the mad scene.

Wasserman notes that in the letter accompanying *The Cenci*, Shelley compares the Peterloo Massacre to the French Revolution.[379] *The Cenci* treats metaphorically the question Shelley raised overtly in *A Philosophical View of Reform*: whether the people have the right to offer armed resistance to an oppressive government. As he believes that 'soldiers [...] would [not] massacre an unresisting multitude', he suggests that a demonstration should 'peaceably [...] risque the danger, & to expect without resistance the onset of the cavalry', but he also says, 'the last resort of resistance is undoubtedly insurrection'.[380] Shelley would therefore have reluctantly supported the taking up of arms in the extreme case of a revolutionary war, although he feels that 'the true friend of mankind & of his country would hesitate before he recommended measures which tend to bring down so heavy a calamity as war' and, in the event of victory, the people 'ought not

376 George Yost, *Pieracci and Shelley: An Italian Ur-Cenci* (Potomac: Scripta Humanistica [c. 1986]), pp. 2, 3.

377 Yost, *Pieracci and Shelley*, pp. 137, 89.

378 Cameron, *The Golden Years*, pp. 398-401; Curran, *Cenci*, pp. 41-45; Alan Weinberg, *Shelley's Italian Experience* (Basingstoke: Macmillan, 1991), pp. 72-77; *SPII*, pp. 865-873.

379 *PBSLII*, p. 118; Wasserman, *Shelley: A Critical Reading*, pp. 92-93.

380 'A Philosophical View of Reform' in *SCVI*, pp. 1054, 1061.

10. 'Beatrice Cenci, an etching by W.B. Scott adapted from the painting that in Shelley's day was commonly attributed to Guido Reni', from *The Cenci*, edited by Alfred Forman and H. Buxton Forman (Shelley Society Publications 1886).

to do or require' 'retribution'.[381] Beatrice's murder of her father ultimately fails because it is an act in isolation against only one tyrant, but tyranny runs through the whole of her society. Her failure warns of the revenge exacted by the oppressors when they are the victors: 'They would calumniate, imprison, starve, ruin, and expatriate every person who wrote or acted, or thought, or might be suspected to think against them'.[382] She does not oppose the Pope, yet her action is crushed by the State since, as Wasserman suggests, it is 'a revolt against all forms of despotism summed up in the idea of paternity and represented archetypally by Shelley's interpretation of the god of organised religion'.[383] Despite Shelley's disapproval of the element of revenge in Beatrice's motive, his sympathies are with her.

Stuart M. Sperry says:

> the fundamental issue upon which the drama turns is [...], was Beatrice wrong in planning the murder of her father, [...] or was she justified in following, like Antigone, the dictates of her conscience and in adopting violent means to relieve both her family and herself from an insupportable tyranny?[384]

Paul Smith's view is that Beatrice's guilt 'is left as a moral paradox, shifting between condemnation and justification', that Shelley implies 'that Beatrice should have endured' but 'perhaps was aware of the highly questionable outcome of this attempt'. Shelley, in the Preface, says that 'no person can be truly dishonoured by the act of another; and the fit return to make to the most enormous injuries is kindness and forbearance'. These characteristics are shown in Lucretia, who takes beatings on herself to protect her step-children (II. i. 1-16) and who attempts to convert Cenci from his crimes (IV. i. 15-23, 34-37), but her actions fail and she conspires in the murder. However, she later regrets her action whereas 'Beatrice never poisons or corrupts her soul with submission or self-contempt'.[385]

The one certainty about a hypothetical 1819 performance of *The Cenci* is that the audience would not have read Shelley's preface but would have decided their opinion by discussing the depiction of the character they saw on stage The tendency of such a discussion is indicated by

---

381 'A Philosophical View of Reform' in *SCVI*, p. 1064, 1065.
382 Ibid., p. 1051.
383 Wasserman, *Shelley: A Critical Reading*, pp. 92-93.
384 Stuart M. Sperry, *Shelley's Major Verse, The Narrative and Dramatic Poetry* (Cambridge: Harvard University Press, 1988), p. 130.
385 Paul Smith, 'Restless Casuistry: Shelley's Composition of The Cenci', *KSJ*, 13 (1964), 77-85, p. 85; *SPII*, p. 730.

some contemporary reactions. Shelley describes the response of Italian acquaintances and Eaton's report, written after seeing Beatrice's 'portrait' and hearing a version of her story less sympathetic than that which Shelley used, is strongly in Beatrice's favour, although she felt that Cenci deserved to lose his life 'from any hand but hers'.[386] Despite Nicoll's argument that 'the play is puzzling in the theatre without a fuller understanding of Shelley's art', Shelley's intentions are revealed more vividly in performance than in examination of the text. He said of O'Neill, the actor of his choice, 'God forbid that I shd. see her play it — it wd. tear my nerves to pieces', which indicates that he thought her performance would be fine enough to arouse strong feelings in the audience. This the actor playing Beatrice must do in order for the moral and political questions raised in *The Cenci* to provoke discussion and sympathy.[387]

Shelley particularly asked Peacock to take *The Cenci* to Covent Garden rather than Drury Lane, but the usual custom was to offer a play to the other house if one turned it down, and Peacock appears to have done this.[388] Covent Garden had an excellent record of performing new plays. Boaden said of its manager, Thomas Harris, 'His judicious adoption of light comedy, with such writers as O'Keeffe, Holcroft, Reynolds, and afterwards Morton, brought him great profit'.[389] Harris paid his writers well and what is more he paid his actors. After putting up with years of unpaid salaries from Sheridan, John Kemble took himself and a number of the Drury Lane company, including Siddons, over to Covent Garden.[390] By 1819, Harris's son, Henry, had taken over the management, assisted by Reynolds and Fawcett. His remark on Sheil's *The Apostate* that 'an altered play never had the attraction of an original one and the dramatist who could write such a scene [...] ought to make the whole play his own' showed him to be knowledgeable about drama and on the lookout for new work.[391] There is no reason to believe him insincere when 'he expressed his desire that the author would write another tragedy on some other subject, which he would gladly accept' as he knew the Examiner of Plays would not have

---

386 Wasserman, *Shelley: A Critical Reading*, p. 101; Charlotte Ann Eaton, *Rome in the Nineteenth Century*, 3 vols (Edinburgh: James Ballantyne, 1820), III, p. 18. It is not Beatrice's portrait, nor is it by Guido Reni, *SPII*, pp. 728-729, 873-874.
387 Nicoll, p. 196; *PBSLII*, pp 102.
388 *PBSLII*, pp. 103, 178.
389 Boaden, *Mrs. Siddons*, II, p. 337.
390 Wyndham, *Covent Garden*, I, p. 293.
391 Macready, *Reminiscences*, I, pp. 125, 176.

allowed a licence for *The Cenci*.[392] Peacock emphasised Harris's admiration for 'the author's powers, and great hopes of his success'. Despite Shelley's teasing accusation that Peacock thought he had 'no dramatic talent', his friend believed that Shelley 'would have accomplished something worthy of the best days of theatrical literature' had he lived, and also believed that this was Shelley's intention because of the 'unwearied devotion' with which he studied the great dramatists.[393]

Neither Shelley nor Harris, therefore, regarded *The Cenci* as a closet play, and they would have judged it by its performance qualities according to the contemporary meaning of the term. Two reviews from April and May 1820 indicate that, subject matter apart, it would have had critical success. *The Theatrical Inquisitor and Monthly Mirror* thought that 'as a first dramatic effort The Cenci is unparalleled for the beauty of every attribute with which drama can be endowed. It has few errors but such as time will amend, and many beauties that time can neither strengthen nor abate', while *The Edinburgh Monthly Review* thought Shelley's 'genius [...] rich to overflowing in all the nobler requisites for tragic excellence, and [...] he might easily and triumphantly overtop all that has been written during the last century for the English stage'.[394] Shelley himself believed *The Cenci* 'singularly fitted for the stage'[395] but this has never been accepted; it is supposed that he did not know enough about the theatre to make an accurate judgment.

The Cenci is the only play of Shelley's to have been regularly and successfully performed, yet it has not been performed by a major English theatre company since 1959. Cameron observes that 'a play starting its career without staging in its author's lifetime is at a disadvantage ever after' but the disadvantage in the case of *The Cenci* is not, as he suggests, that Shelley was unable to make alterations. It requires very little alteration for the stage.[396] The real disadvantages were that, firstly, during its 100-year wait for performance, the play had acquired the stigma of 'closet drama' and, secondly, that the theatre had changed so that it no longer attracted the large cross-section of the population whom Shelley wrote for. Nonetheless, great actors such as Thorndike, Alda Borelli and Eleanora Duse have either

392 *OSA*, p. 337.
393 *PBSLII*, p. 8; Wolfe, II, p. 352.
394 Barcus, *The Critical Heritage*, pp. 186, 174.
395 *PBSLII*, p. 178.
396 Cameron, *The Golden Years*, p. 396; Jocelyn Denford, programme notes, Damned Poets Theatre Company production of *The Cenci* at the Lyric Studio, Hammersmith, August 1992.

seized the opportunity of playing Beatrice, or desired to, and it has attracted great designers. Curran says that whether the play is a great acting drama is 'an impossible question to answer', but that the significant question is rather what attracts 'theatrical minds' to it. The many 'theatrical minds' cited in his masterly stage history offered him his conclusion that 'the play is still dramatic' thereby answering his first question.[397] It is the director who must ask, 'Is *The Cenci* a great acting drama?' If the answer is no, there is little point in staging it professionally.

Curran explains that the criticism of E.S. Bates, followed by N.I. White, was based on the reviews of the first English performance (1886), an amateur one for an uncritical audience, the Shelley Society. The prevailing idea from these early reviews — which has not been corrected — is that *The Cenci* is too long, since that performance ran for four hours. This was not Shelley's fault: material, including a prologue, was added and, since Alma Murray, who played Beatrice, became 'visibly tired', the director, an actor without directorial experience, clearly failed to pace the performance. What is more, the scenery was borrowed and had to be returned between the acts.[398] This gave the stage hands extra work and no time to rehearse the scene changes which, in 1886, were far more complicated than those of 1819. Instead of the swift drawing back of a set of wings to reveal another scene, there was the heavy elaborate Victorian box set which forced Henry Irving and other managers to cut Shakespeare drastically to allow time for scene changes. *The Cenci* takes 2 hours, 10 minutes to read aloud in its entirety.

The Cenci's first professional performance in English came in 1922 from a company without great financial resources, but led by Casson and Thorndike. Thorndike was already an established actor of 20 years' experience who had played Medea and Antigone. Interestingly, she had also recently played Katherine of Aragon in *Henry VIII*, a Siddons role. Sir John Gielgud called her 'unequal in her playing of tragedy' and Bernard Shaw chose her for *Saint Joan* after seeing her Beatrice. Maurice Baring said it was clear that 'we had lost in [Shelley] a great dramatist, but that we had found in Miss Thorndike a tragic actress'. The play had such excellent audiences and reviews that they revived it in 1926. In 1947, Casson, now Sir Lewis, directed it for The Third Programme with Thorndike, now Dame Sybil, playing Lucretia and Rosalie Crutchley Beatrice. Both Dame Sybil, who called it a 'really great play', and Sir Lewis were emphatic about its dramatic

---

397 Curran, *Cenci*, pp. 185, 237, 215.
398 Ibid., pp. 262; 188-193.

quality.[399] Because of their unquestionable pre-eminence in their profession and long association with the play, their views are the most reliable on record. It is inappropriate to give equal validity to the responses of those taking part in an amateur or university production, the contradictory nature of which is shown by a description of the same audience as 'interested but not enthusiastic' but having 'bated breath'. University productions may include talented performers and imaginative staging — such as that at Mt Holyoke College (29 November and 1 December 1949), which had an all-female cast, specially composed music, and projected 'a distant view of the Castle Sant'Angelo Prison' and 'mountainous landscape beyond the Castle of Petrella'. They will not, however, attract major reviewers or have a budget to gain a wider audience, and those taking part may attribute failure to the play when the responsibility lies elsewhere. Criticisms such as 'lacked the humanity which could have made it valuable' and 'stirred very little interest' may arise from poor direction and publicity rather than from the play itself.[400]

Curran supports his opinion that *The Cenci* is more suitable for the modern theatre than for the 1819/20 Covent Garden by citing a 1959 Old Vic production for which the director used 'every artifice [he] could command'.[401] In 1959, this included techniques of lighting and sound unknown in Shelley's day. Stage design and the internal design of the theatre itself had undergone such transformation that the environment of both performers and audience was utterly different. The suggestion in the reviews quoted that the performers were 'melodramatic' implies that the actors adopted an approximation to an imagined Victorian style belonging neither to themselves nor to the actors of Shelley's day. *The Cenci* has been performed successfully in the small venues which Cave suggests are more suitable for the drama of the Romantic poets. Rather than that its techniques were unsuitable in 1819, however, this indicates the continuing relevance of the play and its ease of adaptation to a smaller venue.

---

399 Curran, *Cenci*, pp. 232, 233n., p. 224; Sheridan Morley, *Sybil Thorndike* (London: Weidenfeld & Nicolson, 1999), pp. 67, 147, 68, 84, 168.
400 States, 'Addendum', pp. 638-641; Kessel and States, 'The Cenci as a Stage Play', p. 148.
401 Curran, *Cenci*, p. 252.

Fazio

Milman's *Fazio* is an example of a play which was a success at Covent Garden in 1818 and which has been often compared with *The Cenci*, but its stageworthiness, accounted for by its great roles, has never been dismissed in the way that *The Cenci*'s has.[402] *Fazio*'s route to Covent Garden shows two important factors which have hitherto been overlooked in its discussion: adaptation to the requirements of the stage and the role of the minor and provincial theatres.

Fazio was turned down after discussion by the Drury Lane committee. Fortunately for Milman, Thomas Dibdin — writer, performer and the experienced manager of both Drury Lane and the Surrey Theatres — adapted it for the Surrey as *The Italian Wife*. A version was performed at the Theatre Royal, Bath, the theatre considered the best outside London, where it was noticed by the Covent Garden management.[403] The Italian story, the kind which the Jacobeans adapted for the stage, has dramatic potential. Fazio, who is married to Bianca with two children, appropriates a fortune after the murder of his miserly neighbour, Bartolo, by two ruffians, and claims that he has become rich by alchemy. He now has entry to the court where he rekindles an old passion for Aldabella, with whom he commits adultery. Bianca, in jealousy, tells the officials that Fazio murdered Bartolo, and he is condemned to death. Now mad with grief and remorse, Bianca attempts to save her husband, but Fazio has admitted the theft of Bartolo's gold which bears the same sentence, and he is executed. Bianca accuses Aldabella of alienating Fazio's affection and dies asking that her children are brought up poor.

Fazio gets moving quickly, revealing the plot and main characters within twelve speeches. Bianca is a complex part requiring the expression of intense love, jealousy, madness and remorseful grief and she has been given strong and consistent motivation for her actions; the motivation for Aldabella, on the other hand, is lacking. There are difficulties with the character of Fazio, whose naïveté, perhaps self-deception, about the 'goodness' of Aldabella sits uncomfortably with his cynicism about money and government. A

---

402 E.S. Bates, qtd in Curran, *Cenci*, p. 262; Donohue, *Dramatic Character*, pp. 162-170; Nicoll, p. 167 for his praise of Milman's *Fazio*, while see pp. 196-197 for *The Cenci*; Booth, *English Melodrama*, p. 47, for comments on the Romantic poets including Shelley; Booth, *Prefaces to English Nineteenth-Century Theatre*, pp. 18-19 for comments on *Fazio*.
403 Bernard, *Retrospections*, I, p. 34; Dibdin, *Reminiscences*, II, pp. 134-135.

close reading from the point of view of performance, however, reveals that *Fazio* would need many alterations before it could work on stage. The speeches are long and often repetitive with inappropriate flowery lines in mock Jacobean language. There are characters with little or nothing to do, three of which are merely one-dimensional cyphers. Milman wrote three consecutive scenes in the first act where Fazio enters, makes a speech and exits. If played as written, this would raise a laugh from the audience when the atmosphere should be one of suspense. Unsurprisingly, an examination of the changes made by both the minor theatre and Covent Garden reveals that *Fazio* was not performed at either theatre as Milman published it. Although he claimed to 'totally disdain[s] the alterations made at Bath, and in London'[404] but accepted the Covent Garden version, the versions were not dissimilar and both cut Milman's play heavily. The Larpent manuscripts were submitted with stage alterations, and I have therefore used these texts, referring also to Milman's original publication.[405] I am assuming that the Larpent version of *The Italian Wife* is by Dibdin.

Dibdin would not have found the need for alteration to be a barrier since, if he wished to present it at the Surrey, he was obliged to adapt it into something he could describe as a burletta. To allow *Fazio* to pass as one, and to make a theatrical impact, Dibdin added a ballet, marches and appropriate music to suit the mood: 'solemn' (*The Italian Wife* manuscript, p. 31), 'bacchanalian' (p. 19) 'pathetic' and 'violent agitation' (p. 15). The scenery had variety, from the 'magnificent apartment' with 'every appearance of a ball prolonged to morning' (p. 34) and the 'poor room' with the alchemy instruments where Fazio first appears (p. 1). Dibdin's version allows the actor to perform rather than narrate. He cut speeches in which a character describes his emotions, substituting a stage direction such as 'Enters disturbed' (p. 11). The first scene is a mime depicting the robbers' attack on Bartolo. This would arouse the interest of the audience and add dramatic irony when Bartolo tells Fazio about it with his dying breath (p. 1). Dibdin also gave Aldabella a motivation, absent in the Covent Garden version, for seducing Fazio:

> Rich and renown'd he must be in my train
> Or Florence will turn rebel to my beauty. (p. 15)

---

404 Henry Hart Milman, 'Advertisement' in *Fazio: A Tragedy* (Oxford: Samuel Collingwood, 1815), p. iii.
405 Dougald MacMillan, *Catalogue of the Larpent Plays in the Huntingdon Library 1737-1824* (San Marino, California, 1939), p. viii. The manuscript of *The Italian Wife* does not differentiate acts and scenes clearly, therefore page numbers only are used.

Like Dibdin, Covent Garden cut *Fazio* heavily. Their deletions and retentions were not always more sympathetic than those made by the Surrey. In the original *Fazio* (III. ii, p. 69), Bianca refuses to pause before she denounces her husband in case she changes her mind, which is an attempt at deeper characterisation, however crude. Dibdin kept this speech (*The Italian Wife*, p. 37), which Covent Garden did not, but cut a speech, which Covent Garden kept (*Fazio*, IV. ii, pp.114-115), in which she tells Fazio that she has murdered her children, a cruel lie at a time when she should have the audience's sympathy and an unnecessary plot complication so late in the play. Both theatres were concerned to cut repetitive speeches, lines of 'mere poetry' descriptive to no dramatic purpose such as 'Like sunflowers on the golden light they love' (*Fazio*, IV. ii, p. 100) and unnecessary scene changes, for example, that between IV. iv and V. i. Both merged Fazio's three consecutive solo scenes into one, cut the redundant character of Dandolo and a long, anachronistic, irrelevant song about Italian independence (*Fazio*, pp. 36-39)). In short, *Fazio* was inferior to *The Cenci* not only in poetic and dramatic power but also in technical competence. It needed and received considerable re-working by theatre managements.

Shelley wrote *The Cenci* with the intention of writing not an 'ideal' drama, such as *Prometheus Unbound*, but the best of its kind, with 'better morality than Fazio'.[406] It is ironic that Shelley's own subject was considered 'so objectionable' that the theatre 'could not even submit the part to Miss O'Neill for perusal'.[407] Shelley, as his admiration for Calderón shows, could appreciate a play which had a different moral system from his own but he considered *Fazio* 'miserable trash'.[408] *Fazio*'s moral system is unclear. Donohue says, 'the boldest fact emerging from a comparison of Shelley's and Milman's plays is their common casuistical treatment of a virtuous human being seduced into committing a vicious act'. This suggests that the heroines are alike in virtue, although he remarks that, unlike Bianca, Beatrice 'possesses a commanding intellect'.[409] Yet Shelley's Beatrice is also extraordinarily selfless and courageous, while Milman's Bianca is an ordinary woman who acts out of jealousy. Fazio is greedy and either naïve or self-deceiving about his desire for Aldabella. The Duke, the upholder of law, refuses to lift the sentence of death despite learning that Bartolo was dead when Fazio took his gold, sends Aldabella to a convent and agrees

---

406   *PBSLII*, p. 8.
407   Mary Shelley, 'Note on The Cenci', *OSA*, p. 337.
408   *PBSLII*, p. 290.
409   Donohue, *Dramatic Character*, pp. 171, 176.

to Bianca's request that her children be brought up poor. This unequal and unjust system is not criticised by Milman, thus suggesting authorial approval of the Duke's actions and of the State. In *The Cenci*, on the other hand, Shelley criticises a system in which the State first denies Beatrice protection, then justice and then condemns her for killing a murderer which the State's own laws demanded should be executed.

The 'popular' elements which led to the success of *Fazio*, such as the Renaissance setting, the beautiful distressed heroine, the vehemently expressed passions and illicit sex, can also be found in *The Cenci*. Perhaps in accordance with Schlegel's ideas of the theatrical, however, Shelley avoided 'mere poetry', and 'endeavoured [...] to represent the characters as they probably were'.[410] It is noticeable that, in *The Cenci*, Shelley makes none of Milman's mistakes and he uses spectacular effects reminiscent of *The Italian Wife* in, for example, the Banquet Scene. Although there is no record of it, Shelley, who had already read *Fazio*, did have the opportunity to see *The Italian Wife* while he was staying with Hunt in December 1816.[411] When *Fazio* was performed at Covent Garden, Shelley saw the actor whom he said that *The Cenci* 'might even seem to have been written for' — O'Neill.[412]

The actors

Mary Shelley believed that, without O'Neill, the play 'could [not] be brought out with effect anywhere' and this was perhaps Shelley's own view. He had watched her 'with absorbed attention'[413] and would have recognised that she shared Beatrice's thick blonde hair and blue eyes (as described in the *Relazione*) and the wistful expression in what was thought to be Beatrice's portrait. Shelley's remarks that 'the chief male character I confess I should be very unwilling that any one but Kean shd. play — that is impossible' and that *The Cenci*, 'in all respects' was 'fitted only for Covent Garden,' indicates that it was more important to him for O'Neill to play Beatrice than for Kean to play Cenci, not, *pace* Donohue, that he was unaware that Kean and O'Neill worked at different theatres. As Shelley himself said, Beatrice is the 'principal character', on stage almost throughout the play.[414] The part

410 Schlegel, pp. 36-37; *SPII*, pp. 731, 733.
411 *MWSJ*, p. 662.
412 *PBSLII*, p. 102.
413 *MWSLI*, p.127; Wolfe, II, p. 330.
414 Donohue, *Theatre in the Age of Kean*, p. 171; *PBSLII*, pp. 102-103.

is more complex than that of Cenci, who behaves with consistent villainy.

At the time Shelley saw her, O'Neill had performed most of the tragic parts popular with Georgian audiences: Belvidera in *Venice Preserv'd*, Isabella in *The Fatal Marriage* and Monimia in *The Orphan*.[415] The Shelleys saw her in *The Jealous Wife* in January 1817, but comedy was not her strength. Hazlitt said her 'Lady Teazle [...] appears [...] to be a complete failure' though Crabb Robinson, who usually compared her unfavourably to Siddons, said she 'acted with spirit'.[416] Her attempt to play characters above her age, Constance in *King John*, Lady Randolph in *Douglas*, Volumnia in *Coriolanus* and Mrs. Haller in *The Stranger*,[417] indicates that she needed the challenge of playing a stronger, more mature, tragic role.

Shelley described Beatrice as 'one of those rare persons in whom energy and gentleness dwell together without destroying one another: her nature was simple and profound.'[418] Her admiring biographer, Charles Inigo Jones, describes O'Neill's appearance of 'gentleness' (p. 33) but she could also appear 'dignified and firm' (p. 37) with a 'countenance full of intelligence and sensibility' (p. 11). Her acting was marked by 'chaste simplicity, ingenuous modesty' (p. 14). She had a strong, well-modulated voice which would have been used to advantage in the long speeches (p. 89), but she could also give it a choked hysterical manner and when she portrayed 'indignation contempt and abhorrence' it 'brought forth successive bursts of applause' (p. 56).

The famous Victorian actor, William Macready, described seeing O'Neill as Juliet 'when, with altered tones and eager glance, she inquired [...] the name of Romeo of the Nurse, and bade her go and learn it, the revolution in her whole being was evident, anticipating the worse'.[419] This 'point', as the way of delivering a particular speech was termed, was also mentioned by an anonymous contributor to *Blackwood's*:

> She turned round and stood as if lost in unutterable thought, with her eyes fixed upon the spot where Romeo had lately passed away from her sight; as if her fancy reproduced his form in that very place; [...] Her "rapt soul was sitting in her eyes" her whole body spoke then, with a deep, impatient sigh, she turned away [...]'[420]

415 Jones, *Memoirs of Miss O'Neill*, pp. 24, 35, 73.
416 *MWSJ*, p. 157; Hazlitt, III, p. 123; Crabb Robinson, p. 79.
417 Macready, *Reminiscences*, I, p. 167; Jones, *Memoirs of Miss O'Neill*, p. 48; Genest, VIII, pp. 602, 613.
418 *SPII*, p. 735.
419 Macready, *Reminiscences*, I, p. 95.
420 Qtd in Downer, 'The Painted Stage', p. 529.

Hazlitt said:

> In the silent expression of feeling, we have seldom witnessed any thing finer than her acting [...] her listening to the Friar's story of the poison, and her change of manner towards the Nurse, when she advises her to marry Paris.[421]

The ability to show her feelings and the change which they silently undergo would be effective in the Banquet Scene (I. iii. 99-140), in which Beatrice first pleads with the assembled guests to help her, then realises that they are too afraid of her father to do so. When Beatrice enters with her hair 'undone' (III. i. 6), its unkempt and tousled style reflecting the disorder in her mind, it would have given O'Neill an opportunity to use her long hair to dramatic advantage, as she did in *The Stranger*, 'when she sunk upon the floor, and, clasping her knees, let her head fall upon them, so that her "wild-reverted tresses" hung as a veil before her'.[422] The very last words of the play concern Beatrice's hair, its re-ordering symbolising her firm resignation (V. iv. 160-164).

Although O'Neill cried easily on stage,[423] Beatrice never sheds tears but expresses anger and indignation. Like the traditional tragic heroines, Beatrice has been disappointed in love (I. ii. 20-22) and goes mad (III. i. 1-64) but her strength of mind overcomes both love and madness (I. ii. 24-26, III. i. 64). Shelley was probably justified in believing that 'Beatrice is precisely fitted for Miss O Neil'.[424] Had she performed it, the Christ-like imagery 'overtly identified' with Beatrice would have helped her to take the audience with her, i.e. to keep the sympathy of the audience despite the equivocal attitude they might have towards her actions. Siddons did so in such parts as Elvira in *Pizzarro*, since, as Boaden remarked, 'all characters in her hands receive additional purity'.[425] O'Neill would have had the opportunity to extend her range and to express deep emotion with a young heroine who had the strength of the older tragic characters she had begun to portray. Beatrice's first appearance establishes this strength by direct, brief and to-the-point statements, such as 'Pervert not truth' (I. ii. 1), 'You are a priest./Speak to me not of love' (I. ii. 8-9) and 'Had you a dispensation I have not' (I. ii. 14). O'Neill's warmth in performance would have allowed the audience to recognise Beatrice's courage in the Banquet Scene and her

---

421 Hazlitt, III, p. 30.
422 Downer, 'The Painted Stage', p. 529.
423 *Hunt's Dramatic Criticism*, p. 88.
424 *PBSLII*, p. 102.
425 Bryan Shelley, *Shelley and Scripture*, p. 83; Boaden, *Mrs. Siddons*, II, p. 320; Jones, *Memoirs of Miss O'Neill*, p. 48.

unswerving devotion to her brother and stepmother throughout the play, acknowledged when Bernardo describes Beatrice as 'pure innocence' and 'light of life' (V. iv. 130, 134).

Beatrice is, however, often described as a character who shares her father's evil, who becomes her father by committing his murder and then denying it. Ronald Lemoncelli, for example, believes that even incestuous rape 'is not enough to account for her later acts'.[426] Wasserman suggests Beatrice's claims to innocence should be taken as 'resolute statements' not 'hardened lies or even as casuistry much less as self deception, for they are spoken with the sincerity of conviction and truth'.[427] Yet there is an ambiguity, since Beatrice decides on the murder and the murderers' culpability is brought out in the theatre by the references to *Macbeth* in IV. iii and IV. iv. as Alan Weinberg points out.[428]

There are similarities between Macbeth and the *Relazione*. Shelley clearly intended the audience to notice these Shakespearean references, particularly as the arrival of the Papal legate immediately after the murder (IV. iv) is not in his source but corresponds to the arrival of Macduff and Lennox in *Macbeth*. Shelley knew *Macbeth*, a favourite play from boyhood, far too well for the similarities to be accidental; he quoted from it in a letter to Hunt about *The Cenci* as he was writing it.[429] As *Macbeth* was so popular in the Georgian theatre, the audience would have readily seen the parallels: the fear common to Lucretia and Lady Macbeth that the victim might wake before the deed was done (IV. ii. 4); the resemblance of the victim to the would-be murderer's father (IV. iii. 21); the laugh in the sleep and the blessing (a curse in *The Cenci*, IV. iii. 19); the readiness of Lady Macbeth and Beatrice to commit the murder themselves (IV. iii. 31-33); and the pretence that the murderers have just woken when the visitors arrive (IV. iii. 62). Lucretia's faint (IV. iv. 170) is reminiscent of the fainting of Lady Macbeth, but Shelley relied on his audience knowing this from having read *Macbeth*, since it was not performed in the theatre.[430] Olimpio's description of Cenci's 'stern and reverent brow' (IV. iii. 10) is a reminder of Duncan but one which would also accentuate the difference between the two victims.

---

426 McWhir, 'The Light and the Knife', p. 157; Richardson, *A Mental Theatre*, p. 112; Carlson, *In the Theatre of Romanticism*, p. 194; Lemoncelli, 'Cenci', p. 105.
427 Wasserman, *Shelley: A Critical Reading*, p. 124.
428 Curran, *Cenci*, p. 274; Weinberg, *Shelley's Italian Experience*, p. 89.
429 *PBSLII*, p. 108.
430 *Macbeth, A Tragedy*, in Five Acts by William Shakspeare, printed from the acting copy (London: John Cumberland, [n.d.]).

While both couples are guilty of murder, the Macbeths kill an innocent man for his crown but Beatrice and Lucretia rid themselves of a tyrant as evil as Macbeth becomes.

Shelley is careful not to allow us to see Beatrice decide to murder her father. She does not have a soliloquy in which she considers it, but 'retires' upstage (III. i. 179); the audience would have seen and heard the double image of the dialogue between Orsino and Lucretia while Beatrice prays (III. i. 219) and meditates. To hear Beatrice arguing whether the murder of Cenci is justifiable might have lost her sympathy, and, moreover, since two sides are presented, a discussion between two characters is more likely than a soliloquy to provoke debate. Beatrice never has a soliloquy in the play; the audience is therefore never admitted into her intimate thoughts.

Revenge is only one of Beatrice's motives. She is in danger of repeated assault from her father, from which she has no reason to believe that the law will defend her, and this conflicts with what she sees as her Christian duty to keep her body as God's temple (III. i. 128-129). Furthermore, she is:

> reserved, day after day,
> To load with crimes an overburdened soul,
> And be — what ye can dream not. (III. i. 216-218)

Beatrice is not an ideal heroine; Shelley wrote her as a psychologically believable character as he imagined the historical Beatrice to have been. To give her the endurance and forgiveness of an ideal – and a god - such as Prometheus would not have been appropriate. A different attitude towards the guilt involved in a similar situation is given to the Christian slaves in *Hellas* (675-681).[431]

In the trial scene (V. ii), she has been compared to Vittoria Corombona in *The White Devil* and censured for the 'power of her performance' and her 'unheroic denial in court of patricide'.[432] Yet her words 'Who stands here/As my accuser? Ha! wilt thou be he/Who art my judge?' (V. ii. 173-175) also resemble the words of two innocent defendants. *Henry VIII* was a play frequently performed at Covent Garden and Queen Katherine was a favourite role for Siddons. Katherine says, 'You are mine enemy; and make my challenge/You shall not be my judge' (*Henry VIII*, II. iv. 75-76). Jonson's Silius asks, 'Is he my accuser?/And must he be my judge?' (*Sejanus, His Fall*,

---

431   *SPP*, p. 451.
432   *SPII*, p. 845; Carlson, *In the Theatre of Romanticism*, p. 193; Richardson, 'The Harmatia of Imagination', p. 237.

II. i. 200-201).[433] In *The Cenci*, too, as the audience would have realised, it is an unfair trial, 'a wicked farce' (V. ii. 39), a reminder of the Inquisition since Marzio has been and will be tortured until he says what the judges want to hear.

Beatrice's physical advance towards him across the stage and 'awe-inspiring gaze' are also threatening. When she actually admits, 'thy hand did [...] rescue her' (V. ii. 143), in a context which justifies them both, Marzio says, 'A keener pain has wrung a higher truth/From my last breath' (V. ii. 165-166). The First Judge demanded the 'whole truth' (V. ii. 4), but the judges never hear it, as Beatrice's circumstances are not taken into account. Hunt believed that Marzio, already a dead man in judicial terms, was ennobled by this attempt to save the lives of the Cenci family; this may have been Shelley's view.[434] But another, even higher truth, is present in this scene. Beatrice has committed murder, but she has been 'thwarted from her nature', the courageous virtue which reappears in the final scene. What critics have described as duplicity is in fact a representation of a character with both virtuous and murderous qualities sincerely felt and bound together by Beatrice's strength of mind and conviction that she is right, the presentation of which requires an exceptional actor.

Donohue's claim that 'production records of *The Cenci* indicate that sympathy for Beatrice is lost somewhere toward the end of the drama' is supported by the director, Theodore J. Ritter, for whom Beatrice is 'lying in her teeth', but Kathleen M. Lynch, who co-directed the Mount Holyoke production, found that 'a young actress can make this "weakness" very moving'.[435] His opinion does not appear to be borne out by the research of Curran or Cameron or my own experience. It may be so where the actor is unable to reach the quality of performance Shelley expected from O'Neill.

Other actors

Ervine praised 'Shelley's skill in casting a play', his realisation of 'how excellent Kean would be in the part of Count Cenci'.[436] The Gisbornes, who were qualified to judge, as 'Mr. G's M.S.' contained the source of *The Cenci*, considered Kean ideal for the part.[437]

---

433 Shelley read *Henry VIII* in 1818, *Sejanus* in 1817. *MWSJ*, pp. 656, 673.
434 Johnson, *Shelley-Leigh Hunt*, pp. 51-52.
435 Donohue, *Dramatic Character*, p. 177; States, 'Addendum', pp. 639, 640.
436 Ervine, p. 87.
437 *MWSJ*, p. 211, 211n.; Gisborne & Williams, p. 39.

Like Richard III, Cenci is a villain who involves the audience in his crimes. As already noted, Shelley had read *Richard III* aloud in August 1818 and he had seen G.F. Cooke as Richard and Kean as Shylock.[438] Macready, an admirer of both his predecessors, compared them as Richard:

> There was a solidity of deportment and manner, and at the same time a sort of unctuous enjoyment of his successful craft, in the soliloquizing stage villany of Cooke, which gave powerful and rich effect to the sneers and overbearing retorts of Cibber's hero, and certain points (as the peculiar mode of delivering a passage is technically phrased) traditional from Garrick were made with consummate skill, significance and power.
> Kean's conception was decidedly more Shakespearean. He hurried you along in his resolute course with a spirit that brooked no delay. [...] he was only inferior to Cooke when he attempted points upon the same ground.[439]

A description of Macready's 'most famous point in Werner' in 1831 shows that his style was based on the performances of these actors:

> Carried away by the passion of the scene, he rushed down to Charles Kemble Mason who played Gabor, and demanded 'Are you a father?' Then he whispered 'Say No' whereupon Gabor shouted 'No!' and Macready, in a burst of paternal emotion, rejoined: 'Ah, then you cannot feel for misery like mine' and the pit rose at him.[440]

The attempt of the young Macready to copy Kean was noted by George Daniel.[441] Although Shelley considered Kean the best actor for the role, he recognised that Cenci could be played by an imitator when he said that he 'must be contented with an inferior actor'; as an admirer of Kean, Macready himself would have agreed with this assessment. It is said that he volunteered to come out of retirement to play Cenci, which is all the more likely if he thought that the role might have been written for him. [442]

Cenci begins his first scene at a disadvantage since Camillo, with his message from the Pope, is in the position of authority. Shelley's dialogue skilfully shifts the positions until Cenci finishes by threatening Camillo, who is shown to be a hypocrite and liar. Hazlitt remarked that Kean depicted sarcastic resentment well.[443] There are opportunities for expressing this:

> For you give out that you have half reformed me,

---

438 *SCII*, p. 517; *MWSJ*, p. 222.
439 Macready, *Reminiscences*, I, p. 94.
440 Davies, 'Playwrights and Plays' in *The Revels*, p. 195.
441 D — G — (George Daniel) 'Remarks on *Virginius*' in James Sheridan Knowles, *Virginius: A Tragedy* (London: John Cumberland, [n.d.]).
442 *PBSLII*, p. 103; Curran, *Cenci*, p. 186, 186n.
443 Hazlitt, III, p. 9.

Therefore strong vanity will keep you silent (I. i. 73-74)

and

No doubt Pope Clement
And his most charitable nephews, pray
That the Apostle Peter and the saints
Will grant for their sake that I long enjoy
Strength, wealth, and pride, and lust, and length of days (I. i. 27-31)

The ability to rapidly change mood was described by Hazlitt as Kean's forte. In this scene, Cenci changes to black humour. He has imposed the ultimate restraint on Camillo's conversation by threatening him with death; the ironic lines, 'And so we will converse with less restraint' (I. i. 60) and 'I think they never saw him more' (I. i. 65) give opportunities for a chuckle, perhaps 'fiendish' as was Cooke's in *Richard III*. Cenci's soliloquies have the frankness of Richard's, shocking but also forcing a laugh from the audience in their audacity, for example, when Cenci hopes that his sons' deaths will end the need for supporting them (I. i. 129-134). The stage direction 'looking around him suspiciously' on the line 'I think they cannot hear me at this door' (I. i. 137) allows the actor's body language to reveal what he plans towards Beatrice and his fear of discovery. As 'this door' must lead to Lucretia's apartments, it cannot be the proscenium door through which Camillo exited, so he would have had to cross the stage to the opposite door. A quick, darting move such as Kean, a popular Harlequin, excelled at, would have created a double effect; a glance at the stage box above the door would bring the audience sitting in that desirable position into intimate contact and complicity with Cenci.

In the Banquet Scene, Cenci again exhibits swift changes of mood. Initially conventional and reassuring (I. iii. 1-33), he changes to glee at the shock and alarm his horrifying news causes (I. iii. 44-50) and takes obvious enjoyment in pledging the Devil with his sons' blood (I. iii. 77-90). Taking command of the scene with the powerful threat to 'Think [...] of their own throats' (I. iii. 130-131) when the assembled Nobles suggest seizing him, he changes to menacing fury. In the second act Cenci also has the opportunity for a grand exit (II. i. 192). The word 'walk' allows the actor to physicalise Cenci's evil by moving towards the proscenium door in a sinister way and enables him to deliver the final 'Would that it were done!' as he reaches the door, in a manner effective for gaining applause, or as contemporary critics described it, 'a claptrap'.

The fact that Cenci does not appear in Act III shows Shelley's awareness

11. 'Charles Kemble as Giraldi Fazio' by Thomas Sully, 1833. Courtesy of the Pennsylvania Academy of the Fine Arts, Philadelphia. Gift of Mrs. John Ford.

not only of the demands the part places on the actor, but also the demands such a fanatical character places on the audience. As a result, the part can be played with more subtlety, relying on the audience's grasp of the character for the monomaniacal intensity. This is particularly important, given that in his final scene (IV. i), the actor must express a range of emotions from anticipation, extreme anger, satisfied shock upon hearing he is to die, belief that he is God's scourge and a combination of feelings towards Beatrice which include extreme hatred and tremendous sexual thrill, all before finally appearing overcome by the drug. He has most of the long speeches in this scene, including his curse of Beatrice. The part requires a bravura performance from a compelling actor not afraid of revelling in its wickedness or playing to the gallery. Macready would have been well suited to it, despite his youth.

Kemble, who played the weak but attractive Fazio in Florentine costume and hat, had also played gentlemanly villains such as Don Felix,[444] and his

---

444 Macready, *Reminiscences*, I, p. 83.

charm and good looks would have made him a suitable Orsino who could have inspired the alternation between trust and distrust which Beatrice and Giacomo feel for him. The minor parts, all of which are necessary to the action, are sufficiently well drawn for an actor to make believable. Shelley's economy in having a cast of twelve, some of whom could double, allows the play to be staged today when, generally, casts are small.

The staging

Shelley's stage directions provide suggestions for the scenery which show his awareness of the way in which these effects can emphasise and complement the action. In some cases, as with 'an apartment in the Cenci palace' or 'in the Vatican', a stock scene, though rich and palatial, would suffice, but 'A magnificent Hall in the Cenci Palace. A Banquet.'(I. iii) makes clear that Shelley requires a spectacular scene, something similar to the 'Italian hall' by Charles Pugh (1806-1826).[445] A grand entrance with music would be expected, since Cenci has invited princes, cardinals and everyone of consequence in Rome. Beatrice's reference to 'festival array' (I. ii. 59) suggests fine costumes, accurately designed as in *Fazio*. The richness of the spectacle would have delighted the audience while emphasising the power and grandeur of Cenci's connections and Beatrice's isolation when she is refused help. Similarly, the 'Garden' (I. ii) suggests a wooing scene and a betrayal, such as in *The Fair Penitent* (IV. i). The 'mean Apartment in Giacomo's House' (III. ii) confirms his poverty, contrasting with the preceding palatial setting, his father's abode.

Donohue says the Gothic drama had a 'convention of a stronghold, almost always a castle, within which the villain could exercise his unfettered power [...] a sort of objectified landscape descriptive of the villain's own mind and by extension, of the audience's fearful sense of the human origins of evil.[446] The setting of the Castle of Petrella is directly in line with this. Scene IV. i takes place in Cenci's 'Apartment in the Castle', while the next scene is set 'Before the Castle of Petrella' where Lucretia and Beatrice appear 'above on the ramparts' (IV. ii). The shutters would have parted to

445 Rosenfeld, *Georgian Scene Painters*, p. 87; *The Dramatick Works of Nicholas Rowe* (Facsimile: London, T. Jauncy, 1720; Farnborough, Hants: Gregg International Publishers, 1971).
446 Donohue, *Theatre in the Age of Kean*, p. 99.

reveal it, closing again at the end of the scene to return to the apartment (IV.
iii). It need not have been an edifice such as Capon constructed for Baillie's
De Monfort, although Shelley's setting suggests a similar design with a
back scene painted with mountain scenery by moonlight (IV. iv. 84); only
a front was needed with steps behind for Beatrice and Lucretia to descend
to Olimpio and Marzio, who appear 'below' on the forestage. 'The Cell of
a Prison' (V. iii) is also in the style of Gothic drama. Beatrice 'discovered
asleep on a Couch' is an image reminiscent of *A Sicilian Romance* in which 'a
cave with an iron door fastened with a chain [was] thrown open to discover
a woman sleeping on a stone'.[447]

Curran has criticised Shelley's use of 'thunder and the sound of a storm'
— the lamp and the striking bell — as 'melodramatic paraphernalia' (III. ii.
2, III. ii. 25, III. ii. 9-14, 40). However clichéd these techniques may appear
in modern theatre, when stage and auditorium are equally lit atmosphere
must be created by means other than lighting, and the storm is a strong
theatrical image. The striking bell was part of the tradition of *The Castle
Spectre*.[448] Shelley had recently seen Rossini's *Otello* in which the murder
takes place in a storm and in which Desdemona's Willow song is particularly
poignant; Kimbell describes it as 'a beautiful example of genuinely
expressive variation writing'. Had Shelley seen *Othello* in England he could
not have heard the Willow song (*Othello*, IV. iii, 41-58) since the scene was
cut in performance, but music was used to create atmosphere in all plays
and Henry Bishop, resident composer at Covent Garden in 1819, had used
recurring themes and motives associated with characters and moods.[449]
The dramatic advantage of Beatrice's song of false friendship (V. iii. 130-
145) would have been clear.

Certain speeches in *The Cenci* have an incantatory quality which, so
delivered, would send a shiver down the spines of the audience. In I. iii.
173-178, Cenci believes the wine, transformed into the blood of his dead
sons, a perversion of the Christian sacrament, will act as an aphrodisiac,
the charm which will make Beatrice 'meek and tame'. Beatrice's three
messages in IV. i are like phrases from an old ballad, an effect enhanced by
the medieval setting and Cenci's curse:

---

447   Rosenfeld, *Georgian Scene Painters*, pp. 38, 46.
448   See Chapter 1; Donohue, *Theatre in the Age of Kean*, p. 100.
449   *MWSJ*, p. 230; Robert Lloyd in *Composer of the Week*, trans. 0900-1000 BBC Radio
3, Tuesday 5 August 2003; Kimbell, *Italian Opera*, pp. 458-459; William Shakespeare,
Othello (London: John Cumberland, [n.d.]); Carr, 'Theatre Music 1800-1834' in *Music
in Britain*, pp. 291, 302.

'Go tell my father that I see the gulf
Of Hell between us two, which he may pass,
I will not'. (ll. 98-100)

She said 'I cannot come;
Go tell my father that I see a torrent
Of his own blood raging between us.' (ll. 111-113)

She bids thee curse;
And if thy curses, as they cannot do,
Could kill her soul — (ll. 167-169)

A stage effect often used in plays contemporary with *The Cenci*, such as Inchbald's *Lovers' Vows* or Morton's *Speed the Plough*, was the tableau. Following Lucretia's line 'My dear, dear children!' (II. i. 104) it is probable that the three would have formed a tableau of mutual comfort with Lucretia holding the two young people to her, a physical demonstration of the love between them which provides Beatrice with the strong motivation she needs to believe she can endure all her father's cruelties. This tableau might have been repeated at V. iii. 116-120, when Beatrice, now the strong, comforting one, invites her brother to sit near her and Lucretia to put her head on her lap. During Beatrice's final speech, also the final speech of the play, Shelley enables the actors to show their emotions physically by tying each others' girdles and binding up each others' hair — actions of familiarity and intimacy which actors do for each other every working day, reflected in the lines 'How often/Have we done this for one another' (V. iv. 163-164). They would have thus formed a tableau, perhaps echoing the two earlier tableaux by Giacomo joining them before the guards lead them away. Hunt thought this an ending which would not work on the stage, but W.J. Turner described it as 'the moment when its meaning flowers with a complete and extraordinary beauty', with Casson arguing, 'The great final scene transforms natural speech patterns into pure music'.[450]

It is reported that Marzio has committed suicide by holding his breath until he died (V. ii. 182-184), a physical impossibility, as Shelley, who had some medical training, must have known. The startling dramatic effect may have been prompted by Dibdin's *The Cabinet* (p. 85), where Peter, threatened with torture to reveal a secret, says, 'it would only give me lockjaw'.[451]

---

450 Johnson, *Shelley-Leigh Hunt*, p. 49; qtd in Cameron, *The Golden Years*, p. 411; Curran, *Cenci*, p. 274.
451 Sharon Ruston, *Shelley and Vitality* (Basingstoke: Palgrave Macmillan, 2005), pp. 77-79.

Censorship

Robertson Davies found it a major weakness in the play that 'Shelley is nervous about his theme, perhaps from instincts of delicacy excessive in a playwright. If we are to be shaken by a horror, the horror must not be kept quite so much behind the arras.'[452] Shelley followed his source in suggesting that Beatrice's extra motivation to murder was roused by her horror of incest, but it could not be directly mentioned in a play. Gaull believes that it was not a problem because 'audiences of the period had become acclimated through Gothic melodrama and even found [it] especially appealing.'[453] Certainly, in *The Castle Spectre*, Osmond attempts to force his niece Angela to marry him, but this incestuous element is not focused upon and never carried out. Jewett, following Gaull, describes 'Walpole's *The Mad Mother*' (actually *The Mysterious Mother*) as a 'stage drama' but, precisely because of the incest, Walpole never expected it to be performed publicly, although Worrall has discovered that, in fact, in 1821 Dibdin produced it at the Surrey.[454] This appears to offer the possibility that a minor theatre could have performed *The Cenci*, but these too had to be wary of losing their magistrate's licences.

It is quite clear that fear of censorship prevented *The Cenci* from being accepted at the patent theatres since, despite attempts to counter the ban by theatre companies and the Shelley Society alike, it was not lifted until 1920. Shelley was therefore neither over-cautious nor over-optimistic; he hoped that 'the peculiar delicacy with which I have treated' the subject would enable the play to be 'admitted on the stage'. Mary Shelley pointed out that 'He had never mentioned expressly Cenci's worst crime. Everyone knew what it must be'.[455] His method had a precedent on the stage in Arthur Murphy's *The Grecian Daughter*. Boaden refers to Murphy's way of both revealing and concealing:

> One great difficulty his fable imposed on him — preventing,
> I mean, the *kind* of sustenance which Euphrasia bore

---

452 Davies, 'Playwrights and Plays' in *The Revels*, pp. 196-197.

453 Yost, *Pieracci and Shelley*, p. 2; *SPII*, pp. 868-869; Weinberg, *Shelley's Italian Experience*, note 22; Gaull, *English Romanticism*, p. 103.

454 Jewett, *Fatal Autonomy*, p. 140n.; Horace Walpole, 'Postscript to The Mysterious Mother' in Baines and Burns, p. 65; David Worrall, 'Never Performed Until Now (The Guardian 3 Feb 2001), or, Oops! Losing the Surrey Theatre, 1821: Performances of Horace Walpole's *The Mysterious Mother*' paper given at 'Staging the Page Conference', Swansea University, April 2008.

455 *PBSLII*, p. 102; *OSA*, p. 336n.; Curran, *Cenci*, p. 223.

unperceived to her father from becoming ludicrous — it could never be shewn in action — yet it must be known — it must be described and the language must be so cautious as to throw a transparent veil over what it declares. He prepared the incident even in his first act

'*Euphr:* Yes, Phocion, go;
Go with my child, torn from this matron breast —
This breast that *still should yield its nurture to him.*'

He has thus, by a happy line, invested her with the *unquestioned power* to relieve him; that relief is thus exhibited by Philotas: —

'On the bare earth
Evander lies; and as his languid pow'rs
Imbibe with *eager thirst* the kind *refreshment*
Euphrasia views him with the tend'rst glance,
Even as a MOTHER *doating on her child.*'

I shall, at least, imitate the discretion of the poet, and leave the reader to surmise the terms, which, had they been different, would have ruined the pathos of the scene, and perhaps excited laughter.[456]

In writing about the rape of Beatrice in *The Cenci*, Shelley uses a method similar to Murphy's, revealing what has happened through imagery and the reaction of the other characters but without stating it overtly. Shelley's audience was familiar with *The Grecian Daughter* and would have understood this technique.

The disadvantage is turned to dramatic benefit by Beatrice being, as others have noted, psychologically unable to utter the words.[457] Lucretia's repeated questioning, six times altogether, is not, as Curran suggests, inability to understand. It is clear she knows what has happened since she says, 'Whate'er you may have suffered, you have done/No evil' (III. i. 121-122), close to Shelley's own view that 'no person can be truly dishonoured by the act of another'.[458] When she says, 'Oh my lost child,/Hide not in proud impenetrable grief/Thy sufferings from my fear' (III. i. 104-106), it is to get Beatrice, who can 'feign no image in my mind/Of that which has transformed me' (III. i. 107-108), to speak. Lucretia succeeds sufficiently for Beatrice to be able to tell Orsino that her father has done her a 'wrong so

---

456 Boaden, *Mrs. Siddons*, I, pp. 310-31; see Chapter 2 for the possibility of Shelley's having seen *The Grecian Daughter*.
457 McWhir, 'The Light and the Knife', p. 158; Michael Worton, 'Speech and 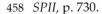 Silence in *The Cenci*' in *Essays on Shelley*, ed. by Miriam Allott (Liverpool: Liverpool University Press, 1982), p. 109; Curran, *Cenci*, p. 269.
458 *SPII*, p. 730.

great and strange' (III. i. 139) and to express anger and sarcasm (III. i. 144). Beatrice's statement that her accusation will not be believed (III. i. 163-164) is confirmed by Orsino's saying 'the strange and execrable deeds alleged' in the petition have 'turned the Pope's displeasure/Upon the accusers from the criminal' (II. ii. 63-66).

Whether or not consciously in accordance with Schlegel's suggestions, Shelley created scenes in *The Cenci* which 'excite interest […] and sympathy' and 'rivet the attention', with 'nothing beyond what the multitude are contented to believe that they can understand'. His contemporaries would, of course, have found less difficulty with the language than today's audience. Shelley wished to use natural language without introducing 'mere poetry', and, compared to that of Milman, Tobin or Baillie, his is very much 'the familiar language of men' while including some concessions to Elizabethanisms which his audience would have expected in a period drama. His verse, as Curran has noted, is very close to speech, therefore easy to learn and to deliver in a natural and modern style. As Dame Sybil told Curran, the speeches are not too long.[459] Neither is the play.

Shelley was working from a consciousness of the contemporary theatre, writing first-class parts for leading performers and good supporting parts and showing understanding of the use of stage effects and scenery. He also tried to avoid censorship problems whilst still putting across his own political views; *The Cenci* was not the only play to fall foul of the censorship issues and a play unperformed for that reason is not inherently unstageable. Its impact in 1819 cannot be judged by modern performance, as a director will alter the play to suit personal interpretation, the company's strengths, the number of actors or the performance space, and the audience will know at least some of its history. It was, however, received enthusiastically by the audience closest to that of 1819 in composition, at the Korsch Theatre, Moscow, in 1920.[460] The philosophical dilemma *The Cenci* poses continues to be relevant to modern society. It deserves to be more frequently performed in the professional theatre and it is largely because of its reputation as a 'closet' play that it has not been.

Shelley was to say that 'The very Theatre rejected it with expressions of the greatest insolence', but this negative view may have been 'the effect of criticism upon the nerves', a result of disappointment at its rejection. While he was writing *The Cenci*, he described it as 'a work of a more popular kind;

---

459   *SPII*, p. 734; Curran, *Cenci*, pp. 49, 262.
460   Curran, *Cenci*, p. 208.

and, if anything of mine could deserve attention, of higher claims' and 'in some degree worthy of' its dedication to Hunt; he had 'some hopes, and some friends here persuade me that they are not unfounded'. It was not until these hopes were disappointed that he said 'I dont think very much of it'. [461] Almost as soon as he had sent it off, on 9 October 1819, he began researching into the period of the English Revolution. This was eventually to result in an attempt to write a more ambitious play, one which might have had a timescale of approximately thirty years and as many characters. Like *The Cenci*, it concerned the right to resist a tyrant. This was *Charles the First*.

---

461 *PBSLII*, pp. 181, 108, 112, 119, 189; Wolfe, II, p. 198.

Chapter Four
Turning History into Art –
Charles the First

Shelley began writing *Charles the First* in January 1822, but at his death he had completed only scenes for a first act, an outline sketch for a second and many notes, jottings and stray lines.[462] As he had not worked on it in the months preceding his death, there is a view that he would not have completed it even had he lived. This view undermines the importance of this project, which he had been researching since 1818, and his competence as a dramatist is challenged by the idea that it may have been laid aside because of difficulties with dramatising the material. It should be borne in mind that there is not yet a modern edition of the play and commentators have not always had all the manuscripts available, but those who believe that he could not have finished it include R.B. Woodings, Jewett and, to some degree, Behrendt, who follow Medwin and Mary Shelley, both of whom were with Shelley in Pisa when he was drafting the play.[463]

In her 'Note to the Poems of 1822', Mary Shelley said that Shelley 'threw aside' *Charles the First* in favour of *The Triumph of Life*, but her supposition that he might not have been able to 'bend his mind away from the broodings and wanderings of thought divested of human interest' is perhaps coloured by her own estrangement from him during the composition; she knew he was capable of writing dramatic characters in *Julian and Maddalo* and *The Cenci*.[464] Jewett, too, believes he abandoned *Charles the First* in favour of

---

462 Bodleian MS. Shelley adds e. 17, pp. 33-51, 52 rev., 55 + stray leaf adds c. 4, fol. 136 rev., 185 rev.-93b rev.(*BSMXII*: 70-109, 114-115, 120-123, 144-327); Bodleian MS. Shelley adds e. 7, pp. 255 rev.-237 rev. (*BSMXVI*: 220-239); Huntington MS HM 2111, fols *1r-*5r (*MYRVII*: 322-339).
463 Jewett, *Fatal Autonomy*, p. 210; R.B. Woodings, 'Shelley's Sources for Charles I', MLR, 64 (1969), 267-275; Behrendt, *Shelley and His Audiences*, pp. 234-235.
464 Mary Shelley, 'Note on Poems of 1822', *OSA*, p. 676.

The Triumph of Life.[465] Shelley, however, frequently wrote more than one work concurrently, as he did *Julian and Maddalo, The Cenci* and *Prometheus Unbound* in 1819. Although he remarked to Hunt on 2 March 1822 that 'a slight circumstance gave a new train to my ideas & shattered the fragile edifice when half built', this 'edifice' could have been rebuilt as he still had the materials, his notes and drafts, from which he had created it. His remark to John Gisborne on 18 June 1822, 'I write little now [...] I do not go on with "Charles the First"' also needs to be taken with caution.[466] At the time Shelley was recovering from grief over the death of Allegra, Byron and Claire's daughter, and Mary's miscarriage and consequent ill-health, by enjoying the beautiful bay of Lerici, sun, music and sailing. At Lerici, he would have found *The Triumph of Life* easier to write in his boat than *Charles the First*, which required reference books, consistency of characterisation, manipulation of historical material and ordering of scenes.[467]

Medwin believed that Shelley had 'formed no definite plan in his own mind' of his subject matter and that he might have abandoned the play because he 'could not reconcile his mind to the beheading of Charles'.[468] Although Shelley said to Gisborne on 26 January 1822, 'I cannot seize the conception of the subject as a whole yet', the 'yet' shows that he expected to overcome the problem and this is borne out by his drafts. The fragments are in themselves carefully structured which indicates that Shelley was developing a structure for the whole play in his head, even if not sketched out on paper. His remark to Hunt that 'Charles the 1st [...] if completed according to *my present idea* [my italics] will hold a higher rank that [than] the Cenci as a work of art' tends to confirm this. Such a pattern of working can be seen in the *Fragments of an Unfinished Drama*. Shelley left only a few speeches, but Mary Shelley knew some of the underlying story which she supplies in her notes.[469]

Medwin incorrectly claims that Shelley 'had no means of procuring' the necessary books of reference. Shelley read numerous works for the play, although some did not arrive until June 1821.[470] As well as Milton's prose and the histories of Clarendon, Hume and Catharine Macaulay,[471]

---

465   Jewett, *Fatal Autonomy*, p. 210.
466   *PBSLII*, pp. 394, 436.
467   *OSA*, p. 676-677; such difficulties are also noted in Scrivener, *Radical Shelley*, p. 297.
468   Medwin, *Life*, II, pp. 163, 164.
469   *PBSLII*, pp. 388, 380; *OSA*, p. 482.
470   Medwin, *Life*, II, p. 164; *PBSLII*, p. 294; *MWSLI*, p. 200.
471   See *MWSJ*, pp. 654, 660.

Shelley read the royalist propaganda, *Reliquiae Sacrae* and *Eikon Basilike*, the *Memorials* of Bulstrode Whitelocke, *The Tryal of Sir Harry Vane*, *Memoirs* of Edmund Ludlow, Lucy Hutchinson's life of her husband, and Charles I's own letters.[472] He was able to gather from these eyewitness accounts a wide range of views which reveal much character and atmosphere invaluable for developing scenes, characters and situations, and before he had read and absorbed them he could not have started writing. If he had an intellectual grasp of the subject matter, he still required an imaginative response to develop the creative impulse. This he explained to his publisher, Charles Ollier, 'when once I see and feel I can write it, it is already written'.[473]

Williams and Trelawny were also in Pisa at the time. Williams said:

As to S[helley]'s "Charles the First" — on which he sat down about 5 days since, if he continues it in the spirit [of] some of the lines which he read to me last night, it will doubtless take a place before any other that has appear[ed] since Shakspeare, and will be found a valuable addition to the Historical Pla[y.][474]

Trelawny reports Shelley as saying:

I am now writing a play for the stage. It is affectation to say we write a play for any other purpose. The subject is from English history; in style and manner I shall approach as near our great dramatist as my feeble powers will permit. King Lear is my model, for that is nearly perfect. I am amazed at my presumption.[475]

Shelley's remarks to Medwin, in July 1820, were:

What think you of my boldness? I mean to write a play, in the spirit of human nature, without prejudice or passion, entitled 'Charles the First'. So vanity intoxicates people; but let those few who praise my verses, and in whose approbation I take so much delight, answer for the sin.[476]

When these passages are read together, it becomes clear that Shelley intended *Charles the First* to be a major work for the stage, Shakespearean indeed in scale and quality. The ambitiousness of the scale would be likely to cause a writer at times to become discouraged and drop the work, but

---

472 The first three were used by Shelley in his notes in *BSMXVI*. Shelley's reading of the last three is here inferred from Mary's having read them after their arrival (*MWSJ*, pp. 374-375, 408); *Eikon Basilike* and *Reliquiae Sacrae* in Walter E. Peck, *Shelley, His Life and Work* (Boston: Houghton Mifflin, 1927), pp. 361-364.
473 *PBSLII*, p. 269.
474 Gisborne & Williams, p. 123.
475 Wolfe, II, p. 198.
476 *PBSLII*, pp. 219-220.

it would also be a reason to return to it, particularly after investing the amount of time in research which Shelley had done.

Peacock implies that *Charles the First* was a response to the invitation from Henry Harris to write upon 'a less repulsive subject' than that of *The Cenci*, and clearly believes it was intended for the stage. Shelley wrote on 22 February 1821 to Ollier, 'I doubt about "Charles the First", but, if I do write it, it shall be the birth of severe and high feelings' and, in September 1821, 'Unless I am sure of making something good the play will not be written.' Yet less than a month later he wrote, 'Expect Charles the Ist [...] in the spring' and, when he had started work in January 1822, 'I ought to say that the Tragedy promises to be good'. This confidence is apparent in his attempt to sell the copyright, perhaps encouraged by the notion that, if it were successfully staged at Covent Garden, as Harris's positive message had given him reason to hope, it would sell well, though he added he could not judge 'how far it may be'.[477] Cameron believes *Charles the First* would have been a 'major historical drama', Scrivener thought it 'would have eventually been finished' and Crook describes Shelley as 'writing at the height of his powers'.[478] Shelley's method of working appears to have been to research the subject thoroughly for a long period before he actually began to write.[479] If Shelley had had a definite plan and had researched the background for *Charles the First* over a number of years, as I believe, it is unlikely that he would have abandoned it.

Shelley's research

There is evidence that in 1819 Shelley was already researching this subject, one he thought suitable for a drama 'full of intense interest, contrasted character, and busy passion'.[480] On 8 June 1818, Godwin had suggested 'a book [...] to be called The Lives of the Common-wealth's Men', as a project for his daughter, Mary Shelley. Shelley's enthusiastic response on her behalf and later insistence that she should write a play ('Charles the 1st') may indicate his interest rather than hers; she never took it up and it

477 Wolfe, II, p. 352; *PBSLII*, pp. 269, 354, 357, 372.
478 Cameron, *The Golden Years*, p. 412; Scrivener, *Radical Shelley*, p. 297; Nora Crook, '"Calumniated Republicans" and the Hero of "Charles the First"', *KSJ*, 57 (2007), 141-158 (p. 143).
479 Curran, *Annus Mirabilis*, p. xvii.
480 Mary Shelley, 'Note on Poems of 1822', *OSA*, p. 676.

is significant that he mentioned himself in connection with it at all despite saying he was 'little skilled in English history' and his interest in the subject 'feeble'.[481] As early as 19 June 1818, the Shelleys began reading aloud Hume's *History of England* which they continued until 15 August,[482] thus commencing the historical research which Shelley was to continue, off and on, for the following three years. His reading appears to bear out Medwin's suggestion that he had 'designed to write a tragedy' on the subject in 1818 and began it at the end of the following year. From August 1819, Shelley read 'about 12' of Calderón's plays including *The Schism in England*, other seventeenth-century dramatists, such as Beaumont and Fletcher, Jonson, and Massinger. He also read Lucan, who influenced seventeenth-century republican writers.[483] On 9 October, Mary notes 'S. begins Clarendon' (Clarendon's *History of the Rebellion and Civil Wars*) and he finished the first volume, some of which he read aloud, by 11 October.[484]

There is an indication that Shelley was then searching for a vehicle for writing a drama about the struggle for liberty. Mary Quinn suggests that he had 'completed *The Cenci* within a month or two of jotting down these notes and *Prometheus Unbound* within weeks or even days'.[485] The notes referred to were as follows:

> On Bonaparte
> A Drama —
> That a bad & weak man is he who rules over bad & wea
> First scene the field of Battle [?]in — one of the first in which Bonapa[r]
> te was conqueror.
> Perhaps in Ægypt
> two wounded men hear ~~his~~ a voice — they first mistake it for each
> others but it is Jacobinism[486]

The wounded men are not given names, but are representative of ordinary people like those in the first scene of *Charles the First*. The 'Voice' of Jacobinism is an abstract one in line with the contemporary theatre, where

481 *PBSLII*, pp. 21, 39-40.
482 *MWSJ*, pp. 215-223.
483 *MWSJ*, pp. 293-302; *PBSLII*, pp. 120, 154; For Lucan's influence, see David Norbrook, *Writing the English Republic: Poetry, Rhetoric and Politics 1627-1660* (Cambridge: Cambridge University Press, 2000), pp. 23-62; for Shelley's reading of Lucan, see *MWSJ*, p. 660.
484 *MWSJ*, p. 298.
485 *The Manuscripts of the Younger Romantics, Percy Bysshe Shelley. Vol VI: Shelley's 1819-1821 Huntington Notebook: a facsimile of Huntington MS. HM 2176* ed. by Mary A. Quinn (New York: Garland, 1994), p. 181.
486 *MYRVI*, pp. 349-348, 347-346.

supernatural elements were created and concealed behind a sidewing, as in *The Castle Spectre* or *The Vampire*. Shelley is writing with awareness of stageability and theatrical effectiveness since there is the basis of a theatrically thrilling scene in the idea of each man thinking the other had spoken and then realising that it was a supernatural voice.

During October and November 1819, Shelley read aloud not only Clarendon's *History* but also de Staël's *Of the Revolution*, from which he drew the parallels with the French and English revolutions in *A Philosophical View of Reform*, a work Donald Reiman believes he continued writing into 1820:[487]

> The revolution in France overthrew the hierarchy, the aristocracy & the monarchy, & the whole of that peculiarly insolent & oppressive system on which they were based [...] The usurpation of Bonaparte and the Restoration of the Bourbons were the shapes in which this reaction clothed itself [...] France occupies in this respect the same situation as was occupied by England at the restoration of Charles the 2d. It has undergone a revolution [...] which may be paralled [sic] with that in our own country which ended in the death of Charles the 1st. The Authors of both revolutions proposed a greater & more glorious object than the degraded passions of their countrymen permitted them to obtain. But in both cases abuses were abolished which never since have dared to show their face.[488]

The news of the Peterloo Massacre raised the possibility of a pre-revolutionary situation in England. On 20 February 1820, Shelley, who had known United Irishmen in Dublin in 1812, discussed the 1798 Rising in Ireland with Lady Mountcashell.[489] The Shelleys' reading aloud in autumn 1819 included Fletcher's 'tyrant plays', *A Wife for a Month* and *Philaster;* they had read these, with *The Maid's Tragedy* and *A King and No King*, alongside Hume in July 1818, so it is interesting that Shelley read them once more alongside Clarendon's history of the period.[490] Reading them was not only invaluable in developing Shelley's dramatic technique but also his historical sense. It gave him an insight into the atmosphere of Charles's court and an awareness of how the theme of tyranny was dealt with in plays, copies of which, incidentally, Charles himself owned and which he saw performed at his father's court.

Andrew Gurr explains that 'Fletcher made tyranny an explicit feature of his tragedies and tragicomedies' and that 'Charles's sexual morality was

---

487 *MWSJ*, pp. 678; *SCVI*, p. 958.
488 'A Philosophical View of Reform', *SCVI*, pp. 980-981.
489 'Stephen Burley, 'Shelley, the United Irishmen and the Illuminati', *KSR*, 17 (2003), 18-26 (pp. 19-20, 23); *MWSJ*, pp. 309, 309n.
490 *MWSJ*, pp. 219, 295.

never in question, but he was seen as a tyrant [...] From *Philaster* and *The Maid's Tragedy* onwards, love at court became a metaphor for the impact of royal misrule on the subject'.[491] The problem is never resolved by a successful rebellion but by the king repenting or the true king returning. Shelley would have realised from this that a certain amount of discussion of the subject was tolerated as long as the conclusion was that rebellion was not tenable. This knowledge would be useful when writing scenes at court.

In January 1820, Shelley continued reading aloud Jacobean drama, particularly that dealing with war, tyranny and rebellion: *King John*, which was frequently played as it provided Siddons with a strong part in Constance, followed by *Henry IV Pt 1* which he almost certainly saw in April 1810. In March he read aloud *Henry V* and, twice, *Henry VI*, plays from which he was able to learn how Shakespeare handled the dramatisation of war and, particularly importantly for *Charles the First*, the problem of several battle scenes in the same play. In March, too, he read aloud Jonson's Roman plays of rebellion and tyranny, *Catiline's Conspiracy* and *Sejanus, His Fall*, and, in the summer, Fletcher's *Bonduca* and Shakespeare's *Troilus and Cressida*, both dealing particularly with aspects of war affecting women.[492] The pattern of reading political works and histories of the English Civil War alongside Jacobean drama was repeated by reading Catharine Macaulay's *History of England*, Clarendon's *Rebellion of Ireland* and Godwin's *Political Justice*.[493] In 1821, the Shelleys again read aloud Jonson and 'Old Plays', almost certainly Scott's new edition of Dodsley's *Old Plays*, retitled *Ancient English Drama*.[494] By immersing himself in Jacobean and Caroline drama for over three years, Shelley became thoroughly familiar with its cadence, vocabulary and manner of writing about political questions; he gained a knowledge of its context by his historical reading, thus preparing the ground for writing a play about the fall of a tyrant and a civil war which warns of the danger of a revolutionary leader who becomes another tyrant. This must have seemed no less necessary in June 1821, when the books he required arrived, since by then he had also received news of revolutionary events in Piedmont, Naples and Greece.

---

491 Andrew Gurr, *The Shakespeare Company, 1594-1642* (Cambridge: Cambridge University Press, 2004), pp. 147, 188.
492 *MWSJ*, pp. 310-312, 317, 333.
493 *MWSJ*: for Macaulay see pp. 326-331, for Clarendon see p. 331, for Godwin see pp. 313-314.
494 *MWSJ*, p. 370.

The theme of the play

By January 1822, therefore, when he began writing *Charles the First*, Shelley was well able to decide his own 'interpretation of events' and would not have been dependent on Hume's history, as Woodings implies. It is true that his notes contain at least twenty page references to it and phrases from Hume appear in the play but, as Crook points out, Shelley refers in his notes to Hume as a 'Tory historian' and clearly did not endorse his views.[495] Cameron, and Crook following him, consider that Shelley would have found those of the Republican Whig, Macaulay, more sympathetic and an examination of Macaulay's *History* bears this out.[496] He read the *Reliquiae Sacrae* and the *Eikon Basilike* because, as a dramatist, he required to know how the King and his supporters thought and felt, not, as Woodings suggests, 'to present the downfall of a suffering king not the overthrow of a harsh despot'.[497] Shelley's portrayal of Charles is more complex and subtle. It shows him to be a loving husband and father and an appreciator of art as a private man, but cruel, autocratic and weak as a ruler. This ambiguity in character was noted by Lucy Hutchinson, for example, who describes Charles approvingly as 'temperate chaste and serious' but also as 'a worse encroacher upon the civil and spiritual liberties of his people by far than his father'.[498] If Shelley's portrayal of Charles followed Hutchinson, Whitelocke's eyewitness reports and the King's own correspondence, this contradiction would be shown by the king's actions. Yet, if Charles was not to be the hero of the play, there is no reason to suppose that Cromwell would have been. Medwin reports Shelley's unwillingness to make him so and the information that we have of the play's structure and the number of characters Shelley planned to include, shows that his intention was in line with Godwin's suggestion of 'the Lives of the Common-wealth's Men', far broader than a mere conflict between two personalities.[499]

Quite apart from the struggle between Parliament and King, there were also the struggles within Parliament, for example those between the

---

495 Woodings, 'Shelley's Sources', pp. 268-269; Nora Crook, *Calumniated Republicans*, p. 146. The edition of Hume which Shelley used consists of slim portable volumes suitable for someone who liked to work outside as Shelley did.
496 *BSMXVI*, pp. 235-234; Cameron, *The Golden Years*, p. 412; *BSMXII*, p. xxix.
497 Woodings, 'Shelley's Sources', p. 273.
498 Lucy Hutchinson, *Memoirs of the Life of Colonel Hutchinson* (London: George Bell & Sons, 1906), pp. 84-85.
499 Medwin, *Life*, II, p. 165; *PBSLII*, p. 21.

Presbyterians and the Independents. Macaulay's *History* provided Shelley with the necessary background information. She regarded the Independents as carrying the struggle for liberty forward, but, although Cromwell was an Independent, she described him as an 'usurper'. Shelley wanted to give an accurate impression of those opposed to the King who also opposed Cromwell's rise to power and the erosion of the liberties won by Parliament, but who were not Puritans like Bastwick, Prynne or Leighton. Macaulay and Whitelocke also provided details about the Levellers and the mutiny in the army. These groups were either silenced by Cromwell or silenced themselves for the sake of peace but did not support bringing back the King.[500] Like Macaulay, Shelley would have supported neither Cromwell nor Charles. The focus of the play was unlikely to have been upon either, but upon the struggle for liberty and the title, as with *Julius Caesar*, justified by the train of events caused by Charles rather than his personal story.

Had Shelley wanted to write a play based on the clash of personalities, he would have structured it as Mitford did her *Charles the First* (1825) which is set in the days leading up to Charles's execution and develops incidents revealing the characters of Cromwell and Charles. Mitford was perhaps using self-censorship; she later felt she had been 'unjust to the memory of a great man' and that her 'drawing of Charles would have been much less amiable, and that of Cromwell much more so' had she portrayed them 'at any other part of their career'. Crabb Robinson thought that she 'sadly profaned [...] the great names of the great era'.[501] Shelley's historical research and political views were sufficiently strong to prevent him from making the mistake of similarly compromising himself. His attitude towards the English Revolution and the trial of Charles I is clear from *A Philosophical View of Reform*:

> By rapid gradation the nation was conducted to the temporary abolition of aristocracy & episcopacy, & the mighty example which, 'in teaching nations how to live', England afforded to the world of bringing to public justice one of those chiefs of a conspirasy of priviledged murderers & robbers whose impunity has been the consecration of crime.[502]

---

500 Catharine Macaulay, *The History of England from the Accession of James I to the Elevation of the House of Hanover*, 8 vols (London: printed for Edward and Charles Dilly in the Poultry, 1771), IV, pp. 267, 303-310, V, p. 201n.; Bulstrode Whitelocke, *Memorials of the English Affairs from the Beginning of the Reign of King Charles the First to King Charles the Second His Happy Restauration* (London: Tonson, 1732), pp. 396-397.
501 'Original Preface' in Mitford, *Works*, I, p. 249; Crabb Robinson, p. 143.
502 'A Philosophical View of Reform', *SCVI*, p. 967.

In September 1820, he said of the revolutionaries at Naples:

> if the Emperor should make war upon them, their first action would be to
> put to death *all* the members of the royal family. A necessary, & most just
> measure when the forces of the combatants as well as the merits of their
> respective causes are so unequal! [503]

A Philosophical View of Reform sets out the case for a redistribution of
wealth from the ruling classes to the poor. Shelley is willing for 'a process
of negotiation' which would occupy twenty years rather than risk civil war,
but he warns that the Government and the richest class must show their
sincerity by granting the demands of the poorer classes.[504] Although he
wrote this in 1819/20, it is unlikely that his view had changed by the time
he came to write *Charles the First* since, on 29 June 1822, he wrote to Horace
Smith essentially what he had stated in that essay:

> England appears to be in a desperate condition, Ireland still worse, & no class
> of those who subsist on the public labour will be persuaded that *their* claims
> on it must be diminished. But the government must content itself with less
> in taxes, the landholder must submit to receive less rent & the fundholder
> a diminished interest, — or they will all get nothing or something worse
> (than) nothing.[505]

A note relating to *Charles the First* ('Monopolies and taxes. See Richard 2d
— See Hume 206 & consider the present time')[506] suggests that he regarded
the play as a suitable vehicle for expressing his views less explicitly than
in *A Philosophical View of Reform*, which Ollier and Hunt were wary of
publishing because of the likelihood of prosecution.[507] It would also have
reached a wider audience than the reformers. 'To Shelley [...] the reform
movement was part of a vast sweep of progressive historical forces out
of the past into the future of a democratic republic and, beyond that, into
a Godwinian equalitarian state'.[508] He may have believed, as Mitford did,
that, since the facts were already in the public domain, a historical drama
based on them would not be refused a licence.[509]

---

503 *PBSLII*, p. 234.
504 'A Philosophical View of Reform', *SCVI*, p. 1061.
505 *PBSLII*, p. 442.
506 *BSMXVI*, pp. 235-234.
507 Behrendt, *Shelley and His Audiences*, p. 224; *PBSLII*, pp. 164, 201.
508 Kenneth N. Cameron, 'Shelley and the Reformers', *ELH*, 12 (1945), p. 85.
509 Mitford, *Works*, I, pp. 243-245.

Scene i

One can see that *Charles the First* was intended for the stage from the first scene. This is based on an actual historical event described in detail in Whitelocke's *Memorials*. It presents a crowd on stage waiting for, and eventually seeing, a procession of pageantry, the Inns of Court masquers travelling to Whitehall for a masque. The masque was presented in honour of Queen Henrietta, ostensibly to distance the Inns of Court from Prynne's *Historiomastix*, since Prynne, a lawyer, by referring to actresses as 'notorious whores', had allegedly attacked the Queen for taking part in masques. Whitelocke, one of the organisers of the masque, explains that it was also a subtle protest against the corruption of granting monopolies. It included an anti-masque of 'cripples and beggars on horseback with musick of keys and tongs [...] mounted on the poorest jades that could be gotten out of the Dirt carts' and the lawyers had oval chariots to indicate that 'there was no precedence in them'.[510]

If *Charles the First* were written for reading only, it would suffice to present the ideas in speeches and to report the procession. Shelley writes an actual procession with spectators watching and commenting, which, on stage, would work on the visual and aural senses, the sharp contrast between masquers and anti-masquers emphasising the symbolic effect of its application to the state of the country and counterpointing the text.

The violent speeches of the Puritans, the eagerness of the Young Man, the brutality of the Pursuivant and the disdain of the royal procession show the distance and hatred between the people and their rulers. Shelley had mastered dramatic technique sufficiently to combine three striking effects in a crowd scene: a procession, a masque and the shocking entry of Leighton, who was mutilated in punishment for speaking out against Laud's policies.

The crowd comments on what the people thought of their government, but it goes beyond the role of a Greek chorus. There is a dynamic within it, the establishment of a group of lively characters who put the point of view of the people in a play ostensibly about a King, in a rapid, clear exposition. Shelley had originally intended to make the opening scene one of Hampden, Vane, Cromwell and other Parliamentarians about to leave England but being prevented by order of the King. This would have been a dramatically effective opening, but the masque scene changes the focus from the Parliamentarians to the citizens of London. As a result, Shelley

---

510 Whitelocke, p. 19.

WEST'S, *Theatrical* PORTRAITS. Nº59.

Mr Elliston as King George the IV.th in the Coronation, at Drury Lane Theatre.
London. Published Nov.r 9. 1821. by W.West. at his Theatrical Print Warehouse, 51, Wych Street, Strand.

12. 'Elliston as George IV', toy theatre illustration, c. 1820. From David
Powell *The Toy Theatres of William West* (London: Sir John Soane's Museum,
2004), p. 54.

introduces the King, Queen, Strafford and Laud and the chief issues of the
play in a scene of brilliant spectacle and lively dialogue; what is more, as it
has an historical basis, its authenticity adds weight to the fictional dialogue.

Several points of view are put: the uncompromising Puritan, the old man who dislikes the injustices, the young man who enjoys the spectacle and believes the King can be won from his counsellors. Through this the audience discovers the attitude of those with no political voice.

Shelley's development of the pageantry shows his knowledge of the resources of Covent Garden's property, musical and scenery painting departments, as he asks for nothing that they could not have delivered. Covent Garden had a large enough backstage to accommodate the pageant through the scenery while the actors in the crowd on the forestage could be heard and seen clearly by the audience. Crowd scenes with amateur extras were used; Kemble had used 240 in *Coriolanus*.[511] In 1820, Covent Garden added to *Henry IV Pt 2* a coronation procession based on George IV's, including scenes created with the help of carpenters by the scene painters, T. Grieve, Capon, Dixon and Pugh: an in depth scene of Westminster Abbey; the cloisters of the Abbey; a banquet in Westminster Hall; and the scene outside 'with tiers of painted spectators'. They had also painted New Palace Yard, the Palace of Westminster, Westminster Council Chamber and a Gothic library based on St. Stephen's, and had the expertise to accurately depict the Banqueting House where the masque took place. Shelley undoubtedly realised the dramatic irony of placing the scene where Charles was executed in 1649.[512]

A director today might present such a scene with sound effects, lights, music and the reaction of the spectators but on the Georgian stage such an impressionistic style did not exist. The pageant would have been staged as realistically and spectacularly as possible, but it is doubtful whether real horses would have been used. Covent Garden had used them for the revival of *Bluebeard* and for *Timour the Tartar* in 1811 but these were the musical extravaganzas not poetic tragedies. Although equestrian drama was extremely popular, it was not without its critics: Hunt considered the use of horses cruel and 'a mark of corrupted taste' while Crabb Robinson found *Bluebeard* 'less impressive than' the original version 'in spight [sic] of the horses'.[513] For a play by a new author, the theatre might have preferred

511 Young, 'Others and Mrs. Siddons', pp. 89-92.
512 Rosenfeld, *Scene Design*, pp. 97-99, 101-102; Nora Crook now considers incorrect her 1991 identification, based on a reading of a doubtful word as 'bargates', of the location of the spectators as Temple Bar, *BSMXII*, pp. 319-318, a sufficient objection being that it would require the Queen to walk along the Strand to the City of London with her ladies; personal communication, November 2004.
513 Cox and Gamer, *Broadview Anthology*, p. 76; *Hunt's Dramatic Criticism*, p. 47; Crabb Robinson, p. 33.

13. 'Interior of Westminster Abbey', toy theatre illustration, c. 1820. From *The Toy Theatres of William West*, p. 54.

to use models on the backstage for this scene rather than incur the expense of strengthening the stage and hiring and stabling the horses from Astley's.

By 1823, Covent Garden was managed by Charles Kemble who loved authenticity. The huge property department, the Painting Room, Decorative Machinery Room and Wardrobe would have been encouraged to create the stately procession with music, flambeaux, period costumes, pasteboard horses and decorated chariots in the shape of half moons and shells, based on those in Whitelocke's description of the historical pageant, which were themselves copied from Roman triumphant chariots. This spectacular visual display would supplement the atmosphere Shelley creates by the increasing excitement in the speech of Young Man. One of the chariots carried the musicians with footmen in scarlet livery holding 'huge flamboys'. The first chariot was silver and crimson, the second silver and blue, with matching costumes and plumes for the horses, spangles and silver and gold lace.[514]

Shelley enhances the dramatic impact upon the audience in sharing the anticipation of a crowd waiting to see a pageant by allowing them to hear music and see the lights which announce it before it is seen. The Law Student says:

---

514 Whitelocke, p. 19.

Even now ye see the redness of the torches
Inflame the night to the eastward, and the clarions
Gust to us on the wind's wave (*BSMXII*, pp. 289-290, 289-288 reverso)

This is based on Whitelocke's 'the torches and flaming huge flamboys born by the sides of each Chariot make it seem lightsome as noonday'. There were 'clarions' and other music, including the 'most excellent musicians of the Queen's chapel' with their '40 lutes besides other Instruments and Voices'[515] which the Covent Garden orchestra was more than adequate to provide.[516]

Shelley shows a mastery of exposition in this scene. With great economy, he sketches in most of the grievances against Charles in the dialogue of the waiting crowd such as the Huguenots Charles failed to relieve at La Rochelle, the 'remnant of the martyred Saints in Rochfort' (pp. 295-294). The speaking parts in the crowd, the Old Man, Young Man, Citizen and Law Student, are large enough to be included in the Dramatis Personae, but only Bastwick and Leighton are named. The Young Man is disposed to think well of the King and approves of the masque, 'a happy sight to see' (pp. 317-316), drawing on Whitelocke's description. The Old Man prophesies of the palace 'nine years more/The roots will be refreshed with civil blood' (pp. 319-318) and that Charles 'must decline/Amid the darkness of conflicting storm'(pp. 309-308). The Young Man believes 'our country's wounds/May yet be healed — The King is just and gracious' but his cry, 'O still those dissonant thoughts' (pp. 285-284) shows that his delight in pageantry surpasses his interest in politics. They are well-contrasted characters.

The discussion of whether the masque is sinful is at the same time a covert criticism of Charles's government and church. The Law Student asks, 'What thinkest thou of this quaint shew?' (pp. 287-288). The replies could apply both to art and Charles's government: the Puritan view, sinful and corrupt in its extravagance and worldliness; the royalist view, harmless in its beauty and escapism, as Henrietta Maria uses art and music in Scene ii. The imagery is reptilian and meteorological. The bishops are 'crocodiles' (pp. 291-290), the Puritan faith the 'serpent creed' (pp. 315-314), the adders

---

515 Whitelocke, p. 19.
516 '6 or 8 first violins, 6 or 8 second violins, 2 tenors, two 'cellos, 3 or 4 double basses, oboe and flageolet, first and second flutes, first and second clarionets, first and second horns, first and second bassoons, trombone, trumpet and bugle, pianoforte, bells, carillons or small bells, and kettledrums', Wyndham, *Covent Garden*, I, pp. 336-337.

which 'doff their skin/And keep their venom' are councillors (pp. 285-284). While Charles is the 'equinoctial sun' (pp. 309-308) the state of the country is associated with 'inclement air' 'whirlwind' and 'the day that dawns in fire will die in storms' (pp. 311-312). The Puritans, Bastwick, Leighton and 'a citizen', are given a suitable idiolect to express their sense of being a righteous remnant, such as calling the Queen a 'Canaanitish Jezebel!' (pp. 321-320), and as in the following exchange:

> 1st Citizen: The root of all this ill is Prelacy
> Bastwick: I would cut up the root
> 1st Citizen: And by what means
> Bastwick: Smiting each bishop under the 5th rib (pp. 291-290)

On the other hand, the masque makes its point through the symbolism of the contrast between the masquers, 'lilies glorious as Solomon' (pp. 275-274), and the anti-masque of 'cripples beggars and outcasts/Horsed upon stumbling jades' (pp. 273-272). [517] Bastwick blames Strafford for the state of the country ('he who poisons/The King's dull ear with whispered aphorisms/ From Machiavel and Bacon', pp. 301-300), and has a characteristic distrust of lawyers (pp. 297-296). Shelley noted that the lawyers were 'among the boldest assertors of public liberty', and also opposed the 'austere & odious temper of the puritans'.[518]

Shelley's indictment of the tyrannical rule of Charles is made visually clear when 'A Pursuivant' enters calling 'Room for the King' (pp. 305-304). Although the audience would realise the necessity of having such an official at a procession, it reveals metaphorically the constant interruption of the lives of ordinary people in England by commands to give way to the King's wishes. Mary Shelley describes seeing 'the Emperor of Austria […] preceded by an officer, who rudely pushes the people back with a drawn sword' when the Emperor visited Rome in 1818.[519] The actions would also recall the violent breaking up of peaceable gatherings in England such as the Peterloo massacre. The word 'pursuivant' is not used in Whitelocke, but Shelley may have taken it from Shakespeare's *Henry VIII* and Fletcher's *A King and No King*. Cancelled lines show that he had in mind more aggressive, insulting commands and possibly was trying to choose the right phrases: 'Thou ragged insolence', 'Fall back', 'Knave', 'off with you', 'Keep from the gate' (pp. 305-304, 303-302).

After the Pursuivant made an effective gap in the crowd, the actors

---

517 Whitelocke, p. 19.
518 *BSMXVI*, Note 14, pp. 235-234.
519 Qtd in *MWSJ*, p. 256n.

forming the richly costumed royal procession would have entered through one of the proscenium doors and proceeded across the stage to the other door, the entrance to the Banqueting Hall. The royal party do not speak and have no contact with the crowd with which they would have formed a striking and colourful contrast. Theatre convention dressed 'common people' in 'good, earthy brown' and this crowd would have included Puritans, dressed in accordance with old prints in black and white with tall hats.[520]

The procession introduces the King and Queen, Strafford, Laud and Sir Henry Vane the Elder, the Earl of Pembroke, Lord Essex and Lord Coventry. Bastwick points them out as they arrive in a Jacobean convention of having notables pointed out by onlookers, as in Shakespeare's *Henry VIII* and *Troilus and Cressida* and Jonson's *Sejanus*. However, his tirade against them is interrupted by a sudden shock at the sight of the mutilated Alexander Leighton:

> What thing comes here[?]
> What image of our lacerated country
> Filling the gap of speech with speechless horror
> Canst thou be —, art thou?

his reply:

> I was (—), Leighton; what
> I am thou seest...

and the response (possibly by another speaker):

> ...Are these the marks
> Laud thinks improve the image of his Maker
> Stamped on the face of man?' (pp. 295-294, 293-292)

The reaction to his appearance shows that, as was the case with the historical Leighton, he has been branded, had his nose slit and his ears mutilated. Shelley wrote an earlier entrance for Leighton and this entrance may be a revision. Leighton's entry is one of the two dramatic events mentioned in Shelley's note for 'Act 1st the Mask Scene 1', and he may have wanted to create the *coup de théâtre* effected by the earlier entrance.[521] This has Leighton, with his mutilated face, entering by the opposite door to that used by the procession at the very moment when the Old Man has pointed out Strafford and turns to indicate Laud (pp. 301-300), the men responsible for Leighton's punishment. Leighton stands unnoticed by the crowd but not by the audience who would, of course, see him plainly on the fully

---

520 de Marly, *Costume on the Stage*, p. 68.
521 *MYRVII*, p. 3.

lit forestage. The contrast between the elegance and richness of the royal party and the victim of their policies creates an anti-masque in itself, and the confrontation of two different processions of oppressor and oppressed is one Shelley uses, although for comic effect, in *Swellfoot the Tyrant*. This violent image may have been influenced by Calderón, who juxtaposes the sight of a mutilated or dead and bleeding body with the symbol of a conservative and cruel ruler or custom. In, for example, *The Physician of his Honour*, the physician shows the body of his wife whom he has bled to death in revenge for her supposed (not actual) infidelity, covered in blood, while, in *The Schism in England*, Anne Boleyn's beheaded body is brought before King Henry.[522]

In Shakespeare's and Fletcher's crowd scenes, the crowd characters have only a few lines and are easily swayed by a Coriolanus or Mark Antony; the main characters are rulers or wouldbe rulers. The subjects of Arbaces in *A King and No King* do not wait in vain for a good word from their King,[523] but the royal party in *Charles the First* do nothing to acknowledge their subjects. Shelley breaks wholly new ground by setting the silence of the lords against the voice of ordinary people who state their own views, supported by their experience of life and their religious beliefs.

Scene ii

This scene unfolds the characters of those in the procession and, as Cameron says, Shelley 'gives a vivid picture of a tyrannical cabal intent at maintaining its own despotic rule no matter what the cost to the country'.[524] It was based on the report of an actual conference produced at Strafford's trial.[525] Shelley made a note of the relevant pages in Hume and Whitelocke.[526]

Like the first scene, it conveys an enormous amount of historical material economically through dialogue and development of character.

---

522 Pedro Calderón de la Barca, *The Physician of his Honour*, trans. by Dian Fox with Donald Hindley (Warminster: Aris & Phillips, 1997), p. 207; Pedro Calderón de la Barca, *The Schism in England*, trans. by Kenneth Muir and Ann L. Mackenzie (Warminster: Aris & Phillips, 1990), p. 185.

523 *A King and No King*, II. ii. 1-74, ed. by George Walton Williams in *Dramatic Works in the Beaumont and Fletcher Canon*, gen. ed. Fredson Bowers, 9 vols (Cambridge: Cambridge University Press, 1970-1994), II.

524 Cameron, *The Golden Years*, p. 416.

525 Macaulay, II, 455; Whitelocke, p. 43.

526 *BSMXVI*, pp. 225-224.

The characters of the King and Queen are shown in their speeches to the Deputation from the lawyers who have come to receive thanks for the masque. The King compares himself to Christ in 'the sharp thorns that deck the English crown' (pp. 269-268). The Queen first claims a role in governing England ('my work/The careful weight of this great monarchy') thereby implying that it is her kingdom, but then suggests it is not by comparing it unfavourably with France (pp. 267-266). Her tearful opposition to a Parliament reveals her manipulation of the King, her desire to lead him to a French despotism and her lack of sympathy for the people. This is in contrast to Queen Katherine, in *Henry VIII*, who protests against taxing the people (I. ii. 47-51) and pleads for Buckingham when he is accused of treachery (I. ii. 109-110, 171-175). Shelley may have seen *Henry VIII*, Katherine being another favourite part of Siddons, and he certainly read it in 1818. Just as with the references to *Macbeth* in *The Cenci*, Shelley alluded to plays which the Covent Garden audience knew, and Queen Henrietta's words, 'the fool of late/Has lost all his mirth' (pp. 165-164) are reminiscent of *Hamlet* I. ii. 314 after the throne of Denmark has been usurped. The historical Charles had usurped not the throne but the rights of the people, having ruled without Parliament for 12 years, imposed cruel punishments, implemented unfair taxes such as Ship Money, and abused the system of Wards of Court.[527]

Shelley establishes Charles's ruthlessness as a ruler by showing him giving orders for expeditions against Ireland and Scotland, for heavy taxation and further oppression through the Star Chamber (pp. 252-248). Charles's complaint that he was forced to 'arm/My common nature with a kingly sternness' (pp. 237-236) shows that these decisions were his own, rather than as a result of being led astray by his advisers as the Young Man claimed. Shelley reveals the weaknesses in Charles's ambiguous personality. He allows Archy to be punished by Laud, despite his traditional licence as fool and, as the audience would have known, his words to Strafford, 'My word is as a wall/Between thee and this world of enemy' (pp. 225-224), were to prove worthless. This ensures that Charles personifies the 'bad and weak' ruler who rules over 'bad and wea' men of Shelley's 'Bonaparte' sketch. Yet Shelley also shows his positive characteristics, such as his generosity and wit. His dialogue with the Queen shows their mutual affection, interest in music and painting and pride in their children.

Shelley reveals Laud's lack of humour and fanaticism directly, when

---

527 Christopher Hill, *The Century of Revolution* (London: Routledge, 2002), pp. 13, 49, 52-55.

he and Strafford are outraged at Archy, and indirectly when the King compares Laud to his supposed opposite, the Puritan, Prynne. In a couple of lines Shelley delineates the practical Cottington. Cottington is concerned to raise money for Charles but does not seem to realise that the purpose of taxation is a 'scourge', since the cost of raising taxes is more than their value, and, when Strafford offers to return all his wealth to the King, he comments dryly, 'All the expedients of my lord of Strafford/Will scarcely meet the arrears' (pp. 195-194).

The vivid jester character of Archy upstages all the others, enlivening the scene and undercutting the pomposity of Laud and Strafford. Archy does more than weave 'about himself a world of mirth/Out of the wreck of ours' (pp. 245-244). He is the thread running through the scene which weaves together the King and the Court and the people, exiting and re-entering. He might also have been the weaver of music throughout the play. His final appearance in the play as we have it is his song, 'Heigho, the lark and the owl' (pp. 159-158), a counterbalance to the touching exchange between the King and Queen which follows his exit. Crook has suggested that the song 'A Widowed Bird' is Archy's comment on Henrietta's taste in music: Archy's song is English while the Queen has ordered 'airs from Italy' to sing and play on the lute.[528] This has a contemporary counterpart in a musical taste which preferred the Covent Garden English operas to the Italian at the King's Theatre.

The juxtaposition in Shelley's note of 'Archy the K's fool/The scene of the mask of the Inns of Court' (pp. 76-77) may be coincidental, but if Archy had been intended to appear in that scene it would have revealed his connection to the people. As it is, he shares their way of thinking. Shelley requires a character in the scene to act as a link between the King and the people and show him what they are thinking and was perhaps intended to undercut what is said at court by presenting the people's view. Archy is not discharged for his insult to Laud as the historical Archibald Armstrong was, but sent to 'stand outside in the rain' (pp. 245-244), a metaphor for the state of the country. He reports more rain tomorrow, the mice waiting to catch the cat, Strafford, and the bankruptcy of Laud's hopes to 'enter the new Jerusalem in triumph', using the imagery of the anti-masque, the 'stinking ditch [...] dead ass, rotten rags and broken dishes' (pp. 167-166). The Queen calls these cryptic remarks 'the echoes of our saddest fears'. Her suspicion of Archy, whom she would be 'loth to think/Some factious

---

528 *BSMXII*, pp. xlviii-xlix.

slave had tutored' (pp. 165-164) emphasises the suspicion underlying the court. Archy's story of the three poets who were to found a 'gynaecocoenic & pantisocratic' Commonwealth shows a parallel between the period of Charles I and the 1790s when Wordsworth, Coleridge and Southey were to have founded a colony on the banks of the Susquehanna River (pp. 181-180). Shelley may have planned to give Archy the device of prophesying to comment on Cromwell and other events and their contemporary relevance.

Medwin suggests, probably correctly, that Shelley based Archy on Pasquin in *The Schism of England* and intended to have given him 'a more than subordinate among his dramatis personae'.[529] Shelley finished reading *The Schism* shortly before starting research on *Charles the First*. Like Archy, Pasquin is banished from the palace by a worldly churchman, offers parables on kingship and makes prophetic statements. Archy uses imagery of eyes and blindness while Pasquin has a story about the blind man giving light to others. However, Archy's close relationship with the King is more akin to that between Lear and his Fool, whose similar attempts to warn his king with witty prophecies are also ignored.[530]

Charles accepts the wisdom of Archy's advice but ignores it when he warns against preventing Hazelrig, Hampden, Pym, Vane and Cromwell from leaving the country — 'If your Majesty were tormented night and day by fever, gout, rheumatism and stone and asthma and you should reason these diseases had secretly entered into conspiracy to abandon you, should you think it necessary to lay an embargo on the port by which they meant to dispeople your quiet kingdom of man?' (pp. 179-178) — picking up Charles's own imagery of 'humours/Of a distempered body that conspire/ Against the spirit of life' (pp. 235-234). When Charles remarks, 'The sheep have mistaken the wolf for their shepherd, my poor fellow', he also ignores Archy's reply, 'And the shepherd the wolves for the watch dogs' (pp. 173-172). Yet there is an understanding between Archy and the King shown by an exchange of wit:

> Archy: What think you that I found instead of a mitre?—
> King: Vane's wits perhaps
> Archy: Something as vain... (pp. 167-166)

It is not possible for Archy to have this relationship with the King's advisers, to whom he appears as a threat. A witty and prophetic dialogue with Laud, developed from the historical Archibald Armstrong's quip, 'Who's fool now,

---

529 Medwin, *Life*, II, p. 166.
530 Calderón, *Schism*, pp. 75-78, 149.

my Lord?' [531] emphasises the mirror-imagery Curran sees in the play. Archy is an image of reflection, as he 'mocks and mimics all he hears'.[532] Taking up 'Mark you what spirit sits in St. John's eyes', Archy remarks:

> Pray your Grace, look for an unsophisticated eye, as those just come from the outside of this empty world which sees everything upside down. You who are wise will discern the shadow of an idiot in lawn sleeves and a rochet setting springes to catch woodcocks in haymaking time. (pp. 263-262)

Laud ('You who are wise') may see the reflection of himself, a wise man who is a fool in his setting of traps and suspicions, in the eyes of a fool. But Archy is a fool who is also a wise man with 'owl eyes' which see better and further. He refers to the wellknown Civil War image of 'the world upside down' and goes on to warn of that coming war by suggesting that a devil 'throws a sword into the left hand scale for all the world like my Lord of Essex's there' (pp. 263-262, 261-260). Essex was later to lead the Parliamentarian army.

Archy's bold and contemptuous attitude is shown when Strafford threatens him with whipping. His retort, 'If all turncoats were whipped poor Archy would be disgraced in good company', refers to 'the apostate Strafford' himself (pp. 259-258). These exchanges are dramatically effective in presenting a tense confrontation on stage between the powerful courtiers and the lowborn but intelligent Archy, which would have been emphasised by the costume: Laud in his ecclesiastical robes, Strafford richly dressed and Archy with his traditional jester's garb.

The head of the deputation in Shelley's source was the royalist Finch, whom he describes in his reading notes as 'a mean, rascally lawyer', responsible for prosecuting Hampden.[533] Shelley replaces him with Hampden's counsel, St. John, later a leading Parliamentarian, which emphasises the masque's subversive intention. St. John's political position is made clear by his riposte to the Queen, 'Madam, the love of Englishman can make/The lightest favour of their lawful King/Outweigh a despot's treasury' (a bold reference to her brother, King of France, pp. 265-264). Crook discusses whether the lines 'We humbly take our leave/Enriched by smiles which France can never buy' (pp. 255-254) were to indicate the exit of the Deputation, but considers the dramatic possibility of their remaining so that two actions, that of the Deputation, King and Queen and that of

---

531 David Hume, *The History of England from the Invasion of Julius Caesar to the Revolution in 1688*, 10 vols (London: Christie & Son, 1819), VII, p. 220.
532 Stuart Curran, 'Shelleyan Drama' in *The Romantic Theatre*, pp. 68-70.
533 *BSMXVI*, pp. 227-226.

Coventry, Archy, Laud and Strafford, occur simultaneously on stage.[534] The farewell lines do not preclude the two actions taking place simultaneously. If the thrones were placed centre-stage and the Deputation exited by the proscenium door after bows, hand-kissing, perhaps backing out, the group, including Coventry could have been placed on the forestage. Coventry could then have observed the spirit 'in St. John's eyes' which he could not have remarked upon on such an occasion in the hearing of St. John or the King.

Scene iii

In order not to lose the dramatic momentum, Scenes iii and iv realise Charles's orders in Scene ii. Scene iii, of which only a dialogue between Hampden and Vane the Younger was written, was originally intended as Scene i,[535] and, as such, a great dramatic effect would have been created by the interruption of the farewells of the wouldbe emigrants by the order to remain. This effect is partially lost by transposing it to Scene iii, as the audience would have seen Charles issue the order in Scene ii. Scene iii establishes the 'characters and intentions' of 'Pym, Hazlerig Cromwell, young Sir H. Vane, Hampden &c.' Their speeches carry the dramatic and emotional impact. The manuscript shows Shelley's difficulty with the speeches in a number of fresh starts; they would undoubtedly have been revised and shortened. The opening speech by Hampden develops into a lively dialogue with Sir Harry Vane the Younger with constant interruption. This is a more natural and more exciting form than set speeches, one that Shelley had developed since writing *The Cenci*. Hampden's reasons for leaving England are opposed by Vane, who feels it is better to remain and 'endure' (pp. 71-107). This incident is reported in Hume, but may not have taken place and, if it had, Vane could not have been present. Shelley's introduction of him suggests his desire to have a character represent the Parliamentarians but who refused to compromise with either Charles or Cromwell.[536] Shelley also needed at least one female character as interesting as the Queen on the Parliamentarian side and he introduces 'Cromwell's daughter' here, perhaps intending her to figure as much as these male characters to show the prominence of women among the Republicans.

---

534 *BSMXII*, p. 254n.
535 Ibid., p. xliv.
536 Ibid., notes through pp. 126-127; Hume, *History*, VII, p. 216.

After reading Hume's description of women petitioning Parliament, Shelley noted 'X^{ist} levelled the sexes', which reflects his own view in *A Defence of Poetry*.[537]

Before 1800, when the West India Docks were begun, all ships left London from the Pool of London.[538] It was usual for passengers to take a boat from Whitehall downriver to embark there and Scene iii takes place at Whitehall Steps since Shelley refers to the 'towers of Westminster'. The scene would have capitalised on the popularity for nautical drama while keeping the action at Whitehall throughout this first act, offering a fine opportunity for the scene painters to paint both Westminster and the Thames with ships and boats.[539] The exchange commencing 'Does the wind hold?' appears a non-sequitur so it may have been intended for another speaker, perhaps another passenger.[540] Shelley possibly had a more complex scene in mind including seamen loading the cargo. The Shelleys read and re-read the Beaumont and Fletcher canon, often aloud, so, although he was away when Claire Clairmont noted reading *Wit Without Money* on 22 April 1820, it is unlikely that Shelley did not know it. In this play, the servants pack the coach with much bustle for the 'Widdow' to leave for the country but, in the midst of this, she changes her mind and decides to stay and everything has to be unloaded. The stage business is therefore a visual counterpoint which emphasises the turmoil caused by the change of plan.[541] The natural verse dialogue carried on between Melchior and Lionel in *The Boat on the Serchio*, interrupting each other, as they and Dominic load stores and set sail, also points to Shelley's capability of creating such a scene.[542]

Scene iv

In Scene iv, Shelley has given the scene painters the opportunity to create yet another spectacular setting well within their capabilities: the Star Chamber. The results of Charles's policies are now enforced by Laud, Strafford and

537 *MYRVII*, p. 337; *BSMXVI*, Note 38, pp. 221-220; *SPP*, pp. 525-526.
538 R. Douglas Brown, *The Port of London* (Lavenham: Terence Dalton, 1978), p. 54.
539 For the popularity of nautical drama and its scenery see Booth, *English Melodrama*; *BSMXII*, p. 126.
540 *BSMXII*, pp. 86-87.
541 *CCJ*, p. 143; *Wit Without Money*, II. v, ed. by Hans Walter Gabler, in *Beaumont and Fletcher*, VI.
542 *The Boat on the Serchio*, 83-114, ed. by Nora Crook, *KSR*, 7 (1992), 85-93 (pp. 91-92).

Juxon in their function as cruel judges of the Puritans, Bastwick, Prynne and Bishop Williams. This scene would be all the more shocking since Shelley probably intended the audience to recall the mutilated Leighton, following Macaulay's remark, 'Whilst the terrors of Leighton's punishment hung yet on the mind of the public, the courage [...] of William Prynne, a barrister at law, give rise to a scene of almost equal butchery'.[543] Those with a knowledge of the period would have appreciated Shelley's wit in obliging Prynne, author of *Historiomastix*, to appear as a character in a play. Bastwick's defiant stand that his judges are the enemy of his God and State, not he, is based on his actual defence recorded in Whitelocke. This defence is responded to with further cruelty from Laud, only prevented by Juxon's concern that it might rebound on themselves. Shelley has the 'turncoat Strafford' point out that Laud owed his advancement to his next victim, Williams. This is an ironical comment, since Williams's arrest on the basis of stolen private papers Shelley had noted as 'the most odious violation of private correspondance — see Hume 217.'[544] It contrasts with the behaviour of the Parliamentarians who excused Whitelocke from duty on the committee which tried Laud since he owed his university education to him.[545] Williams is in his way as defiant as Bastwick. The scene successfully makes concrete Charles's orders in Scene ii, and 'the infernal cruelties of the high commission court' and, although incomplete, does not need to be much longer.[546] Structurally, it would have balanced the trial of the King who also refused to recognise the court which tried him.[547]

Shelley wrote no more dialogue for the play, but he prepared a scheme for Act II — commencing with 'Hampden's trial' and ending with 'Strafford's death'[548] — and left a number of notes concerning most, but not all, of the events and characters depicted in these two acts. A problem would have arisen in dramatising the number of trials and executions. He could hardly have failed to include the King's trial —which had good dramatic material and was historically crucial — but in order not to lose dramatic impact by having too many similar scenes he needed to vary the way in which they were dramatised. Strafford's trial was an important turning point since it showed the King yielding, the increasing confidence of the Parliamentarians

---

543 Macaulay, II, p. 154.
544 Whitelocke, p. 26; *BSMXVI*, pp. 233-232.
545 Ibid., p. 75.
546 *BSMXVI*, pp. 235-234.
547 Whitelocke, p. 75.
548 *MYRVII*, p. 330-331.

and their first significant success. Moreover, Shelley's note 29, 'Whilocke 42. Vanes paper', refers to the historical occasion when Vane the Younger produced the documents found in his father's chest which condemned Strafford.[549] As this is a dramatic surprise event ironically parallel to the case of Bishop Williams, it is likely that Shelley also intended to include it in a scene.

Scene painters had created Westminster Hall where Strafford's trial took place for an earlier play, but Whitelocke's eyewitness account would have provided them with invaluable additional detail. It describes the red cloth covered forms, rows of Lords, Commons, Ladies of Quality, the 'close gallery' for the royal family and the 'place made for the Earl of Strafford with a Seat and Room for the Lieutenant of the Tower; and places for the Earl's secretaries, and for his council to be near him'. Strafford himself is described: 'his habit Black, wearing his George in a Gold Chain... his Person proper, but little stooping with his distemper, or Habit of his Body, his Behaviour exceeding graceful and his speech full of Weight, Reason and Pleasingness'.[550] The sense of mounting excitement when the Parliamentarians decide on Strafford's impeachment is vividly conveyed by Macaulay's *History*.[551] Although 'Strafford's death' rather than his trial was to end the act, this may not have been intended as an execution scene. Shelley's comparison of Strafford with Cardinal Wolsey suggests that he had heeded Whitelocke's description of Strafford's reaction to Charles's betrayal, when he 'rose up from his Chair, lift up his Eyes to Heaven, laid his hand on his Heart and said, "Put not your trust in Princes, nor in the Sons of Man, for in them there is no Salvation."'[552] Shelley noted, 'Strafford passes under Laud's window', when he said farewell on his way to execution.[553] Either incident, or a combination of the action of the first with the words of the second, would both dramatise 'Strafford's death' and make a political point about the trustworthiness of kings.

It appears from Shelley's note 'Hampden's trial & its effects. Reasons of Hampden & his colleagues fo(r) resistance' that, rather than dramatise this trial, he intended writing a scene where the issues were debated among the Parliamentarians. His note referring to 'Young Sir H. Vane's reasons. The

---

549 *BSMXVI*, Note 20, pp. 225-224.
550 Whitelocke, p. 42.
551 Macaulay, II, p. 382-389.
552 Whitelocke, p. 46; *BSMXVI*, Note 25, pp. 227-226.
553 Ibid., p. 46; *BSMXVI*, Note 30, pp. 225-224.

first rational & logical, the second impetuous and enthusiastic',[554] suggests that this debate would reveal contrasting characters and opinions and both types of argument. Other viewpoints would need to be heard in a lively and realistic scene and a note 'The King zealous for the Church inheriting this disposition from his father' indicates possible remarks to be included.

One of the Judges in Hampden's case, Croke, 'suddenly altered his Purpose and Arguments; and when it came to his turn, contrary to Expectation he argued and declared his Opinion against the King'. His wife had said, 'That she hoped he would do nothing against his conscience, for fear of any Danger or Prejudice to him, or his Family: and that she would be contented to suffer Want, or any Misery with him, rather than be an Occasion for him to do, or say anything against his Judgments and Conscience'.[555] Shelley had noted 'Judge Croke alone gives it against ship money. The noble speech of Croke's wife'. [556] This suggests that he believed her support to be a crucial factor, and possibly intended breaking up the all-male debates and displaying the spirit of the Republican women with a domestic scene based on this.

Shelley no doubt envisaged the five-act tragedy customary on the stage of his day. Act I lays the foundation of the play, showing Charles in power and commenting on his reign until 1638; it seems that the timescale is 1634-1638. Act II covers the period when the people begin to take matters into their own hands: Hampden's defiance, the Scottish war and the trial of Strafford (1638-1642). Act III was therefore likely to show the two sides in conflict, but Shelley made only two notes towards it. Note 35, 'Impeachment of the 5 members & Lord Kimbolton [...] His coming in person' refers to Charles's intrusion into Parliament to attempt to arrest five members, an event, one of the precursors of the Civil War, far too important to be omitted from the play. The other note, 'The Queen prepares to retire into Holland. The people hate her; she had born the most contumelious usage with silent indignation' suggests a scene showing her in exile.[557]

The following years were civil war, and most dramatic events took place on the battlefield. Too many battle scenes in a play may become monotonous, but they can be relieved by interspersing domestic scenes or scenes of conferences. Shelley made a note of the Treaty of Uxbridge,[558]

---

554 *MYRVII*, p. 326.
555 Whitelocke, p. 25.
556 *BSMXVI*, Note 18, pp. 232-233.
557 Ibid., Notes 35 and 37, pp. 222-223.
558 BMSXVI, pp. 4, 5.

and perhaps planned to dramatise the conference which led to it. He could have followed Shakespeare's *Henry VI*, with its succeeding short battles, or encompassed several in one long battle scene with intervening short dialogues to show how events had travelled forward in time. He could have used reportage, which he does in *Hellas*, or highlighted events which took place on the battlefield, but not the battle, as he does in the 'Bonaparte' sketch. His political and moral views might have led him to include scenes showing the courage and principled defiance of Sir John Hotham at the gates of Newcastle or, as he had read Lucy Hutchinson's memoirs, the beleaguered John Hutchinson at Nottingham

As the centre of a five-act tragedy, the climax of Act III shows the positions of power reversed. In this play, therefore, Act III should show Charles in the power of the people. Shelley's sources, with variations, give the story of the King's arrest by Cornet Joyce, when the Cornet is said to have interrupted the King at a game of bowls. When the King asked for Joyce's commission, the Cornet indicated his troopers which the King acknowledged to be a very effective one. The story has dramatic elements: the game of bowls and its interruption; the contrast between the King's nonchalant, witty attitude and Joyce's 'plain russet' manner, emphasised visually by their costume; the culmination in the arrest which makes the reversal of fortunes visually clear.[559] This ending for Act III would have been consistent with the time-span suggested for the play by the events covered in the first two acts.

The economy with which Shelley had planned those would have been unbalanced if the rest of the play were to have consisted of an overlong treatment of the King's trial and death, which would have been reserved for a big scene, perhaps to open Act IV. If Act III were to cover, approximately, the first Civil War (1642-1647), it can be assumed that Acts IV and V would each have covered similar periods of activity: Act IV, the Commonwealth years up to Cromwell's seizure of power, including the second and third civil wars (1649-1653), and Act V, the Protectorate and the Restoration (1653-1660). A play which focussed on the liberty of the people and those who fought for it would need to show Parliament's attempts to establish this, for instance by abolishing the House of Lords, and to demonstrate the continuation of this struggle for liberty after its defeat, first by Cromwell's dissolution of Parliament and then by the Restoration, through the fates of those who would not compromise. Shelley may have planned to carry

---

559 Whitelocke, p. 250; Macaulay, IV, pp. 317-318; Hume, VIII, pp. 125-126.

the action on until the Restoration or even after if it were to include Vane's death.

Shelley had already used 'Young Sir Harry Vane' to argue with Hampden in Cromwell's presence (I. iv). He intended to use him to argue the passionate and principled view against the reasonable in Act II and Vane had to appear in the scene of Strafford's trial. Although no one central character is established in Act I, Crook has shown that there are suggestions that Vane might be the hero.[560] It is also possible that Shelley intended his audience to see the hero as a collective one, since he includes so many of the characters who heroically advanced the cause of liberty. His knowledge of the writings of Milton, Hutchinson, Ludlow and Vane himself show he was well able to do this. Shelley indicates the presence of 'Cromwell's daughter' — possibly a composite of daughters which included one who 'opposed to his apostasy from republican ideals' and another who 'deplored his ruthlessness' — and Vane in Act I. This suggests an intention to use the character of the daughter and that of Vane to present an oppositional viewpoint.[561] Shelley, the creator of Cythna and Beatrice Cenci and the admirer of Antigone, did not believe that a woman could not play a major role.

Performance

Shelley became discouraged about the popularity of his writing, partly because he was unaware of the financial problems which made the Olliers unable to pay for the copyright of *Charles the First* and thought it was because they thought the play would not sell.[562] This mood was evident in May 1822, when he wrote to Horace Smith that living near Byron meant 'the sun has extinguished the glowworm', and in June 1822, when he told Gisborne that it was 'impossible to compose except under the strong excitement of an assurance of finding sympathy in what you write', but his statements about giving up writing were not irrevocable. In January 1821, he wrote to Ollier, 'I doubt whether I *shall* write more', but went on to com-

---

560 Crook, 'Calumniated Republicans', pp. 152-156.

561 *BSMXII*, pp. 70-71n.

562 Charles E. Robinson, 'Percy Bysshe Shelley, Charles Ollier, and William Blackwood: The Contexts of Early Nineteenth-Century Publishing' in *Shelley Revalued: Essays from the Gregynog Conference*, ed. by Kelvin Everest (Leicester: Leicester University Press, 1983), p. 200.

pose *Adonais, Hellas, Fragments of an Unfinished Drama, Charles the First* and other poems.[563] Williams said, 'It is exceedingly to be regretted that S. does not meet with greater encouragement. A mind such as his powerful as it is requires gentle leading'.[564] Shelley therefore had the sympathy during the composition of *Charles the First* which he claimed to lack, although he perhaps found this well-meant interest inhibiting rather than encouraging, was distracted by the socialising and constrained by his desire to 'contend' with Byron. He usually did not discuss his work with others, *The Cenci* being the only work Mary Shelley was involved in before its completion.[565] Even though he must have been aware, since Williams was, that *Charles the First* was potentially a much greater play than *Werner*, the apparent ease with which Byron wrote would have been vexing to a writer working on something he had planned over two years before. But the importance of the subject and the amount of research and writing he had completed would have been an incentive to return to it, which he might have done the following autumn, had he lived.

Had he then finished it and sent it to Covent Garden, it would have arrived most opportunely. By 1823, Charles Kemble was the manager and Macready was their leading tragedian.[566] The parts of Charles and Cromwell would have appealed to them as suitable vehicles for their own talents: Kemble's good looks and gentlemanly presence made him the obvious choice to play the King while Macready could show his skill at playing a scheming politician, later revealed in Lytton's *Richelieu*. As children, the Kembles had appeared in Havard's *King Charles the First*, a play sympathetic to the King and royal family, in their parents' touring company.[567]

In 1825, Mary Russell Mitford was commissioned to write *Charles the First*, 'originally suggested to me by Mr. Macready, whose earnest recommendation to try my hand on Cromwell, was at a subsequent period still more strongly enforced by Mr. Charles Kemble'. Mitford points out that Covent Garden would not have commissioned her play had they 'foreseen any objection […] on the part of the Licenser [then Larpent] or the Lord Chamberlain'.[568] Had Shelley's play been delivered to Covent Garden

563 *PBSLII*, pp. 423, 436, 258.
564 Gisborne & Williams, p. 123.
565 *OSA*, p. 335.
566 Wyndham, *Covent Garden*, II, p. 208.
567 William Havard, *King Charles the First: An Historical Tragedy* (Totnes: O. Adams [1775]); Boaden, *Mrs. Siddons*, I, p. 17.
568 Mitford, *Works*, I, p. 243.

in 1823, it would have forestalled hers. As he did not expect the problem of censorship to arise, Kemble may have accepted Shelley's statements that it was 'not coloured by the party spirit of the author' and was written 'without prejudice or passion', and Shelley's sympathetic treatment of the King as a person rather than a monarch might have led him to believe so.[569] Harris had already recognised the quality of *The Cenci*, and Shelley's thorough research methods would have appealed to Kemble's desire for accuracy.

Cameron, although he thought Shelley 'intended to give what he believed was a true portrait of the king and to present royalist views fairly', has argued that 'it is clear [...] that if performed before a contemporary audience [*Charles the First*] would have been understood as advocating parliamentary reform or republicanism'.[570] Even if Larpent had issued a licence, there was the example of James Sheridan Knowles's *Virginius*, set in ancient Rome, which was only allowed on stage in 1819 after the Prince Regent himself had cut out 'some references to tyranny'.[571] It therefore seems inevitable that, even if Shelley's play had been accepted, it would not have been performed at Covent Garden.[572]

A performance of Shelley's *Charles the First* in 1822/1823, then, might have caused the controversy Cameron suggests and Colman feared with Mitford's play. On the other hand, a different route may have been taken. Martin Shee's *Alasco* was submitted to Covent Garden in 1824 but Colman demanded changes unacceptable to the author, who withdrew it and published it. It was 'compressed and arranged as a Melo-Drama at the Surrey' in April 1824 and in December performed in New York. Given the wide interpretation by this time of the term 'burletta', the alterations may have been less destructive than Worrall believes; certainly it seems so since George Bartley, Covent Garden's stage manager, complained of a 'minor theatre' being able to perform 'the play'. Both the Surrey and the New York theatres used the prohibition at Covent Garden to publicise the play.[573] Shelley may not have wished his play to be altered, but, like Byron with *Marino Faliero*, he may not have been able to prevent its performance.

Shelley's notebooks indicate the way in which his play reflects his

569 *PBSLII*, pp. 372, 219-220.
570 Cameron, *The Golden Years*, p. 412.
571 *Representative British Dramas*, ed. by Montrose J. Moses (Boston: Little, Brown, 1920), p. 6.
572 Mitford, *Works*, I, p. 244.
573 Shellard et al., *The Lord Chamberlain Regrets*, pp. 29-31, 52n.; Worrall, *Theatric Revolutions*, pp. 54-56.

146 The Theatre of Shelley

research, the accuracy of which gives it its richness and veracity. Whatever discouragement he had suffered and whatever disappointment he expressed, Shelley's confidence in his powers of developing an idea dramatically had grown by the time he wrote *Charles the First*. He had become adept in writing for the technical requirements of the late Georgian theatre, and incorporating elements of Jacobean drama which its audience would recognise. In *The Cenci* he kept his cast small and confined the scenes chiefly to interiors, but in *Charles the First* he had developed his dramatic techniques sufficiently to write two outdoor scenes, one with a spectacular procession, and another in a busy Thames locality. His cast of at least twenty-four, and probably more, calls for wide differentiation of dialogue and characterisation to allow them to be remembered by the audience, and in this too he was apparently succeeding.

Chapter Five
Ideal Drama – *Prometheus Unbound*

Critics rarely discuss *Prometheus Unbound* from the point of view of performability, although theatre directors such as Paul Fort and, more recently, Madge Darlington, have seen its performance possibilities.[574] Shelley would have realised that it would have been unlikely to have reached the stage in 1818 because its style was based on Greek drama, which would not have been acceptable to the commercial London theatre. Although he published it as a poem for reading, there are signs that he initially conceived it as a performable drama, and he may have hoped that it would be performed in a future theatre. He had recently seen a dramatic form, the ballet of Viganò, which allowed him to realise that the moral and political qualities found in Greek drama could be conveyed effectively with the same beauty and sensitivity as had delighted the huge audience in fifth-century Athens, and this form had been developed in a subsidised theatre.

Shelley described *Prometheus Unbound* as 'a drama' to Medwin, although 'a composition of a totally different character' to *The Cenci*. He also frequently referred to it as a poem but, although he may not have distinguished between the two, as the Greeks did not, an obvious difference between *The Revolt of Islam* or *Queen Mab* and *The Cenci* and *Prometheus Unbound* is that the narrative poems are told directly in verse with reported speech and action and landscape described, while the dramatic have speakers indicated against the dialogue and clear and practical stage directions. The stage directions are particularly numerous in Act I and they run throughout the drama. Yet they do not appear intended to enhance the reading since he cancelled many, but not all, of those he had written for Act I and wrote

---

574 Curran, *Cenci*, p. 200; Cox, 'The Dramatist', p. 83.

fewer in subsequent acts.[575] The cancelled stage directions are extremely suitable for the theatre of his day and do not translate into descriptions of much help to the reader. Shelley did, however, reduce the stage directions, replacing some with lines of verse, as at the entry of the Furies (l. 520), and published *Prometheus* in a volume with other poems. The importance Shelley attached to his poetry being read aloud, however, can be seen by his use of rhetorical punctuation, remarked on by Neil Fraistat, and his opinion that John Gisborne would be better able to revise *Prometheus* for the press, because 'he heard it recited'. [576]

These elements alone do not define a stage drama, but suspense, excitement, mystery and contrast create dramatic effect and these also are all present. Furthermore, Shelley appears to have considered the contributions made by characterisation, scene painting, stage machinery, lighting, music and dance. Certainly, Shelley's remarks to Peacock in April 1818 about his intention of writing for the stage and his subsequent work on *Tasso* suggest that he might have originally conceived *Prometheus Unbound* as a performable drama.[577] Fresh from the experience of seeing the ballet of Viganò at La Scala, he had an example in mind of an extremely beautiful production worthy of his Aeschylean ideal. I suggest that his original idea may have been to write such a drama, but that he changed his mind when he realised that there would have been little point in submitting it to a commercial London theatre since they did not perform Greek drama at that time. He therefore wrote for publication and wished to make it easier for the reader by reducing the stage directions. But it is not impossible to follow them, nor is it impossible to perform *Prometheus Unbound*. Shelley no doubt knew Hunt's *The Descent of Liberty*, and his own scenic effects are never too many to be practically managed or to lose their effectiveness, while his stage directions are sufficient to explain to the professionals in those fields what he required. A director can also infer this from lines which make it clear that a dance or music will take place, or that an actor should have wings or purple and gold sandals. Shelley had planned both publication and production of *The Cenci*; it may be that, despite the publication of *Prometheus Unbound*, he did not rule out an eventual performance. He certainly made no alterations which would have made one impossible.

Shelley knew that *Prometheus Unbound* was 'of a higher character than

---

575 *SPII*, pp. 508n., 503n., 508-510n., 524n. There are further stage directions in *BSMIX*.

576 *PBSLII*, p.196; *SPP*, p. 205.

577 Ibid., p. 8.

any thing I have yet attempted' and 'the best thing I ever wrote', but thought
it could not 'sell beyond twenty copies', perhaps because only a few would
recognise the many allusions to science and philosophy. He had read it to
'many persons', including the Gisbornes, whose response was encouraging,
but it was that of an élite minority.[578] As William Keach suggests, however,
Shelley was aware of posterity and that his future audience would increase.[579]
He knew that his ideal drama was not produced for lack of artists; he lived
'among such philosophers and poets as surpass beyond comparison any
who have appeared since the last national struggle for civil and religious
liberty' and he had seen the greatest performers of his age.[580]

Although theatres in England were not subsidised, many theatres in
Italy such as San Carlo, Naples, La Scala, Milan and Teatro Regio, Turin,
were. These were, of course, court theatres and Milan was once again
under Austrian rule when, at La Scala in April 1818, Shelley saw two
ballets by Viganò which raised dancing to the standard of high art. Viganò
had mounted a ballet, or *coreodramma*, entitled *Prometeo*, at La Scala in the
Napoleonic years, 'one of its most splendid periods, at least in ballet and
scene design', when, as Curran says, and as Shelley most probably knew,
the city was freer than it had ever been.[581] He would therefore have seen
the possibility that theatre could be subsidised in the future and that in
a freer climate political censorship would not be necessary. At the time
when he was writing *Prometheus Unbound* (1818-1819), he believed that
it would not be long before Italy would be free. He also expected reform
or revolution in England, and thus anticipated a favourable political
climate in which a drama such as *Prometheus Unbound* could have been
performed.[582] To a certain extent this was correct since, by 1861, Italy had
gained her independence and unification and, in 1821, Greek drama began
to be performed in London.[583]

---

578 *PBSLII*, pp. 116, 164, 174.
579 William Keach, 'The Political Poet' in Morton, *Companion*, pp. 130-132.
580 *SPP*, p. 535.
581 *PBSLII*, pp. 4, 14; Gatti, p. 58; Curran, 'Prometheus', p. 452; Rosselli, *The Opera Industry*, pp. 29, 74 and Fig. 1 for tables of endowment.
582 See, for example, *PBSLII*, pp. 266-267, 291.
583 Rosselli, *Music and Musicians*, pp. 21- 22; Hall & Macintosh, *Greek Tragedy*, p. 270.

Aeschylus

Putting the commercial stage out of his mind, however, freed Shelley to consider how such a play ought, ideally, to be done. It has often been pointed out that Aeschylus, to whom he refers in title, dedication and preface, is the most important influence on his drama and Shelley's *Prometheus* drew on many of the dramatic elements of Aeschylus. Scholarly work on this subject, however, has not concentrated on dramatic technique but on philosophy, science and politics.[584] Although Tetreault sees *Prometheus Unbound* in terms of opera and ballet, it is as a 'text conceived on the analogue of musical drama'.[585] Wasserman compares Act IV to a masque and Lisa Vargo finds a series of masques throughout the drama, but they are not considered as intentions for performance.[586] Bearing in mind Shelley's requirements for ideal drama, *Prometheus Unbound* might be expected to contain music, dancing, scenic painting and religious (or philosophical) references. It appears to draw on the styles of the melodrama, pantomime and comic opera of the London theatre of Shelley's own period, the Jacobean masque and Viganò's ballet as well as the ancient Greek drama. Yet *Prometheus Unbound* has been considered to lack one essential quality of drama. In Wasserman's words:

> As nearly every critic of *Prometheus Unbound* has observed, the only dramatic struggles in the play take place in Act I, and all the subsequent action, including Demogorgon's almost effortless overthrow of Jupiter, proceeds without worthy opposition and hence without dramatic tension.[587]

Wasserman accounts for this by 'the metaphysical level at which the play is conducted'.[588] This view of drama, however, is from a narrow and modern European perspective, coloured by the idea of 'drama as conflict' or belief that drama must be full of incident and action. Yet the dramas of the ancient Greeks focus very often on one event and do not have subsidiary

---

584 Curran, *Shelley's Annus Mirabilis*; Carl Grabo, *Prometheus Unbound: An Interpretation* (Chapel Hill: University of North Carolina Press, 1935); Desmond King-Hele, *Shelley: His Thought and Work* (London: Macmillan, 1971); Earl R Wasserman, *Shelley's 'Prometheus Unbound'* (Baltimore: Johns Hopkins University Press, 1965); Webb, *A Voice Not Understood*.
585 Tetreault, 'Shelley and the Opera', pp. 144, 154.
586 Wasserman, *Prometheus*, pp. 201-203; Lisa Vargo, 'The Solitary Reformer: A Reading of Shelley's Poetry' (unpublished doctoral thesis, University of Toronto, 1983), pp. 174-202.
587 Wasserman, *Prometheus*, p. 111.
588 Idem.

plots; the same criticism has been made of Aeschylus' *Prometheus Bound*. As H.D.F. Kitto states, Aeschylus' drama takes place in the mind of Prometheus, dramatic effects consisting in 'a series of impacts'; the impact of the Chorus, Oceanus, Hermes and Io contrasts with the initial 'disdainful silence' of Prometheus and his solitude and spurs him to reveal a different aspect of his defiance.[589] Shelley remarks that his own imagery has been 'drawn from the operations of the human mind'.[590] David Grene notes that the complexities of Prometheus have made his story 'significant on a number of different levels [...] rebel against the tyrant [...] Knowledge against Force [...] the champion of man [...] against the would-be destroyer of man [...] Man as opposed to God', adding that Prometheus' suffering equates him with man.[591] Shelley's Prometheus has been described as symbolic in a similar way: 'Regenerator [...] Humanity', 'enlightened thinker', 'the One Mind', 'the mind of Man', 'mankind or the mind of mankind' and, by Shelley himself, the 'Champion of Mankind'.[592] An early nineteenth-century audience would readily see the similarity between Prometheus and Jupiter and the tyranny and oppression of their own time.

Schlegel noted that there was 'little of external action' in Aeschylus' play, but that 'the poet has in a masterly manner, contrived to introduce variety and progress'; he refers to 'the silence of Prometheus', the 'useless compassion' of Vulcan, the 'solitary complainings' of Prometheus, 'the arrival of the womanly, tender ocean nymphs' which causes him 'to give freer vent to his feelings', and of Oceanus and Io.[593] Shelley's play includes the stage effects of earthquake, thunder and lightning in *Prometheus Bound* (1080-1090), Prometheus' complaints of suffering (512-513), his defiance (270-273) and his invocation of the mountains, springs and earth (89-90). Prometheus explains to the Chorus that there are powers which can depose the gods (515-519), and these powers Shelley gives to Demogorgon. Prometheus' dialogue with Hermes (941-1030) is recalled by Shelley's Furies, Shelley's Mercury having more in common with Hephaestus. *Prometheus Unbound* has the layers of dance, drama and poetry which Schlegel found in Greek

---

589 H.D.F. Kitto, *Greek Tragedy* (London: Methuen, 1961), pp. 54-57.
590 *SPII*, p. 472.
591 David Grene, Introduction to *Prometheus Bound* in *Aeschylus II* (Chicago: The University of Chicago Press, 1956), pp. 134, 136.
592 *OSA*, pp. 271-272; King-Hele, p. 198; Wasserman, *Prometheus*, p. 144; Carlos Baker, *Shelley's Major Poetry: The Fabric of a Vision* (London: Oxford University Press, 1948), p. 92; *SPII*, p. 472.
593 Schlegel, pp. 93-94.

drama and I do not consider it lacks dramatic conflict or characterisation.[594]

Shelley spoke of dance and music as elements of drama, but he did not mean that either should convey the whole of the poet's ideas. He thought, rather, that they should accompany words as they had in Greece, where the poetry of dancing and music enhanced but did not replace the poetry of words, creating a multi-layered art form which could truly be described as drama.[595] In this regard, we may see him following Schlegel, who remarks that the delivery of the dialogue in a Greek tragedy could not possibly resemble the modern recitative or opera which he describes as an 'anarchy of the arts, where music, dancing, and decoration are seeking to outvie each other'. He admires the fantasy world the opera creates, but in opera 'the words are altogether lost in the music' whereas in Greek drama 'the primary object was the poetry'. He asks why the Greek poets should have lavished 'such labour and art' on their lyrical songs and choruses 'the most involved constructions, the most unusual expressions, and the boldest images and recondite allusions' if 'it were all to be lost in the delivery' and speaks of the variety of measures the poets use for the dialogue, showing 'the impetuousness of passion' or 'the transition in the tone of mind'.Shelley's contemporaries were also attentive to bold images and recondite allusions, both visual and verbal. Schlegel asks, 'What sort of opera-music would it be which should set the words to a mere rhythmical accompaniment of the simplest modulations?'.[596] He does not envisage Greek drama as being submerged in operatic music, however fine, but that a musical accompaniment should enhance the words.[597] If opera started as an attempt to revive Greek tragedy, it soon developed differently because of the 'primacy of song'.[598] Shelley was certainly aware of this difference. His directions for *Prometheus Unbound* are for a simple musical accompaniment to enhance the poetry as Schlegel suggested the Greeks did.

Curran remarks that 'drama […] was on [Shelley's] mind virtually from

---

594 For a different view, see Peter Cochran, 'Byron and Shelley: Radical Incompat-ibles', *Romanticism on the Net* 43 (2006) <http://www.erudit.org/revue/ron/2006/v/n43/013589ar.html> [accessed 25 January 2007] (para. 53 of 100).

595 *SPP*, p. 518.

596 Schlegel, pp. 63-65.

597 Quillin quotes only part of Schlegel's discussion of opera in relation to Greek drama to support her belief that Shelley turned to music because language was 'no longer an effective mode of aesthetic mediation'. Jessica Quillin, '"An assiduous frequenter of the Italian opera": Shelley's *Prometheus Unbound* and the opera buffa', Opera and Romanticism: Praxis Series *Romantic Circles* <http://www.rc.umd.edu/praxis/opera/quillin.html> (paras. 4, 5, 12, 21 of 21).

598 David Kimbell, *Italian Opera*, pp. 5-6.

the point he arrived in Italy'.[599] As Shelley read Schlegel on the journey, talked of the Alps as being a *corps de ballet* with the Jungfrau as Mlle. Mélanie, and saw the place which gave him his idea for *Prometheus Unbound*, it appears he arrived with his mind already primed. Ballet, the Prometheus story and Schlegel's emphasis upon the value of the Athenian drama — together with the importance of dance to that drama — were linked in his mind when he saw the ballets of Viganò in Milan, *La Spada di Kenneth*, three times and *Otello* twice.[600] Shelley described them to Peacock as:

> the most splendid spectacle I ever saw [...] The manner in which language is translated into gesture, the complete & full effect of the whole as illustrating the history in question, the unaffected self possession of each of the actors, even to the children, made this choral drama more impressive than I should have conceived possible.[601]

To express these changes of mood in mime required acting of a high standard and to bring out the meanings through gesture required a great director. Lady Morgan, too, saw a connection between Viganò's ballet and 'the modern melodrame' and she described Antonietta Pallerini (who danced Desdemona in *Otello* and Elisabetta Wallace in *La Spada di Kenneth*, as well as Eone in *Prometeo*) as 'unquestionably one of the finest actresses in Europe' after seeing her performance in *La Vestale*:[602]

> Suddenly bursting into the conviction of her fatal secret, she exhibits all the struggles between nature and grace, passion and reason, that can agitate the bosom of a devoted woman. The horrible death which awaits the breach of her vow, and the impulses of a passion that is ready even to meet that death, rather than for ever resign its object, alternately madden and dissolve her; till, struggling, reeling, combating, as if her lover was present, she sinks overcome — into his arms...[603]

Lady Morgan's account is borne out by Stendhal, who remarks, 'au troisième acte de la *Vestale*, celle-ci se rend à son amant; la pantomime qui dure un quart d'heure est tellement vraie et tellement gracieuse, que sans indécence, il fa *tirar tutti*.' (In the third act of *La Vestale*, the heroine of the title gives herself to her lover; the pantomime which lasts a quarter of an hour is so true and graceful that without any indecency it tells you everything). For Lady Morgan, Viganò was 'the Shakspeare of his art; and

---

599   Curran, 'Shelleyan Drama' in Cave, p. 63.
600   *CCJ*, p. 88; *MWSJ*, pp. 198-200n., 203-207.
601   *PBSLII*, p. 4.
602   Morgan, *Italy*, I, p. 166.
603   Ibid., pp. 170-171.

with such powerful conceptions, and such intimate knowledge of nature and effect, as he exhibits, it is wonderful that, instead of composing ballets, he does not write epics.'.[604]

Stendhal, too, compared Viganò to Shakespeare, saying 'l'action est profondément vraie' (the action is deeply true) and regretted that 'cet homme de génie ne sait pas composer sur le papier' (this man of genius cannot put his compositions on to paper). Viganò's genius has been lost, as both these writers were afraid it would be, but Stendhal described him, like Rossini and Canova, as an extremely remarkable man, superior to any in Paris in fine arts or literature.[605] Shelley described the opera which preceded *Otello*, Peter von Winter's *Etelinda* (1754-1825), as 'not a favourite'.[606] Stendhal was blunter, 'Une musique détestable est celle de Winter, l'*Etelinda*, sifflée hier soir' (Winter's detestable opera, *Etelinda*, was hissed last night). Shelley thought Camporesi 'a cold and unfeeling singer and a bad actress' and Stendhal said she had 'une voix froide' (a cold voice) though he did add 'et magnifique'. Since Stendhal's opinion coincides with Shelley's in these cases, it may be worth bearing in mind his views when considering Shelley's reaction to the art of Viganò.[607]

Viganò was well-read, knowledgeable about the fine arts and music. His mother was the sister of Boccherini.[608] He had a moral viewpoint which Shelley shared.

> '*Prometeo, Dedalo* and *I Titani* were epic studies of mankind's evolution with the developing, endless, unresolved struggle between his good and evil impulses. Even when the individual confrontations are paramount, in *La Vestale, La Spada di Kenneth*, and *Giovanna d'Arco*, there are always larger ethical issues raised.'[609]

Well-served by his dancers, he was fortunate to be able to work also with an outstanding costume designer, Giacomo Pregliasco, and a legendary scene painter, Alessandro Sanquirico.[610] The reputation of Milan for ballet was pre-eminent: Lady Morgan considered that 'its ballets are superior to every thing of the same kind throughout Europe', and the

---

604 Stendhal, p. 175; Morgan, *Italy*, I, p. 166.
605 Stendhal, pp. 96, 95, 186.
606 *MWSJ*: for *Otello*, 5, 7 April 1818, see p. 203, for *La Spada*, 20, 21, 29 April, see pp. 205-207. Matteo Sartorio, Museo alla Scala confirms that the performance noted on p. 206 was *La Spada*, email 11 July 2005.
607 *PBSLII*, p. 14; Stendhal, pp. 94, 115.
608 Luigi Rossi, *Il ballo alla Scala 1778-1970* (Milan: Edizione della Scala, 1972), p. 53.
609 Winter, The *Pre-Romantic Ballet*, p. 191.
610 Ibid., p. 193.

government of Milan was prepared to allow La Scala the expense of the scenery and costumes which dazzled the visitors. Stendhal describes the court of Neptune in *Dedalo*, 'Rien moins que des poissons dansants dans un palais de madrépores et de corail' (Nothing less than dancing fish in a palace of madrepores and coral) while Lady Morgan described the chariots in *La Vestale* as being 'exactly as they are represented in the ancient bas-relievoes' and 'the living groups [...] formed after the finest sculptures; and down to the bronze vase on the consul's festive board, the lamp, tripod, and consular chair, all seemed borrowed from Herculaneum or Pompeii'.[611]

Despite his high opinion of the ballets, Shelley's descriptions to Hogg and Peacock seem to excuse his enthusiasm: 'strange to say, it left no disagreeable impression' and 'the story is so well told in action as to leave upon the mind an impression as of a real tragedy'.[612] Stendhal, too, repeatedly insisted upon Viganò's genius as if he was not believed: 'L'immortel Vigano [...] Ah! Le grand homme!' (The immortal Viganò [...] Ah! The great man!); 'Dites à vos plats journalistes de vanter un peu les ballets de Vigano et les décorations de Milan' (Tell your journalists to give a bit of a puff to the ballets of Viganò and the scenery of Milan); 'Canova, Rossini et Vigano, voilà la gloire de l'Italie actuelle'. (Canova, Rossini and Viganò, there is the glory of present-day Italy.').[613] Like Shelley, Lady Morgan wondered how Viganò's art produced its effect:

> one is tempted to ask by what lever one's feelings have been so profoundly moved; what poetry, what eloquence, have wound up emotion to such painful excess. It seems incredible that such an effect has been produced, without one word being uttered, one shriek heard; and that the impression is due to the perfection of attitude and gesticulation.[614]

She saw that emotion could be given physical, rather than verbal expression since she remarks, 'In the grand ballet of Othello, the Moor appears literally dancing mad with jealousy'. Stendhal also remarks on *Otello*, 'les sénateurs exprimant leur étonnement; mais *comment*? Voilà le talent de ce grand homme. Il a observé admirablement les gestes humains.' (The senators express their astonishment, but how? There lies the talent of this great man. He has been a wonderful observer of human gesture).[615]

Since Viganò died in 1821, his art died with him and, as his style was

---

611   Stendhal, p. 96; Morgan, *Italy*, I, pp. 166, 169.
612   *PBSLII*, pp. 4, 14.
613   Stendhal, pp. 331, 104, 113.
614   Morgan, *Italy*, I, p. 169.
615   Idem; Stendhal, p. 175.

replaced by the Romantic ballet, it is only from these descriptions and the prints of Sanquirico and Pregliasco that it is possible even to guess its impact. The acting and dancing were excellently performed and the scenery beautiful, with changes 'rapidi, meravigliosi, perfetti' (rapid, marvellous, perfect); La Scala was capable of 11 changes of scene. Shelley's description, 'a combination of a great number of figures grouped with the most picturesque and even poetical effect, and perpetually changing with motions the most harmoniously interwoven and contrasted with great effect', suggests that the combinations created further images which also moved.[616]

As Shelley had done with other performances he had particularly liked, *Fazio* or *Don Giovanni*, he saw the ballets again. Mary Shelley commented that they were 'very much delighted and amused' by *La Spada*.[617] Stendhal saw both ballets which Shelley saw. He described *Otello* and *La Vestale* as Viganò's masterpieces (an opinion shared by Carlo Gatti), saying they were 'chefs-d'œuvre, comme nous n'avons rien en France depuis Voltaire' (masterpieces, such as we have not seen in France since Voltaire) and said, '*La Spada di Kenneth*, roi d'Ecosse, est bien joli. On avait trouvé *Otello* trop fort, trop plein d'action, trop *tetro*, la *Spada* est une fête pour l'imagination.' (*La Spada di Kenneth*, King of Scotland, is very good. One found *Otello* too heavy, too full of action, too intellectual. *La Spada* is a feast for the imagination).[618]

Since these writers from the north of Europe were in agreement about the greatness of Viganò, and had other views in common, it is to be expected that the ballets were discussed at, for example, the house of Signora Dionigi where both the Shelleys and Lady Morgan were entertained at Rome, although they did not meet.[619] As prints were available, and Stendhal sent programmes of the ballets back to France, Curran is probably correct in thinking that Shelley had the opportunity of seeing literature connected with Viganò's *Prometeo* (1813) and perhaps other ballets, such as *Dedalo* and *Mirra* (1817).[620] Apart from his review of the *improvvisatore*, Sgricci, and his negative remarks on Kean's Hamlet, *Otello* and *La Spada di Kenneth* are the only performances upon which Shelley made specific critical observations. Stendhal and Lady Morgan held their high opinion of Viganò not only because of the beauty of the dance but also because of his knowledge of

616 Winter, p. 193; Gatti, I, p. 58; *PBSLII*, p. 14.
617 *MWSJ*, p. 205.
618 Stendhal, pp. 115, 169.
619 *MWSJ*, p. 252n.; Morgan, *Italy*, III, p. 63.
620 Ferrero 'Staging Rossini', p. 207; Stendhal, p. 186; Curran, 'Prometheus', p. 450.

human gestures reflecting the passions, which suggests that Shelley, too, responded to Viganò's psychological insight.[621]

Viganò had arrived in Milan fresh from huge successes in Vienna, where he had already, in 1801 and 1802, produced versions of his *Prometeo, Die Geschöpfe des Prometheus (The Creatures of Prometheus)*, for which Beethoven had written the music. Music for ballet was not considered important, usually selected from popular favourites rather than specially composed. For his 1813 *Prometeo*, Viganò discarded some of Beethoven's music, selecting instead from other great contemporary composers including Mozart. His scenes were taken from famous works of art, at least one of which Shelley had the opportunity of seeing in Milan's Pinoteca Braidense, and which he may have recognised if, as is probable, he had seen prints of *Prometeo*. *Prometeo* had been an outstanding success with audiences who flocked to see it not only from Milan but from the surrounding cities. Over 40 performances were given in that season. Given his interest in both Viganò and Prometheus, it would be rather more surprising if Shelley had *not* heard of this success than if he had. Curran mentions parallels such as Viganò's 'succession of allegorical figures representing Darkness, Dawn, the Hours, Phoebus Apollo, the Year, the Seasons, and the Months', the 'allegorical epithalamial dance' in the fifth act and the name Eone, Ione in Shelley's *Prometheus Unbound*. Despite these similarities, in *Prometeo* it is Prometeo who is hurled from heaven, although he is comforted by humans in his fall to earth, and it is Giove who has the change of heart and forgives Prometeo, prompted by love, although specifically for his son Ercole (Hercules).[622] Shelley, on the other hand, expressed himself as 'averse from a catastrophe so feeble as that of reconciling the Champion with the Oppressor of mankind.' With Giove's change of heart the political system does not change, though it may become a benevolent dictatorship. Shelley did not want tyrants to behave more benevolently, he wanted them abolished.[623]

La Spada di Kenneth

The importance of Viganò's work lies rather in the ballets Shelley did see, which enabled him to understand that it was an art worth taking seriously.

---

621 Morgan, *Italy*, I, p. 166, Stendhal, p. 175.
622 Curran, 'Prometheus', p. 451; Gatti, p. 58.
623 Preface to *Prometheus Unbound*, *SPII*, p. 472.

It is clear from contemporary description that the directing of steps was only one element in a spectacle which drew on exquisite scenery, costume, music, dancing and mime of a very high standard. Schlegel described the Greek chorus as one in which 'their movement kept time with the rhythms of the declamation, and in this accompaniment the utmost grace and beauty were aimed at' and 'a succession of statuesque situations [...] the player remained for some time motionless in one attitude'. Clairmont's remark that Pallerini's 'walk is more like the sweepings of the wind than the steps of a mortal and her attitudes are pictures' suggests that Viganò's ballets followed Schlegel's description.[624] The scenery for *La Spada di Kenneth*, with its story of magic and chivalry, probably used fantasy elements and was close to that for *Prometeo*. This ballet, which has not been previously recognised as an inspiration for *Prometheus Unbound*, is worth describing in more detail.

La Spada di Kenneth is set in Scotland. Elizabeth Wallace, the daughter of William Wallace, has been promised in marriage by her father on his deathbed to Robert Bruce, whom she loves. Scotland is now under the rule of Queen Margaret of Norway, who promises to marry Elizabeth against her will to her own nephew, Balliol (Baliolo). Elizabeth is distraught and Bruce, suspecting the Queen, arrives at the court and challenges Balliol to a trial by combat. Elizabeth, overcome with grief and fear that her beloved will die in this duel, is taken by Gilbert, a faithful old retainer, to a kinsman who is a Druid. When they arrive at his cave the Druid is invoking the Spirits of the Air and playing a harp. In the cave is the sepulchre of Kenneth II, the King who united Scotland, and lying beside him is his magic, invincible sword. The Druid tells Elizabeth that if she has the courage to descend into the tomb and ask for the sword she will be given it. She climbs down the steps below while the Druid and Gilbert pray until she reappears, bearing the sword. The Druid explains that Elizabeth will have to use the sword as it will only work for the person who has claimed it. To prevent Bruce from fighting the duel, she is to give him a magic sleeping potion. She returns to find Bruce armed for the fight. Elizabeth offers him a drink to give him luck, in which she has put the sleeping potion. Although Bruce's suspicions are aroused by her excessive joy when he drinks it, as the trumpet sounds declaring the opening of the tournament, he is overcome by sleep and collapses on a couch. Elizabeth changes into his armour and leaves for the battle on the sound of the second trumpet when Balliol is already claiming

---

624   Schlegel, p. 63; *CCJ*, p. 89n. She mistakenly calls Pallerini 'Maria'.

victory because his opponent has broken his pledge by his non-appearance. Elizabeth is assumed to be Bruce and the fight begins. Balliol fights well, but at last Elizabeth kills him with the magic sword. Bruce arrives at that moment, ready to fight the impostor in the lists. Elizabeth raises her visor and he recognises her. There is general joy and amazement and their marriage is announced.

In both *Prometheus Unbound* and *La Spada di Kenneth* a woman goes to the rescue of her lover who is prevented from playing an active part in the drama. Elizabeth's descent to the tomb on a quest on behalf of Bruce foreshadows Asia's descent to the cave of Demogorgon on behalf of Prometheus. Her scene with the Druid takes place in a mysterious, magical and frightening cave, like Asia's scene with Demogorgon. Elizabeth is like Asia in her loyalty to her lover. Her consultation with the Druid results in finding that she should rely on herself, as Asia discovers in consulting Demogorgon. Both Shelley and Viganò make use of unseen spirits. The Spirits of the Air in Act III of *La Spada* are not mentioned on the cast list, which suggests they do not appear and their voices alone were used. *Prometheus Unbound* can be seen as a response to the visual and aural stimuli of the scenes in *La Spada* combined with a reading of Aeschylus' play and the experience of reports and prints of Viganò's *Prometeo*. The appreciation of how Viganò staged his ballets allowed Shelley to understand the possibility of creating a drama which would allow Greek drama to 'spring again from its seed'. The music, dancing, beautiful scenery and high moral purpose of Viganò's ballets were requirements for Shelley's ideal drama, but excluded the most important: the poetry of words which Shelley was able to supply. By examining what staging he required in terms of what he had seen in the theatre, it becomes clear that *Prometheus Unbound* is Shelley's attempt to put his theory of drama into practice and shows that his ideas, which reveal a knowledge of stagecraft gained by observation, were both practical and dramatic.

Characterisation and dramatic conflict

Although *Prometheus Unbound* has no deep psychological characterisation, Asia, Panthea and Ione all have characters, while the Earth is recognisably an old, sad, weary grandmother in Act I and the Spirit of the Earth an impish child in Act III. Asia's impatience (II. i. 14-25), her complaint (II. i. 32-34) and her questions of Demogorgon (II. iv. 8-128) followed by her glorious — and, in performance, visible — transfiguration (II. v. 16-35) show her development from a rather human sea nymph into the great goddess symbolising love, nature and energy. Demogorgon himself, with his terrifying appearance and laconic answers, appears at times a comic and brutish monster from melodrama. In *Prometheus Bound*, the Oceanides are fiercely loyal and courageous, but Aeschylus does not differentiate them. Shelley distinguishes Panthea's supportive and Ione's more timorous natures. It is his achievement to give them both their own characters and symbolic meaning — they are thus not a chorus as in Aeschylus but defined minor roles in a modern drama.

The defiant and proud character of Prometheus, revealed in the opening of his first speech, is drawn from Aeschylus but is subtly developed to show a character who has remained defiant despite having suffered long. Shelley shows Prometheus change during this first speech in which there are five dramatic moods. In the first (I. i-23) he addresses Jupiter, speaking of his pride and defiance; in the second he bewails his pain (I. 23-30); and in the third tells of his ability to endure (I. 30-53). At the turning point in the speech (I. 53), not just the mood changes but the whole character. Prometheus was able to endure his pain because he knew that Jupiter's fall was at hand, but at this point he begins to consider Jupiter's pain and his wish that no 'living thing' should suffer pain causes him to reject his curse (I. 53-58). To see this rejection as the only action in *Prometheus Unbound* is to use hindsight, for although those familiar with the play realise that this is the turning point from which all else follows, it is by no means established at this point that the release of Prometheus and of mankind will result. In a performance during which the audience does not know, as Earth does not, that it will bring his release, they will share her reaction. The speech changes mood once more to end with an appeal for help in remembering the curse (I. 58-74). Dramatic conflict is revealed through the changes throughout the speech, and its completion engenders yet another, since his request is refused. Other characters are introduced, though these are unseen: the Earth, the Voices from the Mountains, Springs, Air and Whirlwinds.

Mercury's temptation of Prometheus is another example of dramatic conflict and the Chorus of Furies brings yet another since it is clear that Prometheus weakens during their torture and almost succumbs (I. 597-615) until the remaining Fury vanishes or, as Shelley originally wrote, 'exit' (I. 634). The entry of the kind Spirits that bring comfort is dramatic in its contrast with the preceding scene and in the suddenness of their spectacular appearance and disappearance. Mercury had a vivid dramatic, even balletic, gesture here, 'he represses them [the Furies] with his wand'; once again this would be more graphic and effective on stage.[625] Another kind of dramatic effect is seen in Prometheus's longing for Asia, an emotion which he, bound to the precipice, can do nothing to fulfil. Throughout this Act, there are points of dramatic tension and characterisation and it is far from lacking in visual and aural effect to enhance these. There is less of this tension in the following acts but there are different forms of dramatic effect; the shift of emphasis away from Prometheus' struggle as an individual towards that of the struggle of humanity as a whole allows the audience to participate in the cosmic events.

Stage effects

The appearance of the Phantasm demands a huge scenic effect: the ghostly impression achieved with gauze and accompanied by the sound effects late Georgian theatre mechanists did particularly well, whirlwind, earthquake, fire and cloven mountains. Shelley has described the Phantasm's facial expression and frightening demeanour as if to an audience: 'cruel [...] but calm and strong/Like one who does, not suffers wrong' (I. 237-238). He also gives him purple star-inwoven robes (I. 234) with a golden sceptre, the colours he so often uses to denote tyranny. Although we know that the change of heart in Prometheus has taken place, the actual recall of his curse occurs here, in front of witnesses as it were, since he asks the Earth, 'Were these my words, O Parent?' (I. 302). The Earth's distressed reaction, echoed by the Spirits, is one of woe rather than pleasure, yet another dramatic point (I. 303-305). Wasserman pointed out the stage effect in which 'the audience watch[es] the Phantasm uttering the curse against him of whom it is the Phantasm; it also observes Prometheus facing his own former self in Jupiter's ghost since all of Jupiter's nature [...] existed in Prometheus when he cursed his oppressor'.[626] A reader cannot realise this without some thought but it is apparent at once to an audience. A good actor, like Pallerini, can convey a visual impression with body language rather than words and the point can be made by the actors making identical gestures and expressions. Another cancelled stage direction for Prometheus reads

625 *BSMIX*, pp. 152-153.
626 Wasserman, *Prometheus*, p. 38.

'he bends his head as in pain' at the line 'I wish no living thing to suffer pain' (I. 305).[627] This gesture on stage, reminiscent of ballet, would be very moving and convey a great deal in a theatrical representation but it gives nothing extra to the reader.

Immediately afterwards, Mercury enters, wearing gold and purple sandals (I. 320), denoting his attachment to Jupiter, but, as he is not entirely in this livery and his serpent-cinctured wand might suggest he is a free spirit, the effect of his being betrayed by his feet is more readily grasped on the stage. Cancelled stage directions at this point for the Furies (I. 520, I. 538) 'Enter rushing by groupes of horrible forms; they speak as they [rush by *canc.*] pass in chorus and [Another *canc.*] a Fury rushing from the crowd' indicate that Shelley originally thought of this being performed, particularly as he replaced them more suitable lines for a poem (I. 521-524).[628] Again, 'Look' (550) was originally to have had the more dramatic pointing 'Look!'.

Act II concentrates on the journey of Asia and Panthea to Demogorgon. The drama partly lies in the mystery, wonder and sheer beauty of it, which would be created in performance by the actors' gracefulness in their plumed costumes, scene painting, music and sound effects. Dramatic tension is created for the audience by the uncertainty of whether the nymphs are in danger, as they watch them led by invisible forces in a forest of unearthly atmosphere with strange music. The fear is increased when they descend the volcano (II. iii), but the mysterious appearance of Demogorgon is relieved by the comic effect of his brusque oracular answers in his dialogue with Asia. Demogorgon's 'Behold!' and Asia's astonishment (II. iv. 128) lead to the *coup de théâtre*, the volcanic eruption (II. iv. 155). The symbolism of this, the arrival of the charioteers and the struggle with Demogorgon would work on different levels for an audience, as it does for a reader. These effects are similar in a melodrama or an opera, say, *The Magic Flute*. There is no evidence, however, that Shelley — who enjoyed *Don Giovanni* and *The Marriage of Figaro* — ever saw *The Magic Flute*. He did know Kalidasa's *Sakuntala* in Sir William Jones's translation *Sacontala*, and the fact that it may have come to mind would be consistent with the Indian references in *Prometheus Unbound*. In *Sacontala*, there are voices and music 'behind the scenes' (pp. 38, 73-75, 95-96) and a chorus of invisible wood nymphs (p. 85); there are magical elements (pp. 75-77, 109) and Dushmanta travels in a car above the clouds (p. 137); Dushmanta and Sacontala share a poem (pp.

627   *SPII*, p. 495n.
628   *SPII*, pp. 508n., 503n., 510n., also see p. 524n.

61-62) and two Bards repeat stanzas (pp. 94-95).[629]

Geoffrey Matthews cited Shelley's interest in volcanoes and violent geological phenomena, the imagery of which he uses in *Prometheus Unbound*, and his conviction that a tyrant would not allow his own peaceful removal, to show that the struggle between Demogorgon and Jupiter (III .1. 59-82) would have been violent.[630] It is a war between elemental forces — recalling the War of the Titans in which earthquake and thunderbolt contended — which has its basis in the imagery of *Prometheus Bound* and not therefore the unopposed conflict which Wasserman suggests. It would be far more dramatic and exciting to watch than to read as, in performance, the audience would not know the outcome. The scene is one of suspense, a detailed struggle enhanced by Demogorgon first warning Jupiter 'Lift thy lightnings not' (III. i. 56) then conceding that it is 'the destiny/Of trodden worms to writhe till they are dead' (III. i. 59-60). Jupiter is initially confident that he will win (III. i. 63), then pleads for mercy and for Prometheus to judge him (III. i. 63-69). Shrieking and calling for his 'elements' which will not obey him (III. i. 79-80) he sinks 'dizzily down [...] mine enemy above' (III. i. 81-82) in Demogorgon's final victory.

The scenic effects were easily achievable on the late Georgian stage. Shelley had seen spectacular stage struggles in Don Giovanni's descent into hell, both in the opera and Pocock's *The Libertine*, where the Don was carried off by 'fiends come hot from hell with flaming torches', and sank 'into a lake of burning brimstone on a splendid car brought to receive him by the devil, in the likeness of a great dragon, writhing round and round upon a wheel of fire'.[631] He far exceeds them in this scene:

> Sink with me then —
> We two will sink in the wide waves of ruin,
> Even as a vulture and a snake outspent
> Drop, twisted in inextricable fight,
> Into a shoreless sea. Let hell unlock
> Its moulded oceans of tempestuous fire,
> And whelm on them into the bottomless void [...] (III. i. 70-76)

The violence of Jupiter's descent is followed by the contrasting calm of the scene with Apollo and Neptune, which prepares for the long scene of the Caucasus and the unbinding of Prometheus. The dramatic conflict might be said to conclude with this. But the visual and aural impact of the

---

629 *PBSLI*, p. 344; *Sacontala or The Fatal Ring: An Indian Drama by Cálidás* reprinted from the translation of Sir William Jones (London: Charlton Tucker, 1870).
630 Geoffrey Matthews, 'A Volcano's Voice in Shelley' in *SPP*, p. 561.
631 Hazlitt, III, p. 205.

14. 'Mountains', set design undated. Grieve Family Collection. Courtesy of
Senate House Library, University of London, MS1007/409.

combination of poetry, dance, mime, scenery and music is also dramatic.
It is not merely a feast for the senses, but also a profound stimulation to
thought, providing a framework for new moral ideas. *Prometheus* was
recognised to 'end in a mysterious sort of dance' in an early review, and
Act IV, with its celebratory music and dancing, has been seen as a masque
or a ballet following an opera. Yet masque and ballet are combined. Shelley
did not expect his lyrics to be merely read on the page, as Wasserman
and Tetreault appear to suggest.[632] If *Prometheus* was to be performed, he
intended them to be danced.

Scenery

Greek drama was performed in the open. Charlotte Eaton saw open air
theatre on several occasions in Italy but there is no record of the Shelleys

---

632 John Gibson Lockhart qtd in Barcus, *The Critical Heritage*, p. 238; Tetreault,
'Shelley and the Opera', p. 159; Wasserman, *Prometheus*, p. 197.

having done so.[633] The whole of *Prometheus Unbound* is set out-of-doors but this could be recreated on stage by such great scene painters as Sanquirico at La Scala or the Grieves and Greenwood in London.

Each scene is consistent with the style of theatre painting of the period. Not only was mountain scenery popular (an instance is in *Presumption*, a dramatisation of Mary Shelley's *Frankenstein*) but there are many examples of wings painted as part of a forest with standing pieces as rocks, trees or caves, so that actors could move between them, appearing lost in mysterious depths.[634]

The perspective scenery, with wings one behind the other, was suited to creating this effect, as it was for representing a serried mountain range. If depicted on stage, the ravines and mountains of Act I would have formed a spectacular setting, possibly with borders of icicles, and with the precipice to which Prometheus is bound as a standing piece. Asia's vale in Act II creates a contrast by being a spring landscape rather than a wintry one; the setting, however, could be easily adapted with a drop. The wings, however, would not need to be changed since surrounding mountains would be suitable for 'a vale'. The forest scene of II. ii includes caverns and rocks; the rock for the fauns to sit upon and the snowy mountain tops (II. iii, II. v) would have been furnished by standing pieces. For Demogorgon's cave — very dark since he sits on an 'ebon throne' and is a 'mighty darkness' (II. iv. 1, 3) — and the scene in Heaven (III. i), more scenery would be added. Viganò's *Prometeo* was noted for its spectacular scene in Heaven and magnificent Throne for Jupiter. Following the violence of Jupiter's fall, there is the peaceful contrasting setting, 'The mouth of a great river' (III. ii), in Atlantis, offering the scene painter the opportunity for an imaginative response with strange birds and beasts. There is a return to the first scene for III. iii. Prometheus' cave and forest (III. iv) might be slightly adapted for Act IV, with the forest formed of the wing pieces, whereas the cave is 'in the background'. Shelley undoubtedly would have realised that the gradual breaking of the dawn throughout Act I would be best achieved with gas lighting.

As noted in Chapter 1, late Georgian mechanists were easily able to bring about such spectacular scenic and sound effects as whirlwind, earthquake and fire at the appearance of the Phantasm (I. 231-232), 'thunder and

---

633 Eaton, II, p. 42.
634 R.B. Peake, *Presumption*, III, v, in Cox, *Seven Gothic Dramas*; e.g. Thomas Morton, *The Children in the Wood* in Sutcliffe, *Plays by Colman and Morton*.

lightning' required by the partially cancelled stage direction (I. 432n) when the snow-laden cedar is struck (I. 433), earthquake for Demogorgon's chariot arriving (III. i. 46-47) and earthquake and thunder for the fall of Jupiter (III. i. 55-83). There is a volcanic eruption accompanying Demogorgon's 'Behold!' (II. iv. 128) and a sound of waves (III. ii. 48). The wings of the Oceanides themselves make 'Æolian music' (II. i. 26) but, when the Furies enter, Ione hears 'the thunder of new wings'(I. 521). Shelley originally had the direction, 'The Furies having mingled in a strange dance divide, & in the background is seen a plain covered with burning cities' (I. 539n). Since there is no reason to specify the dance dividing to show the back scene purely for the reader, this direction makes more sense as one for performance. As mentioned in Chapter 1, a transparency was commonly used to achieve the effects of 'burning towns', mist for the Furies, 'steaming up from hell's wide gate' (I. 517) and also 'crimson foam' with the addition of coloured silk across a light. The Furies' wings, which are 'blackening the birth of day' (I. 441), and the brilliant colours of the costumes of Jupiter and Mercury would have created a stage effect by their visible contrast to white mountain scenery. When Panthea and Asia descend to Demogorgon, this would have been accomplished, as Elisabetta's descent in *La Spada di Kenneth* no doubt was, by trapdoor, as would Demogorgon's exit with Jupiter and the entrance of The Phantasm and the 'winged child' (III. iii. 147).

Scenes iii and iv in Act II are unusually brief: 53 and 45 lines respectively without their songs. The only happening in Scene iii is the descent of Panthea and Asia into Demogorgon's cave and they do not arrive there until Scene iv. In a poem intended for reading, it makes no sense to split these scenes. However, on stage they cannot be combined as the actors would have to go through a trapdoor in order to descend to the cave, necessitating a scene change so that they can re-enter via the wings as if just descended. Shelley's scene change enables this practical problem to be solved by pulling aside the wings depicting the mountains to reveal the next set: Demogorgon's cave. Panthea and Asia, having exited through the trapdoor, can now enter and, at exactly this point, Shelley has written a song which is long enough to cover the change. When the charioteers leave (II. iv. 135, 174), a similar swift change would have created an impression of flying, a rapid drawing back of the wings allowing them to appear on top of the cloud-capped mountain. Clouds were often hung as borders and, in this case, could give the impression of extreme height as the chariots are now near the top of Olympus. It could also differentiate the location if the same scenery was used as for the 'pinnacle' (II. ii) and for the scene within a cloud on the top of a snowy mountain (II. v). These scene changes suggest that Shelley had performance in mind.

A further suggestion that *Prometheus* would have been staged without difficulty at a theatre of Shelley's time is that the scenes follow in the sequence described in Chapter 1. There is no scene change in the first Act, except for the drops mentioned above, but Act II has four changes. Asia's vale (II. i), like the Caucasus, is a long mountain scene with a vista in the background. Shutters showing a forest would then be pulled across for a short scene (II. ii). For the next long scene (II. iii), Asia's vale could be used again with a built-up practicable piece in the foreground, the 'pinnacle' which is, of course, a volcano. Act III opens with a long scene, Heaven with a large number of gods and goddesses, followed by the short river scene and the long scene of the Caucasus. The forest and cave could easily be drawn across for a short scene to end the act, with adaptations for Act IV.

Dancing, masks, costume and scenery combined to create comic or beautiful effects in the pantomimes Shelley saw, such as *Harlequin Gulliver* on 16 February 1818, when Grimaldi lampooned the 'luxurious narcissism' of fashionable female dress by appearing in a coal scuttle, iron stove pipe and a plum pudding. Crabb Robinson called it one of the best pantomimes he had ever seen, mentioning 'the Laputian masks' and 'the descent of Laputa... a beautiful painting'.[635] Shelley therefore knew the imaginative use to which costume could be put and in a performance of *Prometheus* it is possible for a director to extrapolate how Shelley would have wished the characters to appear. For example, it is clear from the text that the Oceanides have huge wings. Ione's 'wings are folded o'er mine ears/My wings are crossed over my eyes' (I. 221-222). While Ione describes them as giving a 'silver shade' (I. 224), Asia describes Panthea's wings as 'sea-green' (II. i. 26). A combination of sea-green and silver seems intended, giving a shimmering effect. Prints of Pregliasco's costumes for *Prometeo* indicate the flimsy apparel of Viganò's dancers which may have been what Shelley imagined for the Spirits. The Furies would wear wigs to simulate 'hydra tresses' (I. 326). Demogorgon is 'veiled', 'a mighty Darkness' and 'shapeless' (II. iv. 1, 2, 5) which suggests black draperies. In *A Defence of Poetry*, Shelley expresses a preference for masked actors and he may have envisaged the Furies and Demogorgon as masked.[636] The Spirit of the Moon's 'countenance,

635 *MWSJ*, p. 193n.; Moody, *Illegitimate Theatre*, p. 224; Crabb Robinson, p. 81.
636 *SPP*, pp. 518.

like the whiteness of bright snow' could also suggest a mask, as it is entirely in white even to the hair (IV. 220-225).

These would not have been the papier-maché 'big head' masks worn in English pantomime since they were too difficult to dance in, but the type of leather mask worn by *commedia dell'arte* players which are designed to fit the actor's face 'like a shoe', as Dario Fo explains, and must be able 'to breathe' so that it can 'absorb your sweat as well as to live in symbiosis with your body heat and breathing rhythms'.[637] Ione recognises the Hours as charioteers although they have no chariots (IV. 56), which suggests they are wearing a costume like those of the ancient Greek charioteers which Shelley had seen in the Elgin Marbles. Chariots will convey Demogorgon and Asia and Panthea; Asia's, like Aphrodite's, is shaped like a shell just as one of the chariots was in *Charles the First*.[638]

Music

I believe that it is clear from the stage directions and from the many songs that Shelley would have expected a musical accompaniment to the drama, if staged, but it was unlikely to have been orchestral. Ione (I. 669-670) asks if what she hears at the entrance of the Spirits (I. 664-666) is 'the music of the pines?/ Is it the lake? Is it waterfall?' which suggests not orchestral music but a harp which gives a rippling effect. A flute is mentioned (II. ii. 38) and there is also a 'small, clear, silver lute' (III. ii. 38). Off-stage pipes may have sufficed for the 'nightingales' (II. ii. 24). Since the Fauns speak of 'delicate music' (II. ii. 65), it seems Shelley required it to be as Schlegel imagined the music of the Greek theatre: 'not in the slightest degree to impair the distinctness of the words'.[639]

The Spirits are unseen, but they sing. Not all of the verses given to them are specified as sung but they are written in a style easily adapted to music. In some cases, Shelley entitles the verses 'song', as he does with the Song of the Spirits (II. ii. 54-97). Its repetitive refrain 'Down, down' particularly lends itself to the singing style of the late Georgian theatre. Singing indicates the difference between the more abstract and the more developed

---

637 Mayer, *Harlequin in his Element*, p. 28; Dario Fo, *The Tricks of the Trade*, trans. by Joe Farrell, ed. by Stuart Hood (London: Methuen, 1991), pp. 66-67.
638 *MWSJ*, p. 193, 193n.; *SPII*, p. 496n.
639 Schlegel, p. 65.

characters. Although Earth is an unseen Spirit, addressed by Prometheus as 'Melancholy Voice' (I. 152), she is a character who interacts with Prometheus rather than an abstraction and her speeches are in blank verse. However, when the Spirit of the Earth appears in Act IV, it is accompanied by 'music wild' (IV. 252). The Voices of the Mountains, Springs, Air and Whirlwinds are written in short rhyming verses which, especially if sung, make an effective counterpoint to Prometheus's demand, the long speech contrasted with the supernatural singing voices. The Echoes (I. 312-313), repeat Earth's words using the same form as she does. Singers were placed, according to contemporary stage practice, behind the wings or even below or above the stage. The practice of concealing voices behind the scenes occurs in *Sacontala*.[640]

In Act II, Panthea first says the Echoes 'speak' (II. i. 171) but later she speaks of 'the strain' (II. i. 189) and Asia of 'the notes' (II. i. 195). Echo songs were sufficiently popular in the London theatre of the period for Henry Bishop's wellknown one to be re-used for *Presumption* by the composer, Watson.[641] At the beginning of II. ii, there is music since the Fauns are required to be 'listening' (stage directions, p. 539). The Oceanides produce their own music when they move their wings, but no other music is required until the Spirit's song (II. iv. 163-174). The stage directions (p. 571) call specifically for music (II. v. 36) and for the following verses (II. v. 48-71) to be sung, presumably also Asia's verses (II. v. 72-110) in response. This lovely duet, with its imagery of boats and music associated with love while Asia glides in her shell-like chariot across the stage, perhaps drew on Shelley's memory of the candle-lit boats which glided across the stage in Dibdin's *The Cabinet* referred to in Chapter 1. In performance, the sight of both Asia and the boat would reinforce the symbolism of the song.

At the opening of Act IV, the stage direction requires the Voice of Unseen Spirits to 'awaken [Panthea and Ione] gradually during the first song' (p. 612). 'The train of dark Forms and Shadows' also sings (IV. 9-29) and Ione and Panthea have similar verses which suggest they respond in song. The Unseen Spirits (IV. 40-55) and then the Choruses and Semi Choruses of the Hours continue in song. Panthea and Ione hear 'the deep music of the rolling

---

640 Concealed singers in pantomime in Cox and Gamer, *Broadview Anthology*, p. 213; theatre songs, e.g. 'When first to Helen's lute' in *The Children in the Wood*, Elizabeth's song in *Presumption*.
641 Sir H.R. Bishop, 'The Celebrated Echo Song' (William Reeve) (London/ Dublin: Goulding, D'Almaine, Potter & Co., [WM 1820]) BL H.1654 p. (24) 004603022/004832989.

world' (IV. 186) which signifies the presence of the Earth. Since the Earth is on stage until the end of the drama, this music must accompany the poetry and dance but not dominate, perhaps varying so that the Earth and the Moon can dance. There is also the sound of the conch shell, the 'mighty music' which the Spirit of the Hour 'loosens' (III. iii. 81), an instrument which was used in Greek drama and continues to be used in Polynesian drama.

Dancing

Dancing is mentioned throughout the drama. Although Shelley does not specify what 'strangeness' the dance of the Furies consists of (p. 510n), the libretto of *La Spada di Kenneth* shows that even Viganò did not describe dance more fully. If staged, the part of the Furies would require proficient dancers since, whether spoken or sung, the dancing must emphasise the words and change when the metre changes as the chorus in Greek drama did; when they call the second group of Furies, who have a short lined ballad metre, their dancing must be co-ordinated and keep time to continual changes of metre. The dancers would have been expected not to dance in unison but to keep tempo with each other while 'rushing' or darting forward as in the cancelled stage directions (pp. 508 & 510n). The skills of the dancers of the period were very high, even in the minor theatres, as noted by Bush-Bailey.[642]

Shelley admired and described the 'harmoniously interwoven' movements in pictorial groupings and attitudes shown in the prints of Viganò's ballets, and it seems likely that, in a performance version of *Prometheus Unbound*, he would have intended to use this style of dancing to form a dramatic contrast to the Furies and convey the personality of the Spirits. The physical presence of the Oceanides on the stage, visible to the audience from the beginning of the Act (although they are silent until I. 222), compensates for the fact that the Mountains, Springs, Air and Whirlwinds and the Earth are unseen Voices. Ione's first speech mentions her use of her wings and Shelley, having seen Viganò's work, would have no difficulty in imagining how they might perform with these, gracefully miming their reactions to the speeches. Although the performer need not be a trained dancer, a dancer would more easily achieve the desired effect.

642 Gilli Bush-Bailey, 'Still Working It Out' in *Nineteenth Century Theatre and Film*, 29.2 (Winter 2002), p. 15.

15. 'Auguste Vestris', contemporary print (artist unknown. From Ethel L. Urlin, *Dancing, Ancient and Modern* (London: Simpkin, Marshall & Co., 1914), p. 140.

The magical effect of the scenes in which the supernatural beings, Spirits, Oceanides and Fauns, appear throughout the drama, would be lost if the movement were not graceful, suggesting that Shelley had dancers in mind.

The Dreams which enter and 'disappear' (II. i. 115-126, 127-132), must do so swiftly, and Shelley probably intended them to be played by nimble dancers, perhaps children. He had admired the 'unaffected self-possession' of the children from Viganò's La Scala ballet school.[643] A child could also have danced the Spirit of the Earth in III. iv, which, at first, being 'not earthly', 'glides' (III. iv. 1) but finally is 'running' (III. iv. 24).

Shelley was familiar with *Comus* and with the works of Jonson and Beaumont and Fletcher, presumably including their masques. Act IV, like a masque, has characters equivalent to courtiers, Panthea and Ione, asleep in the forest who wake to song. This is followed by 'A train of dark forms and Shadows passes by confusedly, singing' across the backstage (IV. 9-25).

---

643 *PBSLII*, p. 4.

Shelley reverses the seventeenth-century practice; this anti-masque of the gloomy funeral of the hours precedes the masque (IV. 40), emphasising that the following dance can be joy unrestrained as there is no longer any need to mourn. In the theatre, Panthea and Ione would have been placed near a wing painted like a cave opening or a standing piece representing a rock or tree while the ballet took place on the forestage.

The Voices are unseen, but once again dancing is mentioned. The 'charioteers' (Hours) enter (IV. 55) perhaps dancing. Certainly they do so soon afterwards, as indicated by 'leap' (IV. 67, 68) and 'Weave the dance on the floor of the breeze'(IV. 69), repeated by 'weave the mystic measure' (IV. 77) which imply passing deftly between each other. The Chorus of Spirits 'join the throng/of the dance and the song' (IV. 84), both groups of dancers sing and dance together, and 'whirl, singing loud' (IV. 169) suggests they continue to do so. The line 'We are free to dive, or soar, or run' (IV. 137) shows that Shelley thought of very lively dancing as well as singing. Performers with good breath control can do both and, moreover, with a large group of dancers, some can dance more energetically while others can carry the song. This would be necessary in the case of the long dance of the Earth and the Moon, where the words are very complicated to deliver and important to understand. Kelvin Everest considers that Panthea's lines (IV. 514-515, p. 645n) indicate that the singing may have been by 'the bright Visions [...] singing Spirits'.[644] After the chorus of Hours and Spirits end their dance, 'some depart, and some remain' (IV. 176); the only point in some remaining would be to carry part of the singing. The Earth and the Moon may begin by speaking or singing their verses, but their later dancing suggests pirouettes followed by more pirouettes (IV. 444, 457, 470, 477) when it would be impossible for them to speak. A portrait of Auguste Vestris pirouetting at the King's Theatre, indicates the kind of wild joy that Shelley required of the Earth and Moon. As noted in Chapter 2, Shelley had seen Armand Vestris, Auguste's son, equally famous for his pirouette, at the same theatre.

Ethel Urlin calls the tarantella 'the great national dance of the Sicilians and Neapolitans [...] the most passionate and picturesque of all dances' and explains how 'the partners salute each other, draw off, and dance timidly and separately; they then return to each other, stretch out their arms and whirl madly together at the highest possible speed'. She quotes a description from 'an old writer' which she believes shows their Greek origin:

---

644   *SPII*, p. 645.

The Neapolitan girls dance to the snapping of their fingers, and the beat of a tambourine, and whirl their petticoats about them with greater elegance in the position than other Italians, and more airiness in the flow of their draperies; striking likenesses of them may be found in the paintings of Herculaneum.[645]

She also quotes Stolberg's description:

The tambourine is always played by a woman. This is enlivened by the singing of the girls that dance. The songs they sing in general are the complaints of lovers, and the cruelties of the maiden beloved. You imagine you behold a priestess of Apollo seated on the tripod, and that the music is the inspiration of the god [...] No dance is so full of grace and decorum as this. The head inclining, the downcast eyes, the noble dignity of mien and the inimitable elasticity, are indescribable.[646]

At Naples, Shelley re-read de Staël's *Corinne*, in which she describes the tarantella. Shelley had the opportunity to see it there, as it was often performed in the street. In the early nineteenth century there was a belief that the Neapolitans' dances were descended from the Greeks, since the Neapolitans had long preserved the many of the customs of ancient Greece.[647] The belief that the whirling and spinning dance was a form of ancient Greek dancing suggests that the dance of the Moon and Earth originated in the tarantella. The use of this dance in *Prometheus Unbound* would be in perfect accord with Shelley's idea of Greek drama.

The whole drama is not solely masque, opera, poem or ballet, but a new form of drama which combines these, using as its framework the Greek drama from which Shelley took the myth itself. Shelley's scientific and philosophical references show that man could understand natural phenomena and need not be enslaved by religion, war and revenge, but could bring about liberation through forgiveness. *Prometheus Unbound* attempts to provide the 'religious institution' lacking in modern theatre, of which Shelley complained in *A Defence of Poetry*. Despite his admiration for Calderón's Autos, he did not feel they supplied this, but were marred by 'the substitution of the rigidly defined and ever-repeated idealisms of a distorted superstition'.[648] *Prometheus Unbound* in its overthrow of Jupiter, replaces these with 'living impersonations of the truth of human passions',

---

645 Qtd in Urlin, p. 70.
646 Qtd in Ibid., p. 69.
647 *MWSJ*, p. 243; Morgan, *Italy*, III, pp. 197-198; Urlin, p. 68.
648 *SPP*, p. 519.

especially love, and intellectual achievement.[649]

Although he clearly did not intend *Prometheus Unbound* to be performed in the immediate future, Shelley had seen that an audience could appreciate the philosophical and poetical ideas in Viganò's ballets at La Scala. Viganò did not have to commercialise his work as the theatre was subsidised. It is clear that in 1818, the poetry, music, ballet, scene painting and technology required to perform the spectacular effects in *Prometheus Unbound* existed and their existence would have offered Shelley the opportunity of foreseeing the revival of drama not as an imitation of the Greek but as a modern equivalent, retaining aspects of earlier periods but with completely new elements. While this might have been possible at La Scala, however, there was no comparable theatre in England; the theatres were run on a commer cial basis.

It is true that the ideas and poetry of *Prometheus Unbound* are complex and this might appear to contradict Schlegel's theory, since Schlegel emphasises the importance of conveying ideas in the theatre in a very clear way. On the other hand, a physical representation of great beauty and emotional appeal might have clarified aspects which puzzled critics for many years. The earthquakes and volcanoes would have been seen and heard and the scientific and natural phenomena could have been visually portrayed. Perhaps Shelley underestimated his audience, since, as noted in Chapter 2, the poem had favourable reviews in 1820, one of which even acknowledged that the ending appeared to be 'a kind of dance'. As for a wider audience, the radical publisher, William Benbow, brought out a pirate edition of Shelley's poetry in 1826, suggesting that he expected a readership for it not only of a select few but also of the very radicals to whom Shelley wished to appeal in poems such as *The Mask of Anarchy*. Had Shelley been able to arrange a performance, he would have reached an audience wider still.[650]

In the twentieth century, theatrical subsidies allowed such directors as Peter Brook to experiment with innovatory forms which draw on different cultures and myths. It is possible to envisage, even today, a drama such as *Prometheus Unbound* being performed with the sensitivity it requires. Viganò's term *coreodramma* may be a more suitable one to apply to Shelley's 'lyrical dramas', since the songs and dances are an integral part. What is important and extraordinary about them is the extent to which they can stand alone as poetry, yet can be enhanced rather than spoiled by the

649 Schlegel, pp. 56-59.
650 Barcus, *The Critical Heritage*, pp. 225-251; Neil Fraistat, 'Shelley Left and Right' in *SPP*, p. 649.

incorporation of music, dance and stage effects. *Hellas*, also based on an Aeschylean drama, also includes these theatrical elements.

Chapter Six
Drama for a Purpose – *Hellas* & *Fragments of an Unfinished Drama*

Like *Prometheus Unbound*, *Hellas* has a chorus and is modelled on a drama by Aeschylus, in this case very closely. Shelley described it, too, as a 'lyrical drama' and, once again, it has been thought of as a poem rather than a drama. Edward Williams so described it, remarking that it would never be popular as it was 'above common apprehension'.[651] If this is so, it would rule out one of Schlegel's requirements for a successful drama but, like *Prometheus*, it may well have been more accessible to an audience than is generally thought when the visual and performable elements are taken into account.

Shelley does not state that its performance was his intention and called *Hellas* 'a drama from the circumstance of its being composed in dialogue' but he went on to say, 'I doubt whether if recited on the thespian waggon to an Athenian village at the Dionysiaca, it would have obtained the prize of the goat'. As only dramas were entered in the Dionysiaca, this suggests that *Hellas* is a performable tragedy in Greek style, even if not a prizewinner, and the suggestion is reinforced by his comparison to *The Cenci* ('the only *goat-song* which I have yet attempted'), a tragedy successful enough to warrant a second edition. Given his high opinion of the improvisations of Sgricci, his description, a 'mere improvise' may not be as dismissive as it sounds and may be a clue to his dramatic technique.[652] There is no artistic reason why *Hellas* should not have been performed, and successfully, as Shelley knew *The Persians* had been. *Hellas* could be considered as a drama performable

---

651   Gisborne & Williams, p. 111.
652   *SPP*, pp. 430-431.

in a future theatre, like *Prometheus Unbound* but, bearing in mind that the very struggle for which Shelley was writing inspired a fashion for Greek drama,[653] that theatre was close at hand.

Shelley mentions *The Persians* of Aeschylus as 'the first model of my conception' for *Hellas*. It provided the structural basis although other elements were derived from contemporary performances which Shelley saw: Sgricci's *Quattro Etade La morte d'Ettore (The Death of Hector)*, upon which he wrote a review, and Dimond's *The Bride of Abydos*, which has not to my knowledge been discussed at all in connection with *Hellas*.[654] It is not surprising to find that *The Persians*, an especially political play, was an inspiration. The coming popularity of Greek drama shows that this connection was made by others at the time and in fact the awareness of the culture of ancient Greece caused much support for the Greek uprising.[655] The avowed purpose of *Hellas* was to gain sympathy for the struggle for Greek independence. Shelley devoted more of the Preface to the politics than to the drama and urged Ollier to get it printed quickly before it lost its relevance.[656]

Reiman and Michael Neth suggest that Shelley may have begun a draft of a poem on the theme of Greek independence as early as February 1821, and, after a second sketch, laid aside his attempts, while he wrote *Adonais*. They conjecture that 'some time between late July and early September 1821' he began a prologue reminiscent of the 'Prologue In Heaven' of Goethe's *Faust*, which he had read but not yet translated.[657] Although these drafts preceded *Hellas* in the writing, this does not mean Shelley was prevaricating in saying *The Persians* was his first model. It may well have come to mind while he was reading 'fragments of Aeschylus' on 10 January 1821, during a time when Sgricci was visiting the Shelleys. On 22 January, the day of Sgricci's performance of *The Death of Hector*, Alexander Mavrocordato called.[658] The combination of these events suggest that Shelley associated *Hellas* with *The Persians* and Sgricci's improvisation before he put anything on paper, then considered using the technique of a modern poet he admired, Goethe, as a means of bringing his source up to date. For the Greeks, a performance

653   Hall & Macintosh, *Greek Tragedy*, pp. 270-272.
654   *SPP*, p. 430; P.M.S. Dawson, 'Shelley and the Improvvisatore Sgricci: an Unpublished Review', *KSR*, 32 (1981), 19-29.
655   William St. Clair, *That Greece Might Still Be Free. The Philhellenes in the War of Independence* (Cambridge: Open Book Publishers, 2008), pp. 53-54.
656   *SPP*, pp. 431-432; *PBSLII*, p. 365.
657   *BSMXVI*, pp. viii-xxxiii.
658   *MWSJ*, pp. 348, 350.

was a religious occasion which honoured Dionysius, and Shelley may have been experimenting at including a form of religion in the drama by using a parallel to Goethe's 'Prologue in Heaven'. But, as Reiman suggests, this would give an omniscient view which Shelley would wish to avoid.[659] The presence of short lyrics among the speeches may indicate that he intended the Prologue to include a Chorus or they may have been written as they came to mind for another part of the play. Shelley discarded the Prologue, re-used some of the lines in *Hellas* itself and found other ways of making the Greek dramatic model relevant to modern readers..

As Reiman and Neth note, Shelley was unable to predict a Greek victory in *Hellas*; in fact, at this stage in the war, it seemed unlikely that the Greeks would gain their independence, but Shelley felt it important to rouse public opinion on their side.[660] He wrote to Horace Smith in September 1821: 'All public attention is now centred on the wonderful revolution in Greece'. His confidence for Greece, once independent, was founded in the character of Mavrocordato, 'of the highest qualities, both of courage and conduct'. He believed he would 'probably fill a high rank in the magistracy of the infant republic' and dedicated *Hellas* to him, quoting from *Oedipus at Colonus*, 'Prophet I am of noble combats'.[661] He was right about the part Mavrocordato would play, but could not know the factors which meant that independent Greece would not even be a republic, let alone as enlightened as he would have hoped. [662]

Aeschylus inspired Shelley's hope for success. In *The Frogs*, performed in 404 BC when Athens was facing defeat in the war against Sparta, Aristophanes identifies Aeschylus as the tragic poet who can save the polis. In a competition with Euripides for the poets' chair of honour in Hades, Aeschylus claims *The Persians* is 'An effective sermon on the will to win' (II. 1026-1027).[663] He wins the contest and Dionysius returns with him. Thus when Shelley thought of *The Persians* it was not merely as a drama by an admired classical Greek poet, but as a play which represented to the contemporaries of Aristophanes a declaration of the 'will to win' by a man who had fought at Marathon against the Persians. It supplied him with an

---

659 Donald Reiman, 'Tracking Shelley' in *The Unfamiliar Shelley*, p. 321.

660 *BSMXVI*, p. xlvi.

661 *PBSLII*, pp. 350, 368; Herbert Huscher, 'Alexander Mavrocordato, Friend of the Shelleys', *KSMB*, 16 (1965), 29-38.

662 William St. Clair, *That Greece Might Still be Free*, pp. 88-94, 348.

663 Aristophanes, *The Frogs*, in *The Wasps, The Poet and the Women, The Frogs*, trans. by David Barrett (Harmondsworth: Penguin, 1964).

inherited framework which provided an ideal perspective for adumbrating another Greek victory over a tyrannical enemy. As Wasserman says, 'The tacit but presiding presence of Aeschylus' play in Shelley's is the presence of the earliest liberation of the Greeks in their struggle centuries later'.[664]

It has often been said that the model of *The Persians* influenced *Hellas* but it has not been considered in what way the structure of Aeschylus's play may have influenced the performability of Shelley's. He had seen Sgricci's improvisations which were structured 'on the Greek plan [...] without the devision of acts and with chorus's', which showed him how effective this style could be on the stage. By describing *Hellas* as 'short and Aeschylean' and 'full of lyrical poetry', Shelley acknowledged how closely his dramatic technique was related to that of Aeschylus and, although he incorporated dramatic effects into *Hellas* from later periods, he follows *The Persians* closely in structure. This determined what was to be included or discarded; the Prologue was too elaborate for Aeschylean simplicity and economy. .[665]

The structure

The Persians is set in Susa and *Hellas* in Constantinople — both locations would have been exotic to their audiences. In both, messengers bring news of battles and defeat, lists are recited to show the might of the empire and ghosts are raised which forecast the end of an empire. In each play the tyrant learns from his experience. *The Persians* opens with a long choral song by the Chorus of Persian elders, too old to take part in the war, lamenting that the huge army of Xerxes which had set out to conquer Greece has been so long away. They are beginning to lose faith in the victory they had expected.

> Thus sable-clad my heart is torn
> Fearful for those Persian arms. (115/117)[666]

664 Richmond Lattimore, Introduction to *Aeschylus I: The Oresteia* (Chicago: Chicago University Press, 1973), p. 1; Wasserman, *Shelley: A Critical Reading*, p. 378.
665 Webb, *A Voice Not Understood*, p. 199; Wasserman, *Shelley: A Critical Reading*, pp. 377-378; Walker, 'The Urn of Bitter Prophecy', pp. 37-38; *PBSLII*, pp. 364, 357; *MWSLI*, p. 171.
666 Aeschylus, *The Persians*, trans. by Seth G. Bernadete in *Aeschylus II: Four Tragedies* (Chicago: University of Chicago Press, 1975), p. 52. The line numbers cited here, due to complications in the line numbering of the translation, are taken from *Persai in Septem quae Supersunt Tragoedias*, ed. by Denys Page (Oxford: Oxford University Press, 1975).

At the same time, they praise Xerxes as being 'the equal of god' (81), say that 'Persians are never defeated/The people tempered and brave' (191-192) and list the huge number of subject countries which have followed Xerxes to war. This chorus creates an atmosphere of conflict, a kind of disbelieving foreboding, in the minds of the audience before the late entrance of the Queen. Her subsequent speeches parallel the Chorus's song when she describes a dream she has had and a bad omen she has seen which forecast the defeat of her son, Xerxes. She discovers that the Greeks 'are slaves to none', a consequence of which was their victory at Marathon over great King Darius, her husband, and father of Xerxes. A herald enters with the news of the defeat at Salamis, where the Persian ships far outnumbered the Greek.

> Had numbers counted
> The barbarian warships surely would have won; (337-338)

He concludes, 'Some deity destroyed/Our host' (345-346) but, while Xerxes threatened to execute his captains if they lost the battle (370-372), the Greeks in 'a great concerted cry' exhort each other to 'free your fathers' land' (400-402), thus showing the contrast between tyranny and democracy. The Queen, by casting a spell, raises the ghost of Darius whose appearance is a spectacular dramatic effect. Darius prophesies that the unit Xerxes has left behind in Greece will find 'no safe return' (797), forecasting the Battle of Plataea the following year which effectively ended the expansion of the Persian Empire. He descends, leaving the Queen lamenting that her son is dishonoured, and the Chorus that the life they had under Darius is no more. Xerxes returns, and, with the Chorus, performs a long lament which ends the play. Aeschylus reveals the changing emotional states of the Queen and Xerxes through the choruses and the prophecy of Darius. Although Xerxes appears in the play only as the broken man who in Kitto's phrase 'limps home to port',[667] the lessons he had learnt are already clear to the audience. The dramatic structure is therefore one of scenes not merely divided by choruses, but with a parallel theme in the chorus, the dramatic climax being the spectacular raising of a ghost of a great conqueror who prophesies defeat and end of empire.

Shelley also opens his play with a Chorus and a royal Protagonist who does not speak immediately, who has had an ominous dream and wishes to know the future. Both Choruses are unable to take action, Aeschylus'

---

667 Kitto, *Greek Tragedy*, p. 41.

because of their age, Shelley's because they are imprisoned in a seraglio. Shelley keeps to the Greek cast structure of Protagonist and Chorus with the second and third actors being Hassan and Ahasuerus. Both interact critically and sympathetically with Mahmud as the leader of the Chorus does with the protagonist in Greek tragedy. Shelley's theatre employed more performers. This allowed him to increase the number of messengers and fulfil the expectations of his audience by showing them a Mahmud who, in commanding so many, accorded with their idea of an Eastern potentate. The function of the Herald in *The Persians* is performed by Daood and four messengers in *Hellas*, bringing news of Greek victories and revolts taking place in other parts of the Ottoman Empire. These cannot be described by Hassan as he is already on stage, but he remarks on the Greek 'will to win'. The successive appearances of messengers bringing bad news increases dramatic tension, as it does in *Macbeth* (V. iii). The lists of exotic names is reminiscent of the list of the subject peoples which had sent armies to join Xerxes in *The Persians* (30-58). The mention of the Aegean place names in *Hellas* (546-587), which were part of the Persian Empire in the fifth century BC, creates a further reminder of the similarity between the modern struggle and the ancient, and of the vastness of the Ottoman Empire.

The chorus

Shelley used a variety of rhythms and rhyme schemes in the choruses, varying the line lengths to correspond to the different metres used in Greek poetry and probably intending to make up for the comparative paucity of rhythm in the English language by the complexity and richness of the rhyme. They are not intended to be detached from the play since, like their Greek antecedents, they comment on the themes. *The Persians* has a Chorus of Persian elders and *Hellas* one of captive slavewomen.[668] Shelley's Chorus, like Aeschylus', sets up the ambiguous atmosphere of foreboding with the first chorus, ostensibly a lullaby for Mahmud but actually the history of the Greek idea of liberty and the hope that it will triumph. As Constance Walker has noted, the words of the lullaby are ambiguous:[669]

---

668 For clarity, I have used a lower-case 'c' for what is sung and upper-case 'C' for the singers.

669 Walker, 'The Urn of Bitter Prophecy', p. 47; Wasserman, *Shelley: A Critical Reading*, p. 382.

Be thy sleep
Calm and deep
Like theirs who fell — not ours who weep! (*Hellas*, 5-7)

While purportedly lulling Mahmud to sleep, the Chorus are covertly wishing him dead, since 'Theirs who fell' refers to the Greek dead. This song engenders a tension similar to that in *The Persians*, but there is a conflict between what we know the Chorus think of Mahmud and what they are bound as members of a seraglio to perform. This is commented upon by 'the Indian', who accuses the Greek women: they who 'love not/ With your panting loud and fast,/Have awakened him at last' (111-113). But the Indian's own prayers for Mahmud's healthful sleep echoes their 'calm sleep/Whence none may wake, where none shall weep' by her desire for it to be:

Clear and bright, and deep!
Soft as love and calm as death,
Sweet as a summer night without a breath (11-13)

The association with death is repeated by the use of 'dead' and 'weep' in her following verse:

All my joy should be
Dead, and I would live to weep
So thou mightst win one hour of quiet sleep. (24-26)

Thus the Indian echoes the first Chorus when they sing of their lack of sexual freedom, even as she believes she is singing of her love for Mahmud.

The parallels between the sexual enslavement of women and the struggle for liberty sets up the theme for the chorus. The theme of liberty is traced from its birth in Greece, through the medieval Italian republics and a dark age to the early nineteenth-century revolutions in Spain and Greece (45-109). If performed, a Chorus singing of these ideas and dancing before a sleeping Mahmud would be a personification of the ideas themselves, also suggesting that the ideas form part of Mahmud's foreboding dream of defeat and thus arouse his fears, causing him to wake.

In the following scene, Mahmud expresses his fears and desire for reassurance about the future. He hopes that Ahasuerus, whom Hassan suggests is the immortal Wandering Jew but who is certainly a wise, abstemious hermit (136-161), will reassure him. The second chorus sings of immortality, spirituality, and Christianity versus 'the moon of Mahomet'. In parallel to this, Ahasuerus displays a Neo-Platonic philosophy in his words 'look on that which cannot change — the One, the unborn and the undying' (768/769).

Shelley began a chorus which he discarded. Two songs of this link to the preceding scene. 'I would not be a king' reflects Mahmud's belief that kings have 'no repose' (196); 'Judith loved not her enslaver' reminds us of the beheading of Holofernes and echoes Mahmud's casual, tyrannical order of an execution, 'Strike the foremost shorter by a head!'(193).[670] The following verses were intended to be divided between Fatima ('the Indian') and the Greeks, on the subject of the love of a slavegirl for her master, possibly deriving from the Chorus concerning Io in *Prometheus Bound*.[671] The Greeks sing of a preferable love between equals, but begin to limit the choice of partner to those of the same country, religion and rank, approved by their 'friends'.[672] In this they are not expressing Shelley's opinions, since he himself had taken no account of rank or friends' approval in his own marriages, and his infatuation with Emilia Viviani disregarded country and religion. The argument requires to be countered, but a continuation of this chorus would mean that it could not reflect the subject matter of the preceding scene. Moreover, it promised to be lengthy while the previous scene is short. Had Shelley developed this aspect it would have considerably increased the focus on sexual politics, but this would be diverging from his main theme of Greek liberation, in which the possibility of love between despot and slave is only an element.

Shelley evidently saw that these verses would detract from the structure of *Hellas*, since the chorus would no longer reflect the subject matter of the scene. His desire for a structure similar to *The Persians* is shown by his discarding these verses and replacing them with the shorter and more fitting chorus which leads into a scene in which Mahmud's confidence in victory is successively undermined by messengers. They bring news of the defeats of armies bearing 'the crescent moon' (337) by those believing in 'the red cross' (603), and the 'will to win' embodied in those who are defeated and dying on the battlefield. The long third chorus, divided into chorus and semichorus, echoes that spirit of resistance, predicting the end of empire, proclaiming liberty and its continuation through Greece 'Based on the chrystalline sea/Of thought' (699-700) and modified by the warning of 'the small still voice' that 'Revenge and wrong bring forth their kind' (729-732). The ambiguity of the love between master and slave suggested in the opening chorus is now commented upon in the attitude of Hassan, who

---

670 *BSMXVI*, pp. 97, 99.
671 *Prometheus Bound*, 888-905.
672 *BSMXVI*, pp. 97-101.

would 'die for' Mahmud (or Islam), yet whose 'heart is Greek' (456-458). Shelley includes the Chorus's attitude to slavery in:

> Thy touch has stamped these limbs with crime,
> These brows thy branding garland bear,
> But the free heart, the impassive soul
> Scorn thy controul! (678-681)

Mahmud's dialogue with Ahasuerus and the appearance of Mahomet II's phantom prepare him for defeat and the end of empire which the preceding chorus had predicted. The phantom vanishes at the shouts of victory, but although Mahmud's subjects are boasting of this, Mahmud pities them for their self-deception. His reconciliation with his own end and the possibility of defeat is followed by the final heroic and beautiful chorus from the Greeks. In this, they express their determination that 'Another Athens shall arise' (1084), thus repeating the idea of the continuation of the idea of liberty and the belief of the preceding Semichorus that 'Greece, which was dead, is arisen!' (1059) The 'golden years' which will return will be better — 'A brighter Hellas' (1067), 'a loftier Argo' (1072), 'another Athens' (1084) — but the long wars, revenge and cruelty of the ancient Greek world should die. Once again there is a warning from Shelley that revenge brings a continual cycle of war, and an element of foreboding in 'Oh, cease! must hate and death return?' (1096).

Mahmud's resignation and increased self-knowledge, however, show that wisdom is not all on the side of the Greeks and there is therefore a hint at the accordance of mood between Chorus and Protagonist in *Hellas* which unites Xerxes and his Chorus in *The Persians*. As the Greek uprising was only in its early stages, Shelley could not end *Hellas* with a lament for the defeat of the Turks, but, although he would not have claimed to have known what the future held, he could 'suggest the final triumph of the Greek cause' by analogy with the past. He calls the final chorus 'indistinct and obscure' because it is about an optimistic future which is more difficult to portray than war.[673] The last voice heard from the Ottoman side is an ugly threat:

> Oh, keep holy
> This jubilee of unrevenged blood!
> Kill! crush! despoil! Let not a Greek escape!
> (1020-1022)

This may include the Greek harem-girls of the Sultan and is certainly

---

673   *SPP*, pp. 430, 463.

directed at their kith and kin. It does not prevent them singing with the Greek spirit of defiance and bravery. Walker points out that *Hellas* asks the reader to provide a resolution.[674] A performance would end with the menace of their enemy off-stage or perhaps even entering, an imminent massacre which pleads with the audience to prevent it, in the confrontational style now described as Brechtian but not inconsistent with Greek drama.

Shelley followed the simplicity of *The Persians* in *Hellas* which, alone among his plays, keeps strictly to the unities of time, place and action. He does not artificially force his material into these unities: it does not dislocate belief to have all the action taking place in the seraglio, thus keeping to a unity of place. The action is Mahmud's realisation and acceptance that his empire, like all others, is coming to its end, thus the speeches reporting the battles and the ghostly appearance of Mahomet II allow Shelley to use the unity of time without distorting events by huge flashback explanations. This does not contradict his opinion that neo-classical drama was 'the wrong road', for he does not employ this rule unvaryingly throughout his drama. It appears appropriate in *Hellas* where he is following Aeschylus rather than Racine, Dryden or Alfieri. He made certain modifications which fulfil the requirements of contemporary performance practice without losing the spirit of Greek drama. For the Greeks, the drama festivals were religious occasions and Shelley restores this aspect which 'has indeed been usually banished from the stage', in accordance with his ideas expressed in *A Defence of Poetry*, with a philosophy rather than religion.[675]

Although Kitto stresses the religious aspect of *The Persians*, saying that 'Xerxes was to be smitten by heaven because he had committed hybris', Seth G. Bernadete places more importance on the fight for freedom.[676] But religion and patriotism were inevitably intertwined in *The Persians*, as they were for the Greeks, since a certain god or goddess protected a particular city. For example, the Chorus says, 'the gods saved the city/Of the goddess', Pallas Athene (347-348). When Xerxes commits hybris by arrogating to himself the power of a god, he is defeated by the gods, while the enforced Persian army is defeated by the Greek army of free, democratic citizens. Shelley enlarges on the aspects which refer to hybris and the inevitability of the end of empire, and develops the references to Greek courage and the desire to be free. Indeed, the seraglio in *Hellas* is a graphic visual symbol of the Chorus's lack of liberty and their triple oppression as a subject

674 Walker, 'The Urn of Bitter Prophecy', p. 36.
675 *PBSLII*, p. 349; *SPP*, p. 518.
676 Kitto, p. 38; Seth G. Bernadete, Introduction to *The Persians*, pp. 44-46.

race, as slaves and as women. But as he could not expect his audience to share a common religion, as the audience in Athens in 492 BC would have done, the Christianity expressed by the Chorus is made vague enough to be acceptable to groups of differing Christian faith, and does not identify them with the Greek Orthodox church. As a result, the 'religion' in *Hellas* is not Christianity but a philosophical and moral point of view which, when Mahmud is made aware of it, reveals to him his own temporality and frailty and that of his empire.

In *The Persians*, the Queen performs a sacrifice to raise the ghost of Darius. The equivalent action in *Hellas* is Mahmud's request to see Ahasuerus whom he believes to be an immortal, oracular being. Unlike the Queen, who asks advice of her Chorus, Mahmud has no interest in humans; a shout 'bodes/Evil doubtless like all human sounds/Let me converse with spirits' (186/187). In contrast, the following chorus, 'Worlds on worlds are rolling ever' (196-238) glorifies humanity. Ahasuerus, who is the symbol of the continuity of thought, 'The Present, and the Past, and the To-come' (148), induces Mahmud to realise that empires and the whole material universe are temporary whereas thought is permanent, thus foreshadowing the words of the final chorus. Mahmud's dialogue with Ahasuerus allows him, through the suggestion that Mahmud can foretell the future by considering the past, to imagine a dialogue with the ghost of his ancestor, Mahomet II, at the fall of Constantinople, thereby realising what his own place in history is to be.

> Mahomet II, like Darius, is unwilling to return, saying:
> the grave is fitter
> To take the living than give up the dead (*Hellas*, 862-863)

He echoes Darius's words:

> Ascent is not easy
> The chthonic deities more readily
> Receive than give. (*The Persians*, 688-690)

Darius is 'a potentate' among the deities (*The Persians*, 690-1); Mahomet II speaks of reigning over the ruins of his former empire in the world of death (*Hellas*, 887-888). He tells Mahmud:

> The Anarchs of the world of darkness keep
> A throne for thee   (*Hellas*, 879-880)

As Darius explains, Xerxes only hastens an inevitable end so, in *Hellas*:

> The moon of Mahomet
> Arose, and it shall set. (*Hellas*, 221-222)

Like Darius, Mahomet warns of the end of empire and the impermanence of fame and dominion. Ahasuerus tells Mahmud that Mahomet is 'the ghost of thy forgotten dream' and, despite Hassan's suggestion (149-151), says he himself is not the Wandering Jew but 'no more' than a man (739). The ghost of Mahomet II creates a second *coup de théâtre* when, rather than 'entering' and 'exiting', it 'appears' and 'vanishes', suggesting the technique of placing ghosts behind a gauze and a lighting change possible with gas. Shelley makes use of the theatricality of the supernatural in *Hellas*, while insisting that the drama is free from superstition. This accords with the view that his decision to discard the Prologue with its deities was because it might suggest that the Greeks would owe their victory to their faith rather than their 'will to win'.

Mahmud learns compassion and acceptance of his fate from the philosophy of Ahasuerus. He is not in accord with the mood of his subjects at the end of the play when he hears a shout of victory and decides to 'rebuke/This drunkeness of triumph' (928-929). The word 'drunkeness' is a reminder that when a 'drunken crew' had wearied him earlier, he had capriciously ordered a beheading in the style of the historical Xerxes. Now he comments, 'poor slaves'. Despite this maturing sympathy, Shelley is still critical of Mahmud, since, like Xerxes, he is a tyrant. As Bernadete emphasises, Aeschylus shows sympathy for the Persians,[677] but although he shows the Queen as dignified and pities the elders and the men killed in battle, he portrays Xerxes as foolish, greedy and sacrilegious. The Chorus mourns for the dead, but only the Queen begs for the dishonoured Xerxes to be allowed to remain ruler. Mahmud's lines 'tomorrow and tomorrow are as lamps' (649) are reminiscent of *Macbeth* (V. v. 19-23). Had *Hellas* reached the stage, this may have gained audience sympathy, as Wallace suggests, but it would also have helped the audience to see that Mahmud's tyranny, like Macbeth's, is finite, unsustainable and is destroying him (*Macbeth*, III. iv. 41).[678] An audience of Shelley's period might well have reacted vociferously to Mahmud's tyranny, while also sympathising with his later mood. In this they would have resembled the Greek audience who 'wept openly, they applauded, hissed, booed, ate noisily, banged the wooden benches with their heels, threw food at the actors'.[679]

Aeschylus deliberately adapted facts to make the story more accessible

---

677 Bernadete, *The Persians*, p. 44.
678 Wallace, *Shelley and Greece*, p. 203.
679 Paul Cartledge, 'The Greek Religious Festivals' in *Greek Religion and Society*, ed. by P.E. Easterling and J.V. Muir (Cambridge: Cambridge University Press, 1985), p. 127.

to his audience. Detailed accurate information was less important than the essence of what he had to say. Both Kitto and Bernadete point out that the religious sacrifice performed by the Queen in *The Persians* is Greek and that historical references were changed, exaggerated or wrong. Bernadete suggests that this was done to remove the Persian war into the realm of myth: the detail necessary to present a contemporary account being unpoetic. With Shelley, it may have been simply that he was unable to make his account accurate as he was unsure of the truth of his reports.[680] A naval victory and reports of bravery on the battlefield he was sure of,[681] and he may have realised that Aeschylus used no more.

Tommaso Sgricci

Whether or not Shelley had seen Greek drama performed in England, in Italy he saw a version performed by the *improvvisatore*, Sgricci. Shelley's interest in the art of the *improvvisatori* was aroused before his arrival in Italy by a letter from Byron with a 'curious account [...] of the Improvisators and the Curiosities of Milan'.[682] This letter has not survived, but Byron wrote on 6 November 1816 to Thomas Moore that Sgricci's 'fluency astonished me. A few very commonplace mythological images, and one line about Artemisia, and another about Aegius, with sixty words of an entire tragedy about Eteocles and Polynices'.[683] Byron is said to have been 'sceptical' about the *improvvisatori*, saying, 'There is a great deal of knack in these gentry; their poetry is more mechanical than you suppose'.[684] He was presumably referring to their use of stock images, verses and lines, although this was part of their skill. Their subjects, and often the 'rhyme and measure' were chosen for them by the audience, sometimes including a *verso obbligato*, lines which they had to introduce at the end of a stanza. Eaton describes *improvvisatori* as having a 'wonderful talent [...] it is sort of inspiration, or poetic fervour that carries them on'. Their verses are sometimes 'very bad; but they are occasionally wonderfully pretty [...] they have similes and thoughts ready prepared; they are versed in all the commonplace of

---

680   Kitto, pp. 36-37; Bernadete, *The Persians*, p. 45.
681   *SPP*, p. 431.
682   *PBSLI*, p. 514.
683   *BLJV*, pp. 125, 125n.
684   Thomas Medwin, *Conversations of Lord Byron* (London: Henry Colburn, 1824), p. 165.

poetry [...] By far the most interesting performance of the kind is when two sing together, or rather against each other, in alternate stanzas'.[685] Her description is confirmed by a recent eyewitness in Sardinia where the art has recently revived, although it had almost died out. *Cantadori* perform at festivals today, improvising and competing for hours on such themes as 'Hector and Achilles'.[686] It is particularly interesting that this theme is still popular, since it was one chosen for a performance by Sgricci which the Shelleys saw and which Shelley reviewed.

Sgricci's performances were quite unlike those of the *improvvisatori* just described, as he did not use rhyme or music as an aid. Described as a 'shy pretty little man' and 'a sorcerer', dressed in the Byronic style, he was admired for the 'purity of his expression'. He performed on a very simple stage, set with only a chair to which he crossed when he required to change character. He was accompanied by a small boy with an urn containing slips on which the audience could write what they wanted him to improvise.[687] Clairmont described his performance as 'wonderfully fine [...] it seemed not the work of a human mind, but as if he were the instrument [...] of a God; the expression was so strong and fresh, a feature which belongs peculiarly to the art of the Improvisare'.[688] Eaton said he was the only *improvvisatore* who 'attempted tragedy' and was 'most calm in his action — the most free from all those violent contortions or distortions which, whether the effect of natural agitation or affected passion, are peculiarly unpleasant to witness'. She saw him perform *Medea*, with a friend who had heard him perform it before. Sgricci this time introduced two new characters, began the action in a different part of the story and did not repeat 'a single scene nor even speech'.[689] Sgricci could:

> compose entire extempore tragedies, on any given subject, with all the plots, incidents, and dramatis personae, — repeat all the parts himself, and bring the whole to a regular denouement [...] no words can do justice to the perfect ease, the energy, and unhesitating flow of verse.[690]

---

685 Eaton, III, pp. 262-263.
686 Professor Irene Meloni, Facolta di Lingue e Letterature Straniere dell'Università di Cagliari, private communication. On my visit to Sardinia (August 2009), I was unable to see the cantadori but I did hear a folksinger whose chant is similar, according to Professor Meloni.
687 Angela Esterhammer, *Romanticism at the Improvvisatore: Tommaso Sgricci and the Spectacle of Improvisation*, paper given at Romantic Spectacle conference, 8 July 2006.
688 *CCJ*, p. 198.
689 Eaton, III, p. 261-263.
690 Ibid., p. 261.

She thought it 'might have done honour to a drama deliberately finished off in the closet'.[691] Shelley's review also compared it favourably to written dramas:

> The envious perhaps will say that if it were written down, a tragedy produced in this way would display many artistic imperfections which are not noticed in the recital.— But among these who is there who has produced, even with the labour and sweat of a year, a tragedy in which there would not be a crowd of errors, a thousand faults to be forgiven?[692]

Remarking on Sgricci's 'tone of [...] voice, his countenance', Shelley called his performance 'a marvellous exhibition of the power of the human mind' and said that 'the most splendid poetry was united with passion of unexampled tremendousness'.[693]

> Troy resounds with the cry of victory, — in [contrast?] with which, Cassandra rapt by the spirit of prophecy predicting the death of the victor. The effect of this scene was astounding and highly dramatic, and the contrast between the exultant joy of the city and the terrible sorrow of the maddened prophetess, the despairing sister who already sees her own brother and the support of her country staggering beneath the sword of Achilles and dragged around the walls, which the poet depicts in words and gestures, while the very theatre was transformed to that which he was representing, was in the highest style of tragic poetry and electrified the theatre. — from that point onwards the drama continued on its way ever upwards.[694]

Shelley follows this by describing Sgricci's portrayal of Achilles whose 'hatred shines through and bursts out in the most terrible threats', Hector taking his leave of Andromache and his son 'a scene full of tenderness', Paris who, 'bringing the fatal news that Hector is dead', 'depicts, in words whose terror and sorrow made one tremble, the outrage done to the body', and 'the mingled grief of the wife and the mother, the empty consolations, the broken cries [...] dark and sublime distress'.[695] It is clear that Sgricci created these characters in his performance, and Shelley's remarks bear witness to the brilliance of his interpretation. What is more, it showed him that a form of Greek tragedy was still effective, relevant and popular.

Mary Shelley said that in seeing Sgricci's *Inez de Castro* 'when Pietro unveiled the dead Ignez, when Sancho died in despair on her body, it seemed to me as if it were all there; so truly & passionately did his words

691 Eaton, III, p. 261.
692 Shelley's review translated in Dawson, 'Shelley and the Improvvisatore', p. 29.
693 Idem, pp. 27, 28.
694 Ibid., p. 28.
695 Idem.

16. 'Eastern Palace' (watercolour), set design undated. Grieve Family Collection.
Courtesy of Senate House Library, University of London, MS1007/349.

depict the scene he wished to represent'. Like Eaton, Mary believed Sgricci completely original in his performance. As Sgricci visited the Shelleys at least a dozen times, there was opportunity for discussing his art with them both. To Mary Shelley, Sgricci mentioned his inspiration at Cassandra's prophecy and that 'Apollo had also touched his lips with the oracular touch.'.[696] This suggests that Shelley remembered this conversation when writing his review since he comments that 'it was rather a God who spoke in him, and created the ideas more rapidly than the human reason could ever have combined them', adding that in Sgricci's *Hector*, 'the choruses by which the tragedy was divided were without rival in their kind'.[697] Shelley used a similar division by choruses in *Hellas*, and it is probable that the character of Ahasuerus owed something to Sgricci's air of having been divinely inspired. Shelley was aware, however, that performers such as Kean could also achieve this effect.

Sgricci was said to be at least sympathetic to the revolutionary Carbonari and both Mary Shelley and Claire Clairmont saw him on an occasion when 'Sgricci improvisava upon the future independance of Italy'.[698] Mary Shelley

696 *MWSJ*, pp. 341-344, 348-350; *MWSLI*, pp. 176, 182.
697 Dawson, 'Shelley and the Improvvisatore', p. 28.
698 *CCJ*, p. 190.

said, 'He recalled that Petrarch said that neither the very high Alps nor the sea was enough to defend this unsteady and aged country from the foreign masters — But he says — I see the Alps grow — and the sea rise and become agitated in order to impede the enemies'.[699] Shelley's reference to *Hellas* as 'a mere improvise' perhaps should be interpreted as being similar to this, a poem on the future independence of an occupied country, optimistic and inspirational but not precise, such as Adam Mickiewicz's *Improwizacja* (1832), a poem performed in Poland for similar reasons in 1979.[700]

The Bride of Abydos

One of the more important, though hitherto unrecognised, influences on *Hellas* was the melodrama set in modern Turkish Greece, *The Bride of Abydos* (1818), adapted from poems of Byron by William Dimond, which Shelley saw at Drury Lane (23 February 1818).[701] Plays, melodramas and operas with Turkish settings had been performed in Western Europe since at least the mid-eighteenth century, among them Mozart's *Die Entführung aus dem Serail (Flight from the Seraglio)* and Inchbald's *A Mogul's Tale*. Dimond's other plays included *Abon Hassan*, 'derived […] from the Arabian nights', and *Aethiop, or the Child of the Desert*. Presumably, the Shelleys were curious to see *The Bride of Abydos* because of Byron's poem. Dimond did use passages from this, but explained in his preface that the 'characters and events […] were not sufficiently numerous and busy, to supply the material of a stage representation continuing for three hours'. Moreover, he added, 'the catastrophe of the Poem so magnificent in its melancholy — so appalling in its horror was altogether unfitted for a dramatick purpose. An incident from *The Corsair* was made the substitute'. It was, therefore, *The Bride of Abydos* with a happy ending and 'interpolations of the Dramatist'.[702]

Shelley's remarks about Viganò's *Otello* show that he appreciated that stage adaptation need not be literal; the Shelleys may have enjoyed *The Bride of Abydos* for its own sake. It certainly had a distinguished cast including Alexander Pope, Henry Johnston and Mrs. Bland, all popular stars, with Kean as Selim, T.P. Cooke as Osman Bey and the beautiful Mrs. Mardyn as

699 *MWSLI*, p. 165.
700 Seen by me, October 1979.
701 *MWSJ*, p. 194.
702 William Dimond, Preface to *The Bride of Abydos* (London: Richard White, 1818), p. 1.

17. 'View out to sea through colonnade' (watercolour), set design
undated. Grieve Family Collection. Courtesy of Senate House Library,
University of London, MS1007/398.

Zuleika. The scenery by Greenwood was attention-catching and the music
was by Michael Kelly. The eight songs included a 'Duett', a 'Bass solo' and
a 'Glee', with an opening chorus. Each scene ended with a song and, in II.
ii, the song carried the action. There were also dances. Miss Tree led 'the
Almas or Dancing girls of the East'.[703]

There are striking similarities between *Hellas* and *The Bride of Abydos*.
Act II of *The Bride of Abydos* opens in 'a quadrangle of the Haram with a
fountain in centre'. *Hellas* is set 'on a Terrace of the Seraglio', the part of the
Sultan's palace in which the harem was situated. An 1821 audience would
have been unfamiliar with a Greek chorus but they were accustomed to
women dancing and singing in comic opera or melodrama. Shelley's Chorus
of Greek slavegirls, like the 'Almas' in *The Bride of Abydos*, might realistically
be supposed to dance and sing in their official capacity of ministering to
the Sultan. In *The Bride of Abydos* 'female slaves advance joyously some
with musical instruments, others employ themselves in disposing stands
of flowers' (II. ii). Just as Dimond includes 'an Indian maid', Shelley's

---

703   *The Bride of Abydos*, pp. 9, 15, 26, 27, 38, 43, 49, 65.

Mahmud has 'an Indian slave sitting beside his couch'.[704]

Dimond's play makes great use of both sunrise and sunset, no doubt capitalising on the possibilities offered by the introduction of the new gas lighting. Dimond's opening scene has a boat with 'Dawn breaking' and a 'Song (Quartette)' followed by a 'Song chorus', 'the crew betaken themselves to the various morning labours of a seaman's life; climbing the masts and repairing the rigging, &c. &c.'. Dawn 'becomes perfect, and the action of the characters general when the scene closes' and 'sunset fires the west'. In III. v, there is a 'lattice' revealing the sky and the sunset, while IV. iv is set in a 'cave beneath the haram, the Hellespont flows beyond the last of the arched rocks of which it is composed and the tide washes into the centre of the scene. The red glow of departing sunset streaks both sky and wave at the extremity of the perspective'.

In *Hellas*, from its terrace setting, the sun can also be seen at the symbolic time of sunset, recalled when Mahmud directs Hassan to look at the moon (337-348) and at the end of the play when 'the weak day is dead' (1034). Had *Hellas* been performed, the theatre lighting effect would have been used in three ways: as a romantic setting which changes throughout the play; as a visible reminder of time passing which also shows that the unity of time is being adhered to; and metaphorically, to show that the Ottoman Empire was declining. The themes of liberty and end of empire are thus inherent in the staging and casting of *Hellas*.

The Bride of Abydos appears influential in other ways, too, perhaps the most important being in IV. iv, when the trusty Hassan takes Selim — who believes himself to be the illegitimate son of Giaffier, the cruel ruler — to meet Mirza the Pirate Chief.

> Hassan: Youth! now the volume of thy fate unfolds
> And he who reads the past and future, greets thee.
>
> *Mirza slowly emerges form an inner cell, and pausing upon an elevation of the ground stage, gazes intensely upon Selim.*
>
> Hassan: Hail! Lov'd and honour'd! Tis the prosperous hour,
> Sunset and Selim meet thy search together.
>
> *Mirza continues his steadfast gaze. Selim as sway'd by involuntary feelings sinks on his knees beneath the penetrating gaze of Mirza.*
>
> [...]
> Selim: Methinks a prophet rises from the rock,
> Inspired and swelling with eternal will.

---

704 *The Bride of Abydos*, pp. 28, 31; *SPP*, p. 433.

18. T.P. Cooke, toy theatre illustration, c. 1829, unknown artist, private collection.

Mirza's gaze causes Selim to faint. He finds out that Mirza, supposedly murdered by Giaffier, is really his father and the rightful ruler. At this point 'Mirza winds a horn. The blast repeated by small echoes dies away down the distant caverns; suddenly a groupe of Pirate forms protudes from each aperture of the surrounding rock'.[705]

Ahasuerus also has a hypnotic gaze, is believed to know the past and

---

705 *The Bride of Abydos*, IV. iv, pp. 44-48.

future, dwells in just such a cave and can only be questioned by someone willing to 'sail alone at sunset' (*Hellas*, 166) calling 'Ahasuerus' (173) when 'the caverns round/will answer' (175) by echoing the name. Although the powers of Ahasuerus are those of thought rather than of physical power, the resemblances are striking enough to indicate that the melodrama was recalled by Shelley in his own drama. It is possible, also, to read *Hellas* metaphorically; the caverns have a function as the mind and thought of Mahmud, with the Chorus, Hassan and messengers representing his fears and worse actions, and Ahasuerus and Mahomet his better thoughts.

Characters

An awareness that a contemporary audience would expect a greater degree of characterisation than in Aeschylus can be seen in *Hellas*. Mahmud's character, with its foreboding premonitions, sudden rages and exhibitions of power and eventual acceptance of possible defeat, is the only one which has been discussed by critics.[706] Yet an effective play cannot depend upon only one interesting character and Shelley wrote good parts for other actors. In the dialogue between Mahmud and Hassan (260-527), Mahmud is not only a despotic tyrant, but one in the process of change, a character with doubts and fears. In response to this, Shelley develops the character of his servant, Hassan, to take on a protective though still deferential role, persuading his master that he is still strong with his reports of armies and battles. Mahmud's premonition of defeat, and his subsequent doubts and fears, are initially countered by Hassan, who stresses the unassailability of the Ottoman Empire with its 10,000 cannon, full arsenals and armouries and powerful allies. Hassan has a double function for, to comfort the Sultan, he must show pride in Turkish strength but, if he is to report a Turkish victory accurately, he must include the very defiance which shows the spirit of the Greeks and thus reinforces his own 'idiot fear' (357). Mahmud's belief that:

> The spirit that lifts the slave before his lord
> Stalks through the capitals of armed kings (351-352)

accords with Shelley's own belief that 'circumstances make men what they are'.[707] The conflict in this scene is not only between Mahmud and Hassan, but within Hassan himself, servant as he is, torn between loyalty to his

---

706 For example, *BSMXVI*, pp. xlii-xlv.
707 *SPP*, p. 463.

19. 'Sea Battle and sailing ships' (watercolour), , set design undated Grieve Family Collection. Courtesy of Senate House Library, University of London, MS1007/350.

Sultan and Empire and admiration for the Greek spirit which would enable him to gain freedom himself. Mahmud's leadership is undermined by his lack of confidence and the necessity for his lieutenant to put courage into him but Hassan is no mere vehicle for an argument, just as Mahmud is no stereotypical Oriental tyrant.

Shelley wished to suggest that the struggle of the Greeks against the Ottoman Empire was the 19th century counterpart of the defence of Greece against the Persians celebrated by Aeschylus' play and that it would be victorious if inspired with the same spirit of liberty. 'The spirit' has already shown itself on the battlefields where the Turks were victors and the Greeks preferred death to slavery, and the image is actually personified when a dying man is compared to:

> a corpse which some dread spirit
> Of the old saviours of the land we rule
> Had lifted in its anger, wandering by…   (406-407)

It is repeated in the phrase the dying man uses, 'the crushed worm rebels beneath your tread' (425). The tyrant is associated with blood, vultures and dogs while the soldier calls on 'Famine, Pestilence and Panic'. This reported scene is reminiscent of the fragment on Bonaparte discussed in Chapter 4, a voice from among the dead on the battlefield. 'The spirit' enters Hassan himself, who says it 'wrenched me within' (456). His words betray his devotion to Mahmud just as the Indian slave betrays hers by the imagery she uses. The revelation is a shock for Hassan himself as well as for Mahmud, a dramatic revelation in the play and a significant dramatic turning point, particularly when it is followed by Mahmud's insistence that Hassan should 'outlive/Me and this sinking Empire' (458-459). By dramatising such a spirit among the Greeks and such demoralisation among the Turks, *Hellas* reinforces the idea that the Greeks might win their liberty because of this spirit.

Hassan's reports of battles have within them many changes of mood: anticipation, tension, exhilaration, relief and a sudden change to grief. Shelley turns a theoretical disadvantage in his play, a messenger with mere reports to deliver, into an arresting character which gives the scene human interest and dramatic potential. The delivery of the speeches from a forestage was more exciting since the actor was more immediately in contact with the audience. Plays on naval themes were very popular, suggesting Hassan's speech on the sea battle would have met with success had it been performed, particularly by such an actor as T.P. Cooke, whom Shelley had seen in *The Bride of Abydos.*

Cooke's popularity was 'wonderful' and his playing of sailors particularly true to life.[708] 'He was known and idolized for his nautical parts which he performed by the dozen', all the more effectively since he 'really had been in the Navy, gone through a battle and been shipwrecked.'[709]

The speeches lead into the scene with the messengers. The flight of the Russian Ambassador, showing lack of confidence in the Turks, the Greek victories, the revolts in other parts of the Ottoman Empire and finally the defeat at sea are disasters which accord with Mahmud's own premonitions. The superstitious element is emphasised by the omens in the third messenger's speech. Shelley has given each messenger a speech interesting in itself, and sufficiently different from the preceding one for a certain amount of individual characterisation to be possible.

The final speech on the defeat at sea is interrupted by the announcement of Ahasuerus. Mahmud says the shouts of Victory have broken his 'mighty trance', and Shelley, who had himself undergone 'animal magnetism' performed by Medwin,[710] intended Ahasuerus to possess hypnotic powers,

708 Harold J. Nichols, 'The Acting of Thomas Potter Cooke', *Nineteenth-Century Theatre Research*, 5.2 (Autumn 1977) <http://www.english.upenn.edu/Projects/knarf/Articles/nichols.html> [accessed 10 January 2007] (paras 2, 25).
709 Booth, *English Melodrama*, p. 108.
710 *MWSJ*, pp. 342, 342n.-343n.

noting that he was:

> tempting Mahmud to that state of mind in which ideas may be supposed
> to assume the force of sensations through the confusion of thought with
> the objects of thought, and the excess of passion animating the creations
> of imagination. It is a sort of natural magic, susceptible of being exercised
> in a degree by anyone who should have made himself master of the secret
> associations of another's thoughts.[711]

Ahasuerus echoes lines 351-352, 406-407 and 425 when he tells Mahmud
that he does not disdain 'the worm beneath thy feet'. Mahmud disdains the
Greeks as infidels and rebels, but he also fears their rebellion as being the
end of his empire, an end suggested in the first chorus (54-85) where a first
liberation inspires others. In his scene with Ahasuerus Mahmud traces his
own history, a parallel to the Greeks' tracing of theirs in the choruses.

Performance

The apparent influence of techniques from three sources, all of which were
successful on stage, suggests that Shelley intended *Hellas* to be performable,
but he could not have submitted it to a London theatre. Censorship would
have prevented its performance at Covent Garden or Drury Lane, and if,
as Williams thought, the philosophy appeared too difficult, it might not
have been considered suitable at a minor theatre, although the music and
dancing would have enabled it to be described as a burletta. It might have
been suitable for a private theatre such as the West London, but this did not
stage *Oedipus Tyrannus* until November 1821. The fashion for performing
Greek drama increased later in the decade, so Shelley was in accord with his
time, if slightly ahead of actual London theatre practice. Shelley shows skill
in characterisation and was certainly aware of the enhancement brought
to poetic choruses by sympathetic dancing and music, and that scenery
and lighting would form a graceful and metaphorical background to both
chorus and dialogue.[712]

In 1976, the distinguished actor, Paul Daneman, played Mahmud in a
radio performance of *Hellas*.[713] This version confirmed the success of many

---

711   *SPP*, p. 463.
712   Hall & Macintosh, *Greek Tragedy*, p. 241.
713   'Shelley's Hellas ', ed. by Judith Chernaik, with original music by David Cain, produced and directed by John Theocharis, trans. BBC Radio 3, 13 June 1976, 1810-1915.

of Shelley's dramatic techniques since the scene with the messengers did build to a climax, Ahasuerus seemed both hypnotic and wise and the ghost, created with an echo, was effective. The verse was excellently sung and spoken, Daneman's delivery being particularly moving, showing that the sung choruses could be easily understood and that the philosophical argument was clear when spoken. The accompanying music, with Greek and Oriental influences, was atmospheric, rhythmic and sometimes exciting, although three verses of Shelley's famous and beautiful final chorus were inexplicably cut and the setting, although pretty and melodious, did not do it justice.

As a whole, very little was cut, but the alterations shifted the play towards a mystical interpretation which Shelley had taken pains to deny. It opened with verses from the Prologue, 'The curtain of the Universe/Is rent and shattered', followed immediately by the chorus beginning 'In the great morning of the world' (46). Shelley opens with the physical, concrete and sexual image of Greek women dancing and singing with one woman sitting by Mahmud's couch. In a stage presentation, the audience would be constantly aware of the potentially subversive presence of this Chorus. In the radio version, partly because voices on radio are of necessity disembodied, they sounded more like supernatural beings. Mahmud's character was softened by cutting his most bloodthirsty lines (193, 241-249). A Narrator described him as 'long a secret admirer of Western liberalism', although Shelley does not. Hassan's 'Yet would I die for —'(458) was completed by 'Islam'. This introduction of religion emphasised the mystical aspect which contradicts even Shelley's original intention, since the ms. has 'for Islam & for thee'. The final text shows that he preferred to leave the reader, or audience, guessing.[714]

The addition of a Narrator was not only contrary to Shelley's dislike of footnotes in poetry but also increased the number of male voices.[715] There were female voices but, as the main speakers are male and many of the choruses were allotted to men, a uniformity was produced which Shelley's all-female Chorus counteracts. This was, nevertheless, a beautiful interpretation which served to show how much more effective a staging would be, with the visual additions of the *coups de théâtre*, the scenery and the dancing of the Chorus.

Hellas and *Prometheus Unbound* were based on Greek dramatic models

---

714 *BSMXVI*, p. 81; *SPP*, p. 445.
715 *PBSLII*, p. 184.

which were known to have been performed, incorporating elements drawn from theatre of Shelley's time. The very fact that they are great poetry can act as a barrier to seeing them as stage plays of which songs and dances are an integral part, yet it is possible to set great poetry to music without losing the literary effect. Just as the expectation of a ballet is not the same as that of a prose play, so a drama which is a combination of the arts should not be judged by criteria relating to a different single genre. In performance, the way in which music and dance interact with poetry are critical factors. Shelley appears to have planned this interaction of myth, music, poetry, dance and spectacular effects in a play he began to write for his own circle in 1822, but with a bold addition. This was a re-telling of a story which one of his performers had told of himself and a setting in India which made use of the genuine background of two of the others.

The Fragments of an Unfinished Drama

These 'fragments' were 'part of a Drama undertaken for the amusement of the individuals who composed our intimate society', a private performance or reading as Crook and Webb suggest. If a performance was considered, because of so many other events that spring, it was never carried out. Crook and Webb suggest the evidence of Shelley's notebook points to the *Fragments* having been written in April, but they also consider it not unlikely that the idea was conceived as early as February when, with the Carnival in full swing, Byron suggested performing *Othello*.[716] The second suggestion seems more probable. The Shelleys and Williamses were seriously househunting for the summer in April, and were shortly to move to Lerici; it appears too late to begin writing something for their Pisan entertainment. On the other hand, Byron dropped the idea of *Othello* on 28 February which may have encouraged Shelley to begin writing the drama partly to compensate Trelawny, who was to have played Othello, for the loss of this part. As Crook and Webb have shown, there were connections with the *Fragments* and the stories of Trelawny's life with which he had been captivating the Pisan circle, so the part of the Pirate would have allowed him to shine in a role tailor-made for him.[717] As *Othello* was intended to have been performed, so it seems that would have been the case with the

---

716   *OSA*, p. 482; *BSMXIX*, pp. xlix-1i.
717   *BSMXIX*, pp. lxxx, l-li.

Fragments, particularly as Shelley could call on the musical talents of Jane Williams and the artistic talents of Edward Williams to paint the scenery. Shelley characteristically demanded a spectacular entrance for the Spirit, accompanied by 'earthquake and lightning'. Nevertheless, these can be simply managed by shaking the scenery for the first and using a piece of tin for the second.

Shelley probably took part in amateur dramatics as a young man as Byron had done, and as his cousins, the Groves, did. Most amateur theatres then, as now, attempted performances of popular plays. Richard Cumberland, author of *The West Indian* and *The Wheel of Fortune*, and 'one of the very few constructive critics' of the amateurs, considered that they would do better to have plays specially written for them by writers who knew them and their locale, in order to capitalise on their strengths.[718] The belief that it is best to write for or improvise with amateur actors parts which have characteristics associated with their own is endorsed by professionals who work with them today, since amateurs, however, talented, often do not have the training or experience to create a character different from their own. Whether or not Shelley knew this advice, his practice in the *Fragments* accords with it.

There appear to be suitable parts in the *Fragments of an Unfinished Drama* for the members of the Shelley circle. The part of the Pirate was suited to Trelawny with his dark 'half-Arab' looks and tales of 'blood and horror' and a Spirit would have concurred with his friends' perception of Shelley.[719] There are actually two spirits: 'a good Spirit who watches over the Pirate's fate' and 'leads, in a mysterious manner, the lady of his love to the Enchanted Isle'; and the spirit who brews the tempest for the Enchantress.[720] It is possible that Shelley intended both parts for himself, and that they were not to be on stage together, but the 'good Spirit' might have been invisible, its presence created by music and sounds behind the scenery. This would leave the part of the Youth for Williams, with his agreeable nature and pleasant looks. This casting nearly coincides with that of Matthews, but his suggestion of Jane Williams as the Lady and Mary Shelley as the Enchantress appears quite out of accord with the known talents of these women and the parts as they stand.[721] Jane was noted for her

718 *BLJIX*, p. 37; *SCII*, pp. 568, 597; Richard Cumberland, 'Remarks upon the Present Taste for Acting Private Plays', qtd in Rosenfeld, 'Jane Austen', p. 45.
719 *MWSLI*, p. 218; Wolfe, II, p. 172.
720 *OSA*, pp. 482-483.
721 G.M. Matthews, 'Shelley's Lyrics' in *Shelley's Poetry and Prose*, ed. by Donald H.

beauty and musical talents, particularly her ability to play atmospherical Indian melodies. She also had a skill in 'magnetism', the fashionable treatment for ailments.[722] The fascinating Enchantress, who casts spells and sings and perhaps has hypnotic qualities, appears to have been intended for her, while Mary's good memory and 'grace in reading' were strengths more suitable for the speaking part of the Lady, with its long speeches.[723]

A number of scholars have mentioned the attraction that Indian culture had for Shelley. Tilar J. Mazzeo believes that Shelley heard music of this kind before his meeting with Jane Williams, possibly as early as 1804, since it was fashionable for English women to play it, dressed in Indian clothes. Although Sir William Jones had carefully distinguished Hindu music from that of the Moghul court in general, Anglo-Indians did not make any distinction and actually described as 'Indian or Hindustani airs' the love lyrics sung by the Nautch dancers at the Moghul court.[724] This is the case with the one song we are certain that Jane Williams knew, *Tazee be tazee no be no*, although she knew a number of others.[725]

Curran believes Shelley was familiar with 'eastern tonalities and versification' and describes the *Fragments* as 'an attempt to adapt the perfumed, fantastic, and amorous atmosphere of the *Sakuntala* of Kalidasa'.[726] Elements of *Sacontala* are prominent in *Prometheus Unbound* and there are instances in the *Fragments* which resemble not just the style, but the story. King Dushmanta forgets his beloved wife, Sacontala, because he is enchanted by a holy man who felt she had neglected her duty. Sacontala is disconsolate, as is Dushmanta once her memory has been recalled by means of a magic ring. The Pirate 'recalling the memory of her whom he left and who laments his loss, escapes from the Enchanted Island and returns to his lady'.[727] The Indian Youth and Lady may have had a similar memory loss, or the 'mutual *déjà vu*' suggested by Crook and Webb.

Reiman and Sharon B. Powers (New York: Norton, 1977), p. 691.

722   *MWSJ*, p. 342, 342n.

723   *PBSLII*, p. 34.

724   Stuart Curran, *Annus Mirabilis*, p. xvii; Tilar J. Mazzeo, 'The Strains of Empire, Shelley and the Music of India' in *Romantic Representations of British India*, ed. by Michael J. Franklin (London: Routledge, 2006), pp. 181, 184; Bennett Zon, '"From very acute and plausible" to "curiously misinterpreted"/ Sir William Jones's "On the Musical Modes of the Hindus" (1792) and its reception in later musical treatises', in *Romantic Representations*, pp. 200-201.

725   *BSMXIX*, p. 329; *MWSLI*, p. 374.

726   Curran, *Annus Mirabilis*, p. 213; Curran, 'Shelleyan Drama' in *The Romantic Theatre*, p. 65.

727   *BSMXIX*, p. xlix.

The lady tends plants, as it was Sacontala's religious duty to do.[728]

It is supposed that a number of songs were to form part of this play: the Enchantress's invocation 'He came like a dream at the dawn of life' was definitely one; Matthews proposed that 'One Word is Too Often Profaned' as another, to have been inserted in the scene between the Youth and the Lady.[729] Although Jane Williams was the most proficient musician among the group, Edward could also sing. In this context, however, the song would amount to an emotional turning-point in which the Youth sings a formal renunciation of his claims on the Lady except as an unobtainable object of worship, whereas in the existing scene he still seems to cherish some hope of her love, so there is no part of the dialogue which would naturally lead to the song. Shelley integrated songs into the context, although other writers of the period did not, as can be seen from the songs in Dibdin's *The Cabinet*.[730] The poem may, however, have been intended as a song for another part of the play.

Mary Shelley has sketched part of the story which Shelley planned, but not its final resolution or its significance. A magical or supernatural element is clear; there is an Enchantress, Spirits, spectacular stage effects and a magic plant. There is also a suggestion of the events being a dream in the Lady's mind, 'If I be sure I were not dreaming now/I should not doubt to say it were a dream'. The Spirit has its mansion 'within the silent centre of the earth' and may be the Spirit of the Earth as in *Prometheus Unbound* or perhaps the Spirit of Love, since that word is crossed through before the word 'Spirit'.[731] The references to Indian mythology suggested by the setting may have had greater significance. Perhaps the Pirate, who does 'the tasks of Ruin', is connected to the God Shiva, and the theme of the play is to suggest that that which destroys also preserves, as in *The Ode to the West Wind*.

How far the Hutchinson edition is corrupt may be seen by comparing it with Crook and Webb's transcription. Since the drama was unfinished, there are missing sections and different versions of speeches in the manuscript. Hutchinson misattributes speeches which should be divided between the Lady and the Youth. The order is also confusing, suggesting that the 'awful' pirate is also 'a simple innocent child'.[732] In fact:

728 *Sacontala*, p. 26.
729 *BSMXIX*, pp. xlix-l.
730 *The Cabinet*, p. 15.
731 *BSMXIX*, pp. 261-260, 271-270.
732 *OSA*, pp. 484-485; *BSMXIX*, p. lii.

> he was a man of blood and peril;
> And steeped in bitter infamy to the lips.   (pp. 272-273)

Although it is difficult to judge dramatic quality in the case of a drama of which only fragments remain, sufficient speeches remain of the *Fragments of an Unfinished Drama* to warrant discussion of its dramatic potential, with the proviso that Shelley's practice was to revise repeatedly and to discard. It is easier to see his working method by looking at *Hellas*, from which he discarded two sections which have intrigued editors: the Prologue and the debate between Fatima ('The Indian') and the Greek slavegirls. In *Charles the First*, Shelley made repeated attempts at drafting the speeches in Scene III, from which he may have selected or amalgamated parts. The interest of any particular part of a fragment cannot guarantee its forming part of the final version while repetitive and overlong speeches which seem unperformable might be considerably shortened, altered or discarded. Shelley's speeches in his completed plays are not too long to remember, or to speak comfortably. This suggests that the Lady's reply to the Indian Youth's questions, 'when didst thou depart the spring of Indus?' and 'how thence didst pass this intervening ocean'[733] would have been reworked. It appears to be a very long non-sequitur about a magic gourd she tended, although the Indian Youth has occasional interruptions and asides. These could have been developed into a dialogue or the speech might have been shortened or aided by music, props or other effects. Crook has suggested that the end of the speech might have revealed the answer: that the Lady travelled to the Enchanted Island in the gourd which turned into a boat, following the Shelleyan precedent in *The Witch of Atlas*.[734] As the drama contains musical and magical elements and was written to amuse friends, it is probable that the story would have been a fantasy with a happy ending, of the kind that were popular with London audiences.

The scenes show Shelley writing parts for amateur performers which are within their capabilities and display their skills, thus giving them a chance to shine. It is, of course, impossible to know what effect the completed play would have made upon the audience — presumably the Shelleys' Italian, Irish and English friends — but Shelley was offering them something far more interesting than an imitative amateur production of *Othello*; a new and original verse play which wove what Shelley knew of

---

733 *BSMXIX*, pp. 271-270.
734 Nora Crook, 'Shelley's Late Fragmentary Plays; "Charles the First" and the "Unfinished Drama"' in *The Unfamiliar Shelley*, ed. by Alan Weinberg and Timothy Webb (Farnham: Ashgate, 2009), p. 308.

Indian drama and music into the adventures which Trelawny claimed as his own. Whether or not he knew that these stories were invention, Shelley wittily made Trelawny the hero of his own mythology. The resultant play would have given a modern story a mythical perspective derived seemingly from *Sacontala* with its use of music, spectacle, poetry and myth, thus once again conforming to the observations Shelley puts forward in *The Defence of Poetry*. It shows Shelley's grasp of the practical requirements of a playwright: an ability to write for performance in the environment where it was to be shown. The strengths of the drama would be enhanced by the addition of the music and dancing which cannot be shown on the page and therefore are under-estimated by the reader. This is even more true in the case of *Swellfoot the Tyrant*, which depends on comic forms which do not transfer easily to the page, and so it has often been misjudged. To what extent *Swellfoot* would come to life on stage will be discussed in the ensuing chapter.

Chapter Seven
Satirical Comedy – *Swellfoot*
the Tyrant

It was Athenian drama once again that gave Shelley his starting point for *Swellfoot the Tyrant* but this time it was the Old Comedy and the satyr-play. He introduced elements from modern comedy into this too: *commedia dell'arte*, and its deformed but lively descendants, British pantomime, Punch and the eighteenth-century burlesque.

As *Swellfoot the Tyrant* is a satirical response to Queen Caroline's return to England in 1820 to contest George IV's divorce case against her, the play was of course influenced by the popular, political and satirical prints which drew enthusiastic crowds on their publication and exhibition in shop windows, and became part of the life of the street.[735] Printers such as William Hone and Richard Carlile risked and endured imprisonment for publishing the radical point of view, but often the prosecution was literally laughed out of court since the publication submitted as evidence was so funny.[736] Since White's seminal article, many excellent discussions have detailed the similarities between these 1820 pamphlets and *Swellfoot*, suggesting that Shelley saw some of them.[737] The relationship between the radical printers and the private theatres noted by Worrall presents the comic possibilities of a recreation of their grotesque visual effects in a performance. I do not suggest, however, that Shelley expected *Swellfoot* to be performed in a radical private theatre because no evidence has emerged to my knowledge of such performances as early as 1820. It is nevertheless a highly performable play which might have been successful in such a

---

735 E.P. Thompson, *The Making of the English Working Class* (Harmondsworth: Penguin, 1980), p. 810.
736 McCalman, *Radical Underworld*, p. 163; William W. Wickwar, *The Struggle for the Freedom of the Press 1819-1832* (London: George Allen & Unwin, 1928), pp. 58, 70, 163.
737 White, "Swellfoot", pp. 333-335; e.g. McCalman, *Radical Underworld*, p. 169.

milieu since the stage directions are detailed, the characters are written as impersonations offering great scope for comic performance, and the structure and style draw on plays oriented primarily on highly skilled and very successful performance.

Performance would capitalise on a quality which Shelley considered in Restoration comedy to reflect the 'decay of social life'. This was obscenity, which he defined as 'a capability of associating disgusting images with the act of the sexual instinct'.[738] Critics generally sympathetic to Shelley's work, such as Webb and Tetreault, find *Swellfoot* out of character and, in the case of Tetreault, 'repugnant'. Hogg described Shelley as 'in behaviour modest, in conversation chaste' and said that 'the gross and revolting indecency of an immoral wit wounded his sensitive nature'.[739] Shelley was, however, on the side of greater frankness about sex. In writing *Laon and Cythna* and *The Cenci*, he was constrained by concerns about censorship. He disliked the practice of covering nudity in art, remarking, 'Curse these figleaves, why is a round tin thing more decent than a cylindrical marble one?'[740] While he admired Niccolò Fortiguerra's robust and comic *Ricciardetto*,[741] which he was reading at the time of the news of the Caroline affair, he said of Barry Cornwall:

> His indecencies too both against sexual nature & against human nature sit very awkwardly upon him. [...] In Lord Byron all this has an analogy with the general system of his character, & the wit & poetry which surround, hide with their light the darkness of the thing itself.[742]

Shelley's idea of what was acceptable frankness or 'filthy', 'indecent' obscenity therefore varied with the context, and he appears to have linked coarseness with political satire, as did the radical press. In his own satirical poem, *The Devil's Walk* (1810), about the Prince of Wales as George IV then was, George's corpulence and over-indulgence is a legitimate target. Shelley believed that the divorce was 'silly stuff [...] to employ a great nation about',[743] and his attitude to Caroline was that:

> Nothing, I think shows the generous gullibility of the English nation more than their having adopted her Sacred Majesty as the heroine of the day,

738 *SPP*, pp. 520-521.
739 Webb, *Violet in the Crucible*, p. 137; Tetreault, *The Poetry of Life*, p. 159; Wolfe, I, p. 337.
740 'On the Manners of the Ancient Greeks' in *Shelley's Prose*, p. 223.
741 'An Athlete' in *Shelley's Prose*, p. 346; *PBSLII*, p. 207.
742 *PBSLII*, pp. 239-240.
743 *SPI*, pp. 230-237; *PBSLII*, p. 220.

in spite of all their prejudices and bigotry. I, for my part, of course, wish no harm to happen to her [...] but I cannot help adverting to it as one of the absurdities of royalty, that a vulgar woman, with all those low tastes which prejudice considers as vices, and a person whose habits and manners everyone would shun in private life, without any redeeming virtues should be turned into a heroine, because she is a queen, or, as a collateral reason, because her husband is a king;[744]

The Queen, however, had powerful radical supporters who had taken up her cause in an opportunistic way, including William Cobbett and even Carlile, who had originally intended to use the affair as republican propaganda; he complained in December 1820 that the propaganda had diverted attention from other important issues.[745]

Although Shelley thought that the King and his ministers were 'so odious that everything, however disgusting, which is opposed to them, is admirable', he suggests that, by supporting the Queen, the radicals were creating another monster in place of the one they already had. In *Swellfoot*, he directs his humour towards a ruling class whose behaviour deserved to be displayed in all its 'vulgarity' in order to strip away the trappings of 'honourable' and 'majesty' to reveal its corruption, callousness and greed. While Webb finds Shelley 'a highly unlikely translator' for Euripides' *The Cyclops* since, although he succeeds in capturing its freshness he does not catch 'a suitable tone of ribaldry', Reiter remarks that 'it is idle to say that Shelley could not or would not write so, if he did' and draws attention to coarse sexual jokes such as those that occur in the speeches about the Leech and the Rat from Purganax and Mammon (I. 177-192).[746] Hall and Macintosh find resemblances between the Greek satyr-play and *Swellfoot* such as the themes of discovery and transformation and the centrality of the chorus.[747] I would also suggest the cruel, violent and murderous humour and the association of comedy and poetry with cannibalism. Like Swift, Shelley no doubt felt this humour to be appropriate to the situation of the poor in Britain, particularly when contrasted with the extravagant, ostentatious wealth of George IV, and the obscenities justified by the flagrantly adulterous yet hypocritical behaviour of both parties, as well as reflecting the attitudes of his ministers.

---

744 *PBSLII*, p. 213.
745 McCalman, *Radical Underworld*, pp. 169, 162-163, 175.
746 *PBSLII*, p. 213; Webb, *Violet in the Crucible*, p. 134; Reiter, *Shelley's Poetry*, pp. 258, 260, 261, 264.
747 Hall and Macintosh, *Greek Tragedy*, p. 236.

Aristophanes

Mary Shelley's wellknown Note to *Swellfoot* makes the parallels with Aristophanes clear:

> on the day when a fair was held in the square, beneath our windows; Shelley read to us his Ode to Liberty; and was riotously accompanied by the grunting of a quantity of pigs brought for sale to the fair. He compared it to the 'Chorus of frogs' in the satiric drama of Aristophanes; and, it being an hour of merriment, and one ludicrous association suggesting another, he imagined a political-satirical drama on the circumstances of the day, to which the pigs would serve as Chorus.[748]

Shelley was subtly implying that his efforts in reading the poem to the background of the pigs was similar to Dionysius' unaccustomed labour of rowing, which gave him sore hands and blistered bottom, while competing against the Chorus of Frogs. Yet Dionysius not only completes his journey but wins the shouting-match; Shelley, like the god, wins his with the pigs.[749]

Webb notes that Shelley 'scarcely even mentioned Aristophanes in his letters or critical writings'.[750] Yet, between 17 June and 6 July 1818, Shelley read the plays of Aristophanes very thoroughly, taking three days to read *The Clouds* but only a day each to read *Plutus* (20 June) and *Lysistrata* (21 June). He had time to read all Aristophanes' plays at least twice at the same rate, while also reading Barthélemy's *Anarcharsis*, set in ancient Greece, and four comedies by Jonson: *Every Man in his Humour, Epicoene, Volpone* and *The Magnetick Lady*. This reading came shortly after his reading of Schlegel, who praised Aristophanes highly, the previous March, and formed the basis of satirical comedy both ancient and modern which enabled *Swellfoot* to be so swiftly written two years later.[751] There are parallels in 'functional structure' between Aristophanes' comedies and *Swellfoot* which Michael Erkelenz has detailed, but, as Webb and Tetreault have remarked, it does not include typical elements such as witty repartee or an elaborate plot to outwit someone else which ends in hilarious failure and there is not much knockabout fun.[752] Nevertheless, like Aristophanes, Shelley writes about

---

748 *OSA*, p. 410.
749 W.B. Stanford, Introduction to *The Frogs* by Aristophanes (Basingstoke: Macmillan Education, 1958), p. xxi.
750 Webb, *Violet in the Crucible*, p. 137.
751 Schlegel, pp. 153-168; *MWSJ*, pp. 214-217.
752 Michael Erkelenz. 'The Genre and Politics of Shelley's "Swellfoot the Tyrant"', *The Review of English Studies*, n.s. 47, 188 (November 1996), 500-520 (pp. 502-508).

real political events, using an extremely simple plot, archetypal characters, burlesque and rough, physical, coarse humour.

Aristophanes' plays were not performed in England during Shelley's lifetime, but a number of translations had been published. Erkelenz considers that Aristophanes was being associated with Tory politics with the intention of showing that democracy was an 'odious' form of government and that Shelley was claiming Aristophanes for the opposition. Shelley knew that Aristophanes wrote for a mass audience and he no doubt agreed with Schlegel's opinion that the Old Comedy, including Aristophanes, and Athenian liberty 'flourished together' and 'were oppressed under the same circumstances'.[753] Schlegel describes Aristophanes as a defender of that liberty and a pacifist, and, in respect of his supposed immorality, argues for a different attitude towards Greek morals, an attitude which Shelley was to take further in his essay *On the Manners of the Ancient Greeks*.[754] Schlegel also praised the 'elegant' and 'polished' language used by Aristophanes, 'the richest development of almost every poetical talent', praise which would hardly go unobserved by Shelley; in fact, Tetreault has noticed an affinity between Aristophanes' plays and *Prometheus Unbound*.[755] Shelley returns this to comedy by parodying his own *Prometheus Unbound* choruses in *Swellfoot the Tyrant*. The structure of the verses of the Gadfly's song appropriately resembles that of the songs of the Furies in Prometheus (I. 495-520), particularly his invocation, 'Hum! Hum! Hum!', which rhymes with the 'Come, come, come' of the Furies (I. 504). Just as Aristophanes gave *The Frogs* an unusual double Chorus, *Swellfoot* has the Chorus of the Pigs, the Chorus of Priests (II. ii. 1-19) and the Gadfly, Leech and Rat (I. 220-268).

Aristophanes characteristically turned a figure of speech into a literal image. For example, the words of the poets in *The Frogs* are weighed in scales.[756] In *Swellfoot*, Shelley presents the contents of the 'green bag', metaphorically the filthy and poisonous defamatory evidence of spies, literally as a harmful potion which can cause a metamorphosis — or, as when Iona pours it over her enemies, a return to the true nature of the beast (stage directions at I. 361-369, II. ii). Similarly Mammon's disinheritance of his son, Chrysaor, and marriage of his daughter, Banknotina, to the Gallows, producing little gibbets as offspring (I. 195-212) alludes to Cobbett's theory

---

753 Erkelenz, 'Swellfoot the Tyrant ', p. 516; Schlegel, p. 154; *SPP*, p. 520.
754 Schlegel, pp. 155-156; *Shelley's Prose*, pp. 216-228.
755 Schlegel, p. 157; Tetreault, 'Shelley and the Opera', pp. 160-161.
756 Aristophanes, *The Frogs*, p. 206; Also noted by Wallace, Shelley and Greece, p. 77.

that paper money replacing gold caused inflation and brought about increased poverty and crime.

Aristophanes ends his comedies with a celebration: a feast in *The Archarnians,* a dance in *Lysistrata* and a triumphant exit in *The Frogs.*[757] Shelley gives Swellfoot an ironic banquet (stage directions, II. ii), and Iona and the Pigs a triumphant and celebratory exit (II. ii. 129-138), particularly apposite as events proved, for when the bill against the Queen was thrown out on November 11, people rejoiced in the streets and bells rang.[758]

The early Aristophanic comedy included a *parabasis* in which the leader of the chorus speaks directly to the audience expressing his own point of view. The later plays do not, as political commentary was prohibited after the Peloponnesian wars.[759] Shelley does not appeal directly to the audience or make his characters as aware of one as Aristophanes does, perhaps because he wished to create a 'fourth wall' for the drama. But, the speech of Liberty (II. 84-102) is a modern equivalent of *parabasis,* completely in accordance with the spirit of Aristophanic satire, as Steven E. Jones notes, and does not 'alone mar[s] the sustained satire of *Swellfoot the Tyrant*' as Art Young suggests.[760] The need for Aristophanes' actors to be extremely aware of, and responsive to, an audience is shown, for example, in *The Frogs* (I. i. 1-40), when Dionysius and Xanthias discuss which joke should be used — a 'warm-up' technique familiar in modern pantomime. The texts also make it clear that the actors were required to have the skills of acrobatics, stage fighting, dancing, singing and clowning, skills important in *commedia dell'arte,* pantomime and burlesque and usual among the actors of the minor theatres of Shelley's period.[761]

If Aristophanes' plays were straightforwardly bawdy, with jokes about farting, belching, drunkenness and people getting knocked about, they were also boldly political, naming their targets openly as Cleon, Socrates or Euripides. Aristophanes turned the real characters, such as Socrates in *The Clouds* or Euripides in *The Poet and the Women,* into fictional characters

757 Aristophanes, *The Frogs,* p. 212; Aristophanes, *The Acharnians* in *The Acharnians, Lysistrata,* trans. by Alan H. Sommerstein (Harmondsworth: Penguin, 1973), pp. 103, 235.
758 King-Hele, *Shelley and His Work,* p. 263.
759 Helmut Flashar, 'The Originality of Aristophanes' Last Plays' in *Oxford Readings in Aristophanes,* ed. by Erich Segal (Oxford: Oxford University Press, 1996), p. 314.
760 Steven E. Jones, *Satire and Romanticism* (Basingstoke: Macmillan Press, 2000), p. 184; Art Young, *Shelley and Non-Violence* (The Hague: Mouton, 1975), p. 130.
761 Bush-Bailey, 'Still Working It Out', p. 15.

while retaining the real names. Although Shelley does not name his political targets, the success of his satire lies in his depiction of real people by his use of wellknown mannerisms with their names coded rather than disguised. They are meant to be recognised, and have been identified by several critics, although, as Reiter points out, they can also be seen as archetypal abstractions.[762] Dakry (tear) is easily recognisable as Lord Eldon, who wept as he delivered death sentences. As in *The Mask of Anarchy* (14/15), he weeps fatal millstones:

> Morals, and precedents, and purity,
> Adultery, destitution, and divorce,
> Piety, faith and state necessity,
> And how I loved the Queen! — and then I wept
> With the pathos of my own eloquence,
> And every tear turned to a mill-stone, which
> Brained many a gaping Pig (I. 329-336)

The Duke of Wellington was known for his taciturnity, thus the speech of Laoctonos (people-killer) is short and direct. An acquaintance of the Shelleys had seen the Queen in Italy, when she 'had on a black pelisse, tucked up to her knees, and exhibiting a pair of men's boots. A fur tippet that seemed as if it would cover ten such — a white cap, and a man's hat set on sideways'.[763] Though it appears not to have been previously remarked upon, her appearance on that occasion clearly influenced the depiction of Iona Taurina in *Swellfoot the Tyrant*, who wears a 'buckishly cocked' hunting-cap in her final triumphant scene.

Purganax (lord of the tower) is identified as Castlereagh by the wordplay on his name and also by the hypocrisy with which he addressed the Queen. Cameron suggested that the central part of Purganax' speech (II. i. 59-72) was inspired by Castlereagh's speech of 7 June 1820, which Shelley read in *The Examiner*:[764]

> God forbid that he standing on the present situation should say that to be accused was the same thing as to be guilty! But at the same time he thought it proper to say that a charge of crime necessarily implied a presumption of guilt, and that the present charge rested on grave and serious grounds. It would not be expected that he should disclose to Parliament the substance of those documents, but this he would state — that the charges were grave and serious; and, as far as he was at liberty to describe the information on which

---

762 White, 'Swellfoot', pp. 340-341; Cameron, *The Golden Years*, pp. 357-358; Reiter, *Shelley's Poetry*, p. 255.
763 *PBSLII*, p. 216.
764 Cameron, *The Golden Years*, p. 358.

these charges were founded, he would say that it came from individuals who were ready to corroborate by their personal testimony, all the statements which they had made.[765]

While overtly insisting on the Queen's innocence, Castlereagh heavily implies her guilt. A comparison with Purganax' speech will show that he did the same:

> Why, it is hinted, that a certain Bull —
> Thus much is *known*: — the milk-white bulls that feed
> Beside Clitumnus and the crystal lakes
> Of the Cisalpine mountains, in fresh dews
> Of lotus-grass and blossoming asphodel
> Sleeking her silken hair, and with sweet breath
> Loading the morning winds until they faint
> With living fragrance, are so beautiful! —
> Well, *I* say nothing; — but Europa rode
> On such a one from Asia into Crete,
> And the enamoured sea grew calm beneath
> His gliding beauty. And Pasiphae,
> Iona's grandmother, — but *she* is innocent!
> And that both you and I, and all assert.   (II. i. 59-72)

As Reiter says, 'the beauty of the speech subserves the deceit and sharpens the comic climax' of line 72.[766] I would add that Iona's guilt is made to seem practically inevitable by the sexual metaphors of 'the enamoured sea [...] beneath/His gliding beauty' and the sensuous nature of the languid pastoral surroundings of the bulls in the Cisalpine mountains brought to mind by 'lotus-grass' and 'crystal lakes' and phrases such as 'fresh dews', 'blossoming asphodel', 'living fragrance', 'milk-white' and 'silken' which appeal to the senses of touch and smell and suggest the irresistible nature of the temptation.

Shelley suggests by the name of the Chief Wizard, Mammon (wealth), representing the Prime Minister, Lord Liverpool, that members of Parliament 'actually represent a deception and a shadow, virtually represent none but the powerful and the rich'.[767] He satirises its process by making the Cabinet a 'Council of Wizards'. Mammon uses witchcraft to 'coin paper', referring to the current discussion about the value of paper money, and Purganax 'struck the crust o' the earth/With this enchanted rod' (I. 148-149).

By giving his characters the speech mannerisms of the politicians they are representing, Shelley helps the actors playing those parts to give an

---

765 *The Times*, 8 June 1820.
766 Reiter, *Shelley's Poetry*, p. 260.
767 Qtd in Jones, *Shelley's Satire*, p. 100.

accurate impersonation, thus using 'on-stage mimicry as a weapon in political and theatrical dispute'.[768] Erkelenz believes that Shelley, realising the magnitude of the constitutional crisis and the double standard being used to attack Caroline, had 'commitment to [her] cause' by the time he wrote *Swellfoot* and created Iona as its Aristophanic hero. But, on the other hand, the realisation of the popularity of her cause may have been why he felt it necessary to warn the campaigners that it was a diversion and bring their attention back to the more important issues of the day, those he had set out a few months before in *A Philosophical View of Reform*: the abolition of the national debt, sinecures and tithes, the disbanding of the standing army, making all religions equal legally and 'cheap justice, certain and speedy'.[769] Iona's late appearance in the play does not suggest that she is the hero, and her characterisation suggests that Caroline is not to be trusted. Caroline's messages, according to the Parliamentary report, were modest and grateful.[770] Until her trial, Shelley portrays Iona as a demure, dignified wronged queen, a Hermione or Katherine, but her true nature is not revealed until the final scene when she changes into a loud and coarse huntswoman.

In June 1820, Shelley connected Queen Caroline with Greek legend, writing, 'I expect, at least, that the accusation is as terrible as that made against Pasiphae and that a Bill will be passed in Parliament to declare that no Minotaur shall be considered as legal heir to the Crown of *these realms*'.[771] Pasiphae fell in love with the beautiful bull Poseidon had sent her husband King Minos for sacrifice. Minos imprisoned it in the Labyrinth created by Daedalus, who helped Pasiphae to gain access. The offspring of the bull and Pasiphae was the Minotaur, half bull, half man.[772] Purganax refers to this story in his speech (II. i. 70-71). The John Bull Minotaur of the play is Iona's offspring for she helps create the situation in which he takes action. This reinforces the connection between the Queen and her supporters among the common English people. Radical groups such as the Spenceans adopted Burke's insult 'the Swinish multitude' as a badge of honour.[773] Shelley makes it clear that the Swinish multitude is one and

---

768   Bratton, *New Readings*, p. 110.
769   *SCVI*, p. 1027.
770   *The Times*, 7 June 1820.
771   *PBSLII*, p. 220.
772   H.J. Rose, *A Handbook of Greek Mythology* (London: Routledge, 1991), p. 183.
773   Edmund Burke, 'Reflections on the Revolution in France' in Robert B. Dishman, *Burke and Paine on Revolution and the Rights of Man* (New York: Scribner, 1971), p. 114.

the same as John Bull, the sturdy Englishman, 'the salt of the earth', since the Chorus are pigs but those which eat the loaves turn into bulls. Iona's association through the Gadfly with Io and her cow's tail (II. i. 104) suggest she is at least partly cow, though one which wears petticoats (II. i. 96). As the young Boars have cowtails (I. 300-301), however, Iona may have been similarly granted one as a regal honour. The two Goddesses appear human, as Liberty has a 'graceful figure' (II. ii) suggesting a Greek statue, while Famine resembles the skeleton in *Bluebeard* and disappears with the same mechanism.[774]

The MPs are Boars, some of which have been elevated to the Upper Sty:

> [...] fattening some few in two separate sties,
> And giving them clean straw, tying some bits
> Of ribbon round their legs — giving their Sows
> Some tawdry lace, and bits of lustre glass,
> And their young Boars white and red rags, and tails
> Of cows, and jay feathers, and sticking cauliflowers
> Between the ears of the old ones;   (I. 296-302)

The imagery of the ludicrous dressing of animals for display at a show highlights the ridiculous and anachronistic dress of the House of Lords. Purganax here alludes to Castlereagh's implication in the bribery of ennoblement which enabled the Act of Union to be passed,[775] and identifies himself with those in the Common Sty when he says:

> WE believe
> (I mean those more substantial Pigs, who swill
> Rich hog-wash   (II. i. 37-39)

Wallace believes that 'even [Shelley's] heroes are pigs',[776] but, although Swellfoot's greed suggest that he is one, he and his ministers are, from a farmer's point of view, vermin, as finally revealed (II. ii. 116-118), and although they may be the heroes in the sense of their being leading characters, they are not heroic. Iona's calling them 'anything but men', emphasised by the name 'Porkman' which refers to both species, suggests that they have been masquerading as human. The pigs themselves, who have been made to believe themselves pigs though they are truly bulls, are the real heroes of the piece, despite being the chorus. This reading is consistent with Shelley's position in *The Mask of Anarchy*, written the previous autumn.

The non-human characteristics allow the starvation theme to be dealt

774 Kelly, *Reminiscences*, p. 247.
775 Robert Kee, *The Green Flag*, 3 vols (London: Quartet, 1976), I, p. 158.
776 Wallace, *Shelley and Greece*, p. 81.

with ironically rather than tragically by the constant reminder, through terms such as 'dug', 'bristle' and 'brawn', that pigs invariably end up on the table. This leads to the question of how this animal nature would be portrayed in performance. It cannot be established by the 'big head' masks of pantomime, since these do not allow actors to move easily and restrict the voice to too great an extent. If it is shown through costume, the time needed to change renders it impossible to make the sudden transformations required by the play. Shelley is known to have had the opportunity to see a *commedia dell'arte* performance and there is the tradition in *commedia* of associating the characters with particular animals portrayed through 'movement and gait': 'the Doctor [...] is pure pig'.[777] This suggests that *Swellfoot* may have a close connection to this genre through a characteristic not to be found in any other. None of Aristophanes' comedies have such characters; even Tereus in *The Birds* is more of a man than a bird. This style of performance would enable the audience to see human and animal characteristics simultaneously.

Commedia dell'arte

Commedia dell'arte is acknowledged by those working in the theatre as being one of the great genres of acting which deeply influenced European theatre. It is, as Kimbell says, 'next to opera, probably Italy's most brilliant and distinctive contribution to world theatre'.[778] He finds it 'best defined [...] as comedy performed by professional players [...] it depended upon a measure of virtuosity — virtuoso clowning, virtuoso miming, virtuoso facility with the tongue' adding that, 'a good *commedia* performer needed imagination and an inventiveness that was never at rest'.[779] It was dependent upon a professional troupe because it was improvised. It is believed, and was by Shelley's contemporaries, to derive from ancient Roman comedy.[780] Their use of masks was so wellknown that the players were referred to simply as *maschere*. Like actors in Athenian theatre, they danced and performed acrobatics and had a range of sounds and voices they were able to make with the help of the mask, using it as a megaphone or whistle.

The companies started as guilds of professional actors in medieval Italy when scripts were written even by churchmen and 'the obscene always

777 Fo, *Tricks of the Trade*, p. 22.
778 Kimbell, *Italian Opera*, pp. 282-283.
779 Ibid., pp. 286.
780 Pierre Louis Duchartre, *The Italian Comedy* (New York: Dover, 1966), pp. 24-29.

played a liberating role', that role ascribed by Wallace to both Aristophanes and Shelley.[781] During the Counter-Reformation the *commedia* companies were expelled from Italy and in 1675 were expelled from France, where they had shared a theatre for fourteen years with Molière, because of 'their satire on the customs, hypocrisy and the politicking of the age'. Between 1580 and 1780, the *commedia* travelled abroad to France, Spain, Holland and even Russia, and returned to Italy at various times, bringing cross-fertilisation from other cultures. They developed their mimicry and used a language, *grammelot*, based on sounds, real words and seemingly senseless noises so that it was not necessary for their audience to understand Italian, though, like Schlegel, they might not have followed the meaning of every joke. The *commedia* characters had not only human names but also those of an animal whose movements the actor accorded with: 'Capitan Spaventa is also known as Dragonhead or Crocodile while the Pantaloon is also cockerel, turkey or hen, while Harlequin is cat or monkey'.[782]

There were several different plots and speeches which were so well memorised by the actors that they could combine them with others and slip into a completely different and new scenario; as Schlegel, who praised the 'great fund of drollery and fantastic wit' and the diversity of the plots, says, 'an endless number of combinations is possible.'. Schlegel remarks that the Italians were gifted 'from earliest times' in 'a merry, amusing though very rude buffoonery, in extemporary speeches and songs, with accompanying appropriate gestures', noting that Roman mimes had 'the first germ of the *Commedia dell'arte*' and comparing the masks and costumes to those on Greek vases 'never used except on the stage'. He had discovered 'among the frescoes of Pompeji' a figure of Pulcinello and a buffoon with particoloured dress like Arlecchino's. His opinion was that performances during carnivals ensured that the continuity was unbroken and that 'the *Commedia dell'Arte* is the only one in Italy where we can meet with original and truly theatrical entertainment' which should not be 'held in contempt by all who pretend to any degree of refinement, as if they were too wise for it'.[783]

In Milan, Shelley, fresh from reading Schlegel, attended the puppet theatre. It may be assumed that, just as he wished to see *improvvisatori*, he was also curious to see *commedia dell'arte*. The *commedia* shared the spontaneity in improvisation, while the speed and acrobatics of the performers would not have failed to interest someone who at Field Place had been taken with

---

781 Wallace, *Shelley and Greece*, p. 79.

782 Fo, *Tricks of the Trade*, pp. 25, 22, 47, 28, 43; Schlegel, p. 228n.

783 Schlegel, pp. 226, 202-203, 228, 228n.

Arlequin

Avec son habit de facquin,
son geste, et son discours folastre,
chez H. Bonnart, rue S.ᵗ Jacques.

Il faut avouer qu Arlequin
Fait les delices du Theatre
avec privil.

20. 'Arlecchino', 17th century print from Pierre Duchartre, *The Italian Comedy* (New York: Dover Publications, 1966), p. 131.

'a tumbler, who came to the back door to display her wonderful feats'.[784] Mary Shelley's reference to Shelley's dislike of unevenness in performance, and the fact that he was to write in *A Defence of Poetry* of the 'partial and inharmonious effect' of a company of actors without masks, suggest that he would have admired the unity which is characteristic of *commedia dell'arte* companies as well as their wearing of masks.[785] Their unusual ability to portray animal and human characteristics simultaneously and the speed, agility and timing present to a high level in *commedia dell'arte* are necessary elements for a performance of *Swellfoot*. Their ability to communicate in *grammelot* translates easily into the dialogue between Swellfoot and the grunting pigs. These qualities were not, to my knowledge, found in London companies at the time but an Italian scholar, familiar with nineteenth-century British humour and pantomime, immediately connected *Swellfoot* with *commedia*.[786]

Pantomime

The pantomime was only initially inspired by *commedia dell'arte,* having been developed in the eighteenth century by John Rich, himself an excellent acrobat, mime and Harlequin.[787] The names of Pantalone (Pantaloon), Arlecchino (Harlequin) and Colombina (Columbine) were used, but not their characters or the *commedia* scenarios. By 1800, pantomime followed a wellknown formula based on a tale such as *Aladdin*. In the first scene, lovers were separated by the young woman's father, or another authority figure, and a magical being such as a good fairy transformed these three into Harlequin, Columbine, who sometimes sang but did not speak, and Pantaloon.[788] The rest of the show consisted of a chase (harlequinade) with multiple spectacular scene changes, brought about by Harlequin's magic wand or 'slapstick', acrobatic feats, songs, dancing and clowning. The Clown became a major feature during the career of Grimaldi, whose humour was visually witty, satirical and vulgar. Unlike *commedia*, however, the inclusion of humour in pantomime was the responsibility

---

784   *CCJ*, p. 91; Wolfe, I, p. 27.

785   *SPP*, p. 519.

786   Professor Irene Meloni, Facoltà di Lingue e Letterature Straniere dell'Università di Cagliari, private conversation, October 2007.

787   Hughes, 'Afterpieces or That's Entertainment', p. 61; Wyndham, *Covent Garden*, I, p. 4.

788   Mayer, *Harlequin in his Element*, pp. 28-30, 44-47.

of the Clown alone and not of the whole company. Pantomime had neither the verbal wit and repartee of *commedia*, nor its variety of plots.

Just as Byron enjoyed pantomime and carnival, Shelley's interest in pantomime can be assumed from Peacock's writing to him of 'a very splendid' pantomime 'founded on the adventures of Baron Munchausen'.[789] Its mass appeal would have attracted him had he wanted to reach a popular audience; it was the pantomime which balanced the books.[790] In *Swellfoot*, the supernatural figure of Liberty is similar to the good fairy of pantomime. Mammon and Purganax are the bad fairies and the green bag is the magic slapstick which transforms the characters, releasing the pigs from the wizard's spells.

Punch

Polcinello [Pulcinella], a *commedia dell'arte* character from Naples, where he featured in plates, figurines, crockery and frescoes,[791] also became a glove puppet in a floppy white tunic, mask and conical hat with a falsetto voice. He travelled from Italy to France and England and developed into the English Punch, appearing in puppet theatre at eighteenth-century fairs and festivals with his wife Joan (later Judy). They knocked each other about with gusto, Joan giving Punch as good as she got, until the Devil came to her assistance and took both away. Joseph Baretti, the friend of Samuel Johnson, wrote in 1786 that Punch was one who, like Falstaff, always got the worst of a fight but boasted of victory after his attackers had departed. A print of 1785 shows Joan attacking Punch with a stick and it appears that she struck the first blow. Contemporary woodcuts show the pair with similar hooked nose and chin, but only Punch has the massive belly. These shows at the London fairs were 'frequented [...] by children' when Shelley was a child in the 1790s, and in 1804 there was a show in Brighton, not far from Horsham.

Punch was also a familiar sight and introducing new characters and action when Shelley was living in or frequenting London, about which time

---

789 Jones, *Satire and Romanticism*, pp. 170-172; *The Letters of Thomas Love Peacock*, ed. by Nicholas A. Joukovsky (Oxford: Clarendon, 2001), p. 164.

790 Donohue, *Theatre in the Age of Kean*, p. 56.

791 *La commedia dell'arte e il teatro erudito*, a cura di Franco Mancini e Franco-Carmelo Greco (Napoli: Guida, c. 1982); Robert Leach, *The Punch and Judy Show: History, Tradition and Meaning* (London: Batsford, 1985), p. 18.

21. 'Punch and Joan', 18th century woodcuts (artist unknown). From
George Speaight *Punch and Judy, A History* (London: Studio Vista, 1970),
p. 67. Woodcuts now in the possession of the Department of Theatre &
Performance, Victoria & Albert Museum.

Joan's name changed to Judy.[792] Shelley appears uncertain as to her present
name, referring to the royal couple as 'Punch and his wife'. His wishes
that they 'would fight out their disputes in person', and that they should
'beat till [...] they would kiss and be friends' suggests that the version of
the show which he had in mind was the earlier one, where Joan was more
Punch's equal than Judy later became.[793] Dario Fo describes the English
Punch as 'pitiless and hard as Pulcinella, a lineal descendant'.[794] Swellfoot
shares these characteristics, together with Punch's huge belly and Iona's
rumbustious exit suggests 'his wife'. Punch's relationship to Polcinello was
well enough known for Lady Morgan, when describing a performance in
1820, to find it 'scarcely necessary to observe that the Pulchinello of Italy
is not, like the *Polichinel* of Paris, or the Punch of England a puppet; but a
particular character in low comedy, peculiar to Naples'. In Rome she saw
a well-attended satirical outdoor puppet show, and the Shelleys also spent
several months in both cities where they had the opportunity to come
across Polcinello.[795]

---

792 Speaight, *Punch and Judy*, pp. 78, 85, 79, 76; Leach, *Punch and Judy Show*, pp. 15, 40.
793 *PBSLII*, pp. 220, 207.
794 Fo, *Tricks of the Trade*, p. 51.
795 Morgan, *Italy*, II, pp. 291n., 447.

Burlesque

There was yet another influence on *Swellfoot*: the eighteenth-century burlesque. Burlesques were very popular, in particular Fielding's *Tom Thumb* and Henry Carey's *The Dragon of Wantley* and *Chrononhotonthologos*, and had their beginnings in Buckingham's *The Rehearsal*. This parodied the high-flown language, inconsistency of plot and inappropriate timing of music and dance of Dryden's heroic drama by making the characters speak in whispers (II. i. 35-50) or in French 'to show their breeding' (II. ii. 16). Such lines as 'All these dead men you shall see rise up presently, at a certain Note that I have made in *Effaut flat*, and fall a Dancing' (II. v) led to the burlesque convention of the dead coming to life again. Burlesque went on to parody Italian opera, both in respect of plots and music. Shelley, at the very least, knew *The Rehearsal* and *Chrononhotonthologos*. *Chrononhotonthologos* has impossibly long names 'Singing, after the Italian Manner', a silly story with music, dancing and fights. The elegant court dancing is undermined when 'the Queen and ladies dance The [plebeian] Black Joak while the kettle boils' (II. 18). The highflown style is mocked when one of the characters plainly does not understand a word the other is saying, (*Chrononhotonthologos*, I. 53) and a stage direction calls for 'a tragedy groan' (II. 18). The King is woken 'in a burlesque of the traditional scene de sommeil' by 'Rough Musick, viz. saltboxes and Rolling-pins, Grid-irons and Tongs; Sow-gelders Horns; Marrow-bones and Cleavers etc. etc.'[796] 'Marrow-bones and Cleavers', and the Sow-gelder himself, also appear in *Swellfoot the Tyrant* (stage directions, I. 70-95, II. ii).

Although the vogue for writing burlesque had really passed when Shelley attended the London theatre, they were still performed. *Tom Thumb* had been performed at Covent Garden in March 1810. Shelley saw *Bombastes Furioso* by W.B. Rhodes (22 January 1817). Crabb Robinson did not regard it highly, but it was described as late as 1848 as 'a very favourite farce'.[797] Like the earlier burlesques, *Bombastes* has an uncomplicated plot, the incidents illogical or impossible. King Artaximonous fights General Bombastes over his mistress Distaffina and both are killed, but come back to life. Battles take place to the sound of a jig, there are eight songs and a dance at the end. The dialogue is in silly rhymes:

---

796 Introduction to Trussler, *Burlesque Plays*, pp. 2, vii-xii, the references are from *The Rehearsal* and *Chrononhotonthologos* in that edition and from Fiske, *Theatre Music*, pp. 148-149; *MWSJ*, pp. 135, 157.

797 *MWSJ*, p. 165; Crabb Robinson, p. 49; Harcourt, *Theatre Royal, Norwich*, p. 39.

> Who dares this pair of boots displace
> Must meet Bombastes face to face.   (48-59)

> Good night my mighty soul's inclin'd to roam,
> So make my compliments to all at home.   (117-120)

Artaximonous, whose refrain is, 'Get out of my sight or I'll knock you down' shared the characteristic of over-indulgence with the Prince Regent, and the violent knockabout nature of the comedy allows a vicarious disrespect for the monarchy. No criticism of the real monarch could have been made overt at a patent theatre.

Bombastes Furioso was performed by Mathews and Liston, both great comedians. Crabb Robinson, intending to disparage Mathews, said he was 'only excellent as a Mimic or in the rapidity of his transitions in bustle and comic volubility' but these are qualities required by a comedian and, particularly, a *commedia dell'arte* player. Mathews was described as 'the very best actor on the [...] stage' and 'more plastic' than Kean or Dowton'. He had impersonated Lord Ellenborough, another adversary of Shelley, 'in the character of Flexible, the judge in Kenney's comedy *Love Law and Physic*'. Shelley had long appreciated Mathews's talent and been familiar with his work, having sent him an early play. It is highly probable that he would have recalled him when writing *Swellfoot*, which requires the actors to have high skills of impersonation and, in the last scene, the ability to change rapidly. This is not to say that Shelley expected Mathews to perform in *Swellfoot*, but he may have written the play as he did with Kean and Cenci, thinking of what Mathews could do with the part and knowing that others had the required skills, if to a lesser degree.[798] Shelley had the talent of imitation in writing which Mathews had in acting. Just as Aristophanes parodied the style of other writers in a number of comedies, so Shelley was able to write successfully in the same verse forms as Milton, Dante or Spenser and to mock Wordsworth in *Peter Bell the Third*.

Burlesques had a two-act structure with two scenes in each act. Swellfoot's first act has only one scene but the exit at I. 95 clears the stage and divides the act into two parts differing in style: the first short with plenty of physical action, and the second with the drama in the speeches. Burlesques were primarily written for performance and were very popular and successful on the stage; it was this which led to their publication. When published, Fielding's introduction and notes to Tom Thumb in mock-academic style became a tradition of the eighteenth-century burlesque, one

---

798 Crabb Robinson, p. 50; Bratton, *New Readings*, pp. 109-110; *PBSLII*, pp. 102-103.

which Shelley followed.[799] The tradition of burlesque showed Shelley that silly jokes and situations could be successful on stage, that a complicated plot was not necessary for comedy, and that an actor's mimicry could be used to supply the political and social comment that the burlesque lacks.

Act I

As Wallace and Erkelenz have noted, the action of the first scene is a parody of the first scene of *Oedipus Tyrannus* in which Oedipus comes out to greet his supplicants.[800] The comic difference is that, unlike Oedipus, who agrees to help his subjects, Shelley's king first does not even notice the pigs and then behaves towards them with total callousness. Shelley suggests the parody of the magnificence of an exotic temple in his requirements for the scenic presentation — 'tiled with scalps, thigh bones and death's heads'. This may be based on the Church of the Capuchins, Via Veneto, Rome.[801] Swellfoot's comparison of his belly to an Egyptian pyramid emphasises the temple imagery and reminds the audience of the cost of those structures. The visual imagery of the thistle, shamrock and oak makes it clear that the boars, sows and sucking pigs are the people of Scotland, Ireland and England, not of Thebes.

Swellfoot's 'royal robes' of 'gold and purple' are, like Jupiter's in *Prometheus Unbound*, in the colours Shelley associates with power, extravagance and oppression. Swellfoot has what Reiter describes as 'a dictator's contempt for life'.[802] When the pigs plead for a small amount of food, despite the legal and practical benefits of their reasons, his response is 'Kill them out of the way'. The figure of Swellfoot represents both the system, the corruption which offers the dropsical pig to 'serve instead of riot money', and the individual, a satirical portrait of George IV. Like Swellfoot, George was obese. Swellfoot requires the sows to be speyed mentioning their lack of 'moral restraint' and his 'own example' (74-75) just as George cited his wife's adultery as if he were innocent, despite his own numerous affairs.

Just as the Frogs' song 'Brekakek koax koax' represents their croaking, Shelley's Pigs' chorus, 'Aigh! Aigh!', 'Eigh! Eigh!' and 'Ugh! Ugh!' represents their squealing and grunting, a combination of the pathetic and comic.

799 *OSA*, pp. 389-390.
800 Wallace, *Shelley and Greece*, p. 76; Erkelenz, p. 500.
801 *SCX*, p. 805.
802 Reiter, *Shelley's Poetry*, p. 256.

Their dialogue with Swellfoot is at first without words, although Swellfoot's response indicates the meaning of what they say, allowing the actors to express themselves through sounds and body language as the *commedia* players communicate in *grammelot*. This indicates their identity as pigs before line 32 when they confirm it. What should be the graceful dance of the Semi-Chorus is comically parodied and when Moses attempts to spey the sows, the chaos is comic but the situation, a visual portrayal of Malthusianism, has pathos.[803] 'The pigs run about in consternation' while Swellfoot prates about 'moral restraint' and Moses pleads for him to 'Keep the Boars quiet, else —' (I. 79). Swellfoot's order to drive them out to slaughter is a sudden shock climax which effectively divides the act.

The dialogue of Mammon and Purganax unfolds the plot against Iona and also their lying, duplicity, scheming, spying and fear of the people. Shelley shows his command of a dramatic device he used in the first scene of *The Cenci* in which the characters shift position to take up the attitude exhibited at first by the other character. Purganax begins by being despondent and uncertain, saying, 'The future looks as black as death' (I. 96). He is worried about the oracle, an appropriate metaphor for the volatile economic situation in England, (I. 108) and afraid of the Swine (I. 146). But when he begins to report his dealings with his team of spies, he becomes confident. Shelley shows a grasp of technique by allowing the actor playing Mammon time to build his panic while Purganax tells the mock-epic story of the Gadfly. It is now Mammon who begins to panic ('My dear friend, where are your wits?' (I. 181).

Shelley builds the whole scene with dramatic skill to bring Mammon to the level at which he reveals his financial dealings and his fear of 'the Swinish multitude'. He is then interrupted by the entry of the Gadfly and the realisation of all his fears. The great comic potential in a performance of this scene can be appreciated by imagining a masked actor wearing wizard's robes, using the voice of the prime minister, panicking and making sexual puns about leeches and rats.

The style of dialogue also reveals dramatic ability. Mammon and Purganax interrupt each other, breaking up the verse, and use short lines to give a natural feel and create an impression of fear and secrecy appropriate to the subject discussed: 'Now there were danger in the precedent/If queen Iona […]' (I. 146-7) or:

---

803 Scrivener remarks on Malthus's influence, *Radical Shelley*, p. 268.

Mammon: In that fear I have —
Purganax: Done what?
Mammon: Disinherited
          My eldest son.   (I. 195-196)

The Gadfly's entry, preceded by humming, would on stage be both
funny and spectacular. Shelley has described The Gadfly as being 'fed on
dung' (I. 163) 'trailing a blistering slime' (I. 165) with 'convex eyes' which
see 'fair things in many hideous shapes' (I. 160-161) and, like the Leech and
Rat, he is comically sinister and disgusting to look at. This emphasises the
nature of the spying Milan Commission (a Sir John Leach was the chair)[804]
while belittling it through the comedy. The songs, which break up the scene
and vary the action, use such comic invented words and phrases as 'deader'
and 'dumbed her'. Shelley uses the word 'uglification' before Lewis Carroll
and, like Carroll's Queen, Swellfoot cries, 'Off with her head!' (I. 294).[805]

When the Rat emphasises Mammon's fear that the pigs may turn out to
be John Bull after all (I. 276), Purganax realises his spies have failed. His
fuming 'This is a pretty business' (I. 279-280) prompts Mammon's exit line
in keeping with his character as Chief Wizard, 'I will go/And spell some
scheme to make it ugly then' (281). The final part of the scene becomes even
more hectic with Swellfoot's entry, the swine's potential rebellion, and the
introduction of the characters of Laoctonos and Dakry with their news from
the battlefront. The failure of Laoctonos's battalions of 'royal apes' to defeat
the united and determined Swine reflects Shelley's own hope that English
soldiers would not fire on the people, while their succumbing to 'apples,
nuts and gin' shows that he did not think it would be difficult to bribe them.
This was the case, since the soldiers were openly showing their support of
the Queen.[806] The Swine themselves follow good military practice:

> in a hollow square
> Enclosed her, and received the first attack
> Like so many rhinoceroses, and then
> Retreating in good order, with bare tusks
> And wrinkled snouts presented to the foe
> Bore her in triumph to the public sty. (I. 314-319)

Corruption is again revealed in Swellfoot's line 'Pack them then',
an immediate retort to Purganax's desire to have a show of legality by
assembling a jury (I. 295). Mammon's entry with his new magic spell, the

---

804   Cameron, *The Golden Years*, p. 355.
805   Lewis Carroll, *Alice in Wonderland* (London: Collins, [n.d.]), p. 112.
806   Wickwar, *The Freedom of the Press*, p. 161.

Green Bag, and the repetition of the very words 'Green Bag' would have caused certain and repeated laughter in an audience since green bags incurred such notoriety during this trial that lawyers gave up using them.[807] The references to *Hamlet* (I. 199) and *Cymbeline* (I. 205) would also have been recognised and so would the end of the Act with its echo of the witches in *Macbeth*, (I. 414) an appropriate play to parody with its royal murder, oppression of the people and supernatural interventions.

Act II, Scene i

As already mentioned, Purganax's speech, which opens the act, parodies Castlereagh's. The original speech dealt only with the Caroline question, but Shelley had raised questions about why the Council of Wizards behaves as it does which it was dramatically necessary to answer to show the audience the reasons for the oppression of the Pigs:

> Who, by frequent squeaks, have dared impugn
> The settled Swellfoot system, or to make
> Irreverent mockery of the genuflexions
> Inculcated by the arch-priest, have been whipped
> Into a loyal and an orthodox whine   (II. i. 26-30)

He refers to the dissemination of information through pamphlets or papers, which was punished severely even if the distributor knew nothing of the contents.[808] Shelley satirises the hypocrisy of Castlereagh's morality and patriotic virtue with:

> that true source of Piggishness
> (How can I find a more appropriate term
> To include religion, morals, peace, and plenty,
> And all that fit Boeotia as a nation
> To teach the other nations how to live?)   (II. i. 6-10)

The setting is 'The Public Sty' — the House of Commons where the Boars, 'in full Assembly', follow mock Parliamentary procedure. Shelley made use of his early experience of visiting the House of Commons with his father.[809] The scene ridicules the ease with which an orator such as Purganax can win over those like the First Boar, who begins as an aggressive supporter of Iona, saying 'What/Does any one accuse her of?' (II. i. 44-45), and ends

807 White, 'Swellfoot', p. 335.
808 Wickwar, *The Freedom of the Press*, p. 40.
809 Wolfe, I, p. 130.

by calling Purganax 'Excellent, just and noble' (II. i. 94). Shelley does not describe the scenery but allows the scene painter the comic possibilities of combining elements of both a pigsty and the House of Commons. The Boars are better off than 'the Swinish multitude' (II. i. 37-39) and Shelley shows their interests are opposed on class grounds since:

> the Lean-pig faction
> Seeks to obtain that hog-wash, which has been
> Your immemorial right, and which I will
> Maintain you in to the last drop of —'   (II. i. 40-44)

The dialogue which follows (II. i. 95-105) mocks the MPs' conservatism and conformity. Even though the Boars' lines are a feed for Purganax, Shelley has made sure that these small parts are differentiated with comic potential and characterises them in very few lines. While attempting to appear loyal, innocent and intelligent, the Boars reveal their prurience and obtuseness when referring to the 'cow's tail' or 'Her Majesty's petticoats' (II. i. 95, 104), which embarrasses the Second Boar when he realises he will be able to see under them.[810] He is annoyed, snapping 'Or *anything*, as the learned Boar observed' (II. i. 105), when he is outdone by Purganax's description of the glory of her Majesty flying through the sky like an angel.

The Chorus bursts into the Sty at the point when Purganax is to move the resolution that Iona is tried. While they break down the doors, they sing the 'first Strophe', which has only eight words and begins 'No! Yes! Yes! No!' (II. i. 111-114), a potentially very funny scene on stage. Then, excited by their power, they and the alarmed MPs realise that rebellion means they must 'share their wash with the Lean-Pigs'. They confront each other in a dramatically effective comic and musical scene while the First Boar, as Speaker, calls for Order. At the climax, Shelley gives Iona a grand entrance and a fine speech on her innocence and gratitude to her loyal pigs, ending the scene with triumph for Iona and the pigs.

Act II, Scene ii

The scenery for Scene II simply consists of a statue of a skeleton 'clothed in parti-coloured rags, seated upon a heap of skulls and loaves intermingled' (the statue of Famine). Shelley's stage directions and scenery requirements are, as elsewhere, sufficient in their entirety to furnish hints to the scene

---

810 Reiter, *Shelley's Poetry*, p. 260.

painter and to make sure that there is what is needed for the *coup de théâtre* at the end of the scene. It is clear from the stage direction and cue that a trapdoor is required through which Famine will vanish and the Minotaur will rise, the mechanical technique similar to that Kelly describes for the sinking of Blue Beard and raising of the skeleton, though it is to be hoped with more success than Kelly had on *Bluebeard's* first night.[811]

The stage picture of 'exceedingly fat Priests in black garments', 'arrayed' on either side of a skeleton, skulls and loaves shows Shelley's great clarity of conception and regard for grouping, even placing in their hands the marrow bones and cleavers on which they are to perform. He both indulges and makes fun of the audience's pleasure in processions. Mammon, Swellfoot and the other government ministers, together with Iona Taurina and her guards enter to the 'flourish of trumpets' while the swine enter from the other side. There are immense comic possibilities when these two opposing parties see each other and still more when they meet mid-stage, particularly as the expectation is that the King's procession are pompous and stately and the Swine's rough and disorderly. The Chorus of priests satirises the conservative point of view, again making the reasons for opposing reform quite clear:

> The earth pours forth its plenteous fruits,
> Corn, wool, linen, flesh, and roots —
> Those who consume these fruits through thee grow fat,
> Those who produce these fruits through thee grow lean,
> Whatever change takes place, oh, stick to that!
> And let things be as they have ever been;
> At least while we remain thy priests   (II. ii. 8-13)

The 'magnificently covered' table depicts the division of wealth in the country and the 'exceedingly lean' Pigs licking up the wash from what is spilt from the attendants' pails (stage directions following II. ii. 19) contrasts the desperation of starvation and the waste of a banquet for the jaded appetite in a striking visual image placed centrally, since the table is 'at the upper end of the Temple'.

Swellfoot's request to have the Pigs silenced is not granted because their grunting is a tribute to Famine. Their chorus, however, is a clear invitation to rebellion. It refers to 'dividing possessions,' 'uprooting oppressions' and making all 'level' (II. ii. 42-60) instead of 'new churches, and cant', the government's hypocritical programme of churchbuilding in support of a religion one of whose tenets is to feed the hungry. The Chorus alarms the

---

811 Kelly, *Reminiscences*, p. 247.

ministers sufficiently to bring forward Iona's trial. At this point, Shelley allows two actions to run concurrently. Liberty, 'a graceful figure in a semi-transparent veil', passes through the Temple and delivers the *parabasis*, kneeling in genuine prayer. While 'the Veiled Figure has been chanting this strophe', the government ministers have surrounded Iona, whose stance is similar to that required of the hero at the end of *Lovers' Vows*: hands folded on her breast and eyes lifted to heaven' (stage directions following II. ii. 102), but her saintly attitude is only assumed. As movement attracts the eye of the audience and Liberty contrasts so much with Iona in appearance and attitude, Shelley can be sufficiently confident to allow her words to be 'almost drowned' at first. But, being chanted, they are more audible and there is no conflicting dialogue. They become 'louder and louder'.

In *The Mask of Anarchy*, Shelley identifies Freedom with 'clothes, and fire, and food' and in *Swellfoot* Freedom is Famine's 'eternal foe', but in this case Shelley, as Cameron showed, is referring to Coleridge's *Letter from Liberty to her Dear Friend Famine*.[812] Liberty asks Famine to 'wake the multitude' but to 'lead them not upon the paths of blood' (II. ii. 90-91), thus making it clear that it is want which drives people to 'fanatic rage and meaningless revenge' (II. ii. 94). Shelley did not believe in revenge, but that is not to say that he did not want to see Liverpool and Castlereagh brought to justice.

In performance, Liberty's prayer to Famine to 'Rise now!' (II. ii. 102) would be the cue for the stagehands to raise the image of Famine 'with a tremendous sound'. There would be a startling double *coup de théâtre*, since at the same time Iona snatches the green bag with the agility and dexterity of a *commedia dell'arte* player and pours the contents on 'Swellfoot and the whole Court' (stage directions, p. 408). This requires quick nimble playing by the ensemble who are all 'instantly' changed into 'ugly badgers [...] stinking foxes [...] devouring otters [...] hares [and] wolves', while 'all those [pigs] who eat the loaves' are turned into bulls (II. ii. 117-119, stage directions, p. 409). As the 'filthy and ugly animals' rush out, the pigs scramble for the loaves which now can be reached as Famine is no longer seated on them. Famine descends through the trapdoor as the Minotaur rises. The Minotaur, 'in plain Theban, that is to say, John Bull' (II. ii. 107-109), is the revolutionary or reformist spirit in the country, which is why he can 'leap any gate'. He offers aid to Iona who 'leaps nimbly on to his back', but it is clear that he can throw her and that this concession is only 'till you have hunted down your game' (II. ii. 114). The

---

812 Kenneth Neill Cameron, 'Shelley and the Conciones ad Populum', *Modern Language Notes*, 57.8 (December 1942), 673-674.

alliance between Iona and Minotaur, like that between Liberty and Famine, is therefore, as Shelley would have wished that between the people and Queen: temporary. Shelley, although this may have been a second thought, shows his awareness of the requirements of the stage by writing a speech for the Minotaur sufficiently long to allow Iona to put on her hunting costume.[813] She and the Minotaur leave the stage with hounds baying, bells ringing and cries of 'Tallyho!', but the pigs who become bulls 'arrange themselves quietly behind the altar' and take no part in the hunt, suggesting that they are the 'radiant spirits' referred to by Liberty. In performance, this tableau would be the stage picture which the audience would be left with, not the exuberant exit of the hunt.

Swellfoot the Tyrant has been under-rated, since, more than any other of Shelley's dramas, performance is critical to the perception of its quality. The essence of comedy is timing, which cannot exist on a page. The humour added by costumes, scenery, choruses, acting and spectacular stage effects is also easily missed in the reading. There is a great difference between reading dialogue and watching a competent company impersonate the royal family, the cabinet ministers and parliament, mimic the mannerisms of unpopular figures of authority and make the most of Shelley's sexual jokes. Shelley has well-structured scenes and an extremely good grasp of the mechanisms needed at the time for creating an impact with stage effects, skill in writing parts which would have displayed the talents of professional actors and, as I have shown, he exhibits techniques drawn from the comic traditions of Aristophanes, *commedia*, burlesque, pantomime and Punch.

Swellfoot has been described as the 'only great lashing Aristophanic comedy, fantastic and grotesque, in our language',[814] and it is a play for which it is difficult to find parallels either in Shelley's other work or in other plays of the period. Shelley may not have known of a company which could perform it but, had it been staged in 1820, it would have made its points effectively to the audience. The very topicality which would have made it entertaining then has made it unsuitable for performance subsequently, as a knowledge of the contemporary background is required for the audience to understand all the jokes, although there are certainly some perennial issues and recently the issue of royalty and divorce re-awakened interest in this piece of history. It is clear that such a play requires a company with a high level of professionalism, but is, nevertheless, a very performable play.

---

813 *SCX*, p. 813.
814 Reiter, *Shelley's Poetry*, p. 253.

Conclusion

While Shelley's plays have some unchanging aspects, such as the consistent theme of opposition to tyranny, there is also a process of significant development in his dramatic writing. By considering each play individually and in thematic order it has been possible to reveal more clearly the influences on his writing, such as the theatrical practice of his time and the dramatic theory in the work of Schlegel and others. On the other hand, this should not obscure the development of Shelley's dramatic technique or his capabilities as a dramatist, since he never developed his full potential.

The stories and the structures of Shelley's plays were derived from other playwrights. Using structures which had proved successful in the past was a method of learning the craft, and one which Shelley might have dropped as he became more experienced and gained confidence in his ability. On the other hand, Shelley may not have wished to invent his own story, or perhaps he felt that he did not have the ability to do so. As it is not necessary for a play to have an original story, he may have continued to base his stories on legend or historical events. Shelley did not select trivial themes for his dramas. Each one deals, in its own way, with the downfall of tyranny.

Shelley's greatness as a poet gives his drama a strength which his contemporaries could not match since both actors and audiences would appreciate the strength of his verse. He created complex and memorable characters such as Beatrice Cenci and the King, the Queen or Archy from *Charles the First*. Shelley was able to give minor characters individuality, so that roles such as the Old Man in *Charles the First* or Orsino in *The Cenci* would also be interesting to perform. He does not appear to have been gifted in writing witty repartee of the kind occurring in the comedies of manners popular on the English stage, but there are witty rejoinders and exchanges in *Swellfoot the Tyrant* and *Charles the First*. Shelley's awareness of and his readiness to make use of modern and popular theatrical forms, such as the 'improvise' of Sgricci, the ballets of Viganò and the melodrama, burlesque and costume drama of the Georgian stage added freshness while the thorough research on which he based all his plays ensured their solidity. This research is evident from *Tasso* onwards. Although already familiar with the poet's work, he prepared himself by reading biographies and visiting the places connected with Tasso's life. Similar attention to research is evident in *Prometheus Unbound*, *The Cenci*, and *Charles the First* whilst *Hellas* and *Swellfoot the Tyrant* show a familiarity with current affairs and with his theme and style which enabled the dramas to be written quickly.

The development of Shelley's technique is shown in a greater flexibility in use of dialogue, using interruption and a more colloquial style, in suggesting more complicated scenic effects and the use of a greater numbers of actors on stage. The use of set speeches is more prevalent in *The Cenci*, written in 1819, than it is in *Swellfoot* (1820) or *Charles the First* (1822). *The Cenci* concentrates on dialogue between two main characters, even in the trial and banquet scenes, whereas in *Charles the First* there are several characters involved in each scene. He experiments in each play with different requirements for appropriate scenery: simple in *Hellas* but with spectacular effects in *Prometheus Unbound* and *Charles the First*. Each of his plays contain songs. Shelley's dramatic writing, therefore, shows a continuous development of styles, experimenting with dialogue, music, dance and staging techniques.

None of the plays are extant which Shelley and his sister Hellen say that he wrote in 1810. Any discussion of his development as a dramatist must therefore begin with a work of his maturity, the scenes for a historical drama, *Tasso* (1818), but the surprising sophistication of these scenes, despite their fragmentary nature, suggests that he had learnt from earlier attempts. They show an awareness of dramatic tension, character, and technical effects, and his choice of subject allowed him to include poetry and songs, in accord with both Schlegel's theories and those Shelley himself was to express in *A Defence of Poetry*. I have suggested that he did not finish this promising drama because the theme was to be tyrannical oppression and he found Tasso's flattery of his oppressor inconsistent with the defiant hero he required. He went on to write *Prometheus Unbound*, which he was to refuse to end with a reconciliation of oppressor and oppressed according to what was known of Aeschylus' tragedy. Even as Shelley was researching *Tasso,* he had absorbed ideas about the drama from Schlegel and had been inspired by the art of Viganò. I believe that his creative impulse had been strongly stimulated by both the story of Prometheus and the ballets he had just seen. The attractiveness of writing in a new style was too urgent to allow him to carry on any further work on *Tasso,* given his change of mind about the appropriateness of his hero to his theme. If Shelley had initially thought of *Prometheus Unbound* as a drama which could be performed, he discarded a comparatively conventional drama in form and content for one that is unique and consistent with ideas about the drama which he had expressed in *A Defence of Poetry.*

Whilst *Prometheus Unbound* (1819) demanded a style harmonious with Athenian drama and legend, Shelley's own times demanded one which took it further in terms of philosophy and dramatic technique. It is notable that Shelley requested information about Aeschylus' drama before beginning his own play. He had researched modern science and modern moral and political views which he added to that framework, drawing upon Schlegel's theories and his own observations of the ballets of Viganò. He thus attempted something completely original as a dramatist. If my supposition that Shelley saw a Vigano ballet in October 1819 and went to see *Otello* in January 1820 is correct, then Viganò's ballets both preceded and complemented his work on *Prometheus.*[815] I consider that the stage directions, the gestures, the dances and song which Shelley included in *Prometheus* were inspired by Viganò and his company and the designs of Sanquirico and Pregliasco and technical expertise of the La Scala stagehands. Certainly, awareness of the importance of silence, gesture and movement can be seen in Shelley's later work, and the idea of developing in modern form a reply to or reflection upon an Athenian drama was one he was to use again. He took the opportunity to work on a grand scale, to develop the dramatic techniques of characterisation, contrast and suspense, but, although he had written a performable play in *Prometheus Unbound,* it was not one which could have been staged at the time.

Despite developing this original style of dramatic writing, Shelley returned to the conventional five act tragedy of the London stage for *The Cenci* (1819) in which he once again dramatised the problem of tyranny and oppression. As in *Tasso,* he took a subject from Italian history, and, once again, the story had been well researched: Shelley was familiar with other versions, had discussed it with acquaintances, had visited the Colonna Palace and owned a copy of what was believed to be Beatrice's portrait. He developed character to a greater extent than he had done in *Prometheus.* His use of stage technique was in accordance with contemporary theatre practice; he wrote competently for the resources of the Covent Garden

---

815 *SPII,* pp. 456, 462.

stage and its actors. He was able to write both grand scenes, such as the trial and the banquet, and intimate scenes such as those between Beatrice and Orsino. He tried to avoid the constraints of censorship and used English dramatic techniques from Shakespeare to 'Monk' Lewis to develop a theatrical metaphor in sympathy with the tragedies then performed at the London theatres. It was not until it was performed in the following century that *The Cenci* was shown to be effective in performance, but while it was not accepted for censorship reasons, the Covent Garden manager recognised its quality and offered the opportunity to submit a second script.

Shelley continued to have ideas for plays, as the sketch for the Bonaparte scene shows. He now had two styles at his command. In writing *Swellfoot the Tyrant* (1820), he blended Athenian Old Comedy with burlesque, pantomime and *commedia dell'arte*; he probably saw these modern elements as being directly descended from the ancient. The fact that it was very quickly written suggests that his confidence in his ability as a dramatist had increased and that the form was becoming easier for him. Whether or not it was ever performed, *Swellfoot* is a performable play and made use of contemporary techniques such as trapdoors and processions as well as the dancing choruses of Aristophanes. His familiarity with Aristophanes' comedy enables him to use that structure and combine it with popular burlesque with complete assurance. The animal elements which appear to derive from the *commedia dell'arte* enable him to reveal the ruling class as vermin, while the pigs are changed, pantomime fashion, into symbols of virtue. The mock processions produce a comic result, yet, in his initial parody of *Oedipus*, they have a pathos derived from the awareness of the underlying historical reality which shows that *Swellfoot* has a similar serious intent to the comedies of Aristophanes. The dialogue for *Swellfoot* shows progress in a readiness to use interruption and a greater naturalism, and the dialogue is modern and colloquial so that the poetical passages heighten the humour by contrast.

In *Hellas* (1821), Shelley returned to Aeschylus, remaining faithful to the structure of *The Persians* but this time refreshing the form with the dramatic techniques of the contemporary London stage, the chorus of dancing girls and the scenery of a popular melodrama rather than the style of Italian ballet or opera used in *Prometheus Unbound*. Shelley had also seen the popularity of Sgricci's performance which may have given him confidence to bring the Athenian drama up to date. He developed the characters but limited the stage effects to the gradual change of light and the appearance of the phantom of Mahomet. The careful structure of reflecting chorus and dialogue enhances the simplicity of the staging, with its gradually setting sun, allowing Mahmud's changing state of mind to symbolise the end of empire. The youth, physical energy and defiance of the dancing Chorus are in sharp and constant contrast. The reports of battles by messengers reflect the unreliability of the newspaper reports, and also add an immediacy. *Hellas*, *Prometheus Unbound* and *Swellfoot the Tyrant* were not sidelines or diversions, but an exploration of the adaptation of classical forms to modern practice which enabled Shelley to gain greater confidence with his dramatic technique. They were, and are, performable.

All the techniques Shelley developed re-appear to serious purpose in *Charles the First* (1822). His recognition of the importance of visual effect and of humorous situation in *Swellfoot*, use of spectacular scenery, music and dance in the lyric dramas and characterisation in *The Cenci* enabled him to conceive *Charles the First* on a grand scale. He had trained himself to create a drama in which the scenery was to provide a metaphorical theatrical commentary and in which characters were brought to life with a few lines of characteristic language. The fragment suggests that everything Shelley had been learning would have been put to good effect had he been able to finish the drama. I believe that he had overcome some of the difficulties of creating a coherent plot and selecting characters out of the history of the chaotic years of civil war and revolution. He had thoroughly researched this period and the scenes he wrote show that he had mastered character, exposition and dialogue. The spectacular opening scene, a masterpiece of theatrical style, emerged out of the two processions of oppressors and oppressed in *Swellfoot the Tyrant*. It both symbolises the gulf between ruler and ruled and allows a mass of difficult historical information to be given in a naturalistic and vivid way. The intricate court scene, with its group dialogues, shows that Shelley had also acquired the technique of coping with a large cast on stage. The Westminster scene is building up to a climax of interrupted action, that is, an event which the audience expects but which does not take place. The anticipation of the audience is that the characters will board the ship and the drama lies in their being unexpectedly prevented. The complex characterisation of Charles and the well-defined lesser characters show that Shelley was far from being unable to write about real people. He takes the figure of Archy, no more than a slight reference in his sources, and develops him into a pivotal figure, suggesting a semi-fantastical character from Shakespeare and Calderón. Among these realistically drawn portraits,

Archy would provide music and satirical humour in a way that allows the songs and wit to comment upon rather than interrupt the action. Edward Williams believed Shelley, perhaps in response to Schlegel, was writing a Shakespearean drama. The full title, *The Historical Tragedy of Charles the First*, and the unfinished scenes certainly seem to indicate that this was the case, but it was not to be a mere Shakespearean imitation.

His final play, *Fragments of an Unfinished Drama* (1822), a magical fantasy with music, was intended for private performance. It shows his interest in yet another dramatic genre and one which was very popular on the contemporary stage. Once again the combination of poetry, song and spectacular effect was used, but the reference this time was to Hindu rather than ancient Greek mythology, showing that Shelley had sufficient dramatic knowledge at his disposal to adapt to another tradition. Writing for specific talents, the intimacy of the situation allowed an underlying humorous comment in the casting. The fact that he also gave his story an Indian setting when some of his intended performers had an Indian background suggests that he might have used their memories, stories and local knowledge to create incidents in the play. This indicates a further advance in his dramatic techniques and his choice of style and method shows that he is conversant with the fashion of London theatre which enjoyed such musical fantasies as *Oberon*.

Study of the manuscript of *Hellas*, for example, reveals that Shelley carefully edited his dramas, discarding material which did not accord with his plan, and it would appear that he generally based his work on thorough research. His method, then, seems to have been to research, having a rough mental plan, even if no written plan has survived, to write and to subsequently thoroughly edit the text. His achievement in dramatic writing was in the versatility of style, including verse drama appropriate for performance at the patent theatres and a more innovatory style which drew on international and classical sources. Had he lived to continue this dramatic practice, I believe it would have influenced the British theatre, perhaps sufficiently to maintain the tradition of verse drama and to prevent the divorce of music and dance from dialogue.

Although revivals of Jacobean and Restoration drama previously thought unperformable took place in the 20th century, the professional theatre took little notice of the drama of the late Georgian period though exceptions were made for the comedies of Sheridan and O'Keeffe's *Wild Oats*. As a result, the late nineteenth century belief lingers that the plays were not worth reviving. The Orange Tree Theatre, Richmond, Surrey, however, set a trend by producing Arthur Murphy's *All in the Wrong* in 1991 and following it with other Georgian plays including Holcroft's *The Road to Ruin* (2003) and Baillie's *De Monfort* (2008). The Theatre Royal, Bury St Edmunds, a restored Georgian theatre, has produced Douglas Jerrold's *Black Ey'd Susan* (2007). Inchbald's *Wives as They Were, Maids as They Are* (2008) and Holcroft's *He's Much to Blame* (2009). There have been recent productions of Schiller, for example, *Maria Stuart* at the National Theatre (1995) and the Donmar Warehouse (2005) and the Sheffield Crucible production of *Don Carlos* (2004). It is to be hoped that other companies follow in giving audiences the opportunity to experience the drama of this era, including Shelley's.

The Cenci, of course, is the most famous play from the period and was revived in the twentieth century, though the last large-scale production was 1959, a time when Shelley's reputation as a poet was at its nadir.[816] Now that he is again recognised as the great poet he is, there should be a prospect of his dramatic talent also being honoured by further productions of this play.

Two of Shelley's other completed plays, *Hellas* and *Swellfoot the Tyrant*, have not to my knowledge been performed on stage. They are both short, but they present more problems than *The Cenci* in being less wellknown and less conventional in style. The BBC radio production with Paul Daneman showed *Hellas* to be dramatically effective and it could be more so on stage with a similarly compelling actor as Mahmud and good singers and dancers. *Swellfoot* is more likely to be performed than it would have been fifty years ago since there is a greater availability of young actors trained in physical theatre and early twenty-first century audiences are more familiar with the historical background and, indeed, the prints. It could be coupled with a farce from the same period, another Shelley play, or even a play by Dario Fo whose style would not be incongruous and could even be considered a modern equivalent. However, both *Hellas* and *Swellfoot* present economic difficulties because of their large casts.

There have been productions of *Prometheus Unbound*, one of which is discussed by Cox.[817] Much of Shelley's scientific discussion is out-dated, however, and if few would have understood it in 1820, even fewer would now. Nevertheless, it may be possible to include a modern equivalent of the scientific data with the help of researchers. It would be a major project

816 See Donald H. Reiman, 'Shelley's Reputation Before 1960: A Sketch', *SPP*, pp. 539-349.
817 Cox, 'The Dramatist', p. 83.

for a company to interpret Shelley's mythological vision on stage, but one achievable given the multicultural nature of British theatre and its high skills of dancing and singing, and with a company having a sensitivity to Shelley's original stage directions and a willingness to re-create them in a modern idiom.

Among the uncompleted dramas, clearly *Tasso* and the *Fragments of an Unfinished Drama* would not be possible to perform as there is not enough available to tell a story. But the first act of *Charles the First* very clearly sets the scene of what was wrong with Charles's rule and what was making his subjects wish to rebel. It could not be staged in the style of the late Georgian Covent Garden unless a Georgian theatre were used, though there are modern equivalent ways of achieving its stage effects. While a group of fine actors would show the quality of this piece, even with doubling the cast would be very large. Nevertheless, if what there is of this play were shown, its quality would be as much of a revelation to audiences and critics as was *The Cenci* when the Cassons performed in 1922. The shortness of the fragment, however, would require it to be performed with another piece. A double bill with *Swellfoot* might be an appropriate choice, since both plays, though in contrasting styles, deal with the misrule of a king and the rebellion of the subjects.

With the publication of *The Unfamiliar Shelley* just as I was completing this study, it is clear that Shelley's drama is beginning to be accepted by scholars, and that interest in Shelley's work in all areas is increasing. I therefore believe that the theatre will not continue to ignore his drama, and the desire to investigate it more will be prompted by the coming publication of full and accessible texts from which performance texts can be made.

Appendix I
List of Performances Seen
by Shelley

This appendix is intended as a list of the performances seen by Shelley. It is not intended to replace the information given by Paula R. Feldman and Diana Scott-Kilvert in their edition of Mary Shelley's journal or Marion Kingston Stocking in her edition of Claire Clairmont's, but to gather it together with information from Harriet Grove's journal and from newspapers in both Italy and England to give a fuller picture of Shelley's theatre-going. Those titles I have been able to identify which are not included in the above sources I have marked with an asterisk.

It is not intended to give detailed information about the performances. I have classified these according to the way they were described by their contemporaries, but I should add a warning about interpretation. 'Opera' did not always mean a sung-through musical drama and a 'comic opera' was probably closer to what was later described as a 'musical comedy', a light play with songs. A 'pantomime ballet' or *ballet d'action* was close to what is now described as a ballet in that it told a story, but 'ballet' might also be a series of dances, closely linked in theme. 'Pantomime' at this time exhibited spectacular scenic effects in a sequence of magical transformations which displayed the acrobatic skills of the Harlequin, although Grimaldi added his inimitable humour: it was not *commedia dell'arte*. Particular care should be taken with 'melodrama' and 'burletta', which appear to be changing in meaning at this period and might conceal what might otherwise be called a play.

Key

B	Ballet	Int	Interlude
Ball	Masked ball	M	Melodrama
Bur	Burlesque	O	Opera
C	Comedy	P	Pantomime
Cmd	Commedia	PB	Pantomime Ballet
CB	Comic Ballet	Play	Play (kind unknown)
CO	Comic Opera	Pup	Puppet show
F	Farce	T	Tragedy
Imp	Improvvisatore	*	Not in *MWSJ* or *CCJ*

Notes

at K = The company were performing at the King's Theatre

at L = The company were preforming at the Lyceum.

Plays Shelley Saw

Date	Place	Type	Title	Author & Notes	Source
1802-1804	Richmond Theatre	C	*The Country Girl*	David Garrick, adapted from Wycherley's *The Country Wife*. Dorothy Jordan performing (Peggy).	(Medwin, p. 52)
1809	London				
Apr 9	Covent Garden (at K)	T	*Richard III*	William Shakespeare. *G.F. Cooke performing (Richard).	
		P	*Harlequin and Mother Goose, or The Golden Egg*	Thomas Dibdin. Music: Ware. Performers: Grimaldi (Clown), Jack Bologna (Harlequin), Luigi Bologna (Avaro), Miss Searle (Colinette), Samuel Simmons (Mother Goose).	(*SCII*, p. 517)
Apr 18	King's Theatre	O	*Teresa e Claudio*	Giuseppe Farinelli. Performers: Naldi, Morelli, Siboni, De Giovanni, Collini, Griglietti.	
		O	*I Villeggiatori Bizzarri*	Vincenzo Pucitta. Performers: Naldi, Morelli, Righi, Rovedino, De Giovanni, Brighetti, Pucitta, Griglietti, Collini.	
		B	*Le Mariage Secret, ou les habitants du Chêne*	Ballet: James Harvey D'Egville. Music: Federigo Fiorillo. Auguste Armand Vestris ballet master 1809-1817, (Smith, p. 50).	(*PBSLI*, p. 4; *The Times*, 18 April 1809; Smith, pp. 96-97, 100)
Apr 19	Drury Lane	CO	*The Cabinet*	Thomas Dibdin. Music: William Reeve.	
		B	*Love in a Tub*	Possibly based on Etherege's play.	
		F	*The Virgin Unmasked*	Henry Fielding. Included 'the favourite song of Timothy'.	(*SCII*, p. 517; *The Times*, 19 April, 1809)
1810	London				
It is not certain which theatre the Groves and Shelleys attended in April/May 1810, although I think Covent Garden more likely. *See Chapter 2*					
April 26	Covent Garden (at K)	C	*The Grecian Daughter*	Arthur Murphy. Performers: Mrs. Siddons (Euphrasia), Charles Young (Evander), Charles Kemble (Dionysus).	

Date	Place	Type	Title	Author & Notes	Source
		PB	*Oscar and Malvina	Music: Reeve. 'Taken from Ossian'; Glee 'Oscar the Defendant of Fingal'; Song 'I am a jolly gay pedlar'; Trio 'Come every jovial fellow'; Duet 'O ever in my Bosom Live'.	
	or Drury Lane *(at L)*	C	*Riches	Adapted from Massinger's *The City Madam* by James Bland Burgess. 'His alteration is very inferiour to the original play'.	(Genest, p. 163, who records *Hit and Miss* as the afterpiece that night with Charles Mathews)
		CB	*The Village Doctor	Possibly based on the burletta, *The Village Doctor, or Killing No Cure* by John Cartwright Cross (1796).	
		CO	*No Song No Supper	Music: Stephen Storace. Libretto: Prince Hoare.	
Apr 27	Covent Garden	T	*Henry IV Pt I	William Shakespeare. Performers: C. Murray (Henry IV), C. Kemble (Henry, Prince of Wales), Menage (Prince John of Lancaster), Waddy (Earl of Westmorland), John Kemble (Hotspur), G.F. Cooke (Falstaff).	
		PB	*Paul and Virginia	Probably James Cobb's 2-act "Musical Drama" based on Bernardin de St Pierre's novel. Performers: Charles Incledon (Paul), Mrs. H. Johnston (Virginia)	
	or Drury Lane *(at L)*	C	*The Honeymoon	John Tobin. Elliston performing.	
May 2	Covent Garden	T	*Douglas	John Home. Performers: Mrs. Siddons (Lady Randolph), C. Kemble (Norval).	
		CO	*Lock and Key	Music: William Shields. Libretto: Prince Hoare. Mr. Munden performing as Captain Queerly.	*See Appendix II*
	or Drury Lane *(at L)*	C	*Hypocrite	Isaac Bickerstaffe, after Colley Cibber, based on Moliere's *Tartuffe*.	

Date	Place	Type	Title	Author & Notes	Source
		F	*Honest Thieves	Thomas Knight, taken from Sir Robert Howard's *The Committee* (1710).	
		Int	*Croaking	Taken from Oliver Goldsmith's *The Good-natur'd Man*.	
May 3	King's Theatre	O	*La Vestale	Vincenzo Pucitta. Catalani's benefit night. 'Went to the Opera I hate it more than ever, so does P.' Catalani's voice was 'extremely rich, powerful and of great compass and flexibility' ... 'of a most uncommon quality, and capable of exertions almost supernatural'.	
		Div	*A Scotch divertissement		
		B	*Psiché	Ballet composer: Pierre Gardel. Deshayes performing.	(*SCII*, p. 577; Smith, pp. 83, 99, 103, 147; *The Times*, 26, 27 April, 2, 3 May 1810)
1811 -1813					
	Although there are no recorded theatre visits between 1810 and 1814, Shelley's sojourns in London, Bath and Edinburgh allow for theatre-going. It also seems that he saw productions at Drury Lane 1812/13 since he knew of the 'bronze lamps' later removed. (*PBSLII*, p. 71)				
1814	London				
Oct 14	Drury Lane	T	Hamlet	William Shakespeare. Edmund Kean performing (Hamlet).	(*MWSJ*, p. 35)
1815	Windsor				
Aug 21	Theatre Royal	C	A School for Scandal	The Theatre Royal, Windsor opened with this play on this date which probably was the occasion Peacock records seeing it with Shelley. The story that Shelley appeared onstage here suggests the possibility that he was recognised in the audience.	(Wolfe, II, p. 330; Bebbington, p. 215)

Date	Place	Type	Title	Author & Notes	Source
There are no more records until 1817, but Shelley stayed with Leigh Hunt in Hampstead during the winter of 1816/1817 when he may have attended performances not recorded in Mary Shelley's journal. As she did not record *La Molinara*, noted in Claire Clairmont's journal, it is likely that she did not record performances Shelley attended when they were apart. The evidence of 'all' and lists of names included in a party for the opera from Claire Clairmont's journal, and Peacock's corroboration of other attendance suggests that Shelley's presence can be assumed at a performance entered in Mary Shelley's journal unless they were apart.					
1817	London				
Jan 28	Drury Lane	C	*The Jealous Wife*	George Colman the Elder. *Eliza O'Neill performing (Mrs. Oakley).	
		C	*The Ravens*	Isaac Pocock.	(Genest, p. 600; *MWSJ*, p. 157)
Feb 11	Drury Lane	T	*The Merchant of Venice*	William Shakespeare. Kean performing (Shylock).	
		B	*Patrick's Return*	Hazlitt reviewed *Patrick's Return* very favourably.	
		F	*The Panel*	Isaac Bickerstaffe (adapted by Kemble for Dorothy Jordan), based on Calderon's *El Escondido y la Tapada*.	(*MWSJ*, p. 164)
Feb 22	Drury Lane	C	*The Beggar's Opera*	John Gay.	
		Burl	*Bombastes Furioso*	W.B. Rhodes. Mathews and Liston performing.	
		B	*The Flight of the Zephyr*	Mélanie performing.	(*MWSJ*, p. 165)
Mar 11	Drury Lane	T	*Manuel*	Charles Maturin (author of *Bertram*). Kean performing.	(*MWSJ*, p. 166)
May 23	King's Theatre	O	*Don Giovanni*	Mozart.	
		B	*Zulica, ou les Peruviens*	Mary arrived from Marlow on this day. She particularly mentioned Shelley as her companion; perhaps it was a celebration.	(*MWSJ*, p. 170)
1818	London				
Jan 29	King's Theatre	O	*La Molinara*	Giovanni Paisiello. 'Go to the Opera with Hogg - Shelley Peacock & the Hunts.'	(*CCJ*, p. 82)

Date	Place	Type	Title	Author & Notes	Source
				La Molinara was considered by the Earl of Mount Edgcumbe (amateur musician and critic) one of two 'best comic' operas of the 1791 season, but in 1817 a duet by Rossini was added. Fodor performing.	(Smith, pp. 17, 143)
Feb 10	King's Theatre	O	*Don Giovanni*	Mary arrived from Marlow. 'We all go to the Opera in the Evening.'	(*CCJ*)
		B	*Acis & Galatea*		
Feb 14	King's Theatre	O	*Don Giovanni*	With Clare (Mary did not go). 'Peacock & Hogg' too.	(*CCJ*)
Feb 16	Covent Garden	T	*Fazio*	Milman. Eliza O'Neill performing. Claire mentions 'all'.	(*CCJ*)
		P	*Harlequin Gulliver, or the Flying Island*	John O'Keeffe. Grimaldi performing.	
Feb 21	King's Theatre	O	*Don Giovanni*	'We all go'.	(*CCJ*)
		B	*Zephyr, ou La Retour du Printemps*	Louis Duport (rev. by Guillet). Mélanie performing.	(Smith, p. 155)
Feb 23	Drury Lane	M	*The Bride of Abydos*	'They go' must refer to both Shelleys.	(*CCJ*)
Feb 24	King's Theatre	O	*The Marriage of Figaro*	'All go'. Claire notes the opera as *Don Giovanni*. Mary had already seen it on 1 February 1817 with the Hunts.	(*CCJ*)
Feb 28	King's Theatre	O	*Griselda ossia la virtu al cimento*	Ferdinando Paër. 'We all go'. Performers: Fodor, probably also Angrisani, Begrez, Crivelli, Naldi. Paër's music was 'of not the highest order'. Fodor's voice had 'sweetness' but her style was 'not truly Italian'; she was Russian.	(*CCJ*) (Smith, p. 151) (*The Times* qtd in Smith, p. 146) (Mount Edgcumbe, qtd in Smith, p. 136-137).
		B	*Zephyr, ou La Retour du Printemps*		

Date	Place	Type	Title	Author & Notes	Source
Mar 2	Drury Lane	C	*The Castle of Glendower*	Samuel William Ryley. Performers: Dowton, Harley, Knight, S. Penley, Wallack, Mrs. Allsop, Mrs. Orger, Mrs. Sparks. 'This was acted but once'	(Genest, VIII, p. 643)
Mar 5	Covent Garden	T	*Fazio*	Milman. Performers: C. Kemble (Giraldi Fazio), W. Blanchard (Bartolo), Egerton (Duke of Florence), Miss O'Neill (Bianca), Mrs. Faucit (Aldabella).	(Genest, VIII, p. 656; also mentions the Bath production, p. 669)
		C	*The Libertine*	Pocock, adapted from Shadwell, with music from *Don Giovanni*.	
Mar 7	King's Theatre	O	*Don Giovanni*	'Peacock and Shelley'.	(*MWSJ*)
		B	*Zephyr, ou La Retour du Printemps*		(*MWSJ*, pp. 193-196; *CCJ*, pp. 83-86)
Mar 10	King's Theatre	O	*The Barber of Seville*	Gioachino Rossini.	(Wolfe, II, p. 330; *CCJ*, p. 86)
1818	Turin				
Apr 1	Teatro Regio	O	[no title]	'We do not know the name of it & cannot make out the story - The two principal singers are very good'.	(*MWSJ*)
1818	Milan				
Apr 5	La Scala	O	*Etelinda*	Peter von Winter.	
		B	*Otello*	Salvatore Viganò.	
Apr 7	La Scala	O	*Etelinda*		
		B	*Otello*		
Apr 13	Marionetti	Pup	[no title]		(*CCJ*)
Apr 20	La Scala	O	*Il rivale di se stesso*	Joseph Weigl.	
		B	*La spada di Kenneth*	Viganò.	
Apr 21	La Scala	O	**Il rivale di se stesso*		
		B	**La spada di Kenneth*		
Apr 29	La Scala	O	*Il rivale di se stesso*		

Date	Place	Type	Title	Author & Notes	Source
		B	*La spada di Kenneth*		(*MWSJ*, pp. 203-207; *CCJ*, pp. 89-92)
				Matteo Sartorio (Archivio Museo Scala; email, 11 July 2005) has confirmed that the Shelleys saw *La Spada di Kenneth* three times; once an opera was introduced there was no change in programme. Disappointingly, they did not see the great Carlo Blasis, who created the role, dance 'Otello' as he did not perform in April.	
1818	**Venice**				
Oct 14	San Benedetto	O	*Otello*	Rossini. *Tacchinardi sang.	
Oct 21	Vendramin S. Luca	C	**L'Anno 1835*	Comica compagnia Petrelli e Fabrizi. It is not certain that Shelley saw either of these.	
Oct 22	Vendramin S. Luca	Cmd	**Arlecchino flagellò dei Cavallieri Serventi*		(*MWSJ*, pp. 230, 233; La Gazzetta Privilegiata di Venezia, N. 229-237, 13-22 October 1818)
1818	**Rome**				
Nov 22		O	[no title]	'The worst I ever saw'.	(*MWSJ*, p. 238. There were a number of opera houses in Rome, so it has not been possible to trace this)
1818	**Naples**				
Dec 13	San Carlo	O	*Ricciardo e Zoraide*	Rossini.	
		B	*La festa della rosa*	Salvatore Taglioni (uncle of Marie).	(*MWSJ*, pp. 243, 243n)

Date	Place	Type	Title	Author & Notes	Source
1819	Florence				
Oct 9	?Pergola	O	[no title]	'A beautiful ballet' probably at Teatro della Pergola, the main theatre for opera and ballet. Unfortunately, the *Gazzetta di Firenze* for this date is missing, so titles could not be ascertained. The ballet may have been by Viganò's company, which toured and was at Venice earlier in the year for the Carnival.	(*MWSJ*, p. 298; Archivio storico La Fenice <http://www.archivio storico lafenice. org:49542/ ArcFenice/> [accessed 9 Dec 2010])
		B	[no title]		
1820	Florence				
Jan 3	Pergola	O	*La rosa bianca, e la rosa rossa*	Giovanni Simone Mayr. It is not certain which theatre Shelley attended on this occasion but I believe this performance is most likely.	
		B	*Otello*	Viganò (almost certainly, see above)	
	or Cocomero	P	*La Lusinghiera*	Nota.	(*MWSJ*, p. 304; information from Professor Marcello de Angelis, email 13 June 2006)
It has been suggested that the reason Mary Shelley entered so few titles of the operas she saw in Pisa was that they were not as good as elsewhere.					(*MWSJ*, p. 390)
However, in 1820, Angelica Catalani, the famous soprano, settled in Pisa and herself sang in *Aureliano in Palmira* which Claire saw on 11 March 1820. During this period, Teatro Rossi also passed to a different committee, who allotted 200 scudi per annum to the theatre.					(dell'Ira, pp. 14, 39n)
Both these events suggest a rise in standard. I suggest that perhaps the reason for not entering a title is that the opera was one they had already seen, operas being run in repertoire. Mary did not note the title of *Fazio* on her second visit, but noted *The Libertine*, the afterpiece, which she had not already seen. Tacchinardi is noted, but not the opera, but, as he was famous for his singing in *I Misteri Eleusini*, she would have associated his name with the title. As the Shelleys now had a group of friends to accompany them to the theatre, they occasionally went without each other, but as usual the journal entries do not make it clear.					

Date	Place	Type	Title	Author & Notes	Source
1820	Pisa				
Feb 8	Teatro Rossi	O	*La Cenerentola*	Rossini.	(*MWSJ*, p. 308; *CCJ*, p. 122)
Dec 21	Teatro Rossi	Imp	*Pyramus and Thisbe*	Sgricci.	(*MWSJ*, p. 343; *CCJ*, p. 198)
		Imp	*Iphigenia in Tauris*	Sgricci.	
1821	Pisa				
Jan 21	Teatro Rossi	O	[no title]	With the Williamses.	(*MWSJ*, p. 350)
Jan 22	Teatro Rossi	Imp	*Quattro Etade La morte d'Ettore*	Sgricci.	(*MWSJ*, p. 350)
Feb 2	Teatro Rossi	O	*Il Matrimonio Segreto*	Domenico Cimarosa. Based on *The Clandestine Marriage* by George Colman the Elder and David Garrick.	(*MWSJ*, p. 352)
Mar 25	Teatro Rossi	O	[no title]	'With W. and Laurette'.	(*MWSJ*, p. 358)
Apr 2	Teatro Rossi	O	**I Misteri Eleusini*	Mayr. This had its Teatro Rossi premiere on 27 January 1821 with the following performers: Giovanna Girare, Teghil, Nicola Tacchinardi, Maddalena Albertini, Pio Botticelli, 1 violini direttore Raniero Quercioli. Tacchinardi's performance in this opera was much praised.	(*MWSJ*, p. 359; dell'Ira, p. 38) (Review of Otello, Gazzetta Privilegiata di Venezia, N. 224, 9 October 1818)
Dec 26	Teatro Rossi	O	[no title]	John Sinclair performing.	(*MWSJ*, p. 388, Williams, p. 120)

Date	Place	Type	Title	Author & Notes	Source
1822	Pisa				
Jan 13	Teatro Rossi	O	*Maria Stuarda	Saverio Mercadante. Performers: Serafina Rubini, Vittorio Isotta, Giovanni Ascolese, Gaetano Ghedini, Pio Botticelli 1 violino direttore Raniero Quercioli. The Williamses dined with the Shelleys, implying that they all went together to the opera.	(*MWSJ*, p. 389; Williams, p. 124; dell'Ira, p. 38)
Jan 15	Teatro Rossi	O	[no title]	'They all dine with us. The opera in the evening' suggests the whole party went.	(*MWSJ*, p. 390)
Jan 17	Teatro Rossi	O	[no title]		(*MWSJ*, p. 390; Williams, p. 125)
Jan 19	Teatro Rossi	O	*Il gioventu di Enrico*	Giovanni Pacini. Williams considered it 'dull, insipid'. Again, the Williamses dined with the Shelleys, suggesting they all went.	(*MWSJ*, pp. 390, 390n; Gisborne & Williams, p. 126)
Jan 27	Teatro Rossi	O	[no title]	Williams's entry suggests everyone went but him. 'The S[helley]'s Tom [Medwin] and T.[relawny] dined here, who went to the opera'.	(*MWSJ*, p. 393; Gisborne & Williams, p. 127)
Jan 29	Teatro Rossi	O	[no title]	It is not clear if Shelley saw this, as Williams does not say who went.	(*MWSJ*, p. 393; Gisborne & Williams, p.127)
Feb 19	Teatro Rossi	Ball	Veglione	'To the Veglione with Jane, T.[relawny] and S.' Opening masked ball of carnival, which always took place in the theatre auditorium.	(*MWSJ*, p. 398) (John Rosselli, *Musicians*, p. 57)

Date	Place	Type	Title	Author & Notes	Source
Mar 9	Teatro Rossi	O	*Ginevra de Scozia*	Probably Johann Simon Mayr, but Vincenzo Pucitta also wrote an opera with this title. 'Returned home in the boat and went to the theatre with Jane and Mary' implying that he and Shelley, after a day sailing and shooting together, went to this with Jane Williams and MWS.	(Gisborne & Williams, p. 133)
Mar 12	Teatro Rossi	Play	[no title]	'At the Theatre with Shelley'	(Gisborne & Williams, p. 134)
Mar 14	Teatro Rossi	O	[no title]	'Go to the theatre with the W. & T'; 'Sail'd with S[helley] [and] Trelawny - we afterwards went to the Theatre' implies Shelley and Trelawny also went.	(*MWSJ*, p. 402; Gisborne & Williams, p. 134)
Mar 19	Teatro Rossi	Play	[no title]	'Dined at S[helley]'s and went with S[helley] to the Threatre - Good acting in parts'.	(Gisborne & Williams, p. 135).
Mar 21	Teatro Rossi	Play	[no title]	'To the Theatre in the evening'.	(*MWSJ*, p. 403)
April 26	Teatro Rossi	P	*Rosmunda*	Alfieri. 'S[helley] dined here and with Jane we went to see the performance of Alfieri's "Rosamunda" - did not understand a word'. MWS already at Lerici	(Gisborne & Williams, p. 145)

Plays Shelley Did Not See

The following plays are ones that might be thought to have been seen by Shelley. Close attention to the journal entries, however, indicates that he was not at these performances for the reasons given.

Date	Place	Type	Title	Author & Notes	Source
1817	London				
Feb 1	Drury Lane	O	*The Marriage of Figaro*	Mozart. 'Mrs. H. and I go to the opera - Figaro' suggests that Shelley was not at this performance. It was reviewed in *The Examiner* (9 February 1817); these were probably reviewer's seats.	(*MWSJ*, p. 161)
May 27	Drury Lane	P	*Barbarossa*	Dr. John Brown.	
		CO	*Paul and Virginia*	Probably James Cobb, see 27 April 1810. Shelley did not see this as he had returned to Marlow on May 26.	(*MWSJ*, p. 171)
1821	Lucca				
Jan 12		Imp	*Inez di Castro*	Sgricci. Shelley was unwell at the time and did not accompany Mary.	
1822	Pisa				
Feb 6	Teatro Rossi	O	*La Pittura d'Amore*	Williams 'went with Mary and & Jane', implies that Shelley did not attend this.	(*MWSJ*, p. 394; Gisborne & Williams, p. 128)
Mar 28	Teatro Rossi	P	[no title]	'Mary dined... went to theatre', implies she went with the Williamses. Shelley may not have gone because of being hurt in the Masi scuffle.	(*MWSJ*, pp. 404n, 405; Gisborne & Williams, p. 140)
April 8	Teatro Rossi	P	[no title]	'Trelawny dined and with Mary we went to the Play', apparently not Shelley.	(*MWSJ*, p. 407; Gisborne & Williams, p. 142)

Appendix II
The Programme of Songs with the Performance of *Douglas*

As *Douglas* was a special benefit night 'Under the Patronage of his Royal Highness the Prince of Wales, for the Benefit of the Fund of the Relief of Aged and Inform Actors, and the Widows and Children of Actors dcd.' there were songs between the acts sung by the great singers of the day, which, according to *The Times*, Wednesday 2 May 1810, were:

'Says a Smile to a Tear' sung by John Braham 'accompanied by himself on the pianoforte'

'O Quanto L'Anima' sung by Angelica Catalani

The Song of 'Victory' from *The Travellers* sung by John Braham

probably 'The Glad Trumpet Sounds a Victory' from *The Travellers* by Mr Cherry and Domenico Corri

Mozart's Celebrated Air 'O Dolce Concento with Variations' sung by Angelica Catalani

'And By Particular Desire' The Comic Song of 'Sly Renard' by Mr. Munden

The Bay of Biscay-O from *Spanish Dollars, or the Priest of the Parish* by Andrew Cherry, music by John Davy, sung by Charles Incledon

Select Bibliography

Aeschylus I: Oresteia, trans. by Richmond Lattimore (Chicago: Chicago University Press, 1953)

Aeschylus II: The Suppliant Maidens and *The Persians*, trans. by Seth G. Bernadete, *Seven Against Thebes* and *Prometheus Bound*, trans. by David Grene (Chicago: Chicago University Press, 1956)

Allott, Miriam, ed., *Essays on Shelley* (Liverpool: Liverpool University Press, 1982)

Amedei, Maria Grazia, *Il Teatro Goldoni di Venezia* (Università degli Studi di Urbino, Anno Accademico 1969-1970)

(Anon) *Authentic Memoirs of the Green Room* (London: J. Roach, [1815(?)])

Archivio Storico La Fenice http://www.archiviostoricolafenice.org:49542/ArcFenice

Aristophanes, *Lysistrata, The Acharnians, The Clouds*, trans. by Alan H. Sommerstein (Harmondsworth: Penguin, 1973)

—, *The Wasps, The Poet and the Women, The Frogs*, trans. by David Barrett (Harmondsworth: Penguin 1964)

Arundell, Dennis, *The Story of Sadler's Wells* (London: Hamish Hamilton, 1965)

Baer, Marc, *Theatre and Disorder in Late Georgian London* (Oxford: Clarendon Press, 1992)

Baker, Carlos, *Shelley's Major Poetry* (Princeton, NJ: Princeton University Press, 1948)

Baines, Paul and Edward Burns, eds, *Five Romantic Plays 1768-1821* (Oxford: Oxford University Press, 2000)

Barcus, James E., *Shelley: The Critical Heritage* (London: Routledge, 1995)

Beaumont and Fletcher, *Dramatic Works in the Beaumont and Fletcher Canon*, gen. ed. Fredson Bowers, 9 vols (Cambridge: Cambridge University Press, 1970-1994)

Bebbington, William, 'Shelley and the Windsor Stage', *Notes and Queries*, n.s. 2 (May 1956), 213-216

Behrendt, Stephen C., *Shelley and His Audiences* (Lincoln: University of Nebraska Press, 1989)

Bergman, Gösta, *Lighting in the Theatre* (Totowa, NJ: Rowman and Littlefield, 1977)

Bernard, John, *Retrospections of the Stage*, 2 vols (London: Henry Colburn, 1827)

Bishop, Sir H.R.,'The Celebrated Echo Song' (William Reeve) (London and Dublin: Goulding, D'Almaine, Potter & Co. WM 1820) BL H.1654 pp. (24.) 004603022/004832989

Boaden, James, *Memoirs of Mrs. Siddons*, 2 vols (London: Henry Colburn, 1827)

—, *The Life of Mrs. Jordan*, 2 vols (London: Edward Bull, 1831)

Bodleian Shelley Manuscripts, The, gen. ed. Donald H. Reiman, 22 vols (New York and London: Garland, 1986-1997); Index vol. (New York and London: Routledge, 2002): *Volume IX: The Prometheus Unbound Notebooks: a facsimile of Bodleian MSS. Shelley e. 1, e. 2, and e. 3*, ed. by Neil Fraistat (New York: Garland, 1991); *Volume XII, 'Charles the First' Draft Notebook, A Facsimile of Bodleian MS Shelley adds. e. 17*, ed. by Nora Crook (New York: Garland, 1991); *Volume XVI: The Hellas Notebook, A Facsimile of Bodleian MS. Shelley adds. e. 7*, ed. by Donald H. Reiman and Michael Neth (New York: Garland, 1994); *Volume XIX: The Faust draft notebook: a facsimile of Bodleian MS. Shelley adds. e. 18*, ed. by Nora Crook and Timothy Webb (New York: Garland, 1997)

Booth, Michael R., *English Melodrama* (London: Herbert Jenkins, 1965)

—, *Prefaces to English Nineteenth-Century Theatre* (Manchester: Manchester University Press, 1980)

—, Richard Southern, R. Davies, and F. and L.L. Marker, eds, *The Revels History of Drama in English, IV*, 6 vols, 1750-1880 (London: Methuen, 1975)

Borer, Mary Cathcart, *The Story of Covent Garden* (London: Robert Hale, 1984)

Bradby, David, Louis James and Bernard Sharratt, eds, *Performance and Politics in Popular Drama: Aspects of Popular Entertainment in Theatre, Film and Television, 1800-1976* (Cambridge: Cambridge University Press, 1980)

Bratton, Jacky, *New Readings in Theatre History* (Cambridge: Cambridge University Press, 2003)

Brown, R. Douglas, *The Port of London* (Lavenham: Terence Dalton, 1978)

Burley, Stephen, 'Shelley, the United Irishmen and the Illuminati', *KSR*, 17 (2003), 18-26

Burroughs, Catherine B., *Closet Stages: Joanna Baillie and the Theater Theory of British Romantic Women Writers* (Philadelphia: University of Pennsylvania Press, 1997)

Burroughs, Catherine B., ed., *Women in British Romantic Theatre: Drama,*

Performance, and Society, 1790-1840 (Cambridge: Cambridge University Press, 2000)

Bush-Bailey, Gilli, 'Still Working it Out' in *Nineteenth Century Theatre and Film*, 29.2 (2002)

Byron, George Gordon Noel, *Byron's Letters and Journals*, ed. by Leslie Marchand, 12 vols (London: John Murray, 1973-1994)

—, *Poetical Works*, ed. by Frederick Page, new edn rev. by John Jump (Oxford: Oxford University Press, 1970)

Calderón de la Barca, Pedro, *The Physician of his Honour*, trans. by Dian Fox with Donald Hindley (Warminster: Aris & Phillips, 1997)

—, *The Schism in England*, trans. by Kenneth Muir and Ann L. Mackenzie (Warminster: Aris & Phillips, 1990)

Cameron, K.N., *Shelley: The Golden Years* (Cambridge, MA: Harvard University Press, 1974)

—, 'Shelley and the Reformers', *ELH*, 12 (1945), 85

—, 'Shelley and the *Conciones ad Populum*', *Modern Language Notes*, 57.8 (December 1942), 673-674.

— and Horst Frenz, 'The Stage History of Shelley's "The Cenci"', *PMLA*, 60 (1945), 1088

Carlson, Julie A., *In the Theatre of Romanticism: Coleridge, Nationalism, Women* (Cambridge: Cambridge University Press, 1994)

Campbell, Thomas, *Life of Mrs. Siddons*, 2 vols (London: Effingham Wilson, 1834)

Carroll, Lewis, *Alice in Wonderland* (London: Collins, [n.d.])

Cave, Richard, ed., *The Romantic Theatre: An International Symposium* (Gerrards Cross: Colin Smyth, 1986)

Cheeke, Stephen, 'Shelley's *The Cenci*: Economies of a "Familiar" Language', *KSJ*, 57 (1998) 142-160

Chernaik, Judith, ed., 'Shelley's Hellas', BBC transcript, BBC Radio 3, 13 June 1976, 1810-1915

Cochran, Peter, 'Byron and Shelley: Radical Incompatibles', *Romanticism on the Net*, 43 (2006) <http://www.erudit.org/revue/ron/2006/v/n43/013589ar.html> [accessed 25 January 2007]

Coleridge, Samuel Taylor, *Remorse and Zapolya, or a Christmas Tale* in *The poetical works of Samuel Taylor Coleridge: including poems and versions of poems now published for the first time*, ed. by Ernest Hartley Coleridge (Oxford: Oxford University Press, 1912)

Colman, George, the Elder, *The Jealous Wife* (London: T. Becket, 1777)

Colman, George, the Younger, *Who Wants A Guinea?* (London: Longman, Hurst, Rees, Orme, and Brown, 1808)

Conticello, Baldassare, *Pompeii Archaeological Guide* (Novara: Istituto Geografico de Agostini, 1989)

Cox Jeffrey N., 'Re-viewing Romantic Drama', *Literature Compass* 1.1 (2004) <doi:10.1111/j.1741-4113.2004.00096.x>

— and Michael Gamer, eds, *The Broadview Anthology of Romantic Drama* (Peterborough: Broadview Press, 2003)

—, ed., *Seven Gothic Dramas 1789-1825* (Athens: Ohio University Press, 1992)

Cox, Philip, *Reading Adaptations: Novels and Verse Narratives on the Stage, 1790-1840* (Manchester: Manchester University Press, 2000)

Crochunis, Thomas C. and Michael Eberle-Sinatra, gen. eds, *British Women Playwrights around 1800* <http://www.etang.umontreal.ca/bwp1800/essays/crochunis_nassr99.html> [accessed 13 January 2007]

Crook Nora, ed., *The Boat on the Serchio*, KSR, 7 (1992), 85-93

—, 'Calumniated Republicans and the Hero of 'Charles the First', *KSJ*, 57 (2007), 141-158

— and Guiton, Derek, *Shelley's Venomed Melody* (Cambridge: Cambridge University Press, 1986)

Curran, Stuart, 'The Political Prometheus', *SIR*, 25.3 (Fall 1986), 429-455

—, *Shelley's Annus Mirabilis: The Maturing of an Epic Vision* (San Marino, CA: Huntington Library, 1975)

—, *Shelley's Cenci: Scorpions Ringed with Fire* (Princeton, NJ: Princeton University Press, 1970)

Davis, Tracy C. and Ellen Donkin, *Women and Playwriting in 19th Century Britain* (Cambridge: Cambridge University Press, 1999)

Dawson, P.M.S., 'Shelley and the Improvvisatore Sgricci: An Unpublished Review', *KSMB*, 32 (1981), 19-29

de Angelis, Marcello, et al., *Lo spettacolo maraviglioso: il Teatro della Pergola, l'opera a Firenze* (Florence: Archivio di Stato di Firenze, 6 ottobre-30 dicembre 2000)

de Marly, Diana, *Costume on the Stage 1600-1940* (London: Batsford, 1982)

dell'Ira, Gino, *I teatri di Pisa (1773-1986)* (Pisa: Giardini Editori, 1987)

Denford, Jocelyn, Programme Notes, Damned Poets Theatre Company production of *The Cenci* at the Lyric Studio, Hammersmith, August 1992

Dibdin, Thomas, *The Reminiscences of Thomas Dibdin*, 2 vols (London: H. Colburn, 1827; repr. New York: AMS Press, 1970)

—, *The Cabinet: An Opera in Three Acts etc.* (London: Longman, Hurst, Rees & Orme, 1805)

—, *The Italian Wife*. From H.H. Milman's Fazio. No. 1998 Larpent Plays in the Huntington Library, British Library microfiches 254/.819, 254/.820

Dimond, William, *The Bride of Abydos: A Tragick Play, in Three Acts; as performed at the Theatre Royal, Drury Lane* (London: Richard White, 1818)

Dishman, Robert B., *Burke and Paine on Revolution and the Rights of Man* (New York: Scribner, 1971)

Donkin, Ellen, *Getting into the Act* (London: Routledge, 1995)

Donohue, Joseph W. Jr., *Dramatic Character in the English Romantic Age* (Princeton, NJ: Princeton University Press, 1970)

—, *Theatre in the Age of Kean* (Oxford: Blackwell, 1975)

Dowden, Edward, *The Life of Percy Bysshe Shelley*, 2 vols (London: Kegan Paul, Trench, 1886)

Downer, Alan S., 'Nature to Advantage Dress'd', *PMLA*, 58 (1943), 1002-1037

—, 'Players and the Painted Stage', *PMLA*, 61 (1946), 522-570

Duchartre, Pierre Louis, *The Italian Comedy*, trans. by Randolph T. Weaver (New York: Dover, 1966)

Duthie, Peter, ed., *Joanna Baillie's Plays on the Passions (1798 edition)* (Peterborough, Ont.: Broadview Press, 2001), pp. 108-109.

Earl, John, 'The Rotunda; Variety Stage and Socialist Platform' *Theatre Notebook*, 58.2, (2004), 71-90

Easterling, P.E., and J.V. Muir, *Greek Religion and Society* (Cambridge: Cambridge University Press, 1985)

Eaton, Charlotte Ann, *Rome in the Nineteenth Century; Containing a Complete Account of the Ruins of the Ancient City, the Remains of the Middle Ages, and the Monuments of Modern Times with Remarks on the Fine Arts, on the State of Society, and on the Religious Ceremonies, Manners and Customs of the Modern Romans, in a Series of Letters Written During a Residence at Rome, in the Years 1817 and 1818*, 3 vols (Edinburgh: James Ballantyne, 1820)

Erdman, David V., 'Byron's Stage Fright: The History of his Ambition and Fear of Writing for the Stage', *ELH*, 6 (1939), 219-243

Erkelenz, Michael, 'The Genre and Politics of Shelley's "Swellfoot the Tyrant"', *The Review of English Studies*, n.s. 47.188 (November 1996), 500-520

Erne, Lukas, *Shakespeare as Literary Dramatist* (Cambridge: Cambridge University Press, 2003.

Ervine, St. John. 'Shelley as a Dramatist' in *Essays by Divers Hands* (London: Royal Society of Literature, 1936)

Esterhammer, Angela, *Romanticism at the Improvvisatore: Tommaso Sgricci and the Spectacle of Improvisation*, paper given at Romantic Spectacle conference, 8 July 2006

Everest, Kelvin, ed., *Shelley Revalued: Essays from the Gregynog Conference* (Leicester: Leicester University Press, 1983)

Fielding, Henry, *An Old Man Taught Wisdom: or The Virgin Unmask'd, A Farce* (London: J. Watts, 1735)

Finberg, Melinda C., ed., *Eighteenth Century Women Dramatists* (Oxford: Oxford University Press, 2001)

Fiske, Roger, *English Theatre Music in the Eighteenth Century* (Oxford: Oxford University Press, 1986)

—, ed., *Reminiscences of Michael Kelly* (London: Oxford University Press, 1975)

Fo, Dario, *The Tricks of the Trade*, trans. by Joe Farrell, ed. by Stuart Hood (London: Methuen, 1991)

Franklin, Michael J., ed., *Romantic Representations of British India* (London: Routledge, 2006)

Ganzel, Dewey, 'Patent Wrongs and Patent Theatres: Drama and the Law in the Early 19th Century', *PMLA*, 76 (September 1961), 387-388

Garrick, David, *The Plays of David Garrick*, ed. by H.W. Pedicord and F.W. Bergmann, 8 vols (Carbondale and Edwardsville: Southern Illinois University Press, 1982)

Gascoigne, Bamber, *World Theatre* (London: Ebury Press, 1968)

Gay, John, *The Beggar's Opera* in *The Beggar's Opera and Other 18th Century Plays*, ed. by John Hampden (London: Dent, 1968)

Gatti, Carlo, *Il Teatro alla Scala: nella storia e nell'arte, 1778-1963* (Milano: Ricordi, 1964)

Gaull, Marilyn, *English Romanticism: The Human Context* (New York: Norton, 1988)

Genest, John, *Some Account of the English Stage*, 10 vols (Bath: H.E. Carrington, 1832)

Grabo, Carl, *Prometheus Unbound: An Interpretation* (Chapel Hill: University of North Carolina Press, 1935)

Guest, Ivor, *The Ballet of the Enlightenment* (London: Dance Books, 1996)

—, *The Romantic Ballet in England: Its Development, Fulfilment, and Decline* (London: Pitman, 1954)

—, *The Romantic Ballet in Paris* (London: Pitman, 1966)

Gurr, Andrew, *The Shakespeare Company, 1594-1642* (Cambridge: Cambridge University Press, 1992)

Hall, Edith, and Fiona Macintosh, *Greek Tragedy and the British Theatre 1660-1914* (Oxford: Oxford University Press, 2005)

Hancock, Stephen, '"Shelley Himself in Petticoats": Joanna Baillie's *Orra* and Non-violent Masculinity as Remorse in *The Cenci*', *Romanticism on the Net*, 31.8 (2003) <http://www.erudit.org/revue/ron/2003.html> [accessed 21 September 2004]

Harcourt, Bosworth, *Theatre Royal, Norwich: The chronicles of an old playhouse* (Norwich: Norfolk News Co., 1903)

Havard, William, *King Charles the First: An Historical Tragedy Written in Imitation of Shakespeare; as it Was Acted at the Theatre Royal in Lincoln's Inn Fields* (Totnes: O. Adams [1775?])

Highfill, Philip, Kalman A. Burnim and Edward J. Langhans, eds, *A Biographical Dictionary of Actors, Actresses, Musicians, Dancers, Managers and Other Stage Personnel in London, 1660-1800*, 22 vols (Carbondale: Southern Illinois University Press, 1963)

Hill, Christopher, *The Century of Revolution* (London: Routledge, 2002)

Hoagwood, Terence Allan, and Daniel P. Watkins, *British Romantic Drama* (London: Associated University Presses, 1998)

Holcroft, Thomas, *The Life of Thomas Holcroft Written by Himself Continued by William Hazlitt* (Oxford: Oxford University Press, 1926)

—, *Love's Frailties* (London: Shepperson & Reynolds, 1794)

Hume, David, *History of England* (London: Christie, Regent's Edition, 1819)

Hume, Robert D., ed., *London Theatre World 1660-1800* (Carbondale & Edwardsville: Southern Illinois University Press, 1980)

Hunt, James Henry Leigh, *Critical Essays on the Performers of the London Theatres, including general observations on the practise and genius of the stage* (London: [n. pub.], 1807)

—, *Leigh Hunt's Dramatic Criticism 1808-1832*, ed. by L.J. and C.W. Houtchens (New York: Columbia University Press, 1949)

—, *The Descent of Liberty* (Philadelphia: for H. Hall, 1816)

Huscher, Herbert, 'Alexander Mavrocordato, Friend of the Shelleys', *KSMB*, 16 (1965), 29-38

Hutchinson, Lucy, *Memoirs of the Life of Colonel Hutchinson* (London: George Bell & Sons, 1906)

Inchbald, Elizabeth, *The British Theatre, or a Collection of Plays, which are Acted at the Theatres Royal, Drury Lane, Covent Garden, and Haymarket, Printed under the Authority of the Managers from the Prompt Books. With Biographical and Critical Remarks, by Mrs. Inchbald*, 25 vols (London: Longman, Hurst, Rees, 1808)

—, *The Plays of Elizabeth Inchbald*, ed. by Paula Backscheider (New York: Garland, 1980)

—, *Lovers' Vows* (Dublin: Thomas Burnside, 1798)

Ingpen, Roger, *Shelley in England* (London: Kegan, Paul, Trench, Trubner, 1917)

Jewett, William, *Fatal Autonomy: Romantic Drama and the Rhetoric of Agency* (Ithaca: Cornell University Press, 1997)

Johnson, R. Brimley, *Shelley-Leigh Hunt: How Friendship made History* (London: Ingpen & Grant, 1928)

Jones, Charles Inigo, *Memoirs of Miss O'Neill Containing her Public Character, Private Life and Dramatic Progress, from her Entrance upon the Stage; with a Full Criticism of her Different Characters, Appropriate Selections from them, and Some Account of the Plays she has Performed for her Representations* (London: D. Cox, 1816)

Jones, F.L., ed., *Maria Gisborne and Edward Elleker Williams, Shelley's Friends, Their Journals and Letters* (Norman: University of Oklahoma Press, 1951)

—, ed., *The Letters of Percy Bysshe Shelley* (Oxford: Oxford University Press, 1964)

Jones, Steven E., *Satire and Romanticism* (Basingstoke: Macmillan Press, 2000)

—, *Shelley's Satire, Violence Exhortation and Authority* (Illinois: De Kalb Northern Illinois University Press, 1994)

Kalidasa, *Sacontala or The Fatal Ring: An Indian Drama by Cálidás reprinted from the translation of Sir William Jones* (London: Charlton Tucker, 1870)

Kee, Robert, *The Green Flag*, 3 vols (London: Quartet, 1976)

Kessel, Marcel and Bert O. States, 'The Cenci as a Stage Play', *PMLA*, 72 (March 1960), 147-149

Kimbell, David, *Italian Opera* (Cambridge: Cambridge University Press, 1991)

King-Hele, Desmond, *Shelley: His Thought and Work* (London: Macmillan, 1971)

Kitto, H.D.F., *Greek Tragedy* (London: Methuen, 1961)

Knight, W.G., *A Major London 'Minor' The Surrey Theatre 1805-1865* (London: The Society for Theatre Research, 1997)

Lamb, Charles, *The Works of Charles and Mary Lamb*, ed. by E.V. Lucas, 3 vols (London: Methuen, 1903)

Leach, Robert, *The Punch and Judy Show* (London: Batsford Academic and Educational, 1985)

Leacroft, Richard, *The Development of the English Playhouse* (London: Eyre-Methuen, 1973)

Lemoncelli, Ronald L., 'Cenci as Corrupt Dramatic Poet', *ELN*, 16 (1978), 103-117

Lewis, Matthew Gregory, *The Castle Spectre* (London: J. Bell, 1798)

Macaulay, Catharine, *The History of England from the Accession of James I to the Elevation of the House of Hanover*, 8 vols (London: printed for Edward and Charles Dilly in the Poultry, 1771)

McCalman, Iain, *Radical Underworld* (Cambridge: Cambridge University

Press, 1988),

MacMillan, Dougald, *Catalogue of the Larpent Plays in the Huntington Library 1737-1824* (San Marino, California, 1939)

Macready, William, *Macready's Reminiscences*, ed. by Frederick Pollock, 2 vols (London: Macmillan, 1875)

McWhir, Anne, 'The Light and the Knife/Ab/Using Language in The Cenci', *KSJ*, 37 (1989), 145-161 ⟨Keats/Shelley Journal Oa⟩

Mancini, Franco, and Franco-Carmelo Greco, eds, *La commedia dell'arte e il teatro erudito* (Naples: Guida, c. 1982)

Mander, Raymond and Joe Mitchenson, *The Artist in the Theatre* (London: Heinemann, 1955)

Mangini, Nicola, *I teatri di Venezia* (Milan: Mursia, 1974)

Manuscripts of the Younger Romantics: Percy Bysshe Shelley, gen. ed. Donald H. Reiman, 9 vols (New York and London: Garland, 1985-1997): *Volume VII, Shelley's 1821-1822 Huntington Notebook: a facsimile of Huntington MS. HM2111*, ed. by Mary A. Quinn (New York: Garland, 1996); *Volume VI, Shelley's 1819-1821 Huntington notebook: a facsimile of Huntington MS. HM 2176*, ed. by Mary A. Quinn (New York, London: Garland, 1994)

Mason, William, *Caractacus, a Dramatic Poem... Altered for Theatrical Representation* (London: [n. pub.], 1777)

Marchand, Leslie, ed., *Byron's Letters and Journals*, 12 vols (London: John Murray, 1973-1994)

Matthews, G.M., 'A new Text of Shelley's Scene for Tasso', *KSMB XI*, 39-47

Meredith, Michael, *Five Hundred Years of Eton Theatre* (Eton: Eton College, 2001)

Milman, Henry Hart, 'Advertisement' in *Fazio: A Tragedy* (Oxford: Samuel Collingwood, 1815)

—, Preface to *Fazio*, 4th edn (London: [n. pub.], 1816)

Moore, Doris Langley, *Lord Byron – Accounts Rendered* (London: John Murray, 1974)

Lewis, Matthew Gregory, *The Castle Spectre* (London: J. Bell, 1798)

Maturin, Charles Robert, *Bertram; or the Castle* (London: John Murray, 1817)

Mayer, David, *Harlequin in his Element: The English Pantomime 1806-1836* (Cambridge, MA; Harvard University Press, 1969)

Medwin, Thomas, *Conversations of Lord Byron Noted During a Residence at Pisa in the Years 1821 and 1822* (London: Henry Colbourn, 1824)

—, *The Life of Percy Bysshe Shelley*, 2 vols (London: Thomas Cautley Newby, 1847)

Milman, Henry Hart, *Fazio* in *Romantic Context: Poetry - Significant Minor Poetry 1789-1830*, ed. by Donald H. Reiman (New York and London:

Garland, 1977)

Mitford, Mary Russell, *The Dramatic Works of Mary Russell Mitford*, 2 vols (London: Hurst and Blackett, 1854)

Moody, Jane, *Illegitimate Theatre in London 1710-1840* (Cambridge: Cambridge University Press, 2001)

Morgan, Lady (Sydney Owensen), *Italy*, 3rd edn, 3 vols (London: Henry Colburn, 1821)

Morley, Sheridan, *Sybil Thorndike: A Life in the Theatre* (London: Weidenfeld & Nicolson, 1999)

Morton, Thomas, *Columbus* (London: W. Miller, 1792)

Morton, Timothy, ed., *The Cambridge Companion to Shelley* (Cambridge: Cambridge University Press, 2006)

Moses, Montrose J., ed., *Representative British Dramas* (Boston: Little, Brown, 1920)

Mullini, Roberta, e Romana Zacchi, eds, *Traduzioni, echi, consonanze dal Rinascimento al Romanticismo* (Bologna: CLUEB, 2002)

Murphy, Arthur, *The Grecian Daughter* (London: [n. pub.], 1792)

Nichols, Harold J., 'The Acting of Thomas Potter Cooke', *Nineteenth-Century Theatre Research*, 5.2 (Autumn 1977) <http://www.english.upenn.edu/Projects/knarf/Articles/nichols.html> [accessed 10 January 2007]

Nicoll, Allardyce, *A History of Early Nineteenth Century Drama 1660-1900: IV, Early Nineteenth-Century Drama, 1800-1850* (Cambridge: Cambridge University Press, 1955)

Norbrook, David, *Writing the English Republic: Poetry, Rhetoric and Politics 1627-1660* (Cambridge: Cambridge University Press, 1999/2000)

Noverre, Jean Georges, *Letters on Dancing and Ballets* trans. By Cyril W. Beaumont (London: C.W. Beaumont, 1951)

Pascoe, Judith, '*Proserpine* and *Midas*' in *The Cambridge Companion to Mary Shelley*, ed. by Esther Schor (Cambridge: Cambridge University Press, 2003)

—, *Romantic Theatricality: Gender, Poetry and Spectatorship* (Ithaca: Cornell University Press, 1997)

Page, Denys, ed, *Persai* in *Septem quae Supersunt Tragoedias* (Oxford: Oxford University Press, 1975)

Peacock, Thomas Love, *The Letters of Thomas Love Peacock*, ed. by Nicholas A. Joukovsky (Oxford: Clarendon, 2001)

Peck, Walter E., *Shelley, His Life and Work* (Boston: Houghton Mifflin, 1927)

Quillin, Jessica, '"An Assiduous Frequenter of the Italian Opera": Shelley's *Prometheus Unbound* and the *Opera Buffa*', Opera and Romanticism: Praxis Series, *Romantic Circles* <http://www.rc.umd.edu/praxis/opera/

quillin html> [accessed 9 June 2006]

Ranger, Paul, *'Terror and Pity Reign in Every Breast': Gothic Drama in the Patent Theatres, 1750-1820* (London: Society for Theatre Research, 1991)

Rasi, Luigi, *I comici Italiani*, 2 vols (Firenze: Fratelli Bocca, 1905)

Reiman, Donald H., and Neil Fraistat, eds, *Shelley's Poetry and Prose* (New York: Norton, 2002)

— and Sharon B. Powers, eds, *Shelley's Poetry and Prose* (New York: Norton, 1977)

Reiter, Seymour, *A Study of Shelley's Poetry* (Albuquerque: University of New Mexico Press, 1967)

Richardson, Alan, *A Mental Theatre* (University Park, PA and London: The Pennsylvania State University Press 1988)

Richardson, Donna, 'The Harmatia of Imagination in Shelley's *Cenci*', *KSJ*, 54 (1995), 216-239

Robinson, Henry Crabb, *The London Theatre 1811-1866: Selections from the Diary of Henry Crabb Robinson*, ed. by Eluned Brown (London: The Society for Theatre Research, 1966)

Rose, H.J., *A Handbook of Greek Mythology*, 6th edn pbk (London: Routledge, 1991)

Rosenfeld, Sybil, 'Jane Austen and Private Theatricals' *Essays and Studies*, English Association, n. s. XV (London: John Murray, 1962)

—, *A Short History of Scene Design in Great Britain* (Oxford: Blackwell, 1973)

—, *Georgian Scene Painters and Scene Painting* (Cambridge: Cambridge University Press, 1981)

—, *Temples of Thespis; Some Private Theatres and Theatricals in England and Wales, 1700-1820* (London: Society for Theatre Research, 1978)

—, *The Georgian Theatre of Richmond and its Circuit: Beverley, Harrogate, Kendal, Northallerton, Ulverston and Whitby* (York: The Society for Theatre Research in association with William Sessions, 1984)

Rosselli, John, *Music and Musicians in Nineteenth-Century Italy* (London: Batsford, 1991)

—, *The Opera Industry in Italy from Cimarosa to Verdi: the Role of the Impresario* (Cambridge: Cambridge University Press, 1984)

Rossi, Luigi, *Il Ballo alla Scala 1778-1970* (Milan: Edizione della Scala, 1972)

Rowe, Nicholas, *The Dramatick Works of Nicholas Rowe* (London, T. Jauncy, 1720; repr. Farnborough, Hants: Gregg International Publishers, 1971)

Ruston, Sharon, *Shelley and Vitality* (Basingstoke: Palgrave, 2005)

Schlegel, A.W., *Lectures in Dramatic Art and Literature*, trans. John Black, 2nd edn, rev. by Rev. A.J.W. Morrison (London: Geo. Bell & Sons, 1904)

Schor, Esther, ed., *The Cambridge Companion to Mary Shelley* (Cambridge:

Cambridge University Press, 2003)

✓ Scrivener, Michael, *Radical Shelley* (Princeton, NJ: Princeton University Press, 1982)

Segal, Erich, ed., *Oxford Readings in Aristophanes* (Oxford: Oxford University Press, 1996)

Senici, Emanuele, ed., *The Cambridge Companion to Rossini* (Cambridge: Cambridge University Press, 2004)

Shellard, Dominic, and Steve Nicholson with Miriam Handley, *The Lord Chamberlain Regrets: A History of British Theatre Censorship* (London: The British Library, 2004)

Shelley and His Circle, 1773-1822, ed. by Kenneth Neill Cameron, Donald H. Reiman and Doucet Devin Fischer, 10 vols (Cambridge, MA: Harvard University Press, 1961-2002), vols 1-4 ed. by Kenneth Neill Cameron, vols 5-8 ed. by Donald H. Reiman, vols 9-10 ed. by Donald H. Reiman and Doucet Devin Fischer

Shelley, Bryan, *Shelley and Scripture: The Interpreting Angel* (Oxford: Clarendon Press, 1994)

Shelley, Mary, *The Journals of Mary Shelley, 1814-1844*, ed. by Paula R. Feldman and Diana Scott-Kilvert (Baltimore: Johns Hopkins University Press, 1995)

—, *The Letters of Mary Wollstonecraft Shelley*, ed. by Betty T. Bennett, 3 vols (Baltimore and London: Johns Hopkins University Press, 1980–1988)

Shelley, Percy Bysshe, *Shelley's Prose, or, The Trumpet of a Prophecy*, ed. by David Lee Clark (London: Fourth Estate, 1988)

—, *The Poems of Shelley*, ed. by Geoffrey Matthews and Kelvin Everest, 2 vols to date (London: Longman, 1989, 2000)

—, *The Poetical Works of Shelley*, ed. by Thomas Hutchinson, corr. by G.M. Matthews (Oxford: Oxford University Press, 1970)

—, *The Boat on the Serchio*, ed. by Nora Crook, KSR, 7 (1992), 85-93

Sheridan, Richard Brinsley, *The School for Scandal*, ed. by C J.L. Price (Oxford: Oxford University Press, 1971)

Simpson, Michael, *Closet Performances: Political Exhibition and Prohibition in the Dramas of Byron and Shelley* (Stanford: Stanford University Press, 1998)

Smith, Marian, *Ballet and Opera in the Age of Giselle* (Princeton: Princeton University Press, 2000).

Smith, Paul, 'Restless Casuistry: Shelley's Composition of The Cenci', KSJ, 13 (1964), 77-85

Smith, William C., *The Italian Opera and Contemporary Ballet in London 1789-1820* (London: The Society for Theatre Research, 1955)

Southern, Richard, *Changeable Scenery* (London: Faber & Faber, 1952)

—, *The Georgian Playhouse* (London: Pleiades, 1948)

Speaight, George, *Punch and Judy: A History* (London: Studio Vista, 1970)

Sperry, Stuart M., *Shelley's Major Verse* (Cambridge, MA: Harvard University Press, 1988)

St. Clair, William, *That Greece Might Still be Free. The Philhellenes in the War of Independence* (Cambridge: Open Book Publishers, 2008)

Stabler, Jane, *Burke to Byron, Barbauld to Baillie 1790-1830* (Basingstoke: Palgrave, 2002)

Stanford, W.B., Introduction to *The Frogs* by Aristophanes (Basingstoke: Macmillan Education, 1958)

States, Bert O., 'Addendum: The Stage History of Shelley's "The Cenci"', *PMLA*, 72 (1957), 633-644

Stendhal (Henri Beyle), *Correspondances (1816-1820)* (Paris: Le Divan, 1934)

Stirling, E., *Old Drury Lane*, 2 vols (London: Chatto & Windus, 1881)

Stocking, Marion Kingston, ed., *The Clairmont Correspondence: Letters of Claire Clairmont, Charles Clairmont, and Fanny Imlay Godwin* (Baltimore: Johns Hopkins University Press, 1995)

—, ed., with the assistance of David Mackenzie Stocking, *The Journals of Claire Clairmont* (Cambridge, MA: Harvard University Press, 1968)

Stone, Geo. Winchester Jr., ed., *The Stage and the Page: London's "Whole Show" in the Eighteenth Century Theatre* (Berkeley: University of California Press, 1981)

Sutcliffe, Barry, ed., *Plays by George Colman the Younger and Thomas Morton* (Cambridge: Cambridge University Press, 1983)

Swindells, Julia, *Glorious Causes: The Grand Theatre of Political Change, 1789 to 1833* (Oxford: Oxford University Press, 2001)

Taylor, George, *The French Revolution and the London Stage, 1789-1805* (Cambridge: Cambridge University Press, 2000

Temperley, Nicholas, ed., *Music in Britain: The Romantic Age, 1800-1914*, 6 vols (Oxford: Blackwell, 1988)

Tetreault, Ronald, 'Shelley and the Opera', *ELH*, 48 (1981), 144-171

Tetreault, Ronald, *The Poetry of Life: Shelley and Literary Form* (Toronto: University of Toronto Press, 1987)

The Favourite Song of Timothy, as Sung by Mrs. Jordan... in the Farce of the Virgin Unmask'd as Revived at Drury Lane Theatre (London: S.A. & P. Thompson, [1790(?)])

Thompson, E.P., *The Making of the English Working Class* (Victor Gollancz, 1963; rev. Pelican Books, 1968; repr. with new preface Harmondsworth: Penguin, 1980)

Tidworth, Simon, *Theatres: An Architectural and Cultural History* (New York: Praeger, 1973)

Trussler, Simon, ed., *Burlesque Plays of the Eighteenth Century* (Oxford: Oxford University Press, 1969)

Tobin, John, *The Honeymoon* (London: Samuel French, [1827(?)])

Urlin, Ethel L., *Dancing Ancient and Modern* (London: Simpkin, Marshall, Hamilton Kent [1911(?)])

Vargo, Lisa, 'The Solitary Reformer: A Reading of Shelley's Poetry' (unpublished doctoral thesis, University of Toronto, 1983)

Viganò, Salvatore, *La Spada di Kenneth* ([Milan(?)]: [Giacomo Pirola(?)], [1818(?)])

Walker, Constance, 'The Urn of Bitter Prophecy: Antithetical Patterns in Hellas' *KSMB*, 33 (1982), 36-48

Wallace, Jennifer, *Shelley and Greece: Rethinking Romantic Hellenism* (London: Macmillan, 1997)

Ward, A.C., ed., *Specimens of English Dramatic Criticism, XVII-XX Centuries* (London: Humphrey Milford, 1945)

Wasserman, Earl R., *Shelley: A Critical Reading* (Baltimore: Johns Hopkins University Press, 1971)

—, *Shelley's 'Prometheus Unbound'* (Baltimore: Johns Hopkins University Press, 1965)

Webb, Timothy, *Shelley: a Voice not Understood* (Manchester: Manchester University Press, 1977)

—, *The Violet in the Crucible* (Oxford: Oxford University Press, 1976)

Weinberg, Alan M., *Shelley's Italian Experience* (London: Macmillan, 1991)

—, and Timothy Webb, eds, *The Unfamiliar Shelley* (Farnham: Ashgate, 2009)

White, N.I., *Shelley*, 2 vols (London: Secker & Warburg, 1947)

—, 'Shelley's "Swellfoot the Tyrant" in Relation to Contemporary Political Satires', *PMLA*, 36 (September 1921), 332-346

Whitelocke, Bulstrode, *Memorials of the English Affairs from the Beginning of the Reign of King Charles the First to King Charles the Second His Happy Restauration* ([n.p.]: [n. pub.],1682; new edn, London: Tonson, 1732)

Wickwar, William W., *The Struggle for the Freedom of the Press 1819-1832* (London: George Allen & Unwin, 1928)

Williams, Raymond, *Drama in Performance* (Harmondsworth: Penguin, 1972)

Wilkinson, Tate, *The Wandering Patentee; or, a History of the Yorkshire Theatres, from 1770 to the Present Time; Interspersed with Anecdotes respecting most of the Performers in the Three Kingdoms, from 1765 to 1795*, 4 vols (York: Wilson, Spence and Mawman, 1795)

Winter, Marian Hannah, *The Pre-romantic Ballet* (London: Pitman, 1974)

Wolfe, Humbert, *The Life of Percy Bysshe Shelley: As Comprised in The Life of Shelley by Thomas Jefferson Hogg, The Recollections of Shelley & Byron by Edward John Trelawny, Memoirs of Shelley by Thomas Love Peacock with an Introduction*, 2 vols (London: J.M. Dent & Sons, 1933)

Woodings, R.B., 'Shelley's Sources for Charles I', *MLR*, 64 (1969), 267-275

Worrall, David, *Theatric Revolution: Drama, Censorship and Romantic Period Subcultures, 1773-1832* (Oxford: Oxford University Press, 2006)

Wu, Duncan, ed., *The Selected Writings of William Hazlitt*, 9 vols (London: Pickering & Chatto, 1998)

Wyndham, Henry Saxe, *The Annals of Covent Garden Theatre*, 2 vols (London: Chatto & Windus, 1906)

Yost, George, *Pieracci and Shelley: an Italian Ur-Cenci* (Potomac: Scripta Humanistica, 1986)

Young, Art, *Shelley and Non-Violence* (The Hague: Mouton, 1975)

Zambelli, Lucia and Francesco Tei, *A teatro con i Lorena: feste, personaggi e luoghi scenici della Firenze granducale* (Firenze: edizioni medicea, 1987)

Horsham Museum MS 333 X.2001.333.1 / 333.2/ 333.3/ 333.4/ 333.5/ 333.6/ 333.7/ 333.8/ 333.11/ 333.13/ 333.15/ 333.16/ 338.9/ 389.16.2 Ms. 289

La Gazzetta di Firenze, 9 October 1819

La Gazzetta Privilegiata di Venezia, N. 224, October 1818, N. 229-237, 13-22 October 1818

The Times, 17 April 1809, 18 April 1809, 19 April 1809, 26 April 1810, 27 April 1810, 2 May 1810, 3 May 1810, 7 June 1820, 8 June 1820

Editions of plays and play collections

Apart from the contemporary editions of plays cited above and numerous others, I have consulted the following collections of plays, from which I have gained information about the performance of plays mentioned in the text: London: John Cumberland, [*c.* 1826-1831] un-numbered volumes of nonce-editions comprising items from various volumes of Cumberland's British Theatre, *c.* 1826-1828, or Dolby's British Theatre, *c.* 1824-1825, bound together, printed from the acting copy, edited and with remarks by George Daniel (D– G–), with 'description of the costume, cast of characters, entrances and exits, relative positions of the performers on stage, and the whole of the stage business' and illustrated with engravings from drawings often made in the theatre:

(A) William Shakespeare, *Othello*; Edward Moore, *The Gamester*; Thomas Otway, *Venice Preserved*; Thomas Southern, *Isabella: Or the Fatal Marriage*

(B) Peter Bayley, *Orestes in Argos*; James Sheridan Knowles, *Caius Gracchus*; Auguste Kotzebue, *Lovers' Vows*, trans. by Mrs. Inchbald; John Brown, *Barbarossa*; Joseph Addison, *Cato*; Auguste Kotzebue, *The Stranger*, trans. Benjamin Thompson; R.B. Sheridan, *Pizzarro*

(C) Thomas Morton, *The Children in the Wood*; John Gay, *Beggars' Opera*; Joseph Lunn, *The Shepherd of Derwent Vale*; R.B. Sheridan, *The Duenna*; R.B. Sheridan, *The Rivals*; George Farquhar, *The Inconstant*

(D) Charles A. Somerset, *Sylvana: An opera*; George Colman, *Who Wants a Guinea?*; James Sheridan Knowles, *William Tell*; Thomas Cooke, *Oberon: or The Charmed Horn*; James Sheridan Knowles, *Virginius*; Carl Maria von Weber, *Der Freischutz*; Charles Dibdin, *The Waterman*

(E) *The Barber of Seville*, adapted by John Fawcett; R.B. Sheridan, *The Critic*; John O'Keeffe, *The Highland Reel*; William Macready, *The Irishman in London*; George Daniel, *The Disagreeable Surprise*

(F) Philip Massinger, *A New Way to Pay Old Debts*; R.B. Sheridan, *The School for Scandal*; William Shakespeare, *The Merchant of Venice*; William Shakespeare, *As You Like It*; William Shakespeare, *Much Ado About Nothing*; William Shakespeare, *King Henry IV Pt. 1*

(G) James Kenney, *The Alcaid: Or the Secrets of Office*; Richard Cumberland, *The West Indian*; Oliver Goldsmith, *She Stoops to Conquer*; Thomas Southern, *Isabella or The Fatal Marriage*

(H) Thomas Morton, *The Children in the Wood*; Richard Ayton, *The Rendezvous*; John Brown, *Barbarossa*; Charles Thompson, *The Gambler's Fate*; W.T. Moncrieff, *Giovanni in London*; Thomas Morton, *The School for Reform*; Auguste Kotzebue, *Lovers Vows*, trans. by Mrs. Inchbald

(I) William Shakespeare, *Romeo and Juliet*; Oliver Goldsmith, *She Stoops to Conquer*; William Shakespeare, *Macbeth*; R.B. Sheridan, *Pizzarro*; William Shakespeare, *King Richard III*; John Home, *Douglas*; Mr. Hoadley, *The Suspicious Husband*

(J) William Shakespeare, *King John*; William Shakespeare, *King Richard III*; William Shakespeare, *Hamlet*; William Shakespeare, *Julius Caesar*; William Shakespeare, *Cymbeline*; William Shakespeare, *Macbeth*

Index

OpenBook Publishers

A new approach to academic publishing

OPEN BOOK PUBLISHERS is dedicated to making high quality research less expensive and more accessible to readers around the world. Set up and run by academics, we produce peer-reviewed monographs, collected volumes and lecture series in the humanities and social sciences.

Open Book speeds up the whole publishing process from author to reader. We offer all the advantages of digital texts (speed, searchability, updating, archival material, databases, discussion forums, and links to institutions' websites) without sacrificing the quality of the traditional university presses.

All Open Book publications are available online to be read free of charge by anyone with access to the internet. During our first year of operation, our free digital editions have been accessed by people in over 120 countries, and are being read by as many people per month as many traditionally printed titles will reach in their entire published life.

We are reliant on donations by individuals and institutions to help offset the production costs of our publications. As a Community Interest Company (CIC), we do not operate for commercial profit and all donations, as with all other revenue we generate, will be used to finance new Open Access publications.

For further information on what we do, how to donate to OBP, additional digital material related to our titles or to order our books, please contact the Managing Director, Dr. Alessandra Tosi (a.tosi@openbookpublishers.com) or visit our website:

www.openbookpublishers.com

Lightning Source UK Ltd.
Milton Keynes UK
18 December 2010

164615UK00001B/5/P